Art in Doubt

SRLT

NORTHWESTERN UNIVERSITY PRESS
Studies in Russian Literature and Theory

SERIES EDITORS
Caryl Emerson
Gary Saul Morson
William Mills Todd III
Andrew Wachtel
Justin Weir

Art in Doubt

Tolstoy, Nabokov, and the Problem of Other Minds

Tatyana Gershkovich

NORTHWESTERN UNIVERSITY PRESS / EVANSTON, ILLINOIS

Northwestern University Press
www.nupress.northwestern.edu

Copyright © 2023 by Northwestern University. Published 2023 by Northwestern University Press. All rights reserved.

Printed in the United States of America

10 9 8 7 6 5 4 3 2 1

Library of Congress Cataloging-in-Publication Data

Names: Gershkovich, Tatyana, author.
Title: Art in doubt : Tolstoy, Nabokov, and the problem of other minds / Tatyana Gershkovich.
Description: Evanston, Illinois : Northwestern University Press, 2023. | Series: Northwestern University Press studies in Russian literature and theory | Includes bibliographical references and index.
Identifiers: LCCN 2022023698 | ISBN 9780810145535 (paperback) | ISBN 9780810145542 (cloth) | ISBN 9780810145559 (ebook)
Subjects: LCSH: Tolstoy, Leo, graf, 1828–1910—Criticism and interpretation. | Nabokov, Vladimir Vladimirovich, 1899–1977—Criticism and interpretation. | Russian fiction—19th century—History and criticism. | Russian fiction—20th century—History and criticism. | Aesthetics in literature. | BISAC: LITERARY CRITICISM / Russian & Former Soviet Union
Classification: LCC PG3415.A3 G47 2023 | DDC 891.733—dc23/eng/20220524
LC record available at https://lccn.loc.gov/2022023698

For Adam, Nina, and Leo

Contents

Acknowledgments		ix
Note on Transliteration and Citation		xi
List of Abbreviations		xiii
Introduction	"Some Better Brick Than the Cartesian One"	3
Chapter One	Tolstoy's Uncertain Artist	24
Chapter Two	Nabokov's Moderate Multiplication of the Self	60
Chapter Three	Atrophied Aesthetic Sense	90
Chapter Four	Suspicion on Trial	125
Afterword	The Artful and the Artless	155
Notes		161
Bibliography		199
Index		217

Acknowledgments

The conversations I had while writing this book were among its greatest joys. My deepest thanks to Justin Weir for a dialogue that began in my undergraduate days and has now stretched into its second decade. I am grateful for his brilliant example as a scholar and teacher, his steadfast support as an adviser and colleague, and most of all his willingness to linger in unhurried discussions that have shaped my views on Tolstoy, Nabokov, and much else. My profound thanks also to William Mills Todd, whose memorable course on Dostoevsky opened a world of intellectual pleasures and challenges; and to Richard Moran, who helped me develop a vocabulary for engaging more rigorously with questions about art and other minds. This project benefited from the support of many other colleagues and friends at Harvard. I am grateful to the faculty of the Harvard Slavic Department, especially Julie Buckler, Stephanie Sandler, and the late Svetlana Boym. My thanks to Daniel Green, Alex Gross, Mihaela Pacurar, Philipp Penka, Maxim Pozdorovkin, Adam Stern, and Lusia Zaitseva for being kind and incisive interlocutors.

A number of colleagues had a transformative effect on this project. I owe an enormous debt of gratitude to Hannah Vandegrift Eldridge, Matthew Handelman, Joela Jacobs, and Sunny Yudkoff, who were often my first readers, and as patient and generous as anyone could wish one's first readers to be; to Stephen Blackwell, who read this book in toto more than once and improved it each time with his keen insights; to Dana Dragunoiu, Chloë Kitzinger, Susan Polansky, and Andreea Ritivoi for their challenging questions and advice on key chapters; to Caryl Emerson and the anonymous reader at *PMLA* for sharp comments that tightened my arguments; to the anonymous reviewers at Northwestern University Press, whose suggestions improved the work a great deal; and finally to my research assistant Marilyn Gao who helped me finalize the manuscript. I am likewise grateful to the many other scholars and colleagues who have generously offered their thoughts and advice at conferences and talks, and in email exchanges and chance conversations. My thanks to Galina Alekseeva, David Birnbaum, Nancy Condee, David Herman, Maria Khotimsky, Ilya Kliger, Olga Klimova,

Acknowledgments

Susan McReynolds, Eric Naiman, Donna Orwin, Lynn Ellen Patyk, Alfia Rakova, Barry Scherr, and Olga Voronina.

I feel immensely fortunate to have found an institutional home at the Modern Languages Department at Carnegie Mellon University. The warmth and decency of my colleagues here has been a great gift. I owe thanks to Stephen Brockmann, Katherine Burns, Simon DeDeo, Sébastien Dubreil, Wendy Goldman, Naum Kats, Khaled Al Masaeed, David Parker, Christopher Phillips, Candace Skibba, and Bonnie Youngs, who helped this work along in ways large and small. A special thanks to Anne Lambright and Gabriele Eichmanns Maier for their unstinting support and mentorship. In the project's final stages, the American Academy in Berlin became my home away from home; I am very grateful to the Academy—especially Berit Ebert, John Eltringham, Johana Gallup, and Carol Scherer—the other fellows, and the friends we made there.

The research and writing of this book were made possible by support from the Harvard Graduate Society, Davis Center for Russian Studies, and Berkman Faculty Development Fund at Carnegie Mellon. Portions of chapter 4 were published in "Suspicion on Trial: Tolstoy's *The Kreutzer Sonata* and Nabokov's 'Pozdnyshev's Address,'" *PMLA* 134, no. 3 (May 2019): 459–74. And passages from chapter 2 appeared in "In Impossible Proximity: How to Read Like Nabokov," *Berlin Journal* 33 (Fall 2019): 55–57. My gratitude to Cambridge University Press and the American Academy in Berlin for permission to republish these texts. Extracts from "Rech' Pozdnysheva" and "Tolstoy: Miscellaneous Lecture Notes" from the Vladimir Nabokov Papers 1918–87, Henry W. and Albert A. Berg Collection of English and American Literature, New York Public Library, are published by permission of the Wylie Agency LLC. I want to express my gratitude to Gary Saul Morson, Trevor Perri, Faith Wilson Stein, Maia Rigas, and other colleagues at Northwestern University Press for helping to bring this book into the world.

Finally, I want to thank my family, whose unflagging support made this work possible. Thanks to my father, Peter Gershkovich, for being the most attentive and receptive of readers; to my mother, Yelena Titko, for her optimism and strength; to Jeffrey and Sonia Sachs for their keen interest and sound advice; to Lisa Sachs, Hannah Sachs, and Matthew Beck for their kindness, sympathy, and good humor. My greatest debt is to my partner, Adam Sachs. Together we have considered every argument—nearly every word!—of this book on runs and bike rides, in cafés, while strolling to the bakery. I feel unbelievably lucky to have you to talk to. Two more conversation partners came into the world as I worked on this project: Nina and Leo Gershkovich Sachs. I could not be more excited for a lifetime of listening to what they have to say.

Note on Transliteration and Citation

In the main text I rely on the Library of Congress transliteration system with modifications for commonly known place names and for first and last names. In such cases, "-ia," "-iu," and "-ë" might for readability appear as "-ya," "-yu," and "yo," respectively, and names beginning or ending with "ii" are written instead with "y" (e.g., Yasnaya Polyana rather than Iasnaia Poliana, Tolstoy than Tolstoi, Fyodor Tyutchev than Fëdor Tiutchev, and Yuly Aikhenvald than Iiulii Aikhenvald). The notes and bibliography defer without exception to the Library of Congress system.

Translations are mine unless noted otherwise. In cases where I offer my own translation, I quote from the original text in the notes. Where I rely on authoritative translations by others, I cite first the translation and then the source of the Russian text. Frequently discussed texts by Tolstoy and Nabokov are referenced with the abbreviations listed on page xiii. For texts from multivolume works, such as the *Polnoe sobranie sochinenii*, I give first the volume number and then the page number. A passage from *Anna Karenina*, for example, will have a reference to the translated text and then to the Russian text and look like the following: (*AK*, 1; *PSS*, 18:1).

Abbreviations

AK   Leo Tolstoy, *Anna Karenina: A Novel in Eight Parts*, trans. Larissa Volokhonsky and Richard Pevear (New York: Penguin Books, 2000)

Gift   Vladimir Nabokov, *The Gift* (New York: Vintage International, 1991)

HM   Leo Tolstoy, *Hadji Murad*, trans. Louise Maude et al., in *Great Short Works of Leo Tolstoy*, 547–668 (New York: Harper Perennial Modern Classics, 2004)

KS   Leo Tolstoy, *The Kreutzer Sonata*, trans. Louise Maude et al., in *Great Short Works of Leo Tolstoy*, 553–450 (New York: Harper Perennial Modern Classics, 2004)

MM   Leo Tolstoy, "Memoirs of a Madman," trans. Louise and Aylmer Maude, in *Tolstoy's Short Fiction*, ed. Michael R. Katz, 303–13 (New York: W. W. Norton, 2008)

PF   Vladimir Nabokov, *Pale Fire* (New York: Vintage International, 1989)

PSS   *Lev Tolstoi: Polnoe sobranie sochinenii* [*Leo Tolstoy: Complete Collected Works*], 90 vols. (Moscow: Gosudarstvennoe izdatel'stvo Khudozhestvennaia literatura, 1928–58)

SS   *Vladimir Nabokov: Sobranie sochinenii v chetyrekh tomakh* [*Vladimir Nabokov: Collected Works in Four Volumes*] (Moscow: Pravda, 1990)

WIA   Leo Tolstoy, *What Is Art?*, trans. Aylmer Maude (Indianapolis: Bobbs Merrill, 1960)

Art in Doubt

Introduction

"Some Better Brick Than the Cartesian One"

LEO TOLSTOY AND Vladimir Nabokov—the moralist and the aesthete—seem to be radically opposed on matters of art. Tolstoy held that true art is immediately comprehensible to everyone. Art is "infection" with feeling, and all that readers have to do to partake of this feeling is "allow the artist to possess [them]."[1] For Nabokov, true art is accessible only to a select, sophisticated group of "good readers," who must in their reading be "active and creative."[2] Tolstoy insisted that art be simple, sincere, and morally unimpeachable. These imperatives were reflected in many of the author's mature works, which drive toward (though do not always achieve) a stylistic asceticism. Tolstoy's late work "Alyosha Gorshok" (1905), for example, tells of a humble young man who spends his life serving others and concludes after only a few pages with an unadorned description of his death: "He said little. He merely asked for something to drink, and felt a growing sense of wonder. Suddenly, overcome with wonder, he stretched out, and died."[3] Nabokov, in contrast, declared that writers who extol simplicity are "traitors, not teachers."[4] His mature style is as baroque as Tolstoy's is ascetic. The critic Mary McCarthy aptly described his *Pale Fire* as "a Jack-in-the-box, a Fabergé gem, a clockwork toy, a chess problem, an infernal machine, a trap to catch reviewers, a cat-and-mouse game, a do-it-yourself novel."[5] Yet this study argues that their rival styles—Tolstoy's simplicity, Nabokov's complexity—were reached by parallel flights from the same fear: that one's experience of the world might be entirely one's own, private and impossible to share through art.

I propose reconceiving the celebrated fiction and often bizarre aesthetic theorizing of these two authors as coherent, career-long attempts to reckon with skeptical despair. Philosophical skepticism is difficult to define succinctly. Different texts, periods, and traditions have defined it differently. For the purposes of this study, skepticism might be defined as doubt that our perceptions of the external world and of other people can grant us adequate

Introduction

knowledge of them. I should say straight away that I do not consider Tolstoy and Nabokov to be skeptics—but of course many of the philosophers who have dwelled on skepticism have done so precisely to try to overcome it. It is the same with these two. My aim will be to demonstrate that the temptation and torments of skepticism, and Tolstoy's and Nabokov's attempts to think and write their way out of it, shaped their fiction in fundamental ways. We cannot fully comprehend their work or make sense of their affinities—Nabokov deemed Tolstoy "the greatest Russian writer of prose fiction"—without recognizing their shared skeptical affliction.[6]

This skeptical affliction, and the fact that it is an affliction at all, has important implications for our contemporary literary-critical debates. A growing number of scholars in literary and cultural studies have argued that these fields have produced readers so well trained in reading below the surface—in identifying what the text ostensibly conceals—that such so-called suspicious critique is now performed on autopilot, deforming our understanding of texts and yielding predictable interpretations of them. Defenders of suspicious interpretation, on the other hand, fear that nonsuspicious reading of whatever form leaves us inattentive to the power structures that shape literary texts and leads in the end to political quietism. But partisans on both sides share a key presumption: that how we read is largely up to us. We can read with less suspicion or more, at the text's surface or beneath it, but however we choose to read—as the critics of suspicious critique would have us do or as its defenders would—the choice remains a choice. Tolstoy's and Nabokov's works, however, illuminate a phenomenology of reading overlooked in this debate: the experience of the reluctant but ineluctable skeptic, the reader whose skeptical impulse is unwanted yet cannot be willed away. They demonstrate that a deep and ineradicable skepticism may lurk behind the more enduring forms of suspicion.

Is it ineradicable? If distrust of a text cannot be overcome by force of the reader's will, can it be overcome at all? For Tolstoy and Nabokov—and here they depart from other modernists who are more often linked with the problematic of doubt—it *can* be overcome, but not by the reader in isolation. The writer has to help. I read their works as a search for formal and stylistic strategies to allay suspicion in themselves and in their readers. I agree with critics of critique who argue that routinized suspicion impedes our capacity to understand and enjoy aesthetic experiences. But to regard suspicion as a mere attitude, which might be adopted or not, these critics tend to cleave it from the metaphysical concerns that animate it. To do so is to radically underrate the hold that it has on readers (both professional and nonprofessional ones). And if, as Tolstoy and Nabokov believed, a literary text can be constructed to do what the will alone cannot—that is, to dispel our impulse to read it suspiciously—then to underrate the perniciousness of suspicion

"Some Better Brick Than the Cartesian One"

is also to underrate this peculiar faculty of good literature. Only by giving suspicion its full due, by grasping it at its metaphysical roots, can we begin to understand why some works seem better than others at helping us subdue it.

My study aims not only to illuminate the works of Tolstoy and Nabokov but also to move past the current postcritique debate by investigating authorial motives and strategies for alleviating readerly skepticism and activating trust. I am sympathetic to postcritical scholars who, after decades of critique, want to return to questions of beauty, judgment, and pleasure. And I share their democratic impulse to recover a much broader range of reading experiences than those of the professional critic. But this objective is ill served by conceiving of suspicious critique as merely an institutional formation or a politically motivated mistake, rather than a body of thought that tells us something true about how we sometimes read. Sometimes we cannot help but read suspiciously, and some texts ought to be read suspiciously—and sometimes we read trustfully, and some texts are beautiful. I examine Tolstoy's and Nabokov's works to ask why certain texts feel communicative, as if in reading them we encounter another person, and some texts do not. How is this effect created? What is the reader's role in creating it, and what is the writer's? Given the radically contrasting mature forms and styles of these two authors, my answer will be formally and stylistically agnostic. Tolstoy and Nabokov stake out two distinct modes of quelling skepticism; against the critical tendency to ascribe a determinative role to form, they show us that very different textual effects can produce fundamentally similar aesthetic encounters.

THE BURDEN OF SKEPTICISM

In their works, as in a strain of thought extending from Stanley Cavell and Ludwig Wittgenstein back into the early history of skepticism, Tolstoy and Nabokov recognize that skepticism resists refutation. It is worth dwelling at some length on a modern philosophical tradition that brings skepticism's irrefutability into focus to then demonstrate how, as artists, Tolstoy and Nabokov diverge from their philosophical counterparts in their response to this problem.

For Tolstoy, René Descartes's antiskeptical arguments are exemplary of the futility of reason against skeptical doubt: "Descartes rejects everything forcefully, correctly, and then resurrects it again arbitrarily, dreamily. Spinoza does the same. Kant, the same. Schopenhauer, the same."[7] Richard Popkin, the philosopher and preeminent historian of skepticism, echoes Tolstoy's assessment when he observes that Descartes set out to refute the skeptical notions of his day but in the end "outdoubted" his opponents.[8] First Descartes

Introduction

put in question the existence and properties of material objects: Can we be certain that we do not merely dream them? Then he cast doubt on rational truths, such as the properties of triangles. All that we take to be true, he proposed, might be an illusion induced in us by an evil demon. Descartes's attempts to refute this hypothesis—through arguments for the existence of a God who would not deceive us—were no match for the demon hypothesis, which Popkin calls his "super-sceptical weapon."[9] Our idea of a God who is not a deceiver might itself be the work of the demon. "Descartes responded to this objection, admitting in effect that it was correct. He agreed that we could never transcend the circle of our ideas," Popkin explains.[10] But Descartes also asserted that to refuse these "merely human certitudes" would be to "entirely close the door to reason."[11] The skeptic's radical doubt cannot be met by reason, but following this doubt to its end has too high a cost.

Schopenhauer, an intellectual touchstone for both Tolstoy and Nabokov, likewise held that doubt about the reality of the external world and of other people—a doubt that ultimately terminates in solipsism, the conviction that one is alone in the world—cannot be disproved. But though irrefutable, the skeptical conviction was, for Schopenhauer, impossible. How can one go about the world convinced that only oneself is real? This is a "sceptical sophism," he insisted.[12] "As a serious conviction . . . it could be found only in a madhouse; as such it would then need not so much a refutation as a cure."[13] Schopenhauer dismisses such radical doubt as "a small frontier fortress." It is "impregnable, but the garrison can never sally forth from it, and therefore we can pass it by and leave it in our rear without danger."[14] But one might wonder, with Wittgenstein, whether Schopenhauer could in fact pass by this fortress. Wittgenstein, as Ernst Michael Lange explains, "had reasons to understand Schopenhauer himself as a solipsist malgré lui."[15] Schopenhauer's arguments for our double knowledge of the self—both as representation and as will—appear aimed precisely at forestalling solipsistic conclusions. His philosophical edifice, one might argue, is a testament to the persistence of his skeptical doubt.

The persistence of such doubts, their ability to survive the efforts of philosophers to disprove them, was a central problem for Wittgenstein, and following him Cavell—both of whom acknowledged learning much from Tolstoy. Like Schopenhauer, Wittgenstein conceived of skepticism as an illness in need of therapy, not refutation. But he, more than Schopenhauer, admitted the gravity of the disease, the temptation to say: "Only what *I* see (or: see now) is really seen."[16] Solipsism—skepticism at its limit—he regarded as "a serious and deep-seated disease of language (one might also say 'of thought')."[17] This indicates both the severity of the problem and the nature of Wittgenstein's proposed remedy: What the skeptic takes to be a metaphysical puzzle is in fact a misuse of language. Consider, for example, a paradigmatic formulation of the skeptical impulse: "I can't feel [another's] pain."[18] By suggesting that pain is analogous to an object within us, this picture misleads us about what Wittgenstein calls the "grammar" of pain. What could it mean for me to "feel another's pain"? If I felt it, wouldn't it be *my* pain? The skeptic's picture mistakes a "logical" impossibility for a "physical" one.[19]

Wittgenstein grapples with skepticism by explicating such mistakes in grammar and thereby revealing various propositions of the skeptic to be meaningless. Yet it is important to note what contemporary readers of Wittgenstein like Toril Moi sometimes do not stress: that he is keenly attentive to the *difficulty* of discarding the misleading pictures created by our misuse of language.[20] We cannot simply leave them behind. Wittgenstein continues his argument with the skeptic, who, captivated by the image of the body as barrier, might be compelled to say that "only my pain is real."[21] In saying so the skeptic believes he is saying something metaphysical, when in fact what he is registering is a "discontentment with our grammar," with our conventional ways of speaking about pain. The skeptic "sees a way of dividing the country different from the one used on the ordinary map. He feels tempted, say, to use the name 'Devonshire' not for the county with its conventional boundary, but a region differently bounded."[22] Wittgenstein offers the following response: "What you want is only a new notation, and by a new notation no facts of geography are changed."[23] But he quickly follows this rejoinder by sympathizing with the skeptic's reluctance to recognize his mistake: "We easily forget how much a notation, a form of expression, may mean to us, and that changing it isn't always as easy as it often is in mathematics or in the sciences. A change of clothes or of names may mean very little and it may mean a great deal."[24] Schopenhauer diagnosed the disease but did not take it too seriously; Wittgenstein takes it seriously and undertakes to furnish a philosophical cure.

A cure, again, is not a refutation. In *The Claim of Reason*, Cavell stresses that Wittgenstein does not so much rebut or resolve skeptical problems as inquire into what gives rise to them in the first place. Cavell orients his own investigation in the same way. Wittgenstein, he writes, takes the claim that "we do not know with certainty of the existence of the external world (or of other minds)" as "*undeniable*, and so shifts its weight."[25] Wittgenstein, as Cavell sees it, starts from the following:

> What the thesis now means is something like: Our relation to the world as a whole, or to others in general, is not one of knowing, where knowing construes itself as being certain. So it is also true that we do not *fail* to know such things. Then the problem is: Why does the skeptic—how can he—take what he has discovered to be some extraordinary, and hitherto unnoticed, fact? Or perhaps we could ask: Why does he take his discovery to be a *thesis*?[26]

Introduction

Wittgenstein's answer has to do with the skeptic's misuse of language, his "discontentment with our grammar"; Cavell is interested in articulating more completely the nature of that discontentment.

Cavell argues that what the skeptic takes to be a limitation of our knowledge is in fact a disappointed metaphysical yearning. The skeptic laments our separateness from one another. In "Knowing and Acknowledging," Cavell turns to the problem of pain. Against one common way of construing Wittgenstein, Cavell argues that the skeptic's statement "I cannot feel his pain" is *not* nonsensical: "There is a fact there to be recorded."[27] Those who would refute the skeptic directly—with the argument, for example, that since my pain and his pain have all the same features, I *can* feel his pain—miss the point. They will not persuade the skeptic because they ignore what he means (however imperfectly) by his statement. What the skeptic wishes to bring out, Cavell explains, is that my relation to my pain is not the same as my relation to another's pain. The skeptic misconceives a metaphysical condition as an epistemic problem, but that does not mean his disappointment can be dismissed: "[T]he formulation 'inability to feel' tries but fails to capture my experience of separation from others."[28] It is not that I cannot know all the qualities of another's pain (and the skeptic will readily admit that I can); it is that his pain will still be *his* pain and not *my* pain.

Cavell's approach to the skeptic thus builds on Wittgenstein's, but with still greater attention to the psychological source of the skeptic's vexations. The asymmetry the skeptic registers is a matter not of knowledge but of "acknowledgement," as Cavell puts it. "Acknowledgement goes beyond knowledge. (Goes beyond not, so to speak, in the order of knowledge, but in its requirement that I *do* something or reveal something on the basis of that knowledge."[29] In other words, we might both know all the features of your pain, but our modes of acknowledging it—revealing it, responding to it—are fundamentally dissimilar. "Of course I do not acknowledge [your pain] the way you do: I do not acknowledge it *by expressing pain*," Cavell explains.[30] I have other means of acknowledging: calling for help, expressing my sympathy, or even neglecting it. But another's pain may also go *unacknowledged*. Cavell praises the skeptic for registering this alarming fact, but rejects his evasive response. By insisting that we can never know another's pain, the skeptic avoids his responsibility to attend to another's pain, with all the risks (being deceived or exposed) and potential for failure that such attentiveness entails. Instead of admitting the possibility of failure, the skeptic asserts the impossibility of success.

Cavell does not foreclose the skeptic's line of questioning, since "to abandon skeptical yearning entirely" would be to abandon "crucial truths about the finitude of human subjectivity," as Hannah Vandegrift Eldridge puts it.[31] At the same time, Cavell places faith in philosophy's capacity to ease the skeptic's predicament by explaining why and how the skeptic conceives of "metaphysical finitude as an intellectual lack."[32] Cavell dedicates much of his work to this task, making use of not only philosophical argument but also literary-critical analysis. With his essays on Shakespearean tragedy, Cavell undertakes to expose what he calls "the cover of skepticism": the evasive shift from the problem of our human condition (as separate but fundamentally mutually dependent beings) to that of epistemological deficiency.[33] Tragedy, he suggests, makes vivid that the skeptic's "terrible doubt cover[s] a yet more terrible certainty," namely, the certainty of our finitude and separateness from others.[34] For Cavell, "human separation . . . can be accepted, and granted, or not."[35] Failing to accept it, as he shows through his readings of *King Lear* and *Othello*, has profound psychological and moral consequences. One can therefore conceive of Cavell's philosophical project as an attempt to bring us closer to acceptance.

"WHAT AM I AFRAID OF? . . . NOTHING . . . MYSELF."

Tolstoy and Nabokov echo the insights of this philosophical tradition, which recognizes radical doubt about the world beyond the self as a persistent, often malign, and self-reinforcing feature of the psyche. And they, too, I will argue, go in search of a cure. But they do not believe the nature of that cure will be a philosophical one, or that it will be once and for all. Wittgenstein and Cavell, though attentive to the grip of skepticism, still believe that elucidating skeptical problems—drilling down into the skeptic's use of language and articulating concepts such as "acknowledgement"—can help us with these problems. Tolstoy and Nabokov are less optimistic about such strategies of conceptual clarification. For them, being aware of the sources (say, misuse of language or metaphysical discontent) and dangers (such as unresponsiveness to others) of one's skeptical yearnings does not make them any less potent. Despite the significance each author attributed to our human capacity for self-reflection, it does not, for either Tolstoy or Nabokov, present a way out of skeptical doubt. In fact, part of the difficulty is that reflexivity itself and the renunciation of habitual modes of perception, two occupational hazards of their chosen profession, are precisely what give rise to doubt. Even more than their philosophical counterparts, Tolstoy and Nabokov regard skepticism as an unshakable burden bestowed on us by the very same sensibilities and wishes that enable aesthetic and ethical achievement.

It might seem odd to stress the dangers Tolstoy—famous for what Viktor Shklovsky called the technique of "estrangement" (*ostraneniia*)—saw in abandoning habitual modes of seeing. It is true that he, like Nabokov, was wary of social forces that adulterate perception. Tolstoy suspected not only

Introduction

social conventions but language itself of dissimulation. Nabokov was less suspicious of language than he was of those who wielded it cynically or clumsily: "All such great words as 'Beauty,' 'Love,' 'Nature,' 'Truth,' and so on become masks and dupes when the smug vulgarian employs them."[36] But for them, the perniciousness and insidiousness of external influence were matched by the danger posed by our own minds, which in the very acts of keen attentiveness and reflexivity distort and eclipse the world, including, most importantly, other people.

In the same diary entry that Shklovsky quotes in his seminal essay "Art as Device" to argue that art's purpose is to reinvigorate our perceptions of the world, Tolstoy subtly registers that vigorous attentiveness to our perceptions might in fact obscure everything but the self. Tolstoy wrote:

> As I was walking around dusting things off in my room, I came to the sofa. For the life of me, I couldn't recall whether I had already dusted it off or not. Since these movements are habitual and unconscious, I felt that it was already impossible to remember it. If I had in fact dusted the sofa and forgotten that I had done so, i.e., if I had acted unconsciously, then this is tantamount to not having done it at all. If someone had seen me doing this consciously, then it might have been possible to restore this in my mind. If, on the other hand, no one had been observing me or observing me only unconsciously, if the complex life of many people takes place entirely on the level of the unconscious, then it's as if this life had never been.[37]

Citing only this first part of the diary entry, Shklovsky underscores Tolstoy's insight that automatized perception creates phantoms of the things that surround us. The critic hints at the aesthetic and moral implications of such unconscious apprehension: "Automatization eats away at things, at clothes, at furniture, at our wives, and at our fear of war."[38] Art's proper task, Shklovsky concludes, is to impede automatized perception—to "estrange" the familiar in order to renew our awareness of it. Using this quote to support his own theory, Shklovsky, however, overlooks its strangeness and excises from his citation text that hints at Tolstoy's discomfort with what he has written.

Tolstoy asserts that dusting his couch unconsciously is tantamount to not having done it at all. But how can that be true? Doesn't it matter—if not to Tolstoy, then to someone visiting him, or tasked with tidying up after him—whether the sofa is dusty or not? By withholding existence from everything that cannot be consciously recollected Tolstoy partakes of the skeptical temptation to accept only one's own experience as real. As Schopenhauer knew, this skeptical mode of thought eats away at things and people no less than habit does. Schopenhauer, John Atwell observes, believed that such a view on the world, which he called *theoretical egoism*, is not only mad but evil, since it entails a *practical egoism* that treats "only [one's] own person

"Some Better Brick Than the Cartesian One"

as a real person."[39] The practical egoist disregards all but his own interests. Given Tolstoy's familiarity with Schopenhauer and his attention to the passages on theoretical egoism in particular, it seems likely he recognized a kinship between his thoughts here and those of the theoretical egoist.[40] This might explain why Tolstoy concludes this diary entry by noting some confusion about what he has written. He struggles to draw out the consequences of his thoughts on habit. He formulates and reformulates the relationship between habit, consciousness, memory, and freedom, and finally appears to throw up his hands. "Seemed clearer as I was thinking it," he writes in a parenthetical at the end of the entry.[41]

Tolstoy and Nabokov knew the creative and moral potential of estranged vision. But each recognized as well that the perceptual process Shklovsky lauded for restoring the external world could also induce a skeptical outlook that, paradoxically, eliminated it again. Two stories of madness offer an initial glimpse of this dilemma, which reappears in one way or another in each chapter of this study. Tolstoy's "Memoirs of a Madman" and Nabokov's "Terror" exist on the margins of each author's immense oeuvre. Compared to the exquisitely crafted works I consider in later chapters, these stories are slight and unpolished. But as Brian Boyd says of "Terror," these short works hit the authors' themes "dead center."[42] They illuminate Tolstoy and Nabokov's treatment of skepticism as a psychic state that can overwhelm us precisely at moments when we attend most closely to our own perceptions.

~

"Memoirs of a Madman" is a framed narrative recounting a series of episodes of estranged perception that culminate in a religious illumination. "Today I was taken to the Provincial Government Board to the certified," begins Tolstoy's unnamed narrator. "Opinions differed" (*MM*, 303; *PSS*, 26:466). The narrator restrains himself and keeps silent during the examination because, as he says, "I am afraid of the lunatic asylum, where they would prevent me from doing my mad work" (*MM*, 303; *PSS*, 26:466). He is declared sane, though as he explains, "I myself know that I am mad" (*MM*, 303; *PSS*, 26:466). The narrator proceeds to give an account of his madness, which, characteristic of late Tolstoy, turns out to be not madness at all but rather moral enlightenment: the narrator, a nobleman and once-savvy landlord, has come to see his mistreatment of those around him; he repents at having treated them as the means to his own ends.

Each episode of estranged perception that brings the narrator closer to enlightenment also inspires unimaginable terror. The first episode, which occurs in a lodging house in the town of Arzamas, has its source in Tolstoy's biography. In 1869, while traveling, like the narrator, to the Penza region

11

Introduction

of Russia to buy an estate, Tolstoy was waylaid for the night in Arzamas. "And something extraordinary happened to me," he wrote to his wife.[43] In the middle of the night, "Suddenly, I was overcome by anxiety, fear, and such terror as I have never experienced. The details of this feeling I will recount to you later, but this kind of torturous feeling I have never experienced and would not, God forbid, wish on anyone."[44] Tolstoy referred to this episode as he drafted "Memoirs of a Madman" in 1884.[45] And notwithstanding Tolstoy's friend and translator Aylmer Maude's sound objection to equating the madman entirely with his creator, it seems likely this story captures something of the feeling Tolstoy could not express in his letter.[46]

The travel-weary narrator finds himself in an unfamiliar place, which for some reason he is compelled to survey with extraordinary attentiveness. A perfectly ordinary lodging house now strikes him as "uncanny." He looks around his rented room, scrutinizing its features: "It was a small square room, with whitewashed walls. I remember being tormented by the fact that it was a square. It had one window with a red curtain, a birchwood table, and a sofa with bent-wood arms" (*MM*, 307; *PSS*, 26:469). He falls asleep and wakes up shortly thereafter to the horrible realization of his own finitude. "Here I am, the whole of me . . . It is myself I am weary of and find intolerable and such a torment. I want to fall asleep and forget myself and cannot. I cannot get away from myself!" (*MM*, 307; *PSS*, 469). The narrator feels oppressed by confinement within the self, and at the same time fearful of the demise of the self in death. It is as though the hyperconscious scrutiny the narrator undertakes just prior to his terror at being unable to escape the self plays some part in catalyzing it. Wittgenstein, owing perhaps to his reading of Tolstoy, likewise underscored the relationship between intense observation and the threat of solipsism.[47]

The second and third episodes of terror recapitulate the first in their emphasis on both the narrator's acuity of vision and his subsequent sense of excruciating isolation. The narrator travels to Moscow and finds himself alone in a hotel room, observing everything from the hotel's smell to the "blue wallpaper with yellow stripes on the partition" in his room. He is wracked by the "same horror as in Arzamas" (*MM*, 309; *PSS*, 471). He asks himself: "What am I afraid of? Why what is it? Nothing. Myself . . . Oh, nonsense!" (*MM*, 310; *PSS*, 471). The final episode of terror occurs during a hunting outing. This time, snow has "altered the look of everything" and helped the narrator see otherwise familiar woods in a new, estranged way (*MM*, 311; *PSS*, 473). He cries out, but "All was still. No one answered" (*MM*, 311; *PSS*, 473).[48] This final episode brings about the narrator's moral transformation: his awakening to "something joyful" that he learns to understand in the final passages of the story (*MM*, 312; *PSS*, 473). This once casual egoist comes to recognize the universal brotherhood of man.

12

"Some Better Brick Than the Cartesian One"

The central irony of the story is that the narrator's estranged vision persuades him of the brotherhood of man while also creating an abyss between himself and others. The narrator only escapes the lunatic asylum by obscuring the state of his soul from his supposed brothers. Henry Pickford in his discussion of this work points out that the narrator's dissimulation as well as the structure of his transformation endorses a "Cartesianism" that opens the door for skeptical doubt. The narrator, as Pickford explains, "withdraw[s] his belief from one set of external behaviors (acquisitive landowner, traditional husband) and eventually invest[s] it in another set of external behaviors."[49] Outward behavior is thus made suspect as an expression of internal states. I would add that the process that decouples the inner and outer is the narrator's keen attentiveness to his own perceptual experience. The separation between inner and outer fuels in turn the skeptical fear that perhaps no outward sign is sufficient to reveal oneself to another. The obscure way the narrator conveys his ultimate spiritual conclusion—"If there is nothing to all that, it certainly does not exist in me"—makes this doubt manifest (*MM*, 313; *PSS*, 26:474). For Cavell, we can ease our skeptical predicament by recognizing the claims others make on us and attempting to meet our responsibilities toward them. This is not to say, of course, that reflecting on our skepticism is always enough to show us what these responsibilities might be or how we can meet them. Still, self-reflection does not lead us in the wrong direction. For Tolstoy, on the other hand, the same self-reflection that reveals to us our responsibilities toward others also underscores our separateness from others, and so amplifies our skeptical fears.

The early twentieth-century philosopher Lev Shestov considered "Memoirs of a Madman" the "key" to Tolstoy's work, suggesting that everything he wrote after *Anna Karenina* might be subsumed under this title. Shestov proposes that in this short sketch Tolstoy allows himself to fully display his most deep-seated fear, a fear that shook him still more than the fear of death: he reveals his "dread of madness—that is, of living not in the common world but in his own individual one."[50] Shestov intends his remark to underscore Tolstoy's dread of moral isolation, the distance between one's sense of right and the moral norms we hold in common. But the choice of words is telling. Invoking the contrast between an individual and a common world, Shestov gestures toward a dread that is as much metaphysical as it is ethical, the dread central to this study: that we are sealed within ourselves, confined by our subjective perspective on the world. Shestov aptly characterizes Tolstoy's apprehension, but mistakenly excludes *Anna Karenina*—the subject of my first chapter—from the corpus of literary texts that imagines the terrifying absence of a common world.

Nabokov's story "Terror" shares much with "Memoirs of a Madman," and, as D. Barton Johnson suggests, may have been inspired by it.[51] Nabo-

13

Introduction

kov's narrator, like Tolstoy's madman, experiences a series of episodes of estrangement from habitual modes of seeing, which culminate in what he calls a "supreme terror, special terror" at seeing "the world such as it really *is*" ("Terror," 174, 176; *SS*, 1:398, 400).[52] He persists in this state as he wanders in an unknown city—"I had no precise recollection of my actions"—and is brought back to ordinary life when he receives news that his lover is dying ("Terror," 177; *SS*, 1:401). Johnson observes the resemblance between Nabokov's story and Tolstoy's in structure and content: both authors give us monologues by "nameless men on the edge of madness" who experience their most excruciating episodes of "existential estrangement" when they are away from home.[53] In the summer of 1926, the year Nabokov likely wrote "Terror," he participated in a mock trial of Tolstoy's *The Kreutzer Sonata* (a performance I examine in chap. 4). Johnson points out that Nabokov surely knew not only Tolstoy's story but also Shestov's interpretation of it, which appeared in *Sovremennye zapiski*, the same Russian émigré journal that would publish "Terror" seven years later. Yet for all the similarities between Tolstoy's and Nabokov's stories, there is an important difference: Nabokov makes his narrator an artist. In doing so he draws our attention to a connection between skepticism and creativity that is less evident in "Memoirs of a Madman" than in Tolstoy's more fully realized works.

In *Anna Karenina*, a novel Nabokov greatly admired, the capacity for creative work such as artmaking is often attributed to the same psychic state that gives rise to skepticism. Here Nabokov attends to the same phenomenon. The narrator, a poet, first experiences a peculiar estrangement while writing poetry. He describes "emerg[ing] from the trance of [his] task at the exact moment when night had reached its summit and was teetering on that crest," and catching sight of himself in the mirror ("Terror," 173; *SS*, 1:397). He fails to recognize himself, as if "during the time I had been deep at work, I had grown disacquainted with myself" ("Terror," 173; *SS*, 1:397). This estrangement from his own image is followed by an episode of estrangement from his lover. He composes while she sits darning a stocking and "all at once, for no reason at all, I became terrified of her presence . . . I am terrified by there being another person in the room with me; I am terrified by the very notion of *another person*" ("Terror," 174; *SS*, 1:399). Though the narrator claims terror overwhelms him for no reason at all, it seems clearly related to the act of composition that immediately precedes it. The artist's work makes him particularly susceptible to solipsism.

The narrator's last and most acute episode of terror, the experience he relates in the narrative before us, is not preceded by creative work but is itself the stimulus for artistic creation. He struggles to put it into words, but nonetheless succeeds: "I wish the part of my story to which I am coming now could be set into italics; no, not even italics would do: I need some

14

"Some Better Brick Than the Cartesian One"

new, unique kind of type . . . Yes, now I think I have found the right words. I hasten to write them down before they fade" ("Terror," 176; *SS*, 1:400). As in Tolstoy, the episode of estrangement entails existential isolation. The narrator's mind "refused to accept" the objects around him as things "connected with ordinary human life" and consequently his "line of communication with the world snapped" ("Terror," 176–77; *SS*, 1:401). As the narrator puts it: "I was on my own and the world on *its* own, and *that* world was devoid of sense" ("Terror," 177; *SS*, 1:401). But Nabokov's madman no less than Tolstoy's receives compensation for this devastating isolation. Only here, that compensation is the artwork he now creates.

Though "Memoirs of a Madman" is more openly concerned with moral questions, it is "Terror" that explicitly draws out the moral consequences of estrangement's double edge. As long as the narrator's mind refuses his ordinary way of seeing, he occupies the position of the Schopenhauerian madman. Only he is real; others are only phantoms: "I understood the horror of a human face. Anatomy, sexual distinction, the notion of 'legs,' 'arms,' 'clothes'—all that was abolished, and there remained in front of me a mere *something* . . . merely *something* moving past" ("Terror," 177; *SS*, 1:401). He grasps for some philosophical notion—"some basic idea, some better brick than the Cartesian one"—but in the end it is only the death of a loved one that brings him back into ordinary life ("Terror," 177; *SS*, 1:401).[54] He learns his lover is dying and races to her side. "Her death saved me from insanity," the narrator explains. "Plain human grief filled my life so completely that there was no room left for any other emotion" ("Terror," 178; *SS*, 1:402). The émigré critic Yuly Aikhenvald, a friend of Nabokov's, seized on this assertion in his review of "Terror" in the émigré paper *Rul'*. "Here is the instructiveness and wisdom of the story," he writes:

> Groundless, mystical terror recedes before the simple terror of human grief, and the death of another cures us of our own fear of death. In our dreadful time, mystical terror is some type of luxury. And madness itself is a certain kind of luxury: madness leads to a sort of confined egoism. Madness seals you away from other people, from close relations. True suffering and sympathy do not permit madness. The madman is guilty before the community.[55]

On this linkage between egoism and madness Aikhenvald echoes Schopenhauer, whom he translated into Russian. The experience of radical skepticism and ordinary human grief exclude each other. Anyone attuned to such grief cannot regard himself as radically apart from others, and anyone who regards himself as radically apart fails to respond to others' suffering.

Yet even in this moment of grief, Nabokov's narrator does not entirely escape the skeptical mode of thought that leads to his solipsistic crisis. He

Introduction

watches as his lover smiles weakly in her delirium and thinks that what she sees "in her dying fancy" is not him but his double, "so that there were two of me standing before her: I myself, whom she did not see, and my double, who was invisible to me. And then I remained alone: my double died with her" ("Terror," 178; *SS*, 1:402). The idea that the person the lover sees—the one she knows—is not him but his double betrays the narrator's sense that our closest companions are still far apart from us; we do not know them. Each of us lives "in our own individual world," as Shestov puts it, and populates it with our own projections.[56] The "special terror" the narrator experiences is not, after all, displaced by plain human grief; it simply acquires another guise. It is not so easy to pass by Schopenhauer's fortress.

In Aikhenvald's reading of "Terror" one sees an argument similar to the one Cavell will make in his reading of *King Lear*:[57] the madman will-fully evades his obligations to others; his mystical terror, the terror of existential isolation, is a cover for his moral failure; the madman is guilty before the community. By calling Nabokov's story "instructive," Aikhenvald (again anticipating Cavell) suggests that grasping this failure might restore sanity—might dispel the temptations of radical skepticism. Nabokov's narrator, however, knows this is not true. Even the death of a loved one does not offer an antidote to his skeptical doubt. He receives at most a temporary reprieve: "But time flows, and her image within me becomes ever more perfect, ever more lifeless . . . I know that my brain is doomed, that the terror I experienced once, the helpless fear of existing, will sometime overtake me again, and that then there will be no salvation" ("Terror," 178; *SS*, 1:402). How does he know that this terror will overwhelm him again? Because he continues to write. And the estranged mode of perception that sustains his creative work is also what fuels his terror. Like Tolstoy—and more so than Schopenhauer, Wittgenstein, and even Cavell—Nabokov fathoms the full extent of not only skepticism's danger but also its implacability.

SUSPICION IS EASY

The tradition of skeptical philosophy that I have sketched above demonstrates the difficulty of resisting distrust of the world beyond the self. Tolstoy and Nabokov supplement the insights of this tradition by attending closely to the ways skeptical doubt shapes aesthetic expression and reception. In examining their treatment of skepticism I aim not only to shed light on their work, artistic practice, and aesthetic pronouncements, but also to challenge a key presumption of our contemporary reading debates. These authors show us that we cannot always read the way we intend to.

In recent years humanities scholars have expressed concern about the pervasiveness in our disciplines of what Paul Ricoeur called "the hermeneu-

"Some Better Brick Than the Cartesian One"

tics of suspicion"—interpretive practices aimed at unveiling what the text ostensibly conceals.[58] Critics of "suspicious" critique argue that it has become a new dogma, an interpretive mode that now obscures more than it reveals. "There is little doubt," write Elizabeth Anker and Rita Felski, "that debates about the merits of critique are very much in the air and that the intellectual or political payoff of interrogating, demystifying and defamiliarizing is no longer quite so self-evident."[59] Bruno Latour worries that instruments of critique are now wielded by unsavory actors to undermine scientific inquiry, such as the science of climate change. "A certain form of critical spirit has sent us down the wrong path," he concludes. "The question was never to get *away* from facts but *closer* to them."[60] Felski proposes that humanities scholars and students adopt the procedures of suspicion unthinkingly and perform them mechanically: they "easily lapse into the complacent cadences of autopilot argument."[61] Felski, and many others, advocate replacing suspicious critique with other modes of reading. Stephen Best and Sharon Marcus suggest that we have "train[ed] ourselves to see *through*" the text. We might, however, relinquish that training to look directly at the "evident, perceptible, apprehensible in texts."[62] We are exhorted to read differently, restoratively, reparatively, postcritically, or on the surface.

These critics seem to presuppose that reading differently is largely a matter of choosing to do so. And so do the critics with whom they quarrel. Indeed, at the very foundation of the concept of suspicious hermeneutics, Ricoeur installed the notion of suspicion as a decision: what united Karl Marx, Friedrich Nietzsche, and Sigmund Freud was "the decision to look upon the whole of consciousness primarily as 'false' consciousness."[63] To read without suspicion, critics of critique suggest, we merely have to let go of the bad habits we acquired from structuralism and poststructuralism.

What is lost in our reading debates—what Tolstoy's and Nabokov's works allow us to recover—is that one might want to read unsuspiciously without being able to. The discourse about our practices of reading is gripped, it seems to me, by a certain picture—a Platonic picture—of aesthetic experience, in which poetry is a form of possession: the reader, according to Plato, is possessed by the poet, who in turn is possessed by the Muse.[64] Proponents of critique recommend that we resist the poet's charisma through detached scrutiny of the poem, so that we avoid becoming enchanted, overwhelmed, and intellectually subjugated. Their postcritical opponents endorse rather than fear the poet's charisma, stressing that pleasure and knowledge might be gained from this experience of possession.[65] But for neither side is it *hard* to get swept up by texts; on the contrary, that seems to be the natural course of things. Receptivity is tacitly held to be more effortless, more elemental, than suspicion. Tolstoy and Nabokov, too, repeated Plato's ideas about the seductive powers of art. Yet in their fiction, discursive writing, and diaries and letters, they keenly and insistently observed how

Introduction

very hard it is for us to attend to other people, and not least to their art. We miss something vital when, possessed ourselves by Plato's picture, we weigh whether to be vigilant against aesthetic possession or to allow ourselves its pleasures. For those pleasures are not, in fact, easily enjoyed; receptivity is far from effortless. Far from being regularly possessed, we spend much of our lives inattentive to others and distrustful of them. Tolstoy and Nabokov recognize that receptivity might not be so simple or so automatic.

By underscoring the labor involved in receptivity, I do not intend to disparage the project of exploring alternatives to suspicious critique. On the contrary, I am profoundly sympathetic to this endeavor and grateful to it for bringing to light the pervasiveness of suspicion. But I am doubtful of the attempt to attribute that pervasiveness merely to institutional forces of the postwar era. The attraction of suspicion, the grip of it, is stronger and deeper than that. The novelist and critic Gabriel Josipovici presents a broader picture of the suspicious condition, one extending further back than the second half of the twentieth century. "[It] is important to realise that the attitude of suspicion not just towards the words and deeds of others but even more towards our own is not simply the result of the awareness of the atrocities of the camps," Josipovici argues; it reaches back to the likes of Stendhal and John Keats.[66] In Josipovici's account, suspicion follows from the uncertain condition of the post-Romantic artist, who makes art after the disappearance of a "craft tradition" that ensured a stable set of criteria for creating and evaluating artistic work: "For a great many writers, from the early Romantics on, suspicion is seen as a kind of blight."[67] Against the postcritical picture of the skeptic who wears his suspicion lightly and might at any moment shrug it off, Josipovici presents a pantheon of artists and thinkers—Søren Kierkegaard, Thomas Mann, Franz Kafka, Samuel Beckett, and Georges Perec, among others—who dwelled painfully in uncertainty, suspecting not only their own words but also the capacities of art altogether.

Josipovici discriminates the deeply felt skepticism of his heroes from the supposed "blitheness" of the poststructuralists: "There is something in itself suspicious about the ease of the solutions proposed by Barthes and Foucault, the triumphalism of their tone."[68] In making declarations such as "writing today 'has freed itself from the dimension of expression,'" do these high theorists "feel vividly enough what this lack entails?"[69] But perhaps they do; other scholars consider their concerns to be rooted just as deeply. Following Cavell, Richard Eldridge and Bernard Rhie argue that "poststructuralist antihumanism is itself but another (very sophisticated) expression of one of the deepest and most characteristic of human impulses—the wish humans have always had to transcend their own finitude."[70] Michael Fischer, again relying on Cavell, explains deconstruction in terms of skeptical disappointment. Why, Fischer asks, does a method ostensibly meant to understand the

"Some Better Brick Than the Cartesian One"

text better end up unraveling it? Because the deconstructionist "may desire the unraveling of the text (really of all our efforts to make ourselves present) that he gets."[71] Taking Paul de Man as his example, Fischer suggests that the deconstructionist critic's epistemological rigor is a cover for his disappointment with our ordinary means of communication: "Disappointed by everyday life, with the apparent mendacity of the vulgar tongue, de Man takes revenge on literature by debunking its pretensions to escape the inauthenticity that for him tarnishes ordinary talk."[72] And one need not read against the grain to recognize the metaphysical yearnings of high theorists. Michael Wood, for example, observes that Barthes, having pronounced the death of the author, continued explicitly to long for a certain authorial presence.[73] "[L]ost in the midst of a text (not *behind* it, like a *deus ex machina*) there is always the other, the author," Barthes wrote. "In the text, in a way, *I desire* the author."[74]

If we acknowledge that the suspicious critics of the twentieth century were often animated by deep-rooted skeptical anxieties, we ought not assume the absence of such anxieties in today's readers, even today's nonprofessional readers. One stated aim of the postcritical turn is to decenter the reading experience of the professional critic and consider a broader range of readers. Critique, according to Anker and Felski, privileges not only certain texts, ones that mimic their own self-reflexivity, but also certain readers. It erects a hierarchy of readers, juxtaposing the knowing, professional, often male, critic with the "naive," nonprofessional, often female, reader.[75] To this end, Felski proposes divorcing suspicion from skepticism. For her, skepticism "implies a world view," while suspicion is an "affective orientation . . . that does not always terminate in the grand abyss of radical doubt."[76] This postcritical stratagem seems bound up with the desire to expose the suspicious critic's pretense to philosophical depth and thus give the lie to his claim to be a superior reader. Yet it risks giving short shrift to not only its academic targets but also the amateur and student readers whose interests it intends to advance. For if Felski is right that "suspicious readers are preceded and often schooled by suspicious writers," then the metaphysical doubts of Kierkegaard, Kafka, Beckett, Tolstoy, and Nabokov surely trouble their readers, even those outside literature departments.[77] In taking up the cause of nonacademic readers, we would be mistaken to underrate or circumscribe the reasons they and we are moved to read.

And one reason many of us are moved to read—one thing good literature is often good at—is to allay our angst at our separateness from one another, or to try to. A chief pleasure of reading is the feeling of encountering a consciousness other than our own. The writer and critic Zadie Smith draws attention to this pleasure in her essay "Rereading Barthes and Nabokov." Despite her early enthusiasm for Barthes, she found that read-

19

ing in the Barthesian way ultimately made her "feel lonely."[78] The loneliness Smith describes is the loneliness of the skeptic, doubtful of the capacity of any mode of expression to reveal oneself to another. Killing the author, for Smith, means "jettison[ing] the very idea of communication, of any possible genuine link between the person who writes and the person who reads."[79] She expresses her gratitude for Nabokov's lingering presence. But Smith attributes this presence primarily to Nabokov's extraliterary authorial persona, the Nabokov we meet in his interviews and critical essays. She underestimates the work that Nabokov's fiction does—and is designed to do—to convince us (at least those of us who might doubt it) that we are not each sealed within ourselves.

Writers like Kafka and Beckett—or, in the Russian tradition, early skeptics like Fyodor Tyutchev and later ones like Daniil Kharms—made skepticism the very subject of their art, whether to celebrate or lament it.[80] Their encounters with skepticism tend to end in absurdity or despair. Tolstoy and Nabokov are different: they investigate the predicament of skepticism in order to formulate artistic strategies that might temporarily keep it at bay. Both hold out hope that suspicion can be overcome—only not by the reader in isolation. Literature can do what the will cannot. Though neither author saw a philosophical cure for skepticism, both wished to find one in art. "The work of thought is to lead us to see the futility of thought," Tolstoy wrote in his note on Descartes. "No need to return to thought. There is another instrument—art."[81] Nabokov, too, searched for "a better brick than the Cartesian one" ("Terror," 177)—and found one in his art.

THE OTHER INSTRUMENT

Tolstoy bemoaned the "wall" that keeps us from knowing "what happens in the souls of other people."[82] Nabokov lamented that nobody can know the "current and substance" of another's thoughts.[83] In chapters 1 and 2, I argue that Tolstoy's and Nabokov's practices as writers and readers were shaped in crucial ways by their doubt about our ability to reveal ourselves to others and to "know" others in turn. This skeptical concern links the two writers more fundamentally than any set of thematic interests, allusions, or intertexts, which are the usual foci of comparison between them.

In chapter 1 I analyze *Anna Karenina* in conjunction with Wittgenstein's and Cavell's writing on solipsism and skepticism and suggest that in addition to the society tale Tolstoy gives us a philosophical drama about the predicament of what I call the "uncertain artist," the artist who cannot be sure that her art has anything more than a private significance. I argue that through his characterization of the novel's two heroes, Anna Karenina and

"Some Better Brick Than the Cartesian One"

Constantine Levin, as well as the artist figure Mikhailov, Tolstoy identifies certain experiential states that induce us to worry that the world and the people around us are only projections of our own minds. Since artmaking requires one to enter these states, solipsistic conclusions plague the artist in particular. By means of the three characters that many consider his avatars in the novel, Tolstoy's narrative probes different ways of escaping—or failing to escape—the menace of solipsism. Yet his own solution differs from that of his characters: in his treatment of art in the novel, Tolstoy, following Kant, maintains that great art affects everyone in the same way. He regards our common aesthetic delight as a sign that we live in a world shared with other people. Resisting aesthetic subjectivism was therefore not merely an artistic or political imperative for Tolstoy but also an existential one. These stakes help explain why the objectivity and universality of aesthetic judgments become desiderata of Tolstoy's aesthetic theory, despite the many interpretive vexations they inspire.

Chapter 2 examines Nabokov's Künstlerroman *The Gift* with its artist protagonist who longs for a spectator with whom to share his perspective completely. Beneath *The Gift*'s tale of artistic triumph, I delineate an undercurrent of distress over the ineradicable gap between author and reader and present a new argument for the source of Nabokov's well-observed attention to doubles. Nabokov, I argue, probes the paradox inherent in longing for a kind of certainty about the success of one's communication with another that can be obtained only if the other is one's perfect double. An other who is one's double ensures perfect communication—but at the cost of eliminating the otherness that makes communication meaningful at all. It therefore plunges the artist back into the very solipsism he wanted to escape. We find a partial solution to this predicament in Nabokov's critical writing. Analyzing his lectures and scholarship on Nikolay Gogol and Alexander Pushkin, I propose that Nabokov's own mode of reading responds to the same skepticism he dramatized in *The Gift*. The stringent empiricism of Nabokov's critical practice, so often mistaken for the whim of a haughty aristocrat, really represents the disappointed desire for an unattainable communion between author and reader, a desire that became even more urgent in the linguistic and cultural isolation of emigration.

Beyond furnishing us with new perspectives on their fiction, each author's entanglements with skepticism clarify the connections between his literary and discursive writing. Tolstoy's desire to articulate an objective aesthetic standard—to determine once and for all "what is and what is not good art"—permeates *Anna Karenina* no less than his essays on art.[54] Nabokov's mode of reading—the esoteric hyperempiricism that compels him in his commentary to *Eugene Onegin* to discuss the number of stoves in the manor house at Pushkin's mother's estate—is already on display in *The Gift*.[55] The

21

Introduction

quixotic attempt to reconstruct the precise movement of Pushkin's thought is, I argue, not far in its underlying impulse from Tolstoy's quest for artistic objectivity. Both authors, stricken by skepticism, were in relentless pursuit of an impossible proximity with others.

Anna Karenina and *The Gift* pose the question: How can I express myself? The works I consider in the second half of the book ask a different question: How can I listen to others? Can I ever hope to attend to anyone but myself? In chapters 3 and 4 I turn from failures of expression to failures of reception—other minds skepticism from the other perspective.

Tolstoy's aesthetic treatise *What Is Art?* is typically read as an account of art's dangerous charisma. Yet it teems most of all with cases of failed aesthetic infection. My revisionary reading in chapter 3 suggests Tolstoy's treatise to be a story about aesthetic unresponsiveness, about the atrophy of receptivity that Tolstoy diagnoses in himself and his peers. Putting Tolstoy's aesthetics in dialogue with David Hume's, I reconstruct the broader discourse they both partake in, one which deems aesthetic receptivity to be an achievement, something to be labored over, rather than our ordinary predisposition. Tolstoy, like Hume, is acutely attuned to the ways we *resist* engaging with an author's expressive gesture. He probes this resistance in *Hadji Murat*, a text not previously recognized for its depiction of aesthetic experience. Tolstoy's novel illuminates his puzzling insistence that a good spectator "must not do anything himself" but only look and listen. True art, Tolstoy suggests, induces a salutary idleness that helps us attend to others rather than ourselves.

But whereas the spectator enjoys this receptive state, the artist is excluded from it, for his work requires a singular focus on his own objectives that Tolstoy (too readily, in Nabokov's view) equated with egoism. With his *Circle of Reading*, Tolstoy seeks a formal solution to the artist's dilemma: in "writing" a calendar of wise sayings, he tries to be artist and reader at once. His initial aim was to assemble a book composed of the wise thoughts of others, starting from the folk wisdom of proverbs and growing to include the reflections of the world's great thinkers. But with each new version of the calendar, Tolstoy's voice increasingly drowns out all others, and his book becomes less a solution to the problem of receptivity than a testament to its intractability.

As Tolstoy demonstrates by his own example, we cannot presume that how we read is wholly up to us. Both he and Nabokov saw that certain dispositions—the skeptical disposition chief among them—impede our capacity to attend to the world beyond the self. The works I analyze in chapter 4—Tolstoy's *The Kreutzer Sonata*, and Nabokov's "Pozdnyshev's Address" and *Pale Fire*—probe the predicament of the mind sequestered by its own skepticism. In trying to reflect on our skepticism, they suggest,

22

"Some Better Brick Than the Cartesian One"

we often burrow deeper into it. But neither author despairs. Although skepticism cannot be willed away, Tolstoy and Nabokov believe that a certain kind of artwork can offer us relief from it, and they endeavor to create such works. *The Kreutzer Sonata* and "Pozdnyshev's Address" (an unpublished dramatic monologue based on Tolstoy's novella) stimulate readerly suspicion in a highly circumscribed way, channeling it toward the reliably unreliable narrator and away from the author and text. A suspect narrator fosters trust in the narrator's creator. But this narrative strategy has a rather different fate in each author's oeuvre. Tolstoy ultimately disavows it and seeks to cultivate trust by writing works he considers "simple" and "sincere."[86] Nabokov goes the other way, writing byzantine texts like *Pale Fire* that intentionally draw out our doubts only to finally diffuse them. Our faith in the communicative capacity of art is thus obliquely reaffirmed.

By illuminating Nabokov's struggle to maintain such faith, I demonstrate how we might reconcile two seemingly opposed perspectives on the author's oeuvre. One school of readers—whether approvingly (e.g., Alfred Appel, Andrew Field) or not (e.g., Richard Rorty, Michael Wood)—regards Nabokov as a composer of intricate aesthetic puzzles aloof from the miseries of human existence. A second, revisionary school, which includes Vladimir Alexandrov, Dana Dragunoiu, Leland de la Durantaye, David Rampton, and Leona Toker, among others, foregrounds the "humanistic value of Nabokov's work"[87]—the attempt to convey human truths from author to reader. My argument suggests a synthesis: the intricate puzzles were developed precisely because Nabokov, haunted by solipsistic doubts and concerned that no one would ever see the world quite the way he does, was unsatisfied and unconvinced by more naive efforts to communicate.

The same doubts led Tolstoy toward quite different forms. My afterword reflects on how the same search led these two authors in such divergent directions. How does the same philosophical concern generate and find expression in such dramatically opposed styles, one of austerity, one of excess? One tries to strip away anything that might induce us to doubt, the other tries to induce our doubts in order to exhaust them, but the impetus and effect are similar. Tolstoy and Nabokov help us see that approaching the text with suspicion is easy; trusting it is hard. It might in fact be so hard that we cannot summon a trustful attitude at will, as hopeful proponents of alternatives to suspicious hermeneutics encourage us to do. Nor, perhaps, can we formalize the way to read trustfully. For Tolstoy and Nabokov, trust is something enacted in each particular instance of reading, with great effort not only by the reader but also by the author, whose work must be designed to withstand our impulse to doubt it.

Chapter One

Tolstoy's Uncertain Artist

TOLSTOY ARRIVED ON the Russian literary scene at a moment when the perennial question "What is art?" acquired renewed prominence. In Europe, as in Russia, this question had gathered urgency throughout the nineteenth century from the erosion of traditional aesthetic hierarchies and systems of patronage, as well as from the advent of realism. Artists increasingly rejected a strict separation between the poetic and the prosaic, and recognized that anything, however ordinary, may be worthy of representation.[1] But what, then, defines the work of art? Three years after the publication of Tolstoy's 1852 debut novel, *Childhood*, Nikolay Chernyshevsky posed this question with fresh force in his much-debated master's thesis, *The Aesthetic Relations of Art to Reality* (1855). Though it would be decades before Tolstoy put forward his own polemical response—in the tract *What Is Art?*—the questions about what art is and is not, what it can and cannot do, were with him from the start.

Chernyshevsky's *Aesthetic Relations of Art to Reality* became the foundational text for the influential school of socially oriented literary criticism practiced by the so-called radical critics of the 1860s, a mode of criticism that would dominate the literary sphere for decades to come. Chernyshevsky interrogated the distinction between aesthetic experience and sensuous pleasure and considered whether such a distinction might be justified at all. "In a word," his thesis declares, "it is evidently impossible to doubt the fact that an aesthetic sensation is a sensation like any other."[2] And a sensation, moreover, that depends on our senses, sight and hearing above all, he argues. As our sense of sight or hearing becomes satiated, overwhelmed, or exhausted, so does our "aesthetic sense" (*esteticheskoe chuvstvo*). The sensuous nature of our aesthetic response suggests to Chernyshevsky that our aesthetic judgments say something about *us*, rather than about the object we call beautiful: "The beautiful is that in which *we* see life as *we* understand it and desire it to be, life as it delights *us*."[3] Although Chernyshevsky was convinced that our aesthetic impressions are determined by our individually constituted senses,

24

he insisted that these impressions are fundamentally shareable. The beautiful is whatever "we" (not "I") understand it to be.

But Chernyshevsky's arguments paved the way for a still more radical reappraisal of the boundary between aesthetic and sensuous enjoyment, undertaken by his disciple Dmitry Pisarev. In his provocative article "The Destruction of Aesthetics" (1865), Pisarev argues:

> Aesthetics or the science of the beautiful has a reasonable right to exist only if the *beautiful* has a meaning distinct from, independent of, the endless variety of personal tastes. But if the beautiful is only what we like, and, consequently, all sorts of notions about beauty are equally valid, then aesthetics turns to dust. Then every single person articulates his own individual aesthetics, and it follows that a shared aesthetics which unites individual tastes is impossible."[4]

If Chernyshevsky is right that aesthetic reflection is nothing but the impressions an object makes on our senses, Pisarev reasons, the intersubjective validity of our judgments about art cannot be guaranteed. Each of us might experience different pleasures and displeasures based on our individual constitutions; there might not be anything that delights *us* collectively. This possibility is enough for Pisarev to declare that any agreement between my response and yours is merely coincidental and trivial. He posits that we can truly share only the conceptual content of art. Only the idea—for which art is a vehicle—is important for us collectively.

Pisarev accepts what one might call "aesthetic skepticism": the view that our aesthetic responses are fundamentally subjective and there is no arguing with individual taste. For the aesthetic skeptic, we have no grounds for defending a given work as more worthy of attention than another, and what we call "judgments" of taste are really only expressions of personal sentiment. Aesthetics, Pisarev proposes, should go the way of alchemy and astrology.[5] What, Pisarev asks, in effect, is specific to art? And he answers: nothing.

Reflecting on Pisarev's writing many years later, Tolstoy admired the bravery with which he spoke.[6] Pisarev's bravery, one surmises, was in his willingness to follow the logic of Chernyshevsky's thesis to its endpoint in aesthetic skepticism. But during the height of his critical work, Pisarev's uncompromising deductions pleased no one. The aesthetic skepticism Pisarev arrived at on the basis of Chernyshevsky's premises interested neither the so-called liberal critics who defended art for art's sake nor the radical and materialist critics who followed Chernyshevsky. The radical and materialist critics, as Boris Sorokin points out, were no more willing to give up "the feasibility of any system of normative aesthetics" than were the liberals;[7] and both

Chapter One

camps were too consumed by political and institutional debates to reflect on the philosophical paradoxes of aesthetic perception and judgment. Chernyshevsky was working to expand the influence of socially oriented criticism by steering the esteemed journal *Sovremennik*, where Tolstoy had published his *Childhood* and other early works. The liberal critics, led by Ivan Turgenev, Vasily Botkin, and Alexander Druzhinin, sought to oppose him.[8]

Despite his later praise for Pisarev, Tolstoy resisted subjectivism in art (and the concomitant aesthetic skepticism) immediately and vehemently. At the time, he waded into aesthetic debates on the side of his friends Turgenev, Botkin, and Druzhinin, defending not only normative aesthetics but also what he called "pure art."[9] In 1859, upon being inducted into the Society of Lovers of the Russian Word, Tolstoy gave a speech criticizing "political literature and especially the literature of [social] accusation" for monopolizing the means of art as well as public attention.[10] He contrasted political literature, which he considered tendentious, with "another literature, which embodies eternal, all-human concerns, the most cherished, intimate consciousness of the people. This literature is accessible to everyone at all times, and no peoples in possession of strength and vitality have developed without such literature."[11] Already in these early statements one sees Tolstoy's rejection of aesthetic subjectivism—that is, the philosophical notion that there can be no agreement about our aesthetic judgments because they are based on individual sensations of pleasure and enjoyment. There *is*, Tolstoy insists, a category of art that offers not subjective pleasures but universal ones, art that affects all humanity in the same way.

Tolstoy's speech was not well received. Before long, Chernyshevsky's critical program dominated literary discourse, and the young Tolstoy, "having just found a place for himself in literature," as Boris Eikhenbaum puts it, "was ejected from it because literature itself in its former aspect had been liquidated."[12] Tolstoy abandoned attempts to affect Russia's literary institutions and moved to his family estate at Yasnaya Polyana. In this sense, Tolstoy was not lying when years later he told his friend Sergei Taneev that he responded to the literary-critical trends of the 1860s with "indifference" (*bezuchastno*).[13] But he was far from indifferent to the aesthetic problems raised by these debates, and in particular to the problem of aesthetic skepticism, which he would continue to probe relentlessly in his fiction.

Four decades later, in 1897, Tolstoy returned more overtly to the stage of aesthetic debate with the publication of *What Is Art?* Here he opposed still more strenuously the idea that aesthetic experiences are reducible to experiences of sensuous pleasure. By defending a distinction between aesthetic and sensuous response, he aimed to stave off Pisarev's conclusion that aesthetic preferences are entirely subjective—expressions of sentiment rather than judgments of worth. He wished to secure the objectivity and uni-

26

versality of aesthetic judgment. To do so, he had to determine once and for all what is and what is not art: "[It] is necessary for a society in which works of art arise and are supported, to find out whether all that professes to be art is really art, whether (as is presupposed in our society) all that which is art is good, and whether it is important and worth those sacrifices which it necessitates" (*WIA*, 16; *PSS*, 30:33). Tolstoy wanted to identify not only what he or his milieu or any given group of appreciators happened to consider good art, but what *all* people *must* consider good art. It was not enough for Tolstoy to say that the poems of the French Decadents were not his cup of tea; he wished to say they were false and bad and anyone who liked them a corrupt, befuddled, opium-smoking fool—and to be justified in saying so. This desire, among other things, motivates Tolstoy's vigorous critique of "beauty" in his treatise. We cannot get away from defining beauty subjectively, he argues, as "that which pleases (without exciting desire)" (*WIA*, 44; *PSS*, 30:58). By the time he wrote *What Is Art?*, beauty fails to offer Tolstoy the firm ground he seeks to resist aesthetic skepticism.

Why did Tolstoy object so strongly to the skeptical position that aesthetic responses are merely expressions of individual sentiment? Why was he so zealous in his rejection of subjectivism in art, when so many other artists, particularly in the later decades of the nineteenth century, accepted it? Such subjectivism, it is true, threatened their status; it demoted poets and painters to the level of chefs, courtesans, and other purveyors of sensuous delights. But in much of his writing on art, Tolstoy railed against the *inflated* status of artists; why would he be so troubled by *this* demotion? Moreover, Tolstoy's own status was hardly in jeopardy. His contemporary and close friend Afanasy Fet suffered much more from the outcomes of literary debates that reduced aesthetic experience to mere sensuous pleasure. Fet was so often accused of creating only trivial, fleeting gratifications of the senses that he finally responded with a defiant "So what?" In his poem "Butterfly," he writes: "You're right. I'm charming with one airy sweep. / All my velvet with its lively sparkling is merely two wings." I am a butterfly, the poet declares, and I offer temporary pleasures to the senses—but so what? I am here, and for a fleeting moment I enchant: "And any moment, flashing, I'll open my wings and fly away."[14] Fet proudly acquiesced, but Tolstoy refused to accept that our aesthetic preferences have so little foundation to them. In *What Is Art?* Tolstoy lamented that "the direction art has taken may be compared to placing on a large circle other circles, smaller and smaller, until a cone is formed, the apex of which is no longer a circle at all. That is what has happened to the art of our times" (*WIA*, 99; *PSS*, 30:111). Artists aim at smaller and smaller audiences; few have faith that they can reach everyone. Fet embraced this fate; why could Tolstoy not? What appalled him about the prospect that art might be made to please only a certain coterie?

Chapter One

Tolstoy offered an answer: he wanted to establish the grounds for objective aesthetic judgment so that society would not squander its resources on what amounted only to the indulgences of the elite. There is little reason to question the sincerity of Tolstoy's rationale, but this motive cannot be his only one. For one thing, Tolstoy wanted to determine what counts as aesthetic delight (rather than pleasures of the senses) in *every* sphere of art, not just those which demanded great resources. He sought the grounding for poetry as well as opera. And though he framed his arguments in terms of the burdens indiscriminate artmaking placed on the laboring class, Tolstoy seemed no less—and perhaps more—concerned about the implications of aesthetic skepticism for the artist's psyche. It is not just society but "every conscientious artist" that must find an objective definition of good art so "that he may be sure that all he does has a valid meaning" (*WIA*, 16; *PSS*, 30:33).

For Tolstoy, resisting aesthetic skepticism was not only an artistic or political imperative but an existential one. Tolstoy saw objective aesthetic judgment as a bulwark against a kind of doubt into which the very process of artmaking threatened to thrust him—doubt regarding the possibility of ascertaining truth about the world and about other people. In other words, resisting aesthetic skepticism went hand in hand with resisting a broader skepticism about our ability to know the external world and other people.

Tolstoy's skepticism is on display in a diary entry from 1870. "In everything there is a limit one cannot get beyond," Tolstoy broods. "And this limit is nowhere more evident for me than in the intellectual activity of man."[15] The finitude of human senses and human reason means that one can never discern a truth beyond the limits of one's own experiences, Tolstoy despairs. He gives full vent to this despair at the limitations of our human knowledge in his autobiographical *Confession* (1884). Tolstoy wanted to know "the meaning of my life beyond time, beyond cause and beyond space," but all his reason could offer was "the meaning of my life within time, within cause and within space."[16] In *Confession*, Tolstoy's external world skepticism is preceded and perhaps even inspired by other minds skepticism: a disappointment in the means of human expression to assure us that our experiences accord with the experiences of others. Disagreements among artists—each of whom claimed to speak a universal truth but in reality expressed ideas that would be "countered by [their] diametrical opposite from somebody else"[17]—help convince Tolstoy that we cannot be certain our experiences agree with those of others. We therefore cannot verify that our experiences are indeed responses to an external, common reality rather than subjective projections.

But whereas in *Confession* artmaking seems only to precipitate skeptical doubt, elsewhere, both before and after this work, Tolstoy renders the relationship between aesthetic experience and skeptical doubt much more

28

ambiguously. In the same diary entry from 1870, Tolstoy proposes that art offers our best hope to transcend the limits of our human knowledge because "[o]nly art knows neither the rules of time, or space, or motion."[18] Three decades later, Tolstoy again places his hopes in art as the means to assuage other minds skepticism. In a diary entry dated December 20, 1896, he polemicizes against his disciple Vladimir Chertkov, who argues that what happens in another's soul is one of the "four walls of the unknown" (*chetyre steny neizvestnosti*). Chertkov is wrong about this fourth wall, Tolstoy argues: "That which happens in the souls of other people, this wall we must break down using all our powers—[we must] aspire to merge with the souls of other people."[19] Tolstoy puts forward art as the way to break down this wall. In *What Is Art?* he contends that "every art causes those to whom the artist's feeling is transmitted to unite in soul with the artist, and also with all who receive the same impression."[20] For Tolstoy, artistic expression has the potential both to motivate and to resolve skeptical doubt.

Although Tolstoy's extraliterary writing gives us some sense of the entanglement in his thought of various forms of skepticism, it is his fiction that explores the dynamics of these relations most fully and vividly. Tolstoy claimed to have "realized his solitude" (*soznal svoe odinochestvo*) in the years he worked on *Anna Karenina*,[21] and so it is to this novel that I turn first to consider the relationship between skeptical doubt and artmaking in Tolstoy. *Anna Karenina* (1878) demonstrates the existential stakes of Tolstoy's encounter with aesthetic skepticism and his vehement, lifelong attempt to reject it.

LEVIN'S SOLITARY GAZE

Constantine Levin can certainly be counted among Tolstoy's greatest skeptics. As we follow Levin from his first failed proposal to Kitty Shcherbatsky to their eventual marriage and the birth of their son, one point of constancy is his abiding doubt. He draws attention to it himself; as Henry Pickford observes, Levin calls his doubt his "chief sin" and admits that "for the most part [he] live[s] in doubt" (*AK*, 788; *PSS*, 19:6). The limitations of his subjectivity distress him until the very end of the novel: "Without knowing what I am and why I'm here, it is impossible for me to live. And I cannot know that, therefore I cannot live" (*AK*, 788; *PSS*, 19:370). Levin recognizes that "when he did not think, but lived, he constantly felt in his soul the presence of an infallible judge who decided which of two possible actions was better and which was worse; and whenever he did not act as he should, he felt it at once" (*AK*, 791; *PSS*, 19:373). Yet he is unsatisfied with this innate moral sense, often perceived *via negativa* by a feeling of "awkwardness" (*neskladno*) at a moral

Chapter One

misstep. He dismisses such knowledge, negative and subjective as it is, as no knowledge at all and is "tormented by [his] ignorance to such a degree that he feared suicide" (*AK*, 791; *PSS*, 19:373). Disappointed with the human intellect, Levin imagines that his inability to see his life from without as well as from within deprives him of some essential knowledge—namely, a supra-individual notion of the good.

Kitty speculates that Levin's doubt has something to do with his solitude. "[W]hy doesn't he believe? Probably because he thinks so much. And he thinks so much because of his solitude. Alone, always alone" (*AK*, 784; *PSS*, 19:366). Indeed, central to Tolstoy's characterization of Levin is the latter's tendency to withdraw from social life and to scrutinize it with an intensity far surpassing that of his fellow characters, with the possible exception of the novel's namesake. Early on, after his first unsuccessful proposal to Kitty, Levin returns to his estate and lives in solitude—"accumulat[ing] a mass of thoughts and feelings that he could not share with anyone around him" to "fight to live a better life" (*AK*, 160, 96; *PSS*, 18:169, 102). As his life changes over the course of the novel, Levin's penchant for solitude remains the same. Even at the end, as a husband and father, he preserves his privacy, wandering in his woods and fields, absorbed as ever in his epistemic conundrums. It might be that his doubts drive him into isolation to find the quiet to contemplate them, but as Kitty suggests, the causation seems to go the other way around: his doubts derive in part from his inclination to retreat from the social world and its practices.

If aloneness in general threatens to spark his skepticism, one aspect of it appears particularly dangerous. It is in moments of intense visual observation—of the kind Levin often engages in—that he feels most constrained by his limited human perspective, most terrified of it, and most desperate to transcend it. Levin has "one of [his] most tormenting days" at the end of the novel, when he cannot stop asking: "What am I? And where am I? And why am I here?" (*AK*, 792; *PSS*, 19:374). These questions arise when rather than partaking in the work of the harvest Levin stands back from it and observes:

> Standing in the cool of the newly covered threshing barn, with fragrant leaves still clinging to the hazel rods pressed to the freshly peeled aspen rafters of the thatched roof, Levin gazed now through the open doorway in which the dry and bitter dust of the threshing hovered and sparkled, at the grass of the threshing floor lit by the hot sun and the fresh straw just taken from the barn, now at the white-breasted swallows with multi-coloured heads that flew peeping under the roof and, fluttering their wings, paused in the opening of the door, now at the people pottering about in the dark and dusty threshing barn, and thought strange thoughts.
>
> "Why is all this being done?" he thought. "What am I standing here and making them work for? . . . What [is this all] for?" (*AK*, 792; *PSS*, 19:374)

Tolstoy's Uncertain Artist

Standing apart from the action, Levin gives his attention not to the work being done but to the *appearance* of the work being done. The doorway conveniently frames his visual field, as though he were looking at a painting. The happenings take on a dreamlike quality, and Levin is compelled to ask what all this is for, as though there were an answer beyond the one he already knows: to gather the harvest. But Levin's queries oppress him only as long as he continues to *stare* at the scene. As soon he recognizes that the peasants are feeding the threshing machine incorrectly and begins to feed it himself, his doubts (which culminate in his wish to "explain his life so that it did not look like the wicked mockery of some devil, or shoot himself") dissipate (*AK*, 796; *PSS*, 19:378).

"The phenomenon of *staring*," according to Wittgenstein, "is closely bound up with the whole puzzle of solipsism."[22] There is, in other words, an intrinsic link perhaps between the kind of Cartesian skepticism Levin experiences on the threshing floor and the kind of intense looking he engages in there. The psychologist Louis Sass, who considers Wittgenstein's insights in the context of schizophrenic delusions, describes a state he calls "passive hyperconcentration." In this state, subjects refrain from interacting with the world, training their attention instead on the details of their own experience. These subjects, like Levin on the threshing floor, stand back and stare. "The more one stares at things," Sass explains,

> the more they may seem to have a "coefficient of subjectivity," to become only "things-seen." When one stares fixedly ahead, the field of consciousness as such can come into prominence. It is as if the lens of awareness were clouding over, losing some of its transparency, and the world beyond were taking on the diaphanous quality of a dream. Then one, so to speak, experiences experience rather than the world.[23]

Directing one's attention to the details of one's own experience makes it appear so vivid that everything outside it seems to pale in comparison. It starts to seem implausible that "other people could have anything like *this*," and one is liable to become convinced that other people are "unbridgeably apart and different, perhaps not really conscious beings at all."[24] In other words, a state of "passive hyperconcentration" fuels both external world and other minds skepticism by fostering the sense that one's experience of the world is inescapably private, impossible to share. (A conclusion that Wittgenstein himself spent a philosophical lifetime resisting.)

Levin, one might say, is prone to "passive hyperconcentration," particularly when gazing at the sky. It stands to reason that the starry sky would inspire episodes of passive staring. For the layperson, at least, the sky is accessible only as a visual perception: What else can one do but stare at it? As a farmer, Levin could conceivably have a practical reason for celestial

Chapter One

scrutiny, such as forecasting the weather. We often do see Levin observing the natural world from this practical perspective. He is irritated by his half-brother Sergei Koznyshev's rhapsodies to the beauty of the family estate, which Koznyshev visits rarely. Surveying the land from the same spot as Koznyshev, Levin attends instead to the work that needs to be done: "at the sight of the meadows his thoughts turned to the mowing" (*AK*, 241; *PSS*, 18:255). Stargazing, however, is associated primarily with a distinctively passive apprehension throughout the novel. Levin stares, and as he stares, he feels the limits of his consciousness and strains against them. Early on in the novel, Levin's contemplation of the morning sky, with its "mother-of-pearl shell of white, fleecy clouds," accompanies his attempt to divine what it means to live a good life (*AK*, 276; *PSS*, 18:291). Here as elsewhere, Levin longs for an external vantage point from which to evaluate his life but must concede the inescapability of his own perspective.

Staring at the sky has a similar effect on Levin even amid his spiritual epiphany at the end of the novel. He lies in the grass looking up at the sky:

> Don't I know that it is infinite space and not a round vault? But no matter how I squint and strain my sight, I cannot help seeing it as round and limited, and despite my knowledge of infinite space, I am undoubtedly right when I see a firm blue vault, more right than when I strain to see beyond it. (*AK*, 800; *PSS*, 19:381–82)

As in the earlier scene, Levin posits that there is something to be gained by stepping outside one's own perspective, by seeing the sky as infinite space. But the more he stares at the sky the more impossible it seems to escape his own subjectivity, to see anything but a blue vault. Levin evidently wishes to be reconciled to his limited perspective—"I am undoubtedly right when I see a firm blue vault"—but he remains troubled by it nevertheless. His anguish at the limits of his own human knowledge reasserts itself in the very last passages of the novel, when he once again stares at the sky. This time he sees a lightning storm raging against the backdrop of the Milky Way. "Well, what is it that disturbs me?" he thinks (*AK*, 815; *PSS*, 19:398). What disturbs him is that he cannot arrive at an objective definition of the "good" that would hold true for all people, including non-Christians. He *has* arrived at a definition of the good, but he cannot be certain that it is the true one, that it is not merely the true one for him. The joy of Levin's spiritual revelation is tempered by its essentially private and unshareable nature. Levin does not dare share it even with Kitty. As he squints and stares at the sky, he contemplates the incommunicability of his revelation.

Levin's inclination to withdraw from others and engage in intense scrutiny of the phenomenal world is both laudable and perilous. Gary Saul Morson has justly identified looking as an action fraught with ethical import in Tolstoy's fiction. For Tolstoy, the "habits of perception we acquire" shape our moral choices.[25] The penetrating gaze Levin trains on his life—his capacity for estranging his experiences—allows him to expose and reject what is false, arbitrary, and pernicious in the conventions of his social set and in his own behavior. Levin's self-scrutiny anticipates Tolstoy's own some years later in *Confession*. As Richard Gustafson has observed, Tolstoy believed that only through "conscious scrutiny" can we judge our habits and alter our behavior in a way that allows us to progress toward greater self-perfection.[26] But there is evident danger in such scrutiny as well. Looking, for one thing, makes consciousness itself a problem, as Wittgenstein and Sass argue. Attending to the experience of one's own experience can render invisible the reality we share with other people; we might even come to doubt that such a shared reality exists at all. We risk succumbing to epistemological skepticism or even, as Wittgenstein suggests, solipsism. In *Anna Karenina*, as Eduard Babaev has noted, Tolstoy explicitly observes our tendency to disregard the experiences of others, as well as our failure to imagine that these experiences resemble our own in vividness or complexity.[27] Tolstoy paraphrases Schopenhauer's reflection on the skeptic's egoism when his narrator suggests that to both Stiva and Levin "it seemed that the life he led was the only real life, and the one his friend led was a mere phantom" (*AK*, 17; *PSS*, 18:20).[28] There is a second danger. If it is shared conventions that most often assure us that the material world has more than a private meaning—that a given object signifies something similar to you as it does to me—then what happens when by distancing oneself from those conventions they come to seem false, arbitrary, and pernicious?

One might object: For Tolstoy, it is not conventions that sanction our common understanding but an immediate attunement between people, an attunement based on our common relation to God. If anything, all forms of mediation, including language, impede that attunement, and so estranging our social conventions only heightens and clarifies the commonality of our experiences. The second proposal scene between Levin and Kitty, conducted almost in silence, is often cited to advance an interpretation along these lines. This interpretation does capture a particular strain of Tolstoy's (perhaps wishful) thinking. Levin and Kitty write in chalk just the first letter of each sentence they wish to express, yet miraculously they understand one another completely. Tolstoy *does* point up the unmediated nature of this exchange by making it so minimally linguistic. Characteristically, though, he simultaneously seeds doubt about the supposed immediacy of Levin and Kitty's common understanding. Far from transcending convention, their exchange here depends crucially on a shared body of tacit knowledge rooted in the couple's common background and customs familiar to them both, such

Chapter One

as the customs of courtship. Part of the reason Levin can understand Kitty is that he understands her social position as an unmarried girl and recognizes her "fear of spinsterhood" (*AK*, 397; *PSS*, 18:418). Other instances of seemingly intuitive insight into the other—at their marriage rites, for example—occur likewise against the background of familiar customs. Anna and Vronsky, too, appear at times to communicate "immediately"—but only so long as they adhere to the social precedents for affairs such as theirs. When their affair is no longer guided by familiar customs, they begin to misunderstand one another. Shared customs and a shared language always precede moments of ostensibly spontaneous and nonlinguistic concord.

Without common customs, Tolstoy's characters often begin to doubt that sharing another's perspective is possible at all. Levin, therefore, who scrutinizes so much and so thoroughly, doubts this possibility more than most; other minds appear frighteningly opaque. When his doubts momentarily recede, as they do during his near-silent exchange with Kitty, Levin marvels. "Levin smiled joyfully: so striking did he find the transition from an intricate, verbose argument with his brother and Pestsov to this laconic and clear, almost wordless, communication of the most complex thoughts" (*AK*, 396; *PSS*, 18:417). But perhaps Levin, like Tolstoy, senses that this moment is less magical than it appears. For despite it and other instances of mutual understanding, Levin continues to question the possibility of a shared world.

MIKHAILOV'S ACUITY OF VISION

With Levin, Tolstoy illustrates the hazards of solitude and of a hypertrophied acuity of vision; with the artist Mikhailov, he illustrates their creative potential. The same tendencies that fuel Levin's skeptical fears are shown to be those indispensable to the work of the artist. Although a relatively minor character, occupying only a dozen or so pages of the novel during Anna and Vronsky's trip to Italy, the painter's importance lies in the "implicit comparison of [his] painted portrait [of Anna] with Tolstoy's verbal one," as Amy Mandelker puts it.[29]

Mikhailov shares both Levin's propensity for solitude and his visual acuity. Solitude seems to be a precondition of Mikhailov's work. He has removed himself twice over from the social world to which he belongs: he not only is a Russian living in Italy but also resides on the very outskirts of his adopted town. His solitude is disturbed when Anna, Vronsky, and the would-be art critic Golenishchev visit his studio. Mikhailov is eager to hear their impressions of his completed paintings but is gladder when they leave. Only then can he look at his work-in-progress "with his full artistic vision and arriv[e] at that state of confidence in the perfection and hence the sig-

34

nificance of his picture which he needed for that tension, exclusive of all other interests, which alone made it possible for him to work" (*AK*, 476; *PSS*, 19:44). Mikhailov's art requires seclusion.

Mikhailov must isolate himself not only physically but also psychologically. To paint, he must become antisocial. "He never worked so ardently and successfully" as after a fight with his wife (*AK*, 469; *PSS*, 19:36). And although he takes on the commission to paint Anna's portrait, his visits to Anna's villa are unpleasant. He is irritated by the attempts of his new patrons to engage him in conversation: "Anna felt from his eyes that he liked looking at her; but he avoided talking with her" (*AK*, 478; *PSS*, 19:46). Mikhailov attends keenly to Anna—but only to her appearance. He refuses social interaction, maintaining his solitude even in the company of others.

Mikhailov's art depends also on his capacity for intense visual scrutiny. His "artistic sense worked incessantly," we are told, and though he does not remember people's names he remembers "all the faces he had ever seen" (*AK*, 470–71; *PSS*, 19:38). Encountering Anna and Vronsky for the first time, Mikhailov "snatched and swallowed" (*skhvatil i proglotil*) the impression made by "the soft lighting on the figure of Anna" and the outlines of Vronsky's jaw, unconsciously stowing these images away "where he could find [them] when it was needed" (*AK*, 471; *PSS*, 19:39). Tolstoy shows how Mikhailov's painting proceeds from just this kind of accumulation of vivid visual impressions. Mikhailov sits down to sketch "the figure of a man in a fit of anger" (*AK*, 469; *PSS*, 19:37). After drawing the figure, he remembers a previous rendering of the same subject. He examines this earlier drawing; it has been altered by a grease spot, which inspires in his mind's eye a third variant of the figure. Suddenly, Mikhailov's imagination is ignited. From memory he conjures up more related images—"the energetic face, with its jutting chin, of a shopkeeper"—and redraws the figure yet again, until finally "the figure, from a dead, invented one, had come alive, and it was now impossible to change it" (*AK*, 469; *PSS*, 19:37). Mikhailov's work on Anna's portrait likely proceeds in a similar way, and when he finishes, Vronsky is awestruck that the artist could capture her so well simply by *seeing* her, without knowing or loving her: "and he just looked and started painting" (*AK*, 477; *PSS*, 19:45). Vronsky, of course, underestimates Mikhailov's labor, which involves not only looking but also obsessive imagining and reimagining the image and making a multitude of minor adjustments. Nonetheless, he is not wrong to observe the significant role played by Mikhailov's acute vision.

In "Preface to the Works of Guy de Maupassant" (1894), an essay on art that Tolstoy composed years later, the author confirmed in his own voice what one surmises from his depiction of Mikhailov: that standing back from social life to engage in a concentrated scrutiny of it is fundamental to the work of the artist. In this essay, Tolstoy goes so far as to define artistic tal-

Chapter One

ent in terms of precisely that, a capacity for "passive hyperconcentration."
He lauds

> that special gift (referred to as talent) that consists in the aptitude for concentrated, intense attention, which depending on the tastes of the author is directed to this or that object. Thanks to this gift, the person endowed with this capacity sees in the objects to which he directs his attention something new—something that others do not see.[30]

Here, as in many other essays, Tolstoy stresses that a real artist must also be clear, sincere, and morally upright. But he nonetheless places talent above these other requirements. Talent, Tolstoy optimistically proclaims, "if it is only given full rein," will not allow an artist to be false or obscure and will inevitably "teach its possessor, put him on the path to moral development."[31] According to Tolstoy, Maupassant had that aptitude for intense attention, but did not know where to direct it. He was seduced by the false conventions of his time, which compelled artists to represent, above all, female beauty. But his talent, his acuity of vision, often elevated him above his own subject matter.

Without denying the literary value of the Mikhailov sections of the novel, we might agree with Rimvydas Šilbajoris that Tolstoy's rendering of the painter serves as a sort of "prototype essay on art."[32] It is the artist's ability to estrange his experience, and thereby perceive its various facets more vividly, which allows him to see "something new" and yet familiar to others. Mikhailov's painting astonishes Vronsky because it captures the "sweetest inner expression of [Anna's]" that Vronsky thought only he, as her lover, knew about (*AK*, 477; *PSS*, 19:45). In fact, the narrator tells us, it is the painting itself that teaches Vronsky this expression, "but the expression was so true that he and others thought they had always known it" (*AK*, 477; *PSS*, 19:45). Mikhailov brings to the surface what Vronsky sees but only dimly or unconsciously. Art, as Tolstoy would later explain, means "taking something formerly invisible, imperceptible, not understood by people, and bringing it to such clarity that it becomes accessible to them."[33] Central to Vronsky's response is the surprise and pleasure that another person has understood Anna in the same way he understands her, that what had seemed to be his own subjective relation to Anna is in fact shared by others. But whereas the spectator's experience of the artwork affirms for him that our experiences of the world are universal, shareable, the artist's *process* brings that very conclusion into question. To create an artwork that convinces others of how much we have in common, Tolstoy suggests, an artist must do things—withdraw from others and stare at life from a remove—that expose him to the menace of solipsism.

LEVIN'S WORK CURE

Through Levin and Mikhailov, Tolstoy identifies experiential states that enable creativity but at the cost of making vivid the limits imposed by one's own consciousness. It is as if Tolstoy is proposing the etiology of his own doubts. By means of these two characters, he also explores whether the skeptical mood that the artistic stance seems to induce can be fended off. Mikhailov, as I will show, succumbs only briefly to it, and Levin, too, however partially and impermanently, overcomes his skepticism at the end of the novel.

Levin's solution to skepticism entails a return to the agrarian traditions of his family. Though he rejects the conventions of the upper classes, he by no means abandons conventions altogether. By adopting the customs of his forefathers, Levin recovers his faith that at least some of the world's most salient features have the same significance to others as they do to him. Consider Levin's conversation with Fyodor, one of his peasants. Fyodor describes another peasant, Platon, as living "for [his] soul" (*AK*, 794; *PSS*, 19:376). This description, Levin thinks, might strike one as "stupid, vague, imprecise" (*AK*, 795; *PSS*, 19:377). How is one expected to understand these words? Yet he feels that he knows exactly what Fyodor means: "I understood fully and more clearly than I understand anything else in life . . . And not I alone, but everybody, the whole world, fully understands this one thing, and this one thing they do not doubt and always agree upon" (*AK*, 797; *PSS*, 19:379). As Morson observes, "What strikes Levin is not what Fyodor says but the fact that he, and everyone, immediately grasps and grants it."[34] This understanding, Levin goes on to reflect, is not deduced or acquired but simply "given by life itself" (*AK*, 797; *PSS*, 19:379). Pickford has argued that Levin anticipates a Wittgensteinian solution to skepticism: He recognizes that "we can question our common background beliefs and practices, but below the level of our shared sense of their necessity, we will find no fixed points."[35] Levin's "solution" to skepticism, Pickford notes, is to subdue his impulse to interpret the world, to stop searching beneath everyday practices for a foundation he will not find. In stilling that impulse, he stills his skepticism. Now he simply "accept[s] what is given."[36]

In practical terms, accepting what is given means reengaging with the world. Instead of staring at the threshing floor as though it were a painting, Levin pitches the grain. Instead of gazing at the sky, he readies his house for visitors. But both Levin and the reader have reason to suspect that Levin's placidity is far from permanent. For one thing, having apparently recovered a faith in our capacity to know others—to share our experiences of the world—Levin feels he cannot share his new spiritual condition with Kitty. It is as though speaking of it with Kitty threatens it in some way. Levin is evidently still far from accepting a Wittgensteinian answer to skepticism. While he os-

37

Chapter One

tensibly affirms the possibility of accessing other minds, he continues to distrust our only human means to do so: language, expressive behavior, and so on. Nonetheless, the practices of daily life do, to some extent, assuage Levin's skeptical doubts. His fears abate thanks to what early on in the novel Levin calls an *Arbeitskur*.[37] The "work cure"—performing the rituals of agrarian life such as mowing with his peasants—offers Levin a source of relief.

A landowner like Levin can renounce his tendency toward "passive hyperconcentration" and embrace the cure of working beside his peasants. Not so an artist—or at least, not an artist who wishes to remain an artist. The artist cannot adopt Levin's work cure because making art requires precisely the practices Levin abandons. Whereas Levin reengages with the social world and embraces its rituals, the artist, according to Tolstoy, can only create something new so long as he continues to stand back from the world, estrange it, and thereby defy its conventions.

THE PROMISE OF ART

In virtually all his essays on art, Tolstoy declares that an artist must create something "wholly new" (*sovershenno novoe*) that is nonetheless "significant to all."[38] This dual emphasis on novelty and broad significance hints at what is at stake in aesthetic experience for Tolstoy and what is threatened by aesthetic skepticism: the possibility of what Tolstoy calls "to mingle souls with another" (*slivat'sia dushoiu s drugim chelovekom*).[39] Aesthetics, as J. M. Bernstein puts it, "has been a mode of revealing how the apparently merely subjective aspects of knowing or meaning (say in sensing and feeling) are not merely so (not merely psychological), but somehow ingredients *in* objective knowings and public meanings that cannot be fully left behind."[40] When I declare a painting beautiful, I do more—on this view—than express a psychological truth about me. Rather, I assume that this object, this "matter of fact," can be significant to both of us in the same way, and I solicit your agreement on its significance. Art serves as "a kind of jointure or convergence of empirical structure and affective significance," in Bernstein's formulation.[41] And so it may help allay the skeptical fear, if we have it, that each of us is separated from everyone else, unable to share our experience of the world.

Not all art can do so, of course. Some art—including, for Tolstoy, many canonical works—we call "art" only out of habit, when in fact we fail to see it at all. For an artwork truly to be seen, and to signal the possibility that I might see the world the same way as its creator, it must depart enough from conventional forms so as to keep me from merely recognizing and categorizing it. To create art, then, the artist's capacity for acute vision must be paired with a disregard for convention. Otherwise, the artist's vision may be clouded. Maupassant is Tolstoy's exemplar of an artist who tragically often allowed convention to obscure his vision. The model artist Mikhailov, in contrast, has precisely the kind of disdain for convention that Tolstoy found wanting in the French writer. The critic Golenishchev denigrates Mikhailov by calling him a "freethinker." He bristles at Mikhailov's indifference to the precedents set by previous artists, accusing him of never having studied the classics and of being a man who "comes straight to nihilistic literature, [and] very quickly learns the whole essence of its negative teaching" (*AK*, 468; *PSS*, 19:35). Though Mikhailov is by no means ignorant of or indifferent to classical artistic precedent—after all, his visitors find him painting an iconic scene of Jesus standing before Pilate—Golenishchev is not so far off the mark. The painter does "negate" in his own work the conventional renderings of Jesus by emphasizing his humanity rather than his divinity. As Alexandrov observes, Mikhailov "is concerned with issues of artistic precedent and genre *only* to the extent that his work transcends them."[42] The amateur and imitative artist Vronsky, who tries his hand at painting while in Italy, believes that one cannot start work before selecting a genre. The genuine artist Mikhailov knows to eschew established generic conventions.

But while rejecting convention allows for the possibility of making real art, it also poses an obvious risk—of creating something that is meaningless to others, something no one acknowledges as art. Stanley Cavell considers this "possibility of fraudulence" intrinsic to the experience of art.[43] Mikhailov is aware of this risk, however dimly. He thinks little of his visitors—"wealthy Russians [who] understood nothing about art but pretended to be amateurs and connoisseurs"—yet awaits their responses to his *Pilate's Admonition* with such trepidation that he can hardly speak: "He always ascribed to his judges a greater depth of understanding than he himself had, and expected something from them that he himself did not see in his picture. And often in the opinions of viewers it seemed to him that he found it" (*AK*, 470–71; *PSS*, 19:38–39). Even with his artistic confidence, at his remove from the world, he remains troubled by the possibility that his painting will not mean to others what it means to him, that if it has any meaning at all it is only a private and subjective one. The artwork might be "new" without being "significant to all."[44]

This scene is as close as Mikhailov comes to discontent over the limits of his own consciousness. Mikhailov echoes Levin's fantasy of seeing the fruits of his mind and his labor from without, to see them with "an indifferent, estranged eye" (*ravnodushnym, postoronnim glazom*). From this perspective, he "forgot everything he had thought before . . . and found nothing good in [the painting]" (*AK*, 472; *PSS*, 19:39–40). But as with Levin staring at the morning sky and fathoming a way to judge his life from without, Tolstoy immediately reveals the painter's vision to be an idle fancy. Mikhailov

Chapter One

discards his imagined appraisal as soon as he hears the first kind word about his painting. Golenishchev notes that Pilate looks like the perfect official, and in response to this remark:

> The whole of Mikhailov's mobile face suddenly beamed; his eyes lit up . . . Mikhailov was delighted with [Golenishchev's] observation. He himself thought the same about the figure of Pilate as Golenishchev did . . . from a state of dejection [he] suddenly went into ecstasy. The whole painting at once came to life before him with all the complexity of everything that lives. (*AK*, 473; *PSS*, 19:41)

Mikhailov is moved by Golenishchev's observation because it seems to echo his own understanding of the Biblical scene. He becomes still more ecstatic when Anna appears to recognize in Jesus's face a feeling of pity for Pilate. That the visitors' remarks are not very clever or insightful does not diminish their importance to Mikhailov, for whom they indicate that someone else has shared at least in part his view of the world. They suggest that Mikhailov's art is not mere personal fancy—that it has the same significance for others as it does for him. Mikhailov receives confirmation that art can demonstrate the accessibility of other minds, and moreover that *his* art can do this. His art really *is* art.

But Tolstoy's narration undermines Mikhailov's conviction with devastating irony. The spectatorial delight and comprehension the artist takes at face value is revealed by the narrator to be feigned. Anna compliments Mikhailov's Christ not because she is truly astounded by the pity expressed in his image but because "she felt it was the centre of the picture, and therefore that praise of it would please the artist" (*AK*, 473; *PSS*, 19:41).[45] She flatters Mikhailov's vanity. Behind Golenishchev's praise is disapproval over this rendering of Jesus as a historical figure, disapproval that ultimately he cannot help but express. These second thoughts of his suggest that Mikhailov is mistaken about the success of his work. As Golenishchev observes, Mikhailov's relation to his subject is unclear, so his spectators cannot understand the subject clearly either. In his critique, Golenishchev refers to the artist Alexander Ivanov, whose history painting *The Appearance of Christ before the People* inspired much controversy at its first exhibition in Russia in 1858 and has continued to be the subject of interpretive debates. Some critics recognized in Ivanov's depiction of Jesus the predominance of the artist's spiritual concern and underscored the sacrality of the image. Others, in contrast, stressed the secular aspects of the painting and the artist's innovation in depicting a human Jesus.[46] Golenishchev accurately describes the reception of Ivanov's painting when he says that spectators wondered what the artist thinks of Christ: "Is he God or not?" (*AK*, 475; *PSS*, 19:43). And, to him, this dissensus among viewers suggests failure—the painting, as Golenishchev says, does not achieve a "unity of impression." He implies that Mikhailov's *Pilate's Admonition* has failed in a similar way. The artist, disturbed, responds that no "educated people" would ask the question: "Is he God or not?" (*AK*, 475; *PSS*, 19:43). But yielding to the opinion of "educated people" (i.e., convention) is always an act of self-deception in Tolstoy's world and a sign of artistic failure. For all his originality and acuity of vision, Mikhailov has gone astray in his painting of Christ and Pilate.[47]

This is not to say that Tolstoy means to discredit Mikhailov as an artist. In fact, Mikhailov's mistake about his *Pilate* is possible precisely because he *is* an artist. Hack artists create art that looks like art but never is. A true artist, like Mikhailov, can make real art, but he can also—and unwittingly—make bad art. Ivan Kramskoy, whom Tolstoy commissioned to paint his portrait in 1873, appraised Ivanov's *Christ* in a way that echoes Tolstoy's appraisal of Mikhailov's *Pilate*. Ivanov, in Kramskoy's view, was unquestionably an artist who defied artistic conventions and created new, true art. But his *Christ*, Kramskoy suggests, was unsuccessful because it inspired incomprehension and "indifference" (*ravnodushie*) among its viewers. Such a reception cannot be blamed on the public, Kramskoy argues. A successful painting arrests the viewer's attention and inspires a pleasure that precludes "evasive exclamations along the lines: 'I don't understand much in art!'" Viewers might not grasp the full extent of the artwork's meaning and its place in the history of art, he says, but "they will always understand and appreciate its vitality and talent, precisely those qualities that cannot leave the viewer indifferent and in the absence of which the artwork does not exist at all for the public."[48] Mikhailov thus resembles Ivanov—one likely model for the character[49]—in his status as a true artist who does not always make good art.

Tolstoy's portrait of the painter suggest that the artist's view of his own work can always be mistaken. Often it is vanity that clouds his judgment; here the subject itself, "the greatest theme available to art," as Mikhailov admits, suggests as much (*AK*, 475; *PSS*, 19:43). The artist can be deceived also by insincere flattery, or even sincere flattery from a corrupted audience that lets convention dictate its response. Such flattery, Tolstoy suggests, was the downfall of Maupassant, who chose his subjects to elicit it. Tolstoy worried that a similar fate might be in store for Kramskoy himself, whom he invoked as an example of a "very good and artistic nature" that had been affected by the "newest Petersburg tendency."[50] Behind Tolstoy's proclamations about the lapses of others lurks a fear, surely, about his own art. Shortly after correcting proofs of the Mikhailov section of the novel, he wrote to Nikolay Strakhov: "Our vile literary profession is corrupting. Every writer has his own atmosphere of flatterers which he carefully surrounds himself with, and he can have no idea of his own importance or the time of his decline."[51]

Chapter One

Tolstoy begged his friend to prevent him from making the kind of mistake we see Mikhailov make in the novel. "Far better to stop at *War and Peace* than to write *The Watch*, etc.,"[52] Tolstoy wrote, worried, perhaps, that *Anna Karenina* might be his own *Pilate's Admonition*.

MIKHAILOV'S FAITH

Mikhailov's disappointment does not last long; in the end, he does not depend on his audience to affirm the significance of his art. Nor does he need the success of his art to affirm the possibility of intersubjectivity. He is convinced of it to begin with. Neither his experiences of withdrawal from society nor his estranged perspective on the world, nor the tepid and unexpected response to his *Pilate*, induce in Mikhailov the skepticism that dogs Levin. Why not?

Mikhailov has recourse to an antidote more potent even than Levin's work cure. He subscribes to Schopenhauer's notion that artistic genius permits one to intuit Platonic Ideas. Schopenhauer believed that aesthetic cognition breaks radically with ordinary cognition and allows the observer to look beyond individual phenomena to the objective truths they manifest. Despite his momentary doubt, Mikhailov remains convinced of his artistic genius and therefore of his extraphenomenal vision, his ability to intuit truths that hold for everyone. His metaphysics resolves at once aesthetic skepticism, as well as external world skepticism, and the problem of other minds.

Echoing Schopenhauer, Mikhailov conceives of his work as the process of "remov[ing] all the wrappings" (*sniat' vse pokrovy*) from an idea revealed to him as an artist (*AK*, 474; *PSS*, 19:42). He silently rebukes Vronsky's comments on the importance of an artist's technique, asserting that it is the artist's ability to intuit ideas that is most essential. Mikhailov thinks:

> If what he saw had also been revealed to a little child or to his kitchen-maid, they too would have been able to lay bare what they saw. But the most experienced and skilful painter-technician would be unable, for all his mechanical ability, to paint anything unless the boundaries of the content were first revealed to him." (*AK*, 474; *PSS*, 19:42)

In the absence of conventions to sanction his work, Mikhailov has recourse to faith in his own genius. Gabriel Josipovici credits Romanticism with sweeping away the traditional institutions that had authorized artistic work and defined aesthetic success: "With Romanticism the ideas of tradition and craft disappeared; they became false, outmoded, and someone like Beethoven sensed that they could no longer support him."[53] But in place of these traditions, Josipovici argues, Beethoven "put his fiery imagination, his hope in the future, his abounding self-confidence."[54] Mikhailov, not unlike Beethoven, authorizes his own art.

Once his visitors are gone, Mikhailov placidly returns to work, convinced once again of his painting's perfection. He is especially taken with the figure of John the Apostle: "As he corrected the leg, he kept looking more closely (*vsmatrivalsia*) at the figure of John in the background, which the visitors had not noticed but which he knew to be the height of perfection" (*AK*, 476; *PSS*, 19:40).[55] Perhaps John is somehow central to the Platonic Idea revealed to Mikhailov. Mikhailov's painting, as Jefferson Gatrall observes, "decenters the Christ image."[56] Perhaps in doing so, Mikhailov intuits that Christ's image must be diminished if his teachings are to come to the fore. John Givens proposes this was Tolstoy's own Christological strategy: he "negated Jesus to save his message."[57] Mikhailov might indeed be delighting in the transcendental truth of his vision. But it is just as plausible that Tolstoy here is pointing up the irony of the artist's self-assurance. In the painting, John's face is "peering (*vgliadyvavsheesia*) at all that was going on" (*AK*, 472; *PSS*, 19:40), and as such an observer he occupies a position similar to that of the artist himself.[58] Tolstoy underscores this similarity by creating a mise en abyme of looking: Mikhailov peers at John while John peers at Christ. Mikhailov's pleasure at John's depiction might suggest a kind of vanity, a delight at what in some sense amounts to a self-portrait. The distracted, almost careless way Mikhailov works on the figure of Christ while admiring John bolsters the suspicion that his pleasure proceeds from vanity rather than some transcendent vision. Mikhailov is sure that he intuits objective truths, but Tolstoy undermines his certainty. What the artist takes for vision might always be delusion. In an echo of the Levin-Kitty engagement scene, this scene proposes a transcendent solution to skeptical doubt only to doubt (with characteristically Tolstoyan ambivalence) the solution itself.[59] Tolstoy's skepticism extends well beyond that of his model artist.

THE UNCERTAIN ARTIST

Tolstoy attempts to resolve his own skeptical doubts in the Levinian way in his *Confession*. He blames his acute skeptical crisis in Arzamas—which later inspired "Memoirs of a Madman"—on his solitude and his estrangement from life's everyday activities. "This trip for the first time made me feel the degree to which I have grown accustomed to you and the children," he explains to Sofia Tolstoy.[60] "I can remain alone only when I am constantly occupied, as I am in Moscow, but without occupation as I am now, I decidedly feel that I cannot be alone."[61] Tolstoy's Arzamas experience echoes Levin's

Chapter One

states of withdrawal and "passive hyperconcentration," which, though dangerous, Tolstoy nonetheless extols for piercing the obfuscations imposed by routine. It is through this kind of experience, as he says in *Confession*, that he came up squarely against the most important question about life's purpose:

> I began to have moments of what first seemed like bewilderment when my life came to a halt as if I didn't know how to live or what to do, and I felt lost and depressed. But it would pass, and I went on living as before. Then these moments of bewilderment became more and more frequent, and they always took the same form. When my life came to a halt, I was faced with the same questions: "What's it all about? and 'So what?'"[62]

Recognizing that he could not live in "bewilderment"—what I have been calling disappointment over the limits of human knowledge—Tolstoy pursues Levin's Rousseauian-primitivist solution. He dismisses the other alternative: Mikhailov's mystical belief in the genius artist's extraphenomenal vision. Tolstoy takes as his model the "toiling people" (*trudiashcheisia narod*) in whose Christian faith he expects to find "the kind of meaning that is not extinguished by death," which does not depend on our own individual perspectives.[63] He wants to renounce his artistic work not because art is compromised but because it is compromising. Tolstoy, as Gustafson observes, "believed that each person had a particular vocation. The work he had to do is derived from some given talent. Everyone pursues perfection but each in his own way. Tolstoy saw his own vocation as a writer and teacher in this sense."[64] In other words, the work of a true artist may be no less worthy than that of a farmer, but artistic toil always compromises the toiler: it requires one to partake of experiential states that induce skeptical doubt. In turning away from art to the agrarian customs of his forefathers, Tolstoy, like Levin, hopes to affirm for himself the possibility of a reality independent of our perceptions and shared with everyone else.

But *Confession*, as Irina Paperno argues, does not proceed neatly from skepticism to belief in an intersubjectively shared truth. Rather, it describes multiple crises and multiple returns to faith. *Confession* ends with the author's supposed renunciation of his craft, yet Tolstoy "contrary to his professed intentions . . . would produce more fiction."[65] The narrative shape of *Confession* and Tolstoy's inability to renounce artmaking both indicate the instability of this Levinian solution and its ultimate inadequacy for Levin's creator. "With everything the author and the character shared," Paperno writes, "there was an important difference: Levin is not a writer . . . The gentleman-farmer might accept, for himself alone, a faith inexpressible in words, but not Tolstoy—the man who, even when writing a letter to an intimate friend, felt that he was reciting a *profession de foi* [profession of faith] to which the whole of humankind attended."[66] By virtue of both his occupation and his personality, Tolstoy could not rest content with the inarticulate truth Levin (ostensibly) embraces.

The work cure won't work for him. He could, however, rely like Mikhailov on the force of his own ego—his artistic self-assurance. Mikhailov's faith in his own genius and the significance of his work (whether or not it really has it) allows him to evade skeptical doubt without renouncing his artistic calling. But Tolstoy evidently cannot always muster such faith in himself. "An artist of sound, lines, color, word, or even thought is in a dreadful position when he doesn't believe in the significance of his own thought," Tolstoy remarks in his diary while at work on *Anna Karenina.* "Sometimes I have it and sometimes not. Why? A mystery."[67] What answer is there, then, for the skeptical artist—the artist who can accept neither Mikhailov's faith in himself nor Levin's faith in convention? Must this artist succumb to his doubts? It is with Anna's story that Tolstoy probes the uncertain artist's "dreadful position."

ANNA'S DOUBT

Reflecting on the structure of *Anna Karenina*, Tolstoy once remarked enigmatically that the seemingly disparate themes of his work are conjoined "not by plot and not by the relationships (acquaintance) of the personages, but by inner linkages."[68] Anna is inherently linked with Mikhailov by way of her artistic capacities and ambitions. With Levin she shares her skeptical inclination. Her closest affinity, however, is perhaps to her creator. Neither possesses the self-certainty of Mikhailov and neither can renounce the states that induce skepticism, as Levin does.

As readers, we become acquainted with Anna's inner life during an instance of the passive, focused viewing to which Levin is also predisposed. Anna's thoughts are first narrated in free indirect discourse during her train journey home to Saint Petersburg after the Moscow ball where she and Vronsky fell in love. She is immobilized in this scene, confined to a small train compartment, her legs wrapped in a rug. A blizzard raging outside her window obscures the passing landscape. There is, as the narrator notes, "nothing to do" (*AK*, 100; *PSS*, 18:107). Anna tries to distract herself by reading, but her book cannot keep her attention long. She turns instead first to thoughts of Vronsky and then to the scrutiny of her surroundings:

> She felt her eyes open wider and wider, her fingers and toes move nervously; something inside her stopped her breath, and all images and sounds in that wavering semi-darkness impressed themselves on her with extraordinary viv-

45

Chapter One

idness. She kept having moments of doubt whether the carriage was moving forwards or backwards, or standing still. Was that Annushka beside her, or some stranger? "What is that on the armrest—a fur coat or some animal? And what am I? Myself or someone else?" (*AK*, 101; *PSS*, 18:107)

We might expect that the more vivid our impressions, the better oriented we become in our surroundings. But the vivacity of Anna's impressions corresponds with a disorientation not only physical but also existential, akin to that experienced by Levin on his "most tormenting days." Peering into the dark threshing barn, Levin asks: "What am I? And where am I? And why am I here?" Scrutinizing her dark train car Anna poses similar questions. In her anxiety about the motion of the train she implicitly echoes Levin's "Where am I?" and the other two questions she poses explicitly: Who is she and what does it mean for *her* (rather than someone else) to occupy precisely this position in time and space? Anna, too, strains against the limits of her subjectivity. To "come to her senses," she stands up and throws off her rug (*podnialas' i opomnilas'*) (*AK*, 101; *PSS*, 18:108). By engaging in action, she disrupts the frightening reverie that for her, just as for Levin, happens in a moment of solitary staring.

Since Anna and Levin are counterpoised in numerous ways in the novel, scholars have tended to contrast their modes of seeing. Levin's intense self-scrutiny, for example, is often juxtaposed with Anna's refusal to see, evinced by her habit of "squinting" (*shchurit'sia*).[69] It is her sister-in-law Dolly who notices this habit when she visits Anna and Vronsky at the latter's estate after Anna has been spurned by society for her affair. It stands to reason that down-to-earth Dolly would equate Anna's inattention to the practical details of her "irregular" family situation—and especially the ambiguous legal status of her children—with blindness (*AK*, 619; *PSS*, 19:193). But it is not entirely accurate to characterize Anna as blind. She is, after all, a keen observer, both literally and metaphorically. We are treated to one of the most vivid panoramas of Tolstoy's novel near the end of it when we follow Anna's gaze on her suicidal journey to the train station. On a metaphorical plane, Anna scrutinizes her own soul more thoroughly than does any other character in the novel save Levin, even if this scrutiny does not prompt her to moral action. It is with good reason that in his discussion of vision in *Anna Karenina*, Thomas Seifrid singles out Mikhailov, Levin, and Anna as exemplary viewers.[70]

Anna is not unseeing. More likely, her vision is marked by the same paradox as Levin's: her intense attention to the details of her own consciousness obscures from view a world shared with other people. This, of course, has undeniable moral consequences for those others, as noted by Dolly as well as many of Tolstoy's readers. It also has epistemological and psycho-

46

logical consequences for Anna herself. Anna first becomes convinced of her solitude in a scene that parallels Levin's scrutiny of the countryside and the mother-of-pearl clouds. As she struggles to reconcile her passion for Vronsky with her religious faith, Anna stops and stares "at the tops of the aspens swaying in the wind, their washed leaves glistening brightly in the cold sun, and she understood that they would not forgive, that everything and everyone would be merciless to her now, like this sky, like this greenery" (*AK*, 290; *PSS*, 18:306). Over the course of the novel, Anna becomes still more isolated and convinced that others cannot share her perspective. "You cannot understand," she tells Dolly, her last female confidant (*AK*, 640; *PSS*, 19:217). Anna fails to trust even Vronsky to grasp her position, particularly regarding her son. Dolly and Vronsky stand at opposite ends of Tolstoy's moral universe. Dolly's ability to forgive her unfaithful husband and her unwavering attentiveness to the routines of motherhood make her, on Morson's view, the "prosaic hero" of the novel—the character "who most embodies the author's values" (*AK*, 640; *PSS*, 19:217). Vronsky, in contrast, epitomizes what Tolstoy considered the corrosive, artificial mores of high society. Yet what these two have in common is their shared adherence to a set of conventions that lets them feel part of a world held in common with others. Anna's capacity for intense scrutiny and estrangement prevents her from fully embracing the conventions either of motherhood or of society life. Ultimately, she becomes convinced that Vronsky cannot understand her any better than Dolly can. Her doubts about the possibility of accessing others or revealing herself to them induce in Anna not only skepticism but a quasi solipsism. She is struck by the idea that her death would resolve her difficult situation: "The shame and disgrace of Alexei Alexandrovich and of Seryozha, and my own terrible shame—death will save it all" (*AK*, 745; *PSS*, 19:324.). This thought, absurd on its face, can only appear reasonable to a solipsist, who does not fully acknowledge that the pain of others—if not perhaps their public shame—will persist even with the extermination of her own self.

Anna, however, cannot avail herself of Levin's work cure to assuage her skeptical doubts. To some extent, she is precluded from it. As other commentators have noted, Levin is privileged by virtue of his gender and his rootedness within the customs of his old, noble family. Justin Weir observes that Levin's family traditions "mak[e] demands on him" and in so doing they anchor his identity.[71] Simply doing what he must do as the patriarch of his family—tending to the estate, arranging the affairs of immediate and distant relatives—draws Levin out of the experiential states that stimulate his doubts. Anna, by contrast, is an urban dweller with little family and still fewer obligations.[72] The few opportunities she has for labor analogous to Levin's work cure diminish over the course of the novel. Sofia Tolstoy's memoirs suggest that Tolstoy conceived of Anna's tragedy, in part, as the

Chapter One

consequence of her exclusion from the world of women's occupations. She reports Tolstoy explaining his heroine's position: "Anna is deprived of the joys of this feminine side of life because she is all alone. All the other women turn away from her, and she has no one with whom to speak about all that comprises the realm of ordinary, purely feminine occupations."[73] Just before her suicide, Anna makes a final visit to Dolly, during which Anna's exclusion from this realm is most poignantly on display. Dolly is the last woman in the novel to maintain her ties with Anna, yet even she keeps Anna at arm's length when Anna interrupts her conference with Kitty about breastfeeding.

Indeed, for Tolstoy, the practices of childrearing come closest to a feminine counterpart to Levin's work cure. When, during her carriage ride to Anna's estate, Dolly is momentarily released from her usual routine, she becomes alienated and echoes Levin's query about life's meaning: "And all that for what?" (*AK*, 607; *PSS*, 19:181). Her answer, like Levin's, comes not in the form of an easily articulated principle but rather through the reimmersion in familial duties.[74] Anna's rootlessness, urbanism, and social disgrace certainly do not make it easy for her to partake of the everyday practices that reassure Dolly and rescue Levin, but she is not entirely barred from them either. Rather, Anna willfully repudiates them in favor of artmaking. She abandons her son, is "superfluous" (*lishniaia*) in her daughter's nursery, and uses birth control to prevent future children. On her visit to Vronsky's estate, Dolly notices that it is Vronsky, not Anna, who organizes the household. Anna is a "hostess only in conducting the conversation" (*AK*, 630; *PSS*, 19:205).

Anna's energies are channeled instead toward making herself and her life into a work of art.[75] Her artistic talents and aspirations are readily apparent in the novel. She is implicitly compared to "the diva in a grand opera," as Julie Buckler has argued.[76] Anna is also an author in both a very concrete sense—she writes a children's book—and a more abstract one: Morson has argued that Anna authors her own romantic love story by choosing at every turn to steer her affair toward a tragic rather than a more mundane conclusion.[77] Her chief art, however, as Amy Mandelker has observed, is the cultivation of her own image, the beauty she knows how to nurture and display.[78] Levin's work cure is as inadequate for Anna as it is for any other artist who does not wish to renounce her vocation.

Of course, Anna's art is not the same as Mikhailov's. For one thing, she does not make art her livelihood. But one's professional status is, for Tolstoy, no measure of one's artistic talent. In *What Is Art?* he suggests repeatedly that it is among the professional artists and critics that one finds those most incapable of understanding and creating art (*WIA*, 118; *PSS*, 30:129). Another distinction: Mikhailov does not *embody* his art the way Anna does, since his work involves making objects rather than transforming the self. But this difference does not discredit Anna's art any more than the first does: her art is just closer to that of an actor than a painter. "If Anna had a talent," Tolstoy writes in a variant of the novel, "it was the talent of an actress."[79]

And so Anna, I suggest, is in important ways Mikhailov's peer. Not only does she share with him her acuity of vision, she also shares with him a willingness (if not eagerness) to defy convention—he in his artistic realm, she in hers. Anna's artistry is first on display at that fateful Moscow ball that inaugurates her affair with Vronsky. Kitty, who has invited her, is dressed in pink tulle and lace, covered in rosettes, and draped with a velvet ribbon around her neck; upon entering the ballroom she joins a similarly "gauzy, ribbony, lacy, colourful crowd of ladies" (*AK*, 77; *PSS*, 18:83). Anna, in contrast, is stunning in black. Anna, of course, is not immune to the vanity that tempts an artist into following conventional models. As the novel progresses, Tolstoy hints that her art becomes ever more imitative and therefore false. She uses artificial means (birth control) to maintain her figure to remain attractive to Vronsky, Dolly cringes at the theatricality of Anna's life on Vronsky's estate, and, as Morson notes, the ending Anna gives her story is a melodramatic cliché.[80] But Mikhailov, too, as we have seen, is not immune to the seductions of vanity; he, too, makes missteps in his art.

The more crucial distinction between the two artists lies in the way that each understands what art is and what it can do. Anna cannot muster Mikhailov's faith that art enables one to channel a transcendent reality. Her implacable empiricism is on display at the end of the novel. Disappointed with her affair, and having fought with Vronsky for the last time, Anna takes a carriage ride to the train station where she will die by suicide. She is again alone and staring. She sees two passersby and thinks: "What can he be talking about so ardently with the other one? . . . Is it really possible to tell someone else what one feels?" (*AK*, 760; *PSS*, 19:340). She observes a man who thinks he recognizes her before realizing he has made a mistake: "He thought he knew me. And he knows me as little as anyone else in the world knows me. I don't know myself. I know my appetites, as the French say" (*AK*, 760; *PSS*, 19:340). Anna then applies her empiricism—the "bright light in which she saw everything"—to her relations with Vronsky, and specifically to her effect on him at that first Moscow ball (*AK*, 762; *PSS*, 19:342). Now, recalling his initial delight in her beauty (her art), Anna sees nothing but the signs of a sensuous satisfaction that has since disappeared: "The zest is gone! . . . Yes, I no longer have the same savour for him" (*AK*, 763; *PSS*, 19:343). She compares her own appeal to that of a tasty morsel, implying that the pleasures of beauty and art are as personal and arbitrary as those of food. Anna's aesthetic skepticism, her conviction that aesthetics amounts to little more than the subjective response of the senses, helps further convince her that she is right to think we can never know others or any truth outside our subjective experiences: we can only know our appetites.

Chapter One

If one hopes to survive in the world, Tolstoy's novel suggests, then one must find a way to quell one's skeptical doubts. But to engage in artistic work is to distance oneself from the conventions that reassure us that we persist in an intersubjectively shared world. Being an artist means making oneself vulnerable to skeptical doubt. Now, an artist might, like Mikhailov, be persuaded that his art channels some otherworldly truth. This faith can confirm for him the commensurability of our experiences as well as the more than merely private significance of his art—its "valid meaning," as Tolstoy puts it in *What Is Art?* In the absence of such faith, however, the artist must find a different means with which to ward off radical skepticism and ground the possibility of a world that is intelligible and held in common. Anna finds no other means. She sits in the train carriage and observes: "Why are those young men in the other carriage shouting? Why do they talk? Why do they laugh? It's all untrue, all a lie, all deceit, all evil!" (*AK*, 767; *PSS*, 19:347). The skeptical fear that Mikhailov through artistic faith and Levin through convention manage to resist—the Cartesian fear that life is "the wicked mockery of some devil"—consumes Anna (*AK*, 796; *PSS*, 19:378). She flings herself under the train.

Morson warns us not to mistake Anna's views for Tolstoy's. The novel undermines her narrative of her life as a tragic romance; its author has no sympathy for the heroine's "self-indulgent and self-destructive" fatalism.[81] Yet readers are not wrong to detect not only Tolstoy's sympathy for his heroine but also an affinity between them. In Anna, Tolstoy recognizes the plight of the uncertain artist, a plight that threatens him too. Tolstoy, like Anna, can avail himself of neither Levin's remedy nor Mikhailov's; he, however, fares better than she.

AGAINST SKEPTICISM

Tolstoy's novel resists the aesthetic skepticism his heroine accepts. Tolstoy defends the objectivity of our aesthetic response and proposes this objectivity as our best proof of the communal nature of the meanings that we ascribe to the things of the world. But Tolstoy strives to defend this objectivity intellectually—to reason his way toward aesthetic objectivity. He cannot accept it on faith as Mikhailov does. Like Anna, Tolstoy is too much of an empiricist to embrace the Platonic-Schopenhauerian idea that objectivity in aesthetic experience is grounded in an eternal, transcendental essence that inheres in the artwork.

From his earliest writing on art, Tolstoy observed that beauty and art appeal to the senses and must therefore depend on the subject. In an unpublished chapter of *Childhood* titled "To Readers," Tolstoy muses on the

50

subjectivity of taste: "One portion of the work might please one person; a different one might please someone else. And what pleased one might even displease the other."[82] And yet, unlike his heroine, Tolstoy wants to claim that our aesthetic responses are not simply expressions of individual sentiment: that a certain kind of art speaks to "all-human concerns" and is "accessible to everyone,"[83] as he says in his Society of Lovers of the Russian Word speech. But how is one to defend the possibility of aesthetic objectivity without recourse to the kind of metaphysics embraced by Mikhailov?

Tolstoy's unpublished address to readers in *Childhood* prefigures his intellectual-philosophical approach to the problem of aesthetic objectivity. Any and all works might please someone in part, but not every work, Tolstoy speculates, will please as a whole: "If the entirety of the work pleases one person, then this work, in my view, is a perfect object of its kind."[84] Tolstoy goes on to consider how an artist, "who always hopes to achieve perfection," can create an artwork that would please someone in its totality. "I find only one means for this: to compose for oneself a clear, definite picture of the mind, the qualities, and tendencies of the intended reader."[85] Tolstoy's intended reader is sensitive, loves his memories, and abounds in "understanding" (*ponimanie*). Weir considers this stylized sentimentality a form of authorial posturing, the young author imitating his literary predecessors—Gogol and Mikhail Lermontov—in hopes of joining their ranks.[86] Yet amid these conventional elements, we recognize Tolstoy's specific approach to distinguishing art from the myriad things that might please us. Tolstoy suspects that this distinction will be secured not by some feature of the object itself but by the nature of the response it elicits.

Although Tolstoy does not embrace the Platonic explanation of aesthetic objectivity, the influence of Plato's thought on beauty is nonetheless apparent in *Anna Karenina*. Tolstoy would eventually seek to avoid the concept of "beauty" in his discussions of art. In *Anna Karenina*, however, an experience of beauty still denotes the particular phenomenological experience associated with aesthetic delight. And like Plato, Tolstoy explores the nature of beauty first by way of the beautiful person, namely Anna herself. The *Symposium*, Plato's dialogue on beauty, is evoked early on in the novel when Levin attempts to draw a contrast between sexual and platonic love. As he speaks in defense of chaste love, Levin remembers his own youthful affairs and becomes embarrassed and confused about the difference between these types of love, both of which, after all, involve desire for the beloved. What Levin forgets, but surely Tolstoy remembers, is Diotima's crucial lesson for Socrates: our love for a beautiful person is the first step on a ladder leading up to the love of beauty as such. A passionate attachment to the sensible can, paradoxically, guide us to love what transcends the sensible.[87] Dispensing with the idea of beauty as an ideal form, Tolstoy nonetheless retains the

Chapter One

Platonic intuition—one also shared by Kant—that the beautiful is something that generates a desire to neglect one's own desires. David Herman has observed the fundamentally paradoxical treatment of passion in *Anna Karenina*: the novel "obviously fears the dangers of passion, yet simultaneously demonstrates that passion and its close ally selfishness are allowable, indeed vitally necessary, to human self-knowledge and well-being, to artists, art, and novels, and even to the search for and articulation of truth."[88] Tolstoy's notion of the beautiful helps to explain his paradoxical rendering of passion. The beautiful allows its observers to escape the dangers of passion—foremost, egoism—precisely by harnessing its energies. It promotes an ardent attachment that directs one's attention away from oneself and one's own demands. Tolstoy underscores this effect of the beautiful through the contrast he draws between Anna and her brother Stiva, who is in many other ways her close likeness.

STIVA THE AGREEABLE

Given Tolstoy's claim that in writing his novel he had "loved the family idea" (*liub[il] mysl' semeinuiu*),[89] it should not surprise us that the novel's aesthetic concerns are filtered through the lens of family relations. Tolstoy previously conscripted family resemblance into symbolic service in *War and Peace*,[90] and Anna Berman has traced the rich symbolism of sibling pairs in *Anna Karenina*. Berman highlights the similarities between the sensuous Oblonskys: "The pair are stuck in the present and—although Anna resists and Stiva does not—they live for their passions, leading them to become the two main adulterers of the novel (both also show a propensity for lying)."[91] But for all their similarities, the differences between the two siblings—their genders, the nature of their desires, their moral commitments—are what critics have used to explain their radically different fates. Stiva's infidelity goes unpunished; Anna's infidelity leads to her suicide.

One important difference has been overlooked: while they are both sensuous and attractive, Stiva and Anna are dissimilar in the way they appeal to other characters in the novel. They inspire in their observers distinct forms of pleasure. Drafts of *Anna Karenina* show that in the course of composing and revising his novel, Tolstoy gradually accentuated this divergence between the Oblonsky siblings.

In early drafts, Stiva is described as strikingly beautiful. Tolstoy uses the word "beautiful" (*krasivo*) five times in a single sentence to describe Stiva's appearance as he wakes from refreshing sleep only to recall the unpleasantness of the night before: his wife, Dolly, had discovered his affair with the family's former governess. In Tolstoy's initial renderings, Stiva pos-

52

sesses both the rich black curls and the "light step" that are emblems of Anna's beauty. Their resemblance is further underscored when we, along with Vronsky (here called Gagin), see Anna for the first time at the Moscow train station. Vronsky/Gagin immediately recognizes the lady stepping off the train as Stiva's sister. Anna and Stiva both have "shining" (*siiaiushchie*) faces that shine still brighter upon their reunion. Anna tenderly recollects her childhood with Stiva, who even then displayed "a weakness in character and a love for everything."[92] Tolstoy hints that Anna might not share Stiva's weakness of character; still, the siblings here are more alike than different.

In subsequent variants, however, Tolstoy emphasizes not Stiva's beauty—though he remains attractive—but rather his affability and his epicurean nature. In rewriting the first chapter, Tolstoy includes the vivid description of Stiva remembering a sensuous dream in which he had delighted in wine, women, and song. In another new scene, Stiva offers chocolates to his favorite daughter. And in a still later draft, Tolstoy adds the detail of a giant pear that Stiva is on the verge of giving his wife when she interrupts him to confront him about his infidelity. Several times Tolstoy has Stiva preside over dinner parties, and he employs a gastronomic metaphor to describe Stiva's effect on society: like a chef, Stiva "kneaded this social dough so well that the drawing room was in fine form and ringing with voices" (*AK*, 381; *PSS*, 18:402). Food is a necessity as well as a pleasure, but Stiva is associated only with the pleasures of food. He offers his wife and children tasty treats but fails to provide them with the necessary provisions for their summer stay in the country. When Levin confesses that he cannot understand Stiva's infidelity because it seems akin to stealing rolls when one is not hungry, Stiva protests: "Why not? Sometimes a sweet roll is so fragrant that you can't help yourself" (*AK*, 40; *PSS*, 18:45).

All the things Stiva delights in—food, wine, sex—provide what Kant referred to as purely subjective, "agreeable" pleasures. Kant's own example of an agreeable pleasure is the pleasure produced by Canary wine.[93] We respond to wine with satisfaction, and we might even express this satisfaction, but we would not demand that others share in our pleasure, Kant argues in his *Critique of Judgment*. "Agreeable" pleasure is characterized by our willingness to grant that our delight in it is purely our own, contingent on the idiosyncrasies of our own senses. Kant distinguishes the pleasures of the agreeable from the pleasures of the beautiful—"aesthetic pleasures." The latter, he suggests, have not only a subjective but also an objective, normative dimension. When we call something "beautiful" we do not merely express our subjective liking, without mandating the agreement of others; rather, we insist that the object somehow *deserves* to be recognized by all as a source of delight.

Tolstoy may not have been directly familiar with this Kantian distinc-

Chapter One

tion, but at the time he wrote *Anna Karenina* he claimed to have read some Kant and was deeply steeped in Schopenhauer's philosophy. As scholars have noted, the epilogue of *War and Peace* grapples with Schopenhauerian ethics and epistemology.[94] *Anna Karenina* shows that Tolstoy also learned from Schopenhauer's aesthetics, which, like the rest of his philosophy, borrowed a great deal from Kant, but also altered Kant a great deal.[95]

Schopenhauer elaborates on Kant's description of "agreeable" pleasures by observing that what we call agreeable appeals primarily to the senses of taste and smell. For Schopenhauer, our delight in wine, food, sex, and so on, is associated with our base animal nature—the blind drive of all beings to preserve and perpetuate their own existence, the unconscious irrational force that he calls "will." He echoes the Kantian idea that agreeable pleasures are purely subjective and adds that, as such, they are "most closely related to the will, and hence are always the most ignoble."[96] Whatever object appeals to taste or smell, he suggests, stimulates our appetites, leaving us in the "throng of desires."[97] In contrast, the beautiful, for Schopenhauer as for Kant, affords us a pleasure with both a subjective and an objective aspect (though, as I will discuss shortly, the philosophers account for the objective aspect in different ways). Whereas agreeable pleasures fuel our relentless, instinctual striving, aesthetic pleasures according to Schopenhauer release us from our subjective perspective and thereby quiet the call of these individual desires. The beautiful enables "pure contemplation"—one is "elevated . . . above himself, his person, his willing, and all willing."[98]

Schopenhauer proposes that aesthetic pleasure is primarily linked with our sense of sight, while our sensory organs are mostly attuned to subjective pleasures and displeasures. Taste, smell, touch, and even hearing "excite pain immediately, and can also be directly agreeable sensuously."[99] Sight, on the other hand, allows for a more objective perception. Sight, "unlike the affections of the other senses, is in itself, directly, and by its sensuous effect, quite incapable of pleasantness or unpleasantness of *sensation* in the organ; in other words, it has no direct connection with the will."[100] As Bart Vandenabeele explains, "seeing something may be neutral" for Schopenhauer "in the sense that it is not pleasurable or painful."[101] The sight of something does not *necessarily* impinge on our senses in a way that would direct our attention immediately to its desirability or undesirability. Consequently, looking (as opposed to tasting and smelling) affords us an opportunity for "a purely objective contemplation."[102] We are not compelled to consider our own needs and so might momentarily forget them: "Then the world as representation alone remains; the world as will has disappeared."[103] For Schopenhauer, this self-forgetting is central to aesthetic pleasure. Schopenhauer's classification of the senses might seem suspect to us[104]—not to mention somewhat at odds with his treatment of music[105]—but this privileging of sight likely appealed

Tolstoy's Uncertain Artist

to Tolstoy, who, as we have already seen, associated artistic talent with visual acuity.[106] Whereas Stiva is closely linked with the senses that respond to the agreeable—taste, smell, touch—Anna is from the first associated with sight, the sense Schopenhauer singles out as most conducive to the kind of abstraction necessary for aesthetic pleasure.

ANNA THE BEAUTIFUL

The reader meets Anna by following Vronsky's gaze as she steps off her train. Tolstoy underscores her appeal to the eyes by framing her in the train doorway. Variants of this scene indicate that the author vacillated between embellishing and paring down the physical descriptions of Anna, thereby emphasizing and deemphasizing the sensuality she shares with Stiva. In one draft she has an "extraordinary slim waist and wide shoulders," as noted by Vronsky.[107] In other drafts she seems plainer, though still "graceful" (*gratsioznaia*). Her resemblance to Stiva diminishes as Tolstoy continues to revise his novel; early on, for example, the siblings have the same eyes, but in a later draft Vronsky observes that Anna has "the same beautiful, bright, and pedigreed face and build [as Stiva], but completely different eyes."[108] What remains unchanged in all variants is that Vronsky is compelled, almost despite himself, to look at Anna and to keep looking at her. As he passes her, he "[feels] a need to glance at her once more," and when Anna reunites with her brother on the platform, "Vronsky, not taking his eyes away, looked at her and smiled, himself not knowing at what" (*AK*, 61–62; *PSS*, 18:66–67). This encounter is only the first of many occasions when Anna's image captivates those who look at her. There was something "riveting" about her (*chto-to prikovyvalo k nei vnimanie*), as Tolstoy writes in one variant.[109]

Although her sensuous (and sexual) appeal is undeniable, Anna produces in her observer an effect more complicated than that produced by her brother. Everyone who meets Stiva responds to him, as though by reflex, with unambiguous delight: "[T]here was in him, in his handsome, bright appearance, shining eyes, black brows and hair, the whiteness and ruddiness of his face, something that *physically* made an amiable and cheerful impression" (*AK*, 15; *PSS*, 18:17; emphasis mine). Stiva's servant Matvey takes "obvious pleasure" in clothing Stiva's "pampered body" (*AK*, 6; *PSS*, 18:8). The Tatar waiter who serves Stiva and Levin their dinner looks at Stiva "with a noticeable smile of pleasure" (*AK*, 35; *PSS*, 18:89). And Levin, who prefers bread to oysters, is pleased nevertheless to see Stiva enjoying them. Acquaintances "would all rejoice . . . when they met him" (*AK*, 15; *PSS*, 18:18). But Anna's appearance both pleases and disturbs Vronsky. Once inside the train, Vronsky watches through the window as Anna greets Stiva on

55

Chapter One

the platform: "[He] saw her go up to her brother, put her hand on his arm, and begin animatedly telling him something that obviously had nothing to do with him, Vronsky, and he found that vexing" (*AK*, 63; *PSS*, 18:68). Vronsky is enthralled by Anna's appearance, but he is hardly cheered by it. He feels instead frustrated at her self-sufficiency.

Anna produces the same effect that Tolstoy, years earlier, had attributed to the muse of "pure art." In his youthful attempts to fight against the tide of politically minded literature, Tolstoy had written to his friend Botkin suggesting that they found a journal devoted to "pure art." "There is positively no room now for literature (*iziashchnoi literature*)," Tolstoy laments, "but don't think that this prevents me from loving it now more than ever."[110] In testament to this love, Tolstoy inserts into the letter a fictional fragment describing an oneiric visit by a muse. In this fragment, called "Dream," the author finds himself speaking before a crowd. His triumph is complete. He is united with the crowd: "They moved me just as I moved them."[111] Suddenly, the author feels behind him "the pull of something separate."[112] It was "an alien happiness" that "compelled me to turn around."[113] As he does so, he notices among the crowd a lone woman. The author cannot recall if this woman was young or old or particularly beautiful. The only thing he knows is that he is drawn "to her with pleasure and pain by an insurmountable force."[114] The muse captivates the author in the same way Anna captivates Vronsky. And like Anna, the muse displays a self-sufficiency that disturbs him. "She was beautiful and happy," the artist explains. She needed no one, and for this reason I felt that I could not live without her."[115] The muse, like Anna, stands at a remove from her observer's desires: she neither notices nor attends to them. In response, the author, like Vronsky, experiences both pleasure and vexation. Upon waking, he is left with a "merciless memory of her" that both brings him to tears and delights him.[116] *Anna Karenina* dispenses with the sentimental style of "Dream." Vronsky does not revel in his own tears. But the novel retains the notion that the beautiful frustrates rather than satisfies the observer.

Tolstoy's treatment of desire in the moment of aesthetic perception suggests that his aesthetics were actually closer to Kant's than to Schopenhauer's, despite Tolstoy's closer knowledge of the latter.[117] Schopenhauer characterizes aesthetic experience as a reprieve from desire, which is a manifestation of the Will. He explains the objective aspect of our aesthetic judgments by positing that in the beautiful we perceive (with the artist's help) timeless Platonic Ideas, which stand beyond the realm of our individual wants. It is these Platonic Ideas that endow aesthetic pleasure with its objectivity. Kant secures the same distinction without recourse to this metaphysics and without denying that desire is part of aesthetic experience.

Kant does not envision aesthetic pleasure as cleansed of desire. As

Richard Moran has argued, aesthetic pleasure in Kant's account includes the sense that one's desires are "guided" by the object of beauty. For Kant, Moran proposes, "a prior sense of necessity or demand . . . characterizes the experience of the beautiful itself."[118] This leads Kant to conclude that our aesthetic judgments demand intersubjective agreement. How does the beautiful elicit this sense of necessity? Precisely by way of the (potentially vexing) feeling—experienced by Vronsky in *Anna Karenina* and Tolstoy's speaker in "Dream"—when we admire something that does not appear to answer to our desires. As Moran puts it, "the idea of something whose status as a value does not depend on my current desires or interests brings to the experience of that value a sense of my being measured by it (rather than my estimating it according to my own needs) and a normative direction of fit from oneself to the beautiful object rather than the reverse."[119] We feel, in other words, as though we do not intend to admire this object but are rather *compelled* to do so. It is as if the demand on our attention and admiration prevails over our particular desires, whatever they may be, and in feeling our desires thus conquered we sense that the object itself has an unconditional value. Our aesthetic judgments thereby acquire a normative aspect.

One might object, perhaps, that Vronsky's response to Anna—as a man, as her future lover, as the untalented artist he later becomes—is unique, unrepresentative. A final example may help dispel that concern. Anna's beauty, it seems, has the same grip on Vronsky as it does on a very different spectator: Kitty. Kitty admires Anna's artistry—her presentation of her own beauty—at the Moscow ball where Kitty expects a marriage proposal from Vronsky but instead loses him to Anna. It is in observing Vronsky observing Anna that Kitty realizes a proposal is not forthcoming:

> What portrayed itself so clearly to Kitty in the mirror of Anna's face, she also saw in him. Where was his quiet, firm manner and carefree calm expression? No, now each time he addressed Anna, he bowed his head slightly, as if wishing to fall down before her, and in his glance there were only obedience and fear. "I do not want to offend you," his glance seemed to say each time, "I want to save myself but do not know how." There was an expression on his face that she had never seen before. (*AK*, 81; *PSS*, 18:87)

In this scene Kitty registers the reversal of "direction of fit." Vronsky's relation to Anna here is obviously not free of desire. But his desire, as Kitty sees it, is less to gratify his own needs than to conform himself to the demands of the admired beauty. Kitty notices that Vronsky's pleasure is accompanied by submission, fear, and agitation, as well as a sense of his own vulnerability. But we must remember that we are seeing this scene through *Kitty's* eyes; it is she who ascribes these feelings of admiration, submission, and vulner-

Chapter One

ability to Vronsky. Perhaps Kitty is giving a faithful account of the scene. More likely, though, this admiration mixed with fear belongs, at least in part, to Kitty herself, whose reaction bears a resemblance to Vronsky's at the train station. Kitty and Vronsky are, in a sense, united by their encounters with Anna's display of beauty. They each understand it in the same way.

Kitty experiences the same compulsion to admire Anna even when Vronsky's gaze no longer mediates her own. Though crushed by the events of the ball—the loss of her suitor to Anna—Kitty cannot help but continue to admire what Mandelker terms Anna's "ekphrastically presented self-portrait":[120]

> Some supernatural force drew Kitty's eyes to Anna's face. She was *enchanting (prelestna)* in her simple black dress, *enchanting* were her full arms with the bracelets on them, *enchanting* her firm neck with its string of pearls, *enchanting* her curly hair in disarray, *enchanting* the graceful, light movements of her small feet and hands, *enchanting* that beautiful face in its animation; but there was something terrible and cruel in her *enchantment.*
>
> Kitty admired her even more than before, and suffered more and more. She felt crushed, and her face showed it. (*AK*, 83; *PSS*, 18:89; emphasis mine)

Kitty experiences her admiration of Anna not as an act of volition but as an obligation imposed from without. The incantatory repetition of the word "enchanting" underscores the extent to which Kitty is mesmerized by Anna's image, which appears cruel because it so thoroughly thwarts Kitty's own desires. Kitty looks "fearfully" (*ispuganno*) at Anna, feeling the same reverence and vulnerability that she had earlier ascribed to Vronsky. She underscores the effects of the beautiful that are central to Kant's account, namely, reverence and demand.

TOLSTOY'S ART CURE

The objectivity of our aesthetic responses *puzzles* Tolstoy in a way that it does not puzzle Plato, Schopenhauer, or their aesthetic disciple Mikhailov. Tolstoy is temperamentally closer to Kant, who also recognized the paradox of our aesthetic reflections and attempted to reason his way to its resolution. Kant famously formulated this aesthetic paradox into the antinomy of taste: "(1) *Thesis.* A judgment of taste is not based on concepts; for otherwise one could dispute about it (decide by means of proofs). (2) *Antithesis.* A judgment of taste is based on concepts; for otherwise, regardless of the variations among [such judgments], one could not even so much as quarrel about them (lay claim to other people's necessary assent to one's judgment)."[121] Our

Tolstoy's Uncertain Artist

aesthetic judgments are based on fundamentally subjective experiences, yet they somehow claim an intersubjective validity.

In *Anna Karenina* Tolstoy secures the distinction between aesthetic and agreeable pleasures in the Kantian way, through the sense that something beautiful compels us to leave off the pursuit of gratification and seek instead to conform ourselves to it. In recognizing that we are answerable to something outside ourselves, something other than our own needs, we register that thing as beautiful rather than just subjectively pleasing. Ironically, the memory Anna recalls to *confirm* her aesthetic skepticism—the scene of her encounter with Vronsky at the ball—is crucial for Tolstoy's *rejection* of the same. Anna's display of beauty offers Vronsky, Kitty, and the reader more than mere gratification. We are compelled to admire her image and expect that other people, if they only look in the right way, would and should respond to Anna's image as we do. This aesthetic experience thereby helps convince us (those of us who doubt it) that we hold in common with other people the meaning we see in the world. For someone troubled by skepticism, such an experience may help keep skeptical doubts at bay.

Tolstoy's solution to the puzzle of aesthetic objectivity is an intellectual one, and as such it cannot grant him the kind of certainty attained by Mikhailov. Reading the novel, one senses Tolstoy's longing to share in Mikhailov's confident, fideistic rejection of aesthetic skepticism—just as one senses Tolstoy's desire to take the Levinian path and abandon those endeavors that inspire his skepticism in the first place. This latter desire, elaborated in Tolstoy's *Confession*, intensifies in the years to come, as Tolstoy turns his attention increasingly to socioreligious concerns. But as I will demonstrate in chapter 3, Tolstoy remained to the end an "uncertain" artist, bound against his wishes to his rationalism and disturbed by doubts that he sought to allay by artistic means.

Chapter Two

Nabokov's Moderate Multiplication of the Self

"THE ARTIST POSSESSED by creation"—this, according to Vladislav Khodasevich, émigré poet and critic and early champion of Nabokov, is Nabokov's great theme. "In this is his passion, his 'burden,' . . . his happiness and grief, his blessed deformity."[1] In his own statements on artistic work, Nabokov stressed the happiness, not the grief, the bliss rather than the burden. He lauded the lone artist, who, with attention turned inward, "makes his own world or worlds."[2] He declared: "I write for myself in multiplicate."[3] He volubly embraced a kind of artistic solipsism: "[An author's] best audience is the person he sees in his shaving mirror every morning. I think that the audience an artist imagines, when he imagines that kind of a thing, is a room filled with people wearing his own mask."[4]

Nabokov's early critics took notice of his confident self-sufficiency. Whether chiding or celebrating Nabokov, who wrote in 1930s Berlin under the penname Sirin, they regarded him as an author happy to be left alone in the world with his own artistic visions. Vladimir Veidle argued, "Sirin attends less to the world that surrounds him and more to his own 'I,' doomed by virtue of his creative calling to reflect the images, visions or phantoms of this world."[5] Alfred Bem praised Nabokov's detachment as a "fitness of spirit" (*zakalennost' dukha*) exemplary in its singularity.[6] Though Georgii Adamovich disparaged what the others praised ("It is more apt to say his mind raves rather than thinks, more apt to say he peers at the phantoms he himself created than at what actually surrounds him"), he, too, emphasized Nabokov's supposed solipsism.[7] From the pens of both sympathetic and adversarial critics, Nabokov emerged as an author indifferent to his readers and their apprehension of his works. Nabokov, as Adamovich puts it, "doesn't bother with anything. He is nourished by his own self, he is turned toward himself."[8]

Nabokov's reputation for lordly disregard toward his audience persists, cultivated in part by the author himself.[9] The notion that a "real writer should ignore all readers but one, that of the future, who in his turn is merely the author reflected in time,"[10] becomes an authorial mantra asserted in both Nabokov's fiction and his extraliterary writing.[11] Nabokov claimed to be "perfectly indifferent to the capacity and condition of the reader's brain."[12] He stressed his own authorial pleasure as his only motive for creative work and often implied that an artwork is perhaps best enjoyed by the author himself, first during composition and then once the work is complete. "My inventions, my circles, my special islands are infinitely safe from exasperated readers," he declared.[13]

Indeed, Nabokov rarely confronted hostile critics even for (what he considered) outright misinterpretations of his works. But, tellingly, he could never ignore even minor misapprehensions by those who were charitable readers, who *wanted* to understand him. He could not forego making "trivial complaints"—both in print and in private correspondence—about readers he considered to have understood him rather well.[14] To the contributors to his festschrift in *TriQuarterly*, Nabokov offered praise as well as correctives, publishing "rough jottings" like the following: "In Miss Berberov's excellent article on *Pale Fire* I find a couple of minute mistakes."[15] In his letters to Appel, he lauded the critic's book *Nabokov's Dark Cinema*, but pointed out that Appel "slant[s] my works movieward" and that Nabokov did not in fact know the films Appel reads into his books.[16] Nabokov praised Page Stegner's *Escape into Aesthetics*, but could not help but note certain misreadings that might be emended in a second edition of Stegner's book: "I would be glad to list them all for you."[17] On one occasion Nabokov went so far as to admonish his own mother—whom, along with his wife Véra and his father, he considered his best reader[18]—for the allegorical way she had read *Priglashenie na kazn'* (*Invitation to a Beheading*), published in 1936. "You shouldn't look for any symbol or allegory," Nabokov explains. "It's extremely logical and real, it is the simplest everyday reality and doesn't need any special explanation."[19] His remark is undoubtedly facetious—or, as Eric Naiman might put it, "perverse"[20]—yet critics can hardly be blamed for seeing beneath the humorous surface Nabokov's desire for "total control . . . of the reading process."[21] A self-conscious and slightly embarrassed desire, perhaps, but nevertheless a real and urgent one.

Scholarly accounts disagree about the benevolence of Nabokov's methods in teaching his readers how to read. Some underscore Nabokov's generosity and patience in guiding us toward a more attentive attitude not just to fictional worlds but also to our own real one (e.g., Boyd and Stephen Blackwell).[22] Others stress the playful derision of his tutelage. Naiman, for example, argues that Nabokov defamiliarizes the process of reading itself by cultivating an interpretive anxiety among his readers.[23] Such accounts break along a familiar fault line in scholarship, construing Nabokov as either the sagacious metaphysician or the unsentimental postmodernist trickster. What none of them seems to question, however, is his self-possession. Whether Nabokov charitably reveals to us the mysteries of this world and the next, or toys with us to disrupt our routinized perceptions, he still always appears

Chapter Two

as a knowing author, helping us to overcome our own ignorance or dullness. To some, Nabokov looks like a Neoplatonist, to others, a happy skeptic. In either case, he seems untroubled by the limits of human understanding because he either believes in transcendence or cheerfully accepts its impossibility. The one way Nabokov *does not* readily present himself to readers is as a desperate seeker in the vein of Tolstoy and his heroes. My aim in what follows will be to show that, paradoxically, we must see him in this unfamiliar guise in order to reconcile his Olympian self-sufficiency with his stringent demands on readers.

Through an analysis of *The Gift*—Nabokov's most autobiographical novel and certainly the one most self-consciously concerned with the relationship between authors and readers—I contest the perception that Nabokov's work shows "very little anxiety . . . as concerns shared conceptions, full communication."[24] In this novel Nabokov explores what, following Cavell, I wish to call a *skeptical disappointment* in the uncertainty inherent in our human relations. Nabokov's artist-hero Fyodor longs for a kind of certainty about the success and completeness of one's communication with an other that can only be achieved if the other is one's perfect double. But can communication take place if the addressee is not truly an other? The very perfection of resemblance threatens to transform the communicative gesture into a solipsistic delusion. Fyodor, I suggest, echoes the skepticism of Tolstoy's Anna Karenina when she asks: "Is it really possible to tell someone else what one feels?" (*AK*, 760; *PSS*, 19:340). Then, turning from Nabokov's novel to his own reading practices, I further suggest that Nabokov, like his hero in *The Gift*, denies the possibility of certainty about another person's meaning while at the same time longing for it. His stringent demands on readers are not incidental to his work, not a quirk of personality or a vestige of his aristocratic upbringing. Rather, they are rooted in a vexing philosophical problem that permeates his criticism and his fiction.

In light of this preoccupation with accessing other minds, Nabokov's proclamation that the author is his own best audience sounds less triumphant. Indeed, it declares both victory and defeat: it is at once a celebration of artistic autonomy and a lament of our incapacity to know others and to make ourselves known. This is perhaps the reason that artistic self-sufficiency always exists in dialectical tension with the threat of solipsism in Nabokov's literary works. Nabokov thus seems less like a "wicked wizard," as Saul Bellow called him, than a spiritual searcher after Tolstoy.[25]

SKEPTICISM AND THE STRUCTURE OF *THE GIFT*

Many readers of Nabokov are likely to be familiar with *The Gift*, his last Russian novel.[26] Nonetheless, I would like to describe the text in some detail: first, to orient the reader within this formally difficult artwork, for even someone well-acquainted with the novel might struggle to recall all its complexities; and second, to demonstrate the novel's evident concern with what it takes to be a good reader, not only of texts but also of other people.

The Gift, often described as a Künstlerroman, tells the story of Fyodor Godunov-Cherdyntsev, a young Russian émigré living in Berlin. Fyodor knows his creative potential and over the course of the novel he realizes it. He also meets the woman who will become his fiancée, Zina Mertz.

The book has five chapters, with each subsequent chapter depicting Fyodor's gift at a higher stage of its development. In chapter 1 we are introduced to Fyodor's talent through his recently published book of poems about his childhood, as well as his first attempt to compose a biographical sketch. He ponders how he would write about the life of his friends' son who died by suicide, but he never actually puts pen to paper. Fyodor makes a second attempt at a biographical work in chapter 2, writing about his father, a famous naturalist who disappeared (and likely perished) during his last expedition in central Asia around the time of the Bolshevik Revolution. From the outset, Nabokov's text alternates between third-person and first-person narration, blurring the distinction between protagonist and narrator, suggesting that the novel's hero also could be its author-narrator. In chapter 2 the identity of the author-narrator is complicated still further, as descriptions of Fyodor's research for his father's biography and Fyodor's recollections of his father flow seamlessly into what appear to be passages of the biography itself. At the end of the chapter Fyodor decides to give up on the project, not wishing to "dilute it with myself" (*rasbavit' vse eto soboi*) the story of his father's travels (*Gift*, 139; *SS* 3:125).

Chapter 3 is dedicated to the romance between Fyodor and Zina. The story of their courtship is told primarily in the third person, though Fyodor's recollections of his youthful poetic experiments and his composition of a love poem to Zina are given in first-person narration. This chapter also describes Fyodor's work on his third biographical text, this time about the life of the nineteenth-century radical critic Nikolay Chernyshevsky. This biography is the only one in the novel that Fyodor completes, and its full text comprises chapter 4 of *The Gift*. In telling Chernyshevsky's life, Fyodor liberally mixes historical facts with fictions, and even invents a fictitious biographer of Chernyshevsky, whom he cites throughout his book. Fyodor's *The Life of Chernyshevsky* lampoons and critiques Chernyshevsky's materialism and his utilitarian aesthetics, which would subordinate art to sociopolitical aims.

The final chapter of *The Gift* describes the reception of Fyodor's book, which most readers fail to appreciate as an imaginative work of art, considering it instead an invective against one of Russia's liberal icons. Fyodor, however, knows that his talent has reached new heights and tells his fiancée, Zina, of his ambitious plan for his next project. He will write a novel about

Chapter Two

the way fate has brought the two of them together—in other words, a novel that could be *The Gift* itself. But he promises to "shuffle, twist, mix, rechew and rebelch everything" in such a way that "nothing remains of the auto-biography but dust" (*Gift*, 364; *SS* 3:328). The shape of Nabokov's text thus comes to resemble what scholars have variously described as a spiral, a nesting doll, a figure eight, and a Mobius strip, sparking debate about whether Fyodor can in fact be the author-narrator of *The Gift*.[27] All can agree, however, that even if Fyodor and the author-narrator are not one and the same, they have a great deal in common, including their interest in writing biographies and autobiographies.

Central to these genres is the question: Is it possible to know others and make oneself known to them? The structure of *The Gift* resists a definitive answer. If Fyodor is indeed the author of *The Gift*—a novel about how he came to realize his talent—then he appears to successfully author an autobiography. The novel suggests that it *is* possible to tell one's life. But then again Fyodor has promised to reshuffle the particulars of his life, leaving only the "dust" of autobiography. So perhaps it is *not* possible to tell one's life, to reveal oneself to another person. In the fictional world of the novel, Fyodor's more earnest and less imaginative biographical projects are unsuccessful, incomplete. It is *not* possible to truly know another person and to tell his life. But of course these biographies are complete as texts within the author-narrator's novel *The Gift*. So perhaps it *is* possible after all. My aim here is not to lose my reader in this metafictional labyrinth, but rather to underscore that inscribed in the very structure of Nabokov's novel is an ambivalence about our capacity to know others and be known by them. A further, thematic analysis of the novel will allow us to appreciate the depth of this ambivalence and to elucidate how it shapes Nabokov's conception of the relationship between authors and readers.

READING OTHER PEOPLE

Nabokov's hero undertakes two forms of reading throughout *The Gift*. The first, his reading (or rather rereading) of the Russian literary canon from "Pushkin Avenue to Gogol Street" and beyond, lends itself to teleological interpretations of the novel (*Gift*, 145; *SS*, 3:131). Fyodor recalls, discusses, and evaluates the prose of Nikolay Leskov, Turgenev, Tolstoy, and Anton Chekhov; the poetry of Fyodor Tyutchev, Fet, and Alexander Blok; and many others, as his own talents mature. At the novel's conclusion, Fyodor's own art appears to be the triumphant culmination of this tradition. The other kind of reading that occupies Fyodor—reading the minds of other people—works against such teleology, undermining the ethos of optimism in *The Gift*.

Fyodor is no better at reading others at the end of the novel than he was at the beginning. Each attempt leaves Fyodor doubtful of his success.

Early in the novel Fyodor spends an evening at the home of his friend Alexander Chernyshevsky, namesake though not a relation of Nikolay Chernyshevsky, who will be the subject of Fyodor's biography. Looking around the room, Fyodor tries to do again what he does "everywhere and always." He tries

> to imagine the inner, transparent motion of this or that other person. He would carefully seat himself inside the interlocutor as in an armchair, so that the other's elbows would serve as armrests for him, and his soul would fit snugly into the other's soul—and then the lighting of the world would suddenly change and for a minute he would actually become Alexander Chernyshevski, or Lyubov Markovna, or Vasiliev. (*Gift*, 35–36; *SS*, 3:33)

Fyodor's purpose in these ventures into other minds is ambiguous, and scholars disagree on whether these are exercises in empathy or fundamentally "*appropriative* gestures," as Naiman suggests, "even when they are tinged by a certain compassion."[28] Probably they are both.[29] More important than the question about whether this attempt to inhabit others is undertaken out of pity or in search of artistic material is that it *fails*—a failure often overlooked in discussions of Fyodor's mindreading.

Fyodor's sense that he has "actually become" (*deistvitel'no byl*) someone else in this scene is fleeting and disrupted by his doubt that he has truly apprehended another's state of mind. Fyodor fits himself into the soul of his friend Alexander Chernyshevsky, imagining Chernyshevsky attending to the ghost of his deceased son Yasha, who became involved in a love triangle and killed himself as a result. Yasha's ghost appears more real to Chernyshevsky than his flesh and blood guests, Fyodor asserts. But having made this assertion, he quickly retracts it, acknowledging that "perhaps this is all wrong," that Chernyshevsky "is not imagining his dead son at all right now as I imagine him doing" (*Gift*, 35; *SS*, 3:33). Chernyshevsky's "wandering" eyes (*begaiut glaza*), which Fyodor takes to be following the ghost of Yasha, may simply be a sign of his "fidgety" nature (*nervnyi*) or boredom in conversation. Or they may not express anything at all. Fyodor is ready to admit that this is only a game of observation, that Chernyshevsky's behavior reveals nothing definitive about the state of his soul.

Fyodor's forays into others' souls not only fail but also warn him against a certain kind of callousness entailed by presuming to know with any certainty the mind of another person. Fyodor is at his most cruel when he forgets to suspect his own mindreading. An otherwise eminently likable hero, Fyodor harbors an ugly prejudice against Germans, to which he gives vent on

Chapter Two

a tram ride through Berlin. He "concentrate[s]" what he calls his "sinful hatred" on a passenger who bumps into him (*Gift*, 81; *SS*, 3:73). "Reading his features" and taking him to be German, Fyodor attributes to this passenger all sorts of unsavory tastes and motives and hates him for "cruelty in everything" (*Gift*, 81; *SS*, 3:73). But then, the man takes out a Russian newspaper and "cough[s] unconcernedly with a Russian intonation" (*Gift*, 82; *SS*, 3:74). The man turns out to be Fyodor's compatriot. Life thus reminds Fyodor that what looks to him like an insight into another person can always be a delusion, and a dangerous one at that, fueling prejudice. Fyodor is bemused and grateful to be reminded to doubt his own powers of observation, which are insufficient to pin down key aspects of this man's social life, let alone the movements of his mind.

It is true that at moments of great self-assurance Fyodor attributes to himself extraordinary powers of perception, claiming to intuit truths beyond phenomenal representations. His aesthetic musings are occasionally marked by a Platonism, which he seems to share with Nabokov. Both author and hero have a sense that their artworks "preexist" their attempts to create them, as Alexandrov has argued.[30] Both also exalt the artist's capacity to perceive a mystical design behind the mundane features of the world. Fyodor calls this "multilevel thinking":

> you look at a person and you see him as clearly as if he were fashioned of glass and you were the glass blower, while at the same time without in the least impinging upon that clarity you notice some trifle on the side—such as the similarity of the telephone receiver's shadow to a huge, slightly crushed ant, and (all this simultaneously) the convergence is joined by a third thought— the memory of a sunny evening at a Russian small railway station. (*Gift*, 163; *SS*, 3:146)

The artist's gift evidently involves attending simultaneously to a multiplicity of impressions separated in space and time and sensing a deeper pattern in the accumulation of these mundane trifles. This is the same experience Nabokov would later describe in his memoir *Speak, Memory* (1951), calling it "cosmic synchronization."[31] In an act of artistic creation, life's mundane trifles coalesce, "all forming an instantaneous and transparent organism of events, of which the poet (sitting in a lawn chair, at Ithaca, NY) is the nucleus."[32] The Platonic undercurrent of Nabokov's thought—expressed especially clearly in this concept—convinces Alexandrov that we should also read his hero as a quasi Platonist.[33]

Fyodor's Platonism, however, runs aground when he entertains the idea that his talent allows him to know what happens in the minds of other people. Whereas in *Anna Karenina* it is the author who undermines the Platonic outlook of his fictional artist Mikhailov, in *The Gift* it is the character who points up the limits of the author's concept of "cosmic synchronization," subverting both the Platonism and the artistic self-assurance it expresses. Fyodor, having posited his power to penetrate the surface of things and people, immediately goes on to suspect his own supposition: "And at the same time he found it amusing to refute himself: all this was nonsense, the shadows of nonsense, presumptuous dreams" (*Gift*, 164; *SS*, 3:147). Perhaps this "multilevel thinking," Fyodor reflects, is only the "play of the mind with its own self" (*Gift*, 164; *SS*, 3:147). As in the Alexander Chernyshevsky experiment, Fyodor recognizes that all sorts of things might be imagined, but another person can never appear as though he were made of glass.

THE DISAPPOINTMENT OF SKEPTICISM

Having identified beneath *The Gift*'s story of successful artistic flourishing an undercurrent of failure, I now want to elucidate the nature of this failure. Fyodor often wears lightly his inability to ascertain the state of another's mind. He is amused and humbled by his mistakes, and in such moments *The Gift* seems to parody skeptical longing. But there are also instances when Fyodor finds uncertainty about the state of another's mind hard to bear. He is distressed most of all by his inability to know his father's mind. While attempting to write his father's biography, Fyodor observes that he can readily conjure up and describe the striking settings of his father's travels through Asia, but he cannot capture how his father must have experienced them: "I continually ask myself what did he use to think about in the solitary night: I try fervently in the darkness to divine the current of his thoughts, and I have much less success with this than with my mental visits to places which I have never seen" (*Gift*, 119; *SS*, 3:108). It is harder to inhabit the mind of another person than a foreign landscape. Fyodor's father, Konstantin Kirillovich, remains inaccessible. It torments Fyodor that, despite all his research about his father's journeys and all his tremendous powers of imagination and recollection, he cannot enter his father's mind now any more than he could when he was with his father years earlier: "and again I ask myself what Father is thinking about when he is not busy collecting and stands there like that, quite still . . . appearing as it were on the crest of my recollection, torturing me, enrapturing me—to the point of pain, to an insanity of tenderness, envy and love, tormenting my soul with his inscrutable solitariness" (*Gift*, 122; *SS*, 3:110). Remarking on Fyodor's attempts to write about his father, Alexander Dolinin proposes that "everyone is transparent for the imagination of a genuine artist except for those whom he loves because their integrity and inner mysteries are sacred and therefore opaque."[34] But what seems unique

Chapter Two

is less his father's opacity—we have seen that Fyodor's conjectures about other people's minds are similarly doubtful—than the way this opacity torments him. It cannot merely interest or amuse him.

Nabokov's rendering of Fyodor in the act of writing about his father captures what Cavell described as the "disappointment" at the core of other minds skepticism. The other minds skeptic in Cavell's account bemoans our inability to know others the way we know ourselves. For Cavell, this is puzzling because most ordinary human interactions show that we are rather successful in our mutual understanding. Instead of refuting the skeptic, Cavell therefore aims to get a better grasp on the kind of problem the skeptic articulates. What is it exactly that troubles him?

Cavell starts from the canonical formulation of the other minds skeptic's position: I cannot share another's pain. The question of pain is central to arguments for and against other minds skepticism in part because pain presents a particularly difficult case for determining a "criterion of identity."[35] Is the identity of pain determined by its position or its description? If my pain is descriptively the same as your pain, does that mean we share one pain? Does it matter that this pain persists in two different locations? Cavell queries the sort of knowledge that would satisfy the skeptic who insists "I cannot know another's pain." Would he be convinced by the argument that if we have two descriptively identical pains we share each other's pain? No, he would not.

No *knowledge* can satisfy the skeptic, Cavell explains, because when the skeptic says that only you can "know" your pain, he uses the verb "to know" in a special way. His usage, according to Cavell, registers something deeply right about what it means for us "to know"—specifically, that knowledge is often not only what is cognized but also our way of responding to what is cognized. Cavell calls this "acknowledgement." The problem is not that I can never know everything there is to know about the quality of your pain; one can imagine a world in which I could do so. The problem is that even if I were to know all about your pain, it would still be *your* pain and not mine. I am not *"impaled* upon . . . knowledge" of your pain the way you are, and my way of acknowledging your pain is necessarily different from yours.[36] Cavell concludes that what the skeptic laments is not an epistemological deficiency but the condition of one's metaphysical separateness from other human beings, a condition that the problem of pain makes particularly vivid and ethically urgent.[37]

In Fyodor's recollection of his father's frequent absences, one observes the same gesture that Cavell observes in the skeptic: an inescapable metaphysical fact is transposed into a problem of knowledge. Having seen his father off on his last journey, Fyodor is left alone in a meadow whose "divine meaning," the narrator explains, "was expressed in its butterflies" (*Gift*,

132; *SS*, 3:120). "Everyone might have found something here," we are told (*Gift*, 132; *SS*, 3:120). The holidaymaker would see it only as a cool place to rest; the artist "screw[ing] up his eyes" might see it as something more. "But [the meadow's] truth would have been probed somewhat deeper by knowledge-amplified love," the narrator claims (*Gift*, 132; *SS*, 3:120). This epistemological ladder from the obtuse tourist to the more attentive artist to the perceiver capable of "knowledge-amplified love" prefigures Nabokov's later remarks about how we come to know the world. "Reality is a very subjective affair," he says. "I can only define it as a kind of gradual accumulation of information; and as specialization. If we take a lily, for instance, or any other kind of natural object, a lily is more real to a naturalist than it is to an ordinary person. But it is still more real to a botanist. And yet another stage of reality is reached with that botanist who is a specialist in lilies."[38] By turning his attention to an epistemological query, the author-narrator (possibly Fyodor himself) avoids contemplating directly the painful separation from Konstantin Kirillovich.

Standing in the meadow amid its butterflies, Fyodor experiences a moment of multilevel thinking or cosmic synchronization, which for him (and Nabokov) is the most profound form of knowledge—one that "suggest[s] the possibility of a complex of unlimited awareness," as J. B. Sisson puts it.[39] "Fyodor perceived in a flash with one penetrating and experienced glance" all the activity of the meadow (*Gift*, 133; *SS*, 3:121). But having experienced this cosmic synchronization, Fyodor "placed a fist against the trunk of a birch tree and leaning on it, burst into tears" (*Gift*, 133; *SS*, 3:121). This epiphanic moment—the attainment of this ultimate epistemological vantage point available to a genius artist alone—is insufficient because it is not a lack of knowledge but an inescapable solitude that Fyodor, like the skeptic, grieves.

Fyodor's intention to write his father's biography is an attempt to suture the metaphysical rift that plagues him. But his method suggests that like the skeptic he confuses (or refuses to face) the source of his grief. He conceives of it as a lack of knowledge and thus works to gather information about Konstantin Kirillovich's expeditions, his friends, his marriage, and the flora and fauna of the landscapes Konstantin Kirillovich had seen. Fyodor then begins to write. First, he describes his father's journey, including himself among the traveling party. He helps his father capture rare butterflies: "he and I would take Elwes' Swallowtail—a black wonder with tails in the shape of hooves" (*Gift*, 122; *SS*, 3:110). Soon the distinction between father and son disappears altogether as though father and son merge into the single "I" of the adventurer-narrator who details the discoveries of his journey. For the duration of Fyodor's composition, the impressions ostensibly shared by father and son "lingered bewitchingly, full of color and air" (*Gift*, 125; *SS*, 3:113).

Chapter Two

But the moment passes and "like smoke from a breeze, [the visions] shifted and dispersed—and Fyodor saw again the dead and impossible tulips of his wallpaper" (*Gift*, 125; *SS*, 3:113). Nabokov's charged language—the description of the wallpaper as "dead and impossible" (*mertvye i nevozmozhnye*)—underscores the irremediable fact of the father's absence. It casts into doubt our capacity to make another's consciousness fully present, even with the help of an artist's powers of perception, even by way of art.

THE HAPPY SKEPTIC?

The abandoned biography of Konstantin Kirillovich is not Fyodor's last literary work, of course. In fact, his next work, *The Life of Chernyshevski*, embraces the skepticism about other minds that troubles Fyodor with regard to his father. Admitting and celebrating that our forays into other lives are merely the "play of the mind with its own self," Fyodor undertakes an artwork that retreats from the project of "divining the current" of another's thought. Instead, his parodic autobiography creates Chernyshevsky from scratch. He begins and ends his Chernyshevsky book with an apocryphal sonnet, underscoring his intention to replace historical truth with his own artistic truth. He explains to Zina that he must "make my way along this narrow ridge between my own truth and a caricature of it" (*Gift*; 200; *SS*, 1:180). Zina also understands the Chernyshevsky of the biography not as a historical figure but as a character who "belong[s] to Fyodor, and partly to her" (*Gift*, 204; *SS*, 1184). The same skepticism that disturbed Fyodor as he wrote about his father now opens up a space for creativity, enabling Fyodor to produce his first prose work. If what we take to be the inner lives of others are always our own inventions, then why not make them extravagant, brilliant inventions?[40]

Fyodor's success in completing his artistic biography of Chernyshevsky would seem to militate against my antiteleological reading of the novel. Since Nabokov himself often appeared in the guise of the happy skeptic—blithely accepting our incapacity to know others—one could argue that with the Chernyshevsky book Fyodor approximates the creative consciousness of his author (Nabokov) and reaches a higher stage of artistic development. Fyodor appears to shed his disappointment and, like Nabokov, to recognize a creative opportunity in an insufficiency of knowledge. In his essay "Pushkin, or the True and the Seemingly True" (1937), for example, Nabokov imaginatively reconstructs the poet, declaring: "I am quite aware that this is not the real Pushkin, but a third-rate thespian whom I pay to play the part. What is the difference! The ruse amuses me, and I catch myself beginning to believe in it."[41] Nabokov, as Galya Diment notes, stakes out a "creative space for himself which lies between the 'invented facts' of fiction and the 'real facts' of one's personal life . . . which he himself called the 'imagined facts.'"[42] She further observes, however, that when it comes to "imagined facts" Nabokov trusts only his own imagination. He warns his future biographers to stick to "plain facts" alone.[43] One can certainly agree with Diment that this inconsistency speaks to Nabokov's mistrust of the creative capacities of others. But there is a deeper ambivalence here as well—about just how far the creative imagination (even a brilliant one) can take us.

Nabokov performs the sort of cheerful skepticism that will become the hallmark of postmodernism without entirely accepting it. Looking closely at what Nabokov wants from "imagined facts," it is clear that he is after more than mere mental play. Imagined facts are meant to augment our ordinary ways of knowing. True, his visions of the poet may be wrong and "the true Pushkin would not recognize himself in them. Yet if I inject into them a bit of the same love that I feel when reading his poems, is not what I am doing with this imaginary life somehow akin to the poet's work, if not to the poet himself?"[44] It should be noted that Nabokov's musings on the knowledge afforded by the artistic imagination take the form of a question, not an assertion. His query expresses only a *hope* (not a conviction) that an artistic way of knowing allows us to get at the truth of another person. But this hope might always be betrayed, just as it is betrayed for Fyodor when even his "knowledge amplified love" does not allow him to share his father's thoughts.

It is significant that in the Chernyshevsky biography the stakes for Fyodor's success or failure in divining some truth about his subject are low. This work, as Fyodor repeatedly stresses, is merely parody, an artistic exercise, or "firing practice" (*uprazhnenie v strel'be*) (*Gift*, 196; *SS*, 3:177). Even if Fyodor gets it all wrong, he can still be pleased with his own mental play. His misapprehensions can amuse him the same way they do when he misreads the passenger on the tram. But what if Fyodor applied his creative imagination to the life of a beloved friend rather than an ideological foe? Would he be satisfied, or troubled by the insufficiency of his methods, as he is when writing about his father? Dolinin proposes that Fyodor's initial disappointment is dispelled by the epiphanic moment in the Grunewald forest when his "artistic consciousness finally bursts out of its cocoon."[45] Through this creative awakening, Dolinin argues, Fyodor "overcomes absence and death."[46] If that is the case, we might speculate that having completed his "firing practice," Fyodor will go on to write the kind of creative biography that can assuage his skeptical longing. Significantly, however, such a book never materializes within the world of the novel.[47] In other words, Nabokov's novel never affirms that "imagined facts"—the products of keen observation enhanced by affection and imagination—can in fact bridge the metaphysical divide between oneself and another. It only longs for this to be true.

Chapter Two

Nabokov rarely expressed in his own voice a disappointment with the insufficiency of imagination. But he did so, quite poignantly, on the occasion of the death of Yuly Aikhenvald in 1928. This dear friend of Nabokov's was struck and killed by a tramcar while walking home one night. Nabokov remembered Aikhenvald in the pages of *Rul'* in an uncharacteristic expression of candid grief, which tellingly takes the form of a discourse on what it means to know another person. "To know a person," Nabokov begins, "means to create him."[48] We create a person by observing his traits, his image, and his voice, and by retaining these things within ourselves. "O yes, there is on earth the possibility of immortality," he exclaims.[49] In a thought similar to ones he would articulate in *The Eye* (1930), Nabokov posits that even after a person dies, "the deceased continues to live fully and concretely in the souls of all the people who knew him."[50] An individual can be preserved through the kaleidoscope of others' perspectives. Nabokov strikes a hopeful chord, which he sounds over and over again in works like *Speak, Memory*, presenting himself as the master artist capable of restoring whatever has been lost in time. Yet in this tribute to Aikhenvald, Nabokov immediately retreats from such hope and claims no mastery. Instead, he suggests that the person one imaginatively creates is not enough—the real human being is gone. Nabokov undermines the faith in earthly immortality that he had just proclaimed:

> No matter how you try to philosophize, no matter how you try to comfort yourself with the receptivity of your five senses, all the same, all the same, the real person, the singular specimen, is now gone. He left for home late at night, walking immersed in his own thoughts, the current and substance of which nobody, nobody can know.[51]

This meditation on death brings Nabokov to a skeptical lament. No amount of sensuous receptivity infused with love can give access to the real current and substance of that beloved, and now absent, person's thought. He is foreclosed to us; we are inescapably apart from him. Death concretizes the metaphysical condition of our separateness that Nabokov, like the Cavellian skeptic, describes in terms of the other's opacity.

THE READER AN AUTHOR NEEDS: ÉMIGRÉ READERS

The Gift shares with *Anna Karenina* the imperative to draw out the consequences of an artist's other minds skepticism for the creation and reception of art. But whereas *Anna Karenina* is primarily concerned with how skepticism shapes the artist's relationship to his own work, Nabokov's novel brings into focus how skepticism shapes the relationship between author and au-

Nabokov's Moderate Multiplication of the Self

dience. Questions pertaining to the reader's attentiveness, his training, his demands, and even his very existence troubled Nabokov in a way that they could not have troubled Tolstoy. Tolstoy presided over half a century of rapid expansion of the reading public.[52] Nabokov, in emigration, faced a rapidly shrinking literary sphere.

Nabokov composed *The Gift* in Berlin between 1933 and 1938 amid heated debates within the Russian émigré community about the health of the émigré reader. Approximately 500,000 Russians arrived in Europe after the Bolshevik Revolution and the Russian Civil War, establishing what Marc Raeff has called a "society in exile."[53] Russian émigrés founded their own schools, political institutions, and social organization, as well as a multitude of cultural publications. Though exact figures are hard to ascertain, Raeff estimates that Berlin, the publishing center in the first decade of the emigration, was home to 188 Russian-language publishing ventures between 1918 and 1928.[54] But such publications, in Berlin, Paris, and elsewhere, faced increasing financial pressures and a waning readership. As a result, established literary periodicals such as *Sovremennye zapiski* preferred to publish well-known writers—Ivan Bunin, Mark Aldanov, Dmitry Merezhkovsky, Zinaida Gippius—who had made their reputations before the revolution. The absence of an audience for a rising generation of writers worried not only the younger writers themselves but also the older writers who took seriously their mission to preserve Russian culture outside the Soviet Union.

In a flurry of articles with titles such as "Without a Reader" (1931) and "In Defense of the Reader" (1931), critics engaged in a reckoning of sorts with the state of Russian culture after more than a decade in exile. They wondered whether dislocation, trauma, and linguistic isolation had made émigré readers uninterested in high literary culture and incapable of supporting the next generation of Russian writers. Georgy Ivanov proposed that a once vibrant and generally well-educated community of émigrés had passed though "the general Russian collapse as though through a meat grinder, and long ago become a formless mass. This mass of readers is painted in one color: the color of indifferent exhaustion."[55] There had never existed a better reader than the "Russian *intelligent* . . . who was the most sensitive, receptive, and grateful reader in the world," but now this reader is a corpse, "fast asleep."[56] Readers are "wilting" (*vianut*) in the suffocating smoky atmosphere of the emigration.[57] Gaito Gazdanov explained this "cultural decline" (*kul'turnoe snizhenie*) differently: the professional class, of which the émigré community was largely composed, was forced to take up menial labor in emigration and thereby lost their cultural sophistication.[58] Khodasevich similarly blamed exhaustion from labor for drawing audiences away from serious literature to light adventure novels and especially to film.[59] But not everyone wished to blame the reader. Mark Aldanov, for example, held that the émigré

Chapter Two

reader remained a "cultured reader" (*kul'turnym chitatelem*), and faulted insufficient support from publishers for the diminishing output of émigré writers.[60] Zinaida Gippius likewise affirmed readers, attributing the stifling atmosphere of émigré letters to various forms of subtle censorship imposed by publishing outlets.[61] Bem blamed readers' dwindling interest on the insularity of the literary community, in which cultural criticism had devolved into writers sniping at each other or praising their friends.[62]

Although Nabokov did not participate in these polemics directly, one hears their echoes in his later sallies against "average" readers and an uncultivated, "poshlaya" reading public. Moreover, these questions of reading and readership manifestly made their way into *The Gift*. Dolinin proposes that the émigré sense of crisis ultimately inoculated Nabokov against anxiety about readership: "Even the lack of readers—the plague of émigré literature—does not trouble [Nabokov] so much."[63] But I suggest that Nabokov did not learn to disregard the problem of readership; indeed, he delved deeper into it. Nabokov does perhaps neglect the contingent, historical question of fellow émigré writers: how many readers does a writer need to survive professionally? Instead, he takes up the transhistorical question: what sort of audience does an artist need to survive existentially?

THE DANGEROUS READER

The Gift offers a comic taxonomy of bad reading, lampooning criticism of all sorts, from that of the careless historian to the amateur psychologist to the committed ideologue. Fyodor disdains such poor readers almost as much as Nabokov himself. He cares little if people "turn away" from him in response to his Chernyshevsky biography, declaring that he "prefer[s] the backs of their heads" (*Gift*, 207; *SS*, 3:187). This disdain, however, obscures a more profound wariness of the reader that reveals itself when Fyodor is confronted not by poor readings of his works but by good ones. Nabokov's artist-hero perceives an existential danger posed by the reader—one that is rooted in other minds skepticism.

My doubt about knowing others, as Cavell explains, is the obverse of my doubt about whether others can know me. "The question whether there are other minds is exactly as much a question about me as about anyone else. If *anyone* is another mind, *I* am one—i.e., I am an other to the others (and of course others are then I's to me)," Cavell argues.[64] "Then the question is: Do others know of my existence?"[65] He calls these the *active* and *passive* aspects of skeptical doubt. The active skeptic proceeds from the intuition that another person might suffer and the skeptic will not be able to know this other person's pain. Fyodor, like the active skeptic, is especially troubled by the inability to know his father's state of mind in the last, possibly painful moments of his life. He has been told that Konstantin Kirillovich was likely killed, and he wonders at his father's attitude in the moments preceding this execution. The passive skeptic, in contrast, proceeds from the "decisively significant" fact that he himself "may be suffering when no one else is, and that no one (else) may know (or care?)"[66] Skeptical doubt in its passive aspect raises questions about whether one's modes of expression—physical, linguistic, and so on—are enough to reveal oneself to others. Anna Karenina succumbs to doubt in this passive aspect, convinced that nothing will allow her to make herself known. Fyodor, too, expresses doubt in this passive aspect. In his case, such doubt takes the form of apprehension toward readers.

Fyodor asks whether it is possible for another person to grasp the current of *his* thought in the opening pages of the novel. Alexander Chernyshevsky alerts him to a supposedly glowing review of the poetry collection Fyodor has just published, and Fyodor wonders: "Can it really be that [the unknown reviewer] has understood everything in [the poems], understood that besides the good old 'picturesqueness' they also contain special poetic meaning (when one's mind, after going around itself in the subliminal labyrinth, returns with newfound music that alone makes poems what they should be)?" (*Gift*, 28; *SS*, 3:26). Fyodor seems to answer in the negative. He cannot imagine a reader who would achieve what he wishes—a reader who would appreciate not just Fyodor's words but the "chinks between words," the movements of his mind (*Gift*, 28; *SS*, 3:26). Instead, the critics conjured up by his imagination laud and critique his poems in the wrong way, making trivial remarks about their picturesqueness or lyricism. One imagined reviewer praises the poems as "disarming by their sincerity" (*Gift*, 11; *SS*, 3:12). Fyodor is shaken by the compliment he himself has just ventriloquized: "no, that's nonsense—Why must one 'disarm' the reader?" (*Gift*, 11; *SS*, 3:12). In the Russian text, the reader is called a "mercenary" and Fyodor declares, "Who needs him" (*SS*, 3:12). In Nabokov's English translation, Fyodor asks of the reader, "Is he dangerous?" (*Gift*, 11). He then immediately rejects the portrait of the reader he has just painted: "Nonsense, I say! He does not write like that my nameless, unknown eulogist" (*Gift*, 11; *SS*, 3:12). The subtle differences in translation notwithstanding, Fyodor's imagination clearly betrays his pessimism about the possibility of being understood in the way he would wish.

Some pages later we learn that there is no actual review of the collection—news of the review was an April Fool's prank played on Fyodor by Alexander Chernyshevsky. Nor are reviews likely to appear. Fyodor has not bothered to send out review copies of the book. One might interpret this negligence as a sign of the artist's inexperience or indifference to readers. But given the ineptitude and misunderstanding of Fyodor's imagined critics,

Chapter Two

one might also see Fyodor's reluctance to send out his works as a sign of the threat the reader poses to him. The reader *is* dangerous after all. Or at least Fyodor thinks so.

Dangerous how? Nabokov frequently denounced two types of reader: the reader who thoughtlessly consumes "buxom best sellers" and one who "begins with ready-made generalizations," treating literature as fodder for the study of history, politics, and so forth.[67] He offered "Kindness to Authors" as a subtitle to his Cornell lectures on good reading, thereby implying that to read to satisfy one's demands for entertainment or information is to mistreat the author. Nabokov's 1944 book on Gogol warns such bad readers to "keep away, keep away" from Gogol's works.[68] And in *The Gift* this type of bad reading is comically personified in a pair of hooligans—a merchant and a locksmith—who set out for some fun on a bright Berlin day: "the merchant and his pal [the locksmith] guzzled beer and drove the horses hard, the weather was beautiful so that, in their high spirits, they deliberately hit a cleverly cornered cyclist, beat him up violently in the ditch, tore his portfolio to bits (he was an artist) and rolled on" (*Gift*, 50; *SS*, 3:47). The merchant stands in for the demands of the appetite, for the bad reader who regards art only in terms of how it satisfies his craving for diversion. The locksmith parodies the Marxist and psychoanalytic readers who, according to Nabokov, seek to unlock every text with the skeleton key of their ideology. Together they are a hazardous duo of philistines or "poshlyaki," which, as Nabokov points out, rhymes with "key."[69]

In Fyodor's view, Nikolay Chernyshevsky embodies both types of readerly transgression, and Fyodor's biography ceaselessly mocks him for it. Like the merchant, Chernyshevsky is a thoughtless consumer—a "glutton for books" (*Gift*, 213; *SS*, 3:191) who "could not bear reading alone; i.e., he invariably used to chew something with a book" (*Gift*, 219; *SS*, 3:195). As a utilitarian critic, Chernyshevsky is also guilty of the crimes of the locksmith. He fits literary works into the procrustean bed of his own ideas, making absurd determinations such as that anapest is the most "democratic" of Russian meters (*Gift*, 241; *SS*, 3:216). But the parodic treatment of such readerly sins, by both Nabokov and his hero, suggests their ultimate triviality. Fyodor does not take Chernyshevsky seriously enough to be troubled by his bad reading. The danger Fyodor perceives in the reader is illuminated not by the comically bad readers but by the good ones.

Fyodor's sister Tanya and his mother Elizaveta Pavlovna are his first readers (or rather, listeners). The intimacy of this family circle would seem to suggest the possibility that these readers will give Fyodor what he desires: they will be able to understand his communication in full. But even here— *especially* here—Fyodor feels the poignant incompleteness of their reception. Fyodor remembers how in childhood, as he and Tanya lay in bed at

76

night, he would compose riddles for her to solve. Occasionally, there would be no response to his composition: "she would fall asleep while I waited patiently, thinking that she was struggling with my riddle, and neither my pleading nor my imprecations would succeed in reviving her" (*Gift*, 16; *SS*, 3:16). Tanya's silence is followed by a series of Fyodor's hellish nightmares, which stand out for their violence in a novel with few violent descriptions. Fyodor sees himself as a horse pulled apart by Mongolian shamans: "its legs would break with a crunch and collapse at right angles to the body—my body" (*Gift*, 17; *SS*, 3:17). The listener's lack of receptivity is figured as physical violence; Tanya's failure to respond to Fyodor feels to him like a physical death.

Fyodor's near telepathic connection with his mother seems to hold even greater promise for making himself known to someone else. The communication between mother and son is described as an "animated silence" (*ozhivlennoe molchanie*), an "almost subgramineal speech which emerged as a single stream, as a word understood to both of them" (*Gift*, 89; *SS*, 3:80). Nabokov, however, subtly punctures even their near-perfect, seemingly "otherworldly" knowledge of one another. Elizaveta Pavlovna listens to her son read his poetry at a literary evening, including a poem about two lovers parting:

> One night between sunset and river
> On the old bridge we stood, you and I.
> Will you ever forget it, I queried,
> —That particular swift that went by?
> And you answered, so earnestly: Never!
>
> And what sobs made us suddenly shiver,
> What a cry life emitted in flight!
> Till we die, till tomorrow for ever,
> You and I on the old bridge one night. (*Gift*, 94; *SS*, 3:84–85)

Although Elizaveta Pavlovna is moved by the poem, Fyodor suspects that "she did not think to connect it with the memory of a young woman, long dead, whom Fyodor had loved when sixteen" (*Gift*, 94; *SS*, 3:85). She had not understood him in full. This is not to say that Fyodor or Nabokov advocates for a bluntly biographical mode of reading, but rather to stress that some particularity, some associations, are inevitably lost on even the most intimate of readers. The poem itself, which Nabokov later recalled as one of his best Russian poems, underscores the kind of particularity that cannot be captured.[70] One lover asks another to remember *that* swallow, and though she says she will, both know it is impossible. Likewise impossible is

Chapter Two

the listener's ability to know Fyodor's poems as he knows them. No matter how great their mental affinity, Elizaveta Pavlovna is not, after all, Fyodor himself, and necessarily experiences the poem from her own perspective.

The same poem highlights the imperfections of Zina's reading, demonstrating that romantic intimacy is also incapable of granting the identity of perspectives between author and reader that Fyodor often desires. Zina is surely among the best readers of Fyodor's work. She is serious, discerning. Tracing her loving attention to Fyodor's writing, Stephen Blackwell argues that she is Fyodor's "first and ideal reader and helps give final shape to his artistic perception."[71] Yet for all her love and understanding, Zina, too, slightly misapprehends the poem. "'I liked very much the one you recited at that evening of poetry,' she says to Fyodor. 'The one about the swallow that cried out'" (*Gift*, 180; SS, 3:162). Zina misremembers the poem. It was not the bird that cried out but life itself: "What a cry life emitted in flight!" This mistake would not be lost on Fyodor, and it would likely remind him of his mother's incomplete understanding of the same poem.

Fyodor recognizes "an extraordinary grace in [Zina's] responsiveness" to his art and even thinks that in some sense she might be steering his creative activity (*Gift*, 205; SS, 3:185). Still, he registers that their perspectives on it do not coincide:

> Gifted with a most flexible memory, which twined like ivy around what she perceived, Zina by repeating such word-combinations as she particularly liked ennobled them with her own secret convolution, and whenever Fyodor for any reason changed a turn of phrase which she had remembered, the ruins of the portico stood for a long time on the golden horizon, reluctant to disappear. (*Gift*, 205; SS, 3:185)

Fyodor's words are altered by Zina's own "secret convolutions." She continues to perceive and appreciate elements of the text that were cancelled by Fyodor. Instead of inhabiting Fyodor's perspective, she reads his text in her own way. It is telling that Zina's reading is compared to the twining of ivy, which, despite its beauty, obscures and sometimes smothers the things it envelops.

The forms of bad reading Nabokov volubly ridicules and denounces in fiction, essays, and interviews appear to be red herrings diverting us from a subtler problem that he was perhaps less keen to disclose. The artist might ignore careless and callous readers; Nabokov certainly did. What is harder to abide is the good reader who nonetheless gets it wrong. Nabokov's own implacable need to correct his most perceptive and generous readers demonstrates this well. The real danger is that a reader—any reader—forces an author to confront the possibility that no amount of readerly intelligence, attentiveness, or affinity will ensure that he has been properly understood. Ap-

Nabokov's Moderate Multiplication of the Self

plying the logic of the Cavellian skeptic to the relationship between author and reader, one might say that what concerns Fyodor (and Nabokov) is that the author cannot count on any reader to share his vision.[72]

NOT OTHER ENOUGH

Nabokov's *The Gift* registers the paradox inherent in the author's desire for an identity of perspectives between author and reader. The artist longs for this because he wishes to be certain that he can make himself understood to another person, the reader. But the identity of perspectives that would grant him such certainty also threatens the otherness of the reader. Fyodor himself recognizes that he idealizes a relationship between author and reader that threatens to lapse into solipsism. The only reader who grants Fyodor the certainty of understanding that he longs for turns out to be a figment of his own imagination. In a gently self-mocking remark, Fyodor refers to the "all-comprehending" Koncheyev—the only poet of his circle whom he (at first begrudgingly) admires and believes capable of grasping his work (*Gift*, 64; *SS*, 3:59). His two conversations with Koncheyev—both of which turn out to be imagined—demonstrate what Fyodor demands of his reader and what this ideal reader grants him.

In their first encounter, the two artists discuss, among other things, the dawn of their love for literature. Fyodor feels that to explain how he was initiated into literary life by his *audition coloreé* (synesthesia), he must make Koncheyev see the precise colors of his, Fyodor's, alphabet. He asks Koncheyev to recall the color of the "insulating cotton wool which was removed with the storm windows in spring" to show him his letter *m* (*Gift*, 74; *SS*, 3:68). "You would appreciate my radiant '*s*,'" Fyodor tells him,

> if I could pour into your cupped hands some of those luminous sapphires that I touched as a child, trembling and not understanding when my mother, dressed for a ball, uncontrollably sobbing, allowed her perfectly celestial treasures to flow out of their abyss into her palm, out of their cases onto black velvet, and then suddenly locked everything up and did not go anywhere after all. (*Gift*, 74; *SS*, 3:68)

To understand Fyodor's love for language, in other words, Koncheyev must perceive the colors of his alphabet, shaded as they are by an impossibly complicated matrix of associations and recollections. He must know the mixture of amazement and fright in Fyodor's radiant *s*, whose color reflects the child's wonder at his mother's sadness, presumably connected in some way with his father's absence. Only then will Koncheyev know Fyodor's work in full.

What does Fyodor want most from his imagined reader's reading?

79

Chapter Two

Not praise. The "real" Koncheyev who moves in Fyodor's social circles does praise the Chernyshevsky book in the press. But the imagined Koncheyev—the one who is Fyodor's ideal reader and interlocutor—does more: he shares almost exactly Fyodor's own perspective on this work. Fyodor marvels that Koncheyev's criticisms of his book "correspond to my own complaints against myself" (*Gift*, 340; *SS*, 3:305) and rejoices at their communion:

> The fact that I know you so well without knowing you makes me unbelievably happy, for that means there are unions in the world which don't depend at all on massive friendships, asinine affinities or "the spirit of the age," nor on any mystical organizations or associations of poets, where a dozen tightly knit mediocrities "glow" by their common efforts. (*Gift*, 341; *SS*, 3:306)

Fyodor thus rejects most of the ordinary ways we have of knowing others. Like the skeptic, Fyodor envisions what Cavell calls "a harmony, a concord, a union, a transparence, a governance, a power—against which our actual successes at knowing, and being known, are poor things."[73] Emerging from his second fictitious dialogue with Koncheyev, Fyodor thinks what a pity it is that this was once again a trick of his imagination, that "a conversation with him never blossom[s] out into reality" (*Gift*, 343; *SS*, 3:308). The conversation cannot blossom into reality, of course, because no reader can satisfy Fyodor as his imagined Koncheyev can—by being Fyodor and yet not being him.

Notably, Fyodor in his fantasy is careful to preserve a certain distance between himself and Koncheyev. The poet is not Fyodor's double but only a near double. He is almost the same age as Fyodor, but a year younger. He publishes in the same émigré publications, but with more success. They disagree on Gustave Flaubert and Fyodor Dostoevsky; Koncheyev confesses to being an "ardent admirer of the author of *The Double* and *The Possessed*" (*Gift*, 341; *SS*, 3:306). When they "meet" for the second time by the Grunewald lake, Fyodor is nearly naked, bronzed by the sun, whereas Koncheyev wears a black suit and tie.

Why take such care to distinguish himself from his imagined Koncheyev? Fyodor recognizes the potential for self-defeat in his desire for a perfect identity between his own perspective and that of the reader. Fyodor longs for another to understand him as he understands himself, because such understanding would dispel his sense that we are each sealed within ourselves. What he wants is to escape succumbing to a solipsistic view of the world. But, as Cavell argues, if it were possible for one to know and be known in the way the skeptic wishes, then the distinction between oneself and another is lost. If it were possible for someone else to know my pain as I know it—that is, to feel *my* pain as if it were *his* pain—then "'his pain' no longer differentiates what he feels from what I feel, him from me; he is

80

not *other* in the relevant sense."[74] This outcome, however, would not please Fyodor (or the other minds skeptic). After all, Fyodor's initial wish is to *escape* solipsism, whereas the absence of a genuine other would only confirm it. To point up the paradox of Fyodor's desire, Nabokov appears in the text in his favored guise of a lepidopteron. Sitting by Koncheyev, Fyodor watches "a little geometrid caterpillar that was checking the number of inches between the two writers," measuring out the minimal distance necessary to separate oneself from an other—from the ideal reader (*Gift*, 338; *SS*, 3:304).

"SOLIPSIZING" THE READER

The awareness of a paradox inherent in the skeptical artist's desire does not, however, dispel it. Nabokov placed tremendous faith in the liberating power of self-consciousness: it is what separates us from animals. "Being aware of being aware of being. In other words, if I not only know that I *am* but also know that I know it, then I belong to the human species," he wrote.[75] Moreover, in Nabokov's fictional universe, self-consciousness facilitates transcendence. Characters who achieve a higher vantage on their own predicaments—for example, as Cincinnatus C does in *Invitation to a Beheading*—are granted the chance to escape the confines of their world. Others (many more) are instead trapped "within an epistemological chamber which both author and reader transcend and view from without," as Thomas Seifrid observes.[76] The author's and reader's "superior vision" correspond to their superior freedom.[77] The fact that Fyodor cannot transcend his desire through self-awareness speaks to its force. Though he recognizes Koncheyev as a solipsistic fantasy—and at times lightly ridicules himself for it—Fyodor still longs for "real" readers like Zina who approximate this ideal.

A disappointment with "real" readers is palpable not only within the world of the novel but also at the metanarrative level. There are two moments when the author-narrator of *The Gift* directly addresses a presumed reader: once when Fyodor is in the process of composing a poem to Zina and again when Fyodor is in the Grunewald forest. In both cases the narration slips from third person into first person. While writing the poem to Zina, Fyodor merges with the author-narrator, and this composite "I" recalls his early experiments with poetry and his first love. As if prompted by a question we do not hear, the author-narrator digresses from the narration to reassure someone that his first lover "was not intelligent, she was poorly educated and banal, that is, your exact opposite" (*Gift*, 150; *SS*, 3:134). The addressee here, as Blackwell points out, must be either the real Zina listening to Fyodor read, or else a Zina whom Fyodor imagines as he composes the work before us. Either way, Blackwell suggests, the inclusion of this descrip-

Chapter Two

tion of Fyodor's first lover demonstrates how the reader influences, if not cocreates, the artwork.[78] I agree with Blackwell that this passage registers the presence of either an actual or an anticipated reader (whether that reader is Zina or, if one believes the text's author-narrator is not Fyodor but only someone *like* Fyodor, her model).[79] Equally important, however, is that the reader whom the author addresses here is evidently *not* his ideal reader. This scene does not celebrate the collaboration of author and reader, but rather demonstrates the latter's intrusion, similar to the intrusions of the phantom reviewers whom Fyodor imagines in the first chapter while rereading his poems. Instead of attending to what the author wishes to express—that is, the coincidence of his first poetic experiments and his first love—the reader here reinterprets the author's words in terms of her own preoccupation. Her concern is how his love for her measures up to his love for this previous mistress. With some exasperation, the author-narrator replies to a question that is again asked offstage: "no, I do not mean at all that I loved her more than you" (*Gift*, 150; *SS*, 3:134). And whether the voice of the reader is real or merely imagined, the author evidently resents its disruption of the flow of his narrative: "What would happen now if she [the first lover] were resurrected—I don't know, you should not ask stupid questions" (*Gift*, 150; *SS*, 3:134). If this passage hints that *The Gift* is being read aloud to a real or imagined Zina, then Zina is not Fyodor's ideal reader, and Fyodor fears as much. The reader-addressee asks the kind of "stupid question" that an ideal reader would never ask, about the way his art pertains to *her* attachments and investments. Whereas the ideal reader completely inhabits the author's perspective, this reader ponders what his work means for her.

The direct address to the reader in the Grunewald forest demonstrates more explicitly how the author-narrator (again merged with Fyodor into a single "I") wishes to be read. "Give me your hand, dear reader, and let's go into the forest together," he says. "Look: first—at these glades with patches of thistle, nettle or willow herb, among which you will find all kinds of junk: sometimes even a ragged mattress with rusty, broken springs; don't disdain it!" (*Gift*, 331; *SS*, 3:297). The author-narrator invites the reader-addressee to share not only his visual impressions but also his tactile ones: The "pinkish scaly trunks" of pine trees, the "feathery foliage" of rowans, the sun's "caress" of the wings of a butterfly that "alighted on my bare chest, attracted by human sweat" (*Gift*, 331; *SS*, 3:297). The author imagines a reader who replicates exactly his own experiences, bringing nothing additional into the text. There is no trace of disagreement between author and reader, no dissatisfaction on the part of the author. Evidently what the author-narrator wants is not just a reader "who senses and works to appreciate [his] every word"[80] but one who *does* understand and appreciate every word. Whereas the first instance of direct address is associated with Zina, this second is linked with

Koncheyev. Fyodor's last imagined conversation with him takes place immediately after this scene. This suggests one of two things. Either the speaker here is not addressing any real interlocutor but rather envisioning the ideal reader he lacks—the reader he suspects Zina cannot be—or he is still addressing Zina, compelling her to be more like Koncheyev, the reader in his solipsistic fantasy.

It is Fyodor's epistemic longing that leads him to slip into a solipsistic relation to Zina. If the problem of knowing others and being known by them is not epistemological but relational—if, as Cavell says, what the skeptic really laments is our metaphysical separateness—then accepting the reader's imperfect understanding amounts to accepting her otherness. Fyodor, however, in subtle ways obliterates the other he wants to reach. When he first tries to kiss Zina, she stops him. Among other reasons, she refuses because "you don't know me at all" (*Gift*, 184; *SS*, 3:165). And even as their romance progresses, Fyodor learns relatively little about Zina. He is grateful that she keeps to herself the details of her former romance. By his own admission, he has a "sluggish and bored . . . reaction to her reminiscences of her father, that is, to the most precious thing she had to show him" (*Gift*, 188; *SS*, 3:168). He is surprised by this, though he need not be. By neglecting Zina's history and her attachments, Fyodor ignores the markers of her otherness.

The most stubborn reminder of their separateness, of course, is Zina's body, which Fyodor frequently refuses to acknowledge. "Visually, Zina is a gracefully ethereal, almost fleshless, creature," Anna Brodsky observes.[81] Zina is at her most ethereal—appearing "out of the darkness, like a shadow leaving its kindred element"—at moments when Fyodor wishes to proclaim "her perfect understanding, the absolute pitch of her instinct for everything that he himself loved" (*Gift*, 177; *SS*, 3:159). When Fyodor sees her in this way—emerging from the shadows—he optimistically declares that "Zina [is] cleverly and elegantly made to measure for him by a very painstaking fate," and together they form "a single shadow" (*Gift*, 177; *SS*, 3:159). But Zina is not always ghostly. Her body is vividly present when Fyodor, in contrast, feels most distant from his beloved, following the departure of her family at the end of the novel. He responds to her ardent kiss with "strange embarrassment" (*Gift*, 360; *SS*, 3:324). And as Fyodor watches Zina groom herself on their way home, the couple's transcendent communion turns into a mundane exchange. Zina "took out a small mirror, looked into it, baring the filling in her front tooth, replaced the mirror inside . . . looked at her shoulder, brushed off a bit of fluff . . . doing all this in rapid succession, with her features in motion, her eyes blinking and a kind of inner biting and sucking in of her cheeks" (*Gift*, 361; *SS*, 3:325). "There's a smut on your cheek," Fyodor tells her. She repeats the procedure again and notices his strange stare. "What?" she asks. "Nothing," Fyodor responds, and agrees to comply

Chapter Two

with her plans for dinner (*Gift*, 361; *SS*, 3:325). With Zina at her most corporeal, there is not a wordless communion between the lovers. Instead, there is a palpable chill in their exchange.

Fyodor thus toggles between two alternatives. Either he faces the disappointment of an imperfect reader or he preserves the fantasy of a perfect one by "solipsizing" Zina—denying not only her particular cares, her family history, and so on, but also her very body, which stands in the way of the kind of communion the skeptic desires. In this denial, Fyodor shares something with other Nabokovian protagonists early and late. The émigré hero of Nabokov's 1926 debut novel, *Mashen'ka* (Mary), painstakingly reconstructs an image of his first love but flees Berlin before the flesh-and-blood woman arrives there to destroy his mental image. Much later, and more malevolently, Humbert "safely solipsize[s]" Lolita, displacing her lived reality with his own fantasy.[82] (Humbert even solipsizes himself: "Imagine me; I shall not exist if you do not imagine me."[83]) Scholars have (rightfully) distinguished Nabokovian heroes like Fyodor from protagonists like Humbert, whom Nabokov labeled one of his "dragons."[84] The former, they argue, avoid the confusions of the latter. They know where to draw the line between art and life, "between insight and solipsism."[85] But just as Nabokov's villains are not simple—"art is never simple"[86]—neither are his heroes. Nabokov endows even his most harmless protagonist, Fyodor, with the seeds of skepticism that in Humbert blossom into a pernicious solipsism.[87] Knowing better might not be enough to resist the urge to "solipsize" an other.

Nabokov's literary treatment of the skeptic's desire to know and be known thereby contests Cavell's effort to domesticate it with a philosophical account. "The cause of skepticism," according to Cavell, is "the attempt to convert the human condition, the condition of humanity, into an intellectual difficulty, a riddle."[88] He suggests that the skeptic's demand for an impossible certainty about the mental state of others is an excuse for avoiding his ordinary responsibilities to other people—his obligation to respond to the everyday claims they make on him. Cavell points up these responsibilities to the skeptic by identifying the true source of his doubt. But Nabokov demonstrates that skeptical desire is not dispelled even when we recognize its roots and its dangers.

Indeed, having plumbed its depths in *The Gift*, Nabokov himself still finds it hard to resist. Like Fyodor, Nabokov wants his reader to be his near double. The reader of *The Gift* is asked to have the same depth of familiarity and recall of Russian and European literature as does Nabokov himself. Simon Karlinsky notes that the reader "is expected to realize that a quoted line of poetry is a fusion of a line of Pushkin with a line of Blok; to know when Gogol' is discussed without being named; or to grasp a point about Rimbaud's 'Voyelles' that is made without the poet or the title of the poem

Nabokov's Moderate Multiplication of the Self

being mentioned."[89] The reader who has followed Nabokov's own career and can identify the allusions to his earlier novels (including *Mary*, *The Defense* (*Zashchita Luzhina*, 1929), and *Invitation to a Beheading*) can achieve a still deeper understanding. But the most profound grasp of the text is afforded to the "intimate circle of readers initiated into Nabokov's private background," as Dolinin describes them, who could identify the autobiographical details that Nabokov bestows on his hero, including his synesthesia.[90] There were a handful of such readers when the novel first appeared, but subsequently, with the memoir *Speak, Memory*, Nabokov widened this intimate circle. Nabokov demands of readers almost as much attention to the particularity of his creative evolution as Fyodor demands of Koncheyev. As readers, we are to immerse ourselves in his art and thought to try to approximate an identity with his perspective. At the same time, we are to recognize that our task is beyond our powers.

DEMANDING TOO MUCH

What of Nabokov as a reader? Nabokov approaches literary works with an idiosyncratic empiricism that must be understood in the context of his skeptical doubt. Otherwise, it might strike readers as baseless pedantry, a pretension of a haughty aristocrat. As many others have observed, Nabokov's quasi-scientific approach to reading resembles that of the Formalists. Paperno points out that he, too, believed that art is not "a direct imitation, or mirror image of reality . . . that artistic representation is a distorted ('shifted') image of the object in reality."[91] He, too, attended foremost to an artwork's materiality, its structure and language, often focusing his analysis on the "how" over the "what." He, too, rejected the idea that a literary work offers us historical, political, sociological, or biographical information. "I am sick of reading biographies in which mothers are subtly deduced from the writing of their sons and then made to 'influence' their remarkable sons in this or that way," he declared in his book on Gogol.[92]

But Nabokov's empiricism is not that of the Formalists. It is both more stringent and more peculiar. The word "information" appears frequently in Nabokov's discussion of his methods for reading in interviews, lectures, and essays on art. He admitted that in his lectures on literary works he aimed to "give factual data only," to "provide students of literature with exact information about details."[93] Asked what he learned from being a literature professor, Nabokov responded that he "amassed an invaluable amount of exciting information in analyzing a dozen novels for my students."[94] Nabokov, however, pursues a rather idiosyncratic knowledge of the text. Any Formalist would agree with him that an analysis of Gogol's use of adverbs and preposi-

Chapter Two

tions is important for understanding *The Overcoat*. But his imperative to "clearly visualize" the arrangement of Anna Karenina's train compartment—the impossibility "to comprehend certain important aspects of Anna's night journey" without it—would exceed the requirements of most Formalist analysis.[95] Few have found Nabokov's diagrams of the Samsa household and his drawings of Kafka's insect ("a domed beetle, not the flat cockroach of sloppy translators") useful, let alone indispensable, to understanding *The Metamorphosis*, as Nabokov insisted they were.[96] And many critics have taken Nabokov to task for the sort of "exact information" he offers in the commentary to his translation of Pushkin's *Eugene Onegin*. In addition to useful literary-historical observations, Nabokov expounds at length on the layout and dimensions of various buildings around Pushkin's Boldino estate, as well as the fact that lilacs surrounded the manor house.[97] We are instructed to "notice and fondle details," but what sort of purpose do these details serve?[98] Despite his admiration for Nabokov's scholarly commentary, Dolinin has suggested that it is marred precisely by such details—by the author's "sporadically flaunting his awesome erudition for its own sake and pouring out irrelevant curiosities upon the reader."[99] But these curiosities are not irrelevant: they indicate the objectives of Nabokov's mode of reading.

Nabokov aspires to the kind of knowledge Fyodor demands of his ideal reader Koncheyev when he dreams of pouring into Koncheyev's hands Elizaveta Pavlovna's sapphires. The desire to know what sort of insect Kafka saw in his mind's eye or what sights and scents surrounded Pushkin during his stays at Boldino suggests an aim beyond determining the function of the text. Readers ought to "discover," as he puts it, "a definite order in the system of [a text's] gaps and odd perches—and this order is a characteristic of the author's individual style."[100] For Nabokov, however, an individual style is coextensive with an author's identity. "The writer's art is his real passport," he explains. "His identity should be immediately recognized by a special pattern or unique coloration."[101] In other words, he aims to discover, if not inhabit, the authorial consciousness. This is a task anathema to Formalism. Indeed, it harkens back to an earlier form of criticism practiced by Nabokov's friend Aikhenvald before the advent of Formalism.

For Aikhenvald, the literary text is a meeting of two souls—the author's and the reader's. It is the formation of a "spiritual dyad."[102] In his essay on Pushkin, Aikhenvald describes how in reading his poetry, we nearly merge with the poet himself: "In his poetry, Pushkin told his biography in such a way that this biography became all human. Change the names, individual details and facts, and it would be you."[103] After cataloguing a few of Pushkin's devices, Aikhenvald insists that any attempt to dissect Pushkin's poems is hopeless. To understand Pushkin "one has to simply read him"—to immerse oneself in the "very flow, the resounding joy of his poetry."[104] For Nabokov,

86

too, "the work of art was unquestionably the expression of a unique and creative consciousness," as Michael Glynn points out. He rejected the Formalist approach to the artist as a "vehicle not [an] agent"[105] and shared Aikhenvald's sentiment that an aesthetic experience is a communion between author and reader—a "spontaneous embrace."[106]

Their aspirations of communion notwithstanding, neither Nabokov nor Aikhenvald had illusions of actually *attaining* any certain knowledge about another's expression, let alone his psyche. But whereas Aikhenvald celebrated this uncertainty, Nabokov found it hard to abide. "The word is elusive, the word is obscure, and we readers do not understand it in the exact way the author meant to say it," Aikhenvald observes.[107] "Only there is no calamity in this—the reader must augment the author or else there would be no literature."[108] Aikhenvald argues that as long as the reader does not deliberately distort the author's work, he should not be ashamed of or deny his subjectivity: "Everyone has a right to himself."[109] Aikhenvald suggests that our goal as readers is to articulate how a text draws out our own judgments and attachments. Nabokov, in contrast, asserts that, yes, our aesthetic impressions are always subjective—"everything that is worthwhile is to some extent subjective"—but "the reader must know when and where to curb his imagination and this he does by trying to get clear the specific world the author places at his disposal."[110] To the extent possible, the reader is to investigate the author's world, not focus on what the text evokes for himself as reader. Aikhenvald stressed the reader's subjectivity, Nabokov the need to restrain it.

It is true that Nabokov, like Aikhenvald, refers to a "creative" reader, arguing for example that "neither the person who wants a good laugh, nor the person who craves for books 'that make one think' will understand what *The Overcoat* is really about. Give me the creative reader; this is a tale for him."[111] Nabokov's further description of this creative reader demonstrates, however, that his idea of readerly creativity is limited to the reader's capacity to abandon habitual modes of perception. For him, creativity does not mean refracting the artwork through the prism of one's own concerns. On the contrary, Nabokov conceives of readerly creativity as the ability to approximate an identity with the mind of the author—to "perform a kind of mental somersault so as to get rid of conventional values in literature and follow the author along the dream road of his superhuman imagination."[112] Reading Gogol, Nabokov's creative reader will allow his eyes to be "gogolized," as he put it.[113]

While denying, with Aikhenvald, the possibility of certainty regarding another's meaning, Nabokov evidently continues to long for it. This longing is manifest in *The Gift* and it is also vividly apparent in Nabokov's most ambitious critical endeavor—the commentary to *Eugene Onegin* (1964). In

Chapter Two

the early essay "Pushkin, or the True and the Seemingly True," Nabokov attempts an Aikhenvaldian approach to Pushkin, even echoing Aikhenvald's rhetoric: "There is certainly nothing more boring than describing a great work of poetry, except perhaps for listening to the description. The only valid method of study is to read and ponder the work itself, to discuss it with yourself but not with others, for the best reader is still the egoist who savors his discovery unbeknownst to his neighbors."[114] But returning to Pushkin years later, Nabokov *does* describe it in painstaking, often esoteric detail. Nabokov's purpose, he claimed, was to enable Anglophone audiences to read Pushkin. Yet the excess of the commentary—an excess that in fact makes it hard for an English reader to appreciate the poet—suggests that Nabokov is driven by a different desire. Like the skeptic, he yearns for certainty in a realm where there can be none. His desire for an impossible proximity with an other, with an author, results in the peculiar, gratuitous empiricism he demands of all readers, including himself.

SONOROUS VOID

"[The] ideal reader is really the author's double," Nabokov told his creative writing students: "the reader an authentic writer imagines is himself or a man like himself, that is, with the same capacity of receiving impressions as he has. Hence the more original his genius is (and original genius is what solely matters in all art) the more limited will be the group of people that he can imagine enjoying his work."[115] This remark sounds triumphant until one considers its consequences. If genius is inversely proportional to the number of others who can share one's vision, then the artist of supreme genius is akin to a madman: he can share his vision with no one at all. Yet as Osip Mandel'stam insists, an artist cannot doubt the existence of an understanding reader—however distant that reader may be in space and time—without "coming to doubt himself."[116] Perhaps this is why Nabokov's later declaration that an author writes to "please one reader alone—one's own self" is immediately followed by an important qualification, omitted in most citations:

> But one also needs some reverberation, if not response, and a moderate multiplication of one's self throughout a country or countries; and if there be nothing but a void around one's desk, one would expect it to be at least a sonorous void, and not circumscribed by the walls of a padded cell.[117]

The author's own creative pleasure is insufficient, except perhaps in the asylum. For Mandel'stam, a poet who truly addressed his words to no one would be indistinguishable from a madman. Nabokov is no madman. The presence

Nabokov's Moderate Multiplication of the Self

or absence of readers is not irrelevant to him, and neither is the condition of their minds. The author is in fact quite particular about what that condition should be: he asks for a "moderate multiplication" of himself. Nabokov's phrasing is telling. With his call for moderation, he describes a relationship between author and reader that borders on the solipsistic without going over the edge. To write for oneself alone, to imagine the reader as one's double, would be to lapse into solipsism, to admit that one is hermetically sealed within oneself and unable to reach other people. What, then, is the minimal distance that must obtain between author and reader?

Nabokov comes closest to an explanation of what he means by a moderate multiplication in a letter he writes to Carl Proffer, whose analysis of *Lolita* he esteemed. First, Nabokov registers his disappointment that he does not fully recognize himself in Proffer's reading. "A considerable part of what Mr. Nabokov thinks has been thought up by his critics and commentators, including Mr. Proffer, for whose thinking he is not responsible," Nabokov writes in response to *Keys to Lolita*.[118] Proffer fails—like all readers necessarily do—to achieve an identity of perspectives with the author. But then Nabokov relents, praising Proffer: "Many of the delightful combinations and clues, though quite acceptable, never entered my head or are the result of an author's intuition and inspiration, not calculation and craft. Otherwise why bother at all—in your case as well as mine."[119] Proffer does not duplicate Nabokov's thought—this is impossible—but neither does he stray too far beyond it. The "combinations and clues" Proffer observes are ones Nabokov is willing to acknowledge as the products of his own mind, even if they were not entirely intentional. Nabokov reluctantly accepts Proffer's *moderate* multiplication. How else is one to avoid solipsism? But his praise contains a warning, too, to readers who would ignore his authorial intention entirely, who would read against the grain of the text. Such a reading is unacceptable to Nabokov not (or not only) because it denies him a monopoly over the text's meaning, but because it fuels his fear that even art is not enough to let us know others or to make ourselves known to them.

89

Chapter Three

Atrophied Aesthetic Sense

TOLSTOY SPENT APPROXIMATELY fifteen years ruminating on the nature of art to set down his thoughts in his 1897 philosophical treatise *What Is Art?*[1] What he produced dismayed his contemporaries and bewildered his future readers. How could Tolstoy not only reject the avant-garde movements of his time but also disparage the most beloved works of European literature, including his own great novels? "I consign my own artistic productions to the category of bad art," Tolstoy declared in a footnote.[2] One eminent aesthetics philosopher, Paul Guyer, has called *What Is Art?* "an attack upon both the art and the aesthetic theory of the nineteenth century."[3] As Caryl Emerson has observed, many of Tolstoy's readers were scandalized by "the spectacle of a great writer turning against himself."[4] Nabokov, for one, marveled at the sight.

In his lecture notes on Tolstoy, Nabokov remarked that most writers tend to admire art that resembles their own. In Tolstoy, however, "we have got the unique case of a writer who wrote in precisely the way he condemned. All the beauty of Tolstoy's work consists exactly in the beauty he refuses to accept in this essay."[5] Nabokov goes on to dissect *What Is Art?*, enumerating instances of flawed reasoning and poor argumentation. He takes the essay to task for failing to define clearly what is meant by art—"the word art is so loosely applied as to become meaningless"—and insists that "you cannot base a philosophical examination of art on something as vague and often false as the term used in everyday speech."[6] Like many readers of *What Is Art?*, Nabokov is disappointed by Tolstoy's aesthetic conclusions, his apotheosis of simplicity in form and content. Parts of the treatise "leave one with the uncomfortable feeling that what is happening is an old man grumbling at youth, a conservative denouncing the moderns."[7] Yet Nabokov, unlike many early critics of *What Is Art?*, recognized the significance of this text in Tolstoy's body of work. "To understand the way Tolstoy's thought moved and the reasons why he put on the breaks so often during his (our) adventures in art, the examination of this essay is very important," Nabokov told his students.[8]

90

Atrophied Aesthetic Sense

My aim in what follows is, in part, to reconstruct this movement of Tolstoy's thought. Unlike previous approaches to his late aesthetics, I want neither to condemn nor to rescue Tolstoy's ideas about art.[9] I do not intend to defend the logic of his aesthetic canon or explain its excesses—like his "overpowering revulsion" (*neotrazimoe otvrashchenie*) at Shakespeare—by means of Tolstoy's personality, his age and class, or even his evolving sociopolitical commitments.[10] Instead, by reading *What Is Art?* in the context of other late writings (*Hadji Murat* and *The Circle of Reading*), I intend to demonstrate that all these late works are shaped by a distinct concern—namely, Tolstoy's anxiety about our capacity to be receptive to other people and their art. Despite his professed worry about our involuntary aesthetic absorption, these late works repeatedly shift to failures of responsiveness—failures physical, psychological, social, and aesthetic. These modes of unresponsiveness are, of course, diverse, and distinct, but for Tolstoy they belong together as manifestations of a deeper incapacity to attend to the world beyond the self. For Tolstoy, as Gennadii Ishuk notes, "the problem of readerly reception was connected with his fundamental philosophical-aesthetic searching and compositions."[11] The problem remains one of other minds, but it is now taken up from the other point of view. If in *Anna Karenina* Tolstoy the doubtful artist wondered how one can ever hope to express oneself to other people, then here the question becomes: Can we ever attend to anyone but ourselves?

Tolstoy spent a lifetime pointing out how external forces (e.g., family traditions, social conventions, or language itself) affect our behavior, and in particular our ethical choices. It might therefore seem counterintuitive to ascribe to him a concern that we are *insufficiently* receptive. "One soul influences another, and the individual is completely free only when he is alone," Tolstoy writes in *The Circle of Reading*.[12] Natasha Rostova is seduced by Anatole in *War and Peace* (1869). Vasiliy Pozdnyshev is debauched by his older friends in *The Kreutzer Sonata* (1890). Eugene Irtenev is persuaded that it is healthy and natural to have extramarital affairs in *The Devil* (1911). The primary danger to the spiritual life of the individual, Tolstoy often suggests, is precisely his receptivity, his vulnerability to the corrosive influences of those around him. Gustafson speculates that in this way Tolstoy turned his personal tendency toward solitude "into a positive force for good."[13] But Tolstoy—perhaps starting from the same experiences of psychic isolation—registers also a countervailing threat to the individual, one that comes not from without but from within. Rather than demonstrating our excessive vulnerability, the texts I consider in this chapter dwell on the problem of resisting too much the world outside the self. They show that an individual can become inured to the world. This threat from within is not wholly unfamiliar to readers of Tolstoy. It inspires what Shklovsky later described as

91

Chapter Three

Tolstoy's "estranging" narration: worried about the way habit blinds us to the world that surrounds us, Tolstoy sought to reinvigorate everyday things and events by describing them as though seeing them for the first time.[14] But the concept of defamiliarization captures only the most benign version of this threat from within: the way we *neglect* to be attentive to the things around us. For Tolstoy, as I will show, the problem of our inurement to the world runs deeper. Tolstoy observes that we do not just neglect but often, and more perniciously, *withhold* our attention. And not only from things, but from other people. Tolstoy, as I will demonstrate, lays bare our impulse to disregard whatever does not pertain to our immediate aims, pleasures, and preoccupations. His late works attest to the labor required to attend to anything other than oneself.

Tolstoy's intuition about the difficulty of receptivity challenges a long-standing assumption that informs our current debates. Our discourse about methods of reading proceeds from the assumption—one that dates back at least to Plato—that texts tend to draw us in, sweep us away.[15] We are captivated, deprived of reason, drawn in by the charisma of the artist as if according to a natural law. If we do nothing, we will succumb to that charisma. By suspecting, by critiquing, we do our best (the thinking goes) to resist this fate, to preserve our intellectual autonomy. The Frankfurt School critics, for example, affirmed critique as the means by which we avoid becoming "victims" of the pseudoart of the culture industry, designed to absorb the spectator's attention completely and "den[y] its audience any dimension in which they might roam freely in imagination."[16] Their late twentieth-century critical heirs prescribed critique still more broadly, holding that all art, not just those forms of it that seemed suspect to the Frankfurt School, must be scrutinized and demystified, if we are to resist unwittingly submitting to the ideology that artworks carry. This procedure, according to Bruce Robbins, is what separates fans from critics, the (presumably naive) "mainstream [that] may flatter itself on improvements and reform" in our society from the vigilant critic who continues to recognize its problems.[17]

Recent advocates of a scholarly turn from critique dispute the association of serious reading with detachment and skepticism. But they tend not to challenge the picture of aesthetic receptivity as somehow more effortless and automatic than detachment. Felski, for example, underscores the bad reputation unjustly bestowed on the experience she terms "enchantment": "a state of intense involvement, a sense of being so entirely caught up in an aesthetic object that nothing else seems to matter."[18] She points to a tradition of linking this state of receptivity to a "low-brow," naive, and female spectator, and linking critique to the sophisticated, serious, male critic. Practitioners of critique, she suggests, recapitulate the very hierarchies they seek to expose. By disavowing enchantment, by exaggerating its dangers—for "even as

92

we are bewitched, possessed, emotionally overwhelmed, we know ourselves
to be immersed in an imaginary spectacle"—we foreclose the intellectual
and affective possibilities it offers.[19] Felski thus presupposes that these possibilities are always open to us in the first place. For all her potent arguments
against the methods of critique, she shares with her opponents the assumption that aesthetic receptivity is more fundamental than suspicion—that enjoying it is merely a matter of relinquishing bad habits.

Tolstoy's late works help contest this assumption shared by partisans
of both sides of the postcritique debate. The conservatism, moralizing, and
self-contradictions of Tolstoy's late aesthetics are indisputable. Nevertheless,
there are, as Wittgenstein suggested, important things to learn from Tolstoy's
"bad theorizing."[20] Tolstoy makes a valuable contribution to our aesthetic
discourse by revealing the difficulty of receptivity. He helps us see that we
cannot take for granted our ability to be attentive to other people or to become absorbed in their art. Receptivity is no less intentional and no less effortful than skeptical detachment; indeed, it might be far more so.

FAILED INFECTIONS

To clarify his own views on art, Tolstoy sought first to familiarize himself
with the English, French, and German traditions of aesthetic philosophy. In
1891 he asked his friend Nikolay Strakhov to send him books that could illuminate "all known definitions" of art.[21] In the opening chapters of *What Is
Art?* Tolstoy summarizes what he learned from these books—by and about
Alexander Gottlieb Baumgarten, Gotthold Ephraim Lessing, Johann Gottfried von Herder, Edmund Burke, Charles Bateaux, Friedrich Schiller, Kant,
Schopenhauer, Georg Wilhelm Friedrich Hegel, Hippolyte Taine, Herbert
Spenser, and many others—only to dismiss it. Thanks to these aesthetic traditions, Tolstoy concludes, people accept the idea that "art is such activity as
produces beauty" (*WIA*, 17; *PSS*, 30:34). But "there is no objective definition
of beauty," he protests (*WIA*, 43; *PSS*, 30:58). Everything amounts to the
same "subjective definition" of beauty as something that "pleases (without
exciting desire)" (*WIA*, 44; *PSS*, 30:58). Aestheticians have felt the "insufficiency and instability" of this definition, he goes on, and, seeking to give it
a "firm basis, have asked themselves why a thing pleases"; they have "converted the discussion on beauty into a question concerning taste" (*WIA*, 44;
PSS, 30:58–59). He rejects this direction in aesthetic discourse, contending
instead that there can be no objective standard for pleasure.

Tolstoy proposes an alternative definition of art. He defines art as "infection" (*zarazhenie*) with feeling: "Art is a human activity consisting in this,
that one man consciously, by means of certain external signs, hands on to

Chapter Three

others feelings he has lived through, and that other people are infected by these feelings and also experience them" (*WIA*, 51; *PSS*, 30:65). Art, he explains, is a mechanism of conveying feeling from one person to another. Tolstoy then goes on to categorize all art along two axes: infectious/not infectious and good/bad. Individual artworks that succeed in the transmission of feeling are "infectious." Those that fail are not infectious and thus cannot be properly considered art; they are what Tolstoy calls "false" art (*lozhnoe iskusstvo*). Art that does produce infection—"true" art (*istinnoe iskusstvo*)—is further categorized as "good" or "bad" depending on the type of feeling it transmits; on whether it transmits the "religious consciousness" (*religioznoe soznanie*) of its time (*WIA*, 72; *PSS*, 30:69). The term "religious consciousness," as Elena Kupreyanova explains, means something greater than religious sentiment for Tolstoy. It "encompasses for Tolstoy the totality of, in his view, progressive ideas—civic, moral, religious—that are the spiritual nerve of the progressive development of a given time."[22] Good art, Tolstoy says, infects with these ideas and bad art infects with their opposite. Tolstoy thus ends up with three operative categories of art: false, true-good, and true-bad.

The contagion model of art Tolstoy puts forward in his treatise echoes Plato's description of the power of art. In the dialogue "Ion," Plato's Socrates explains to his eponymous interlocutor that art acts like a magnet pulling a series of iron rings. "Do you also know then that the spectator is the last of those rings I spoke of as receiving power by the Heraclean stone [magnate]?" Socrates asks.[23] "You, the rhapsode and actor, are the middle ring; the first ring is the poet himself. But it's the god who draws the soul of men through all of them in whatever direction he may wish, making the power of one depend upon the other."[24] Socrates's speech reflects Plato's apprehension of art, its power to persuade people by bypassing human reason. Famously, this fear led Plato to banish poets from his Republic. Tolstoy rejected the Platonic prohibition on art—it would deny people an "indispensable means of communication, without which mankind could not exist"—but expressed sympathy for the concerns that animate it (*WIA*, 53; *PSS*, 30:67). The echoes of Plato in Tolstoy's treatise are undeniable, and as a result most scholarly treatments of *What Is Art?* foreground the author's worry about the "the power of art to change one's mood."[25]

The standard view of Tolstoy's aesthetics is given lucid expression in Gustafson's seminal *Leo Tolstoy: Resident and Stranger*. This view suggest that *What Is Art?* is chiefly concerned with art's thrilling yet frightening capacity to alter consciousness. Gustafson explains the author's attitude toward art by positing that aesthetic experience for Tolstoy is a mode of human relatedness that partakes of two other modes, one of which Tolstoy considers pernicious and sinful ("intoxication") and the other wholesome and redemptive ("ecstasy"). Tolstoy, Gustafson argues, begins from the premise that

Atrophied Aesthetic Sense

people have lost their "natural state of harmony"—a state in which the self is united with others.[26] We are atomized and egoistic, and even hostile to each other. But the originary drive to forget oneself and unite with others—or what Gustafson calls "going forth" from the self—persists in a perverted form as the temptation to become passionately "possessed" or "intoxicated" by other people and things. Intoxication happens when "the loss of self is brought about by something external to it," Gustafson explains.[27] This self-loss is coerced and therefore dangerous: "In the moment of intoxication the sense of who I am and where I must go gets blurred."[28] An altogether different kind of self-loss occurs in a state of "ecstasy." Tolstoy's characters experience ecstasy when their self-forgetting does not involve coercion but instead occurs spontaneously:

> Released from his usual way of being and seeing, the person discovers a new world to which he feels he belongs. In intoxication one is drawn to or driven by others. In ecstasy one is set free to be with and for others. Both are states of relatedness, but intoxication is the foundation of sin, while ecstasy resembles prayer.[29]

Aesthetic experience ("infection") is a third state that mediates between harmful intoxication and virtuous ecstasy, exhibiting facets of both. An artwork is something external that acts on the spectator, so the effect it produces is akin to intoxication in that it comes from without. Yet unlike intoxication, aesthetic experience does not annihilate the self. Instead, it releases the self from egoism and allows it to "go forth" to unite with others; in this way it resembles ecstasy. Tolstoy, in Gustafson's view, wishes to suggest that "Art connects, but it is not coercive. Art does not force you into a position not your own, as [Tolstoy's protagonist] Pozdnyshev claimed. Rather, art leads you into your own position."[30] The psychologically nuanced, if not always convincing, distinctions that Gustafson's account reconstructs evince Tolstoy's wish to neutralize a dangerous potential he saw in art. Gustafson explains that Tolstoy "came to understand the aesthetic experience itself as a most powerful form of [the] loss of self and hence both very important and very dangerous."[31] Delicately calibrated between intoxication and ecstasy, aesthetic experience is capable of promoting human connectedness, but Tolstoy feared it might collapse into intoxication.

In light of Gustafson's reading, we might expect that Tolstoy's aesthetic treatise would offer us ample evidence of art's capacity—for better or worse—to captivate us. It is thus striking that the aesthetic experiences Tolstoy actually *describes* in *What Is Art?* are *not* experiences of possession. Just the opposite: they are experiences of incomprehension and estrangement, as well as the failure to be receptive to art. Tolstoy gives us example after

95

Chapter Three

example of art that does not move its audience, whether that audience is Tolstoy himself or his peers, whether that art is the refined (and therefore suspect) art of the upper classes or the simple folk art of the peasants. This dissonance, I will argue, demonstrates that Tolstoy's worry about the undue influence of art exists in dialectical tension with another set of concerns that have thus far been neglected in scholarship—concerns about our *invulnerability* to aesthetic experience and the limits of art's power to induce self-forgetting. I stress this second element of the dialectic to elucidate the moral and aesthetic consequences Tolstoy discerned in the loss of responsiveness to art.

Tolstoy's treatise begins not with an instance of aesthetic absorption but with one of withdrawal and resistance. In the first pages of *What Is Art?* Tolstoy vividly recounts an opera rehearsal he observed backstage. His trip through the theater evokes a journey through Hades: "By dark entrances and passages I was led through the vaults of an enormous building, past immense machines for changing the scenery and for lighting, and there in the gloom and dust I saw workmen busily engaged" (*WIA*, 10; *PSS*, 30:28). Tolstoy defamiliarizes the scene on stage: "Amid various poles and rings and scattered scenery, decorations, and curtains, stood and moved dozens, if not hundreds, of painted and dressed-up men, in costumes fitting tight to their thighs and calves . . . They all came from one place and walked round and round again, and then stopped" (*WIA*, 10–11; *PSS*, 30:28–29). It is not the happenings on stage that hold Tolstoy's attention but the labor surrounding them—the workmen, the angry director. Tolstoy stresses his confusion: "But what was being done here? For what, and for whom?" (*WIA*, 13; *PSS*, 30:31). A spectator swept up, swayed, overwhelmed with the performance might have emphasized the transformative magic of the costumes and props, or the effect of the music or plot. Tolstoy is decidedly not possessed by this artwork.

One might attribute Tolstoy's unresponsiveness to the fact that this dramatic work is poor or still unfinished. Perhaps it is not a fully realized aesthetic experience capable of sweeping its spectators away—of producing the absorbing effect Tolstoy feared and thereby distracting spectators from the objectionable (in Tolstoy's view) conditions of its making. But similar experiences of incomprehension appear throughout *What Is Art?* even in response to complete and widely acclaimed artworks. For example, Tolstoy devotes several chapters to a discussion of French Symbolism, in which he repeats the words "obscure" (*neiasno*) and "incomprehensible" (*neponiatno*) as though they were an incantation. Tolstoy transcribes the text of Maurice Maeterlinck's song "Quand il est sorti," which is then followed by Tolstoy's own uncomprehending commentary: "Who went out? Who came in? Who is speaking? Who died?" (*WIA*, 89; *PSS*, 30:102). Tolstoy not only cites the poems of Charles Baudelaire, Stéphane Mallarmé, Paul Verlaine, and many others in the body of the treatise, but also produces an appendix with further examples of such "obscure" poetry. He begs his reader to peruse the appendix and experience this confusion firsthand. It is evidently his confusion and disaffection in the face of such art—"what was being done here?"—that compels Tolstoy to write a treatise that endeavors to define the nature of aesthetic experience. Tolstoy's discussion of art proceeds from experiences of aesthetic unresponsiveness. The fact that he asks the same questions of poetic description as of a live performance—paying no attention to the artistic medium—serves as further proof of this unresponsiveness.

If Tolstoy's principal concern were to explicate his Platonic apprehension of art, we might expect him to devote much of his treatise to giving us an account of the frightful effects of true-bad art, the art that threatens to infect with bad feelings. He does not. After defining true-bad art as art that conveys feelings estranging people from God and from one another, Tolstoy offers a short, unspecific list of examples of true-bad art: "in literary art . . . all novels and poems which transmit Church or patriotic feelings, and also exclusive feelings pertaining only to the class of the idle rich such as aristocratic honor, satiety, spleen, pessimism, and refined and vicious feelings flowing from sex-love quite incomprehensible to the great majority of mankind" (*WIA*, 157; *PSS*, 30:164–65). He is similarly vague in his examples from visual art, condemning "all the so-called symbolic pictures, in which the very meaning of the symbol is comprehensible only to the people of a certain circle" (*WIA*, 157; *PSS*, 30:165). In music he is only slightly more specific, listing among true-bad artists Ludwig van Beethoven (in his late period), Robert Schumann, Hector Berlioz, Franz Liszt, and Richard Wagner, whom he ultimately reclassifies as a "false" artist, without a great deal of justification. The reclassification of Wagner is telling, since it shows that Tolstoy's discussion not only neglects to probe the effects of true-bad art but also fails even to articulate precisely the boundaries of this category. Moreover, instead of emphasizing the pernicious influence of true-bad artworks, Tolstoy underscores that these works are incomprehensible to the majority of people. This stress on the hermeticism of true-bad art belies Tolstoy's concern about its potency. If the infectiousness of true-bad art is as limited as Tolstoy suggests, then it can hardly pose the danger Plato envisioned.

In fact, there is in Tolstoy's treatise a surprising dearth of examples of aesthetic infection, good or bad. Having failed to find one in true-bad art, we might look next to true-good art. After all, true-good art, according to Tolstoy, transmits universally comprehensible feelings, so it should infect everyone. But even here we struggle to find a vivid example of successful infection. While Tolstoy devotes several chapters to describing failed infections—by theater, poetry, new musical compositions—he spends only half a dozen paragraphs outlining how true-good art affects its audience. A peasant choir at Yasnaya Polyana singing spontaneously upon his daughter's return

Chapter Three

home, a story Tolstoy finds in a children's magazine, and a theatrical performance by the Siberian Vogul tribe (now known as Mansi) described in a newspaper: these serve as Tolstoy's examples of true-good art. Tolstoy speaks vaguely and briefly of its effects. He says only that the peasant choir made him more cheerful and that he "could not tear [himself] away" from the story of "the children and the chickens" (*WIA*, 136; *PSS*, 30:145). The Vogul performance is discussed in a distinctly removed manner: "The audience, as the eyewitness describes them, are paralyzed with suspense; deep groans and even weeping is heard among them. And, from the mere description, I felt that this was a true work of art" (*WIA*, 138; *PSS*, 30:146). Tolstoy does not experience the infectious power of the performance but only reports that others have experienced it. He wants to posit these aesthetic events as examples of infection, yet his own pale descriptions of them hardly suggest a spectator swept up by the artist's feeling.

The passages of *What Is Art?* devoted to Wagner's opera offer Tolstoy yet another opportunity—perhaps the best opportunity—to discuss the sort of potent possession Plato imagined. After all, Wagner's productions have inspired in their many fans the aesthetic absorption that concerned the philosopher. Tolstoy's Wagner chapter, as Stephen Halliwell puts it, "sets up a stark and perplexing (or perplexed) antithesis . . . between the failure of the operatic work to engage a particular individual's mind, and on the other hand, its ostensibly seductive, 'hypnotic' effect on the rest of a large audience."[32] Tolstoy, however, refuses to grant that Wagner's work possesses the power Plato feared. Instead, he denies its "infectiousness," slotting it into the category of "false" art, which only *mimics* infection without producing it. Tolstoy compares the effect of Wagner's productions to that of hypnosis, alcohol, and opium—things that befog consciousness, as he explains in another tract called "Why Do People Stupefy Themselves?" (1891). There, Tolstoy argues that people "stupefy" themselves for the sole purpose of concealing from themselves their own thoroughgoing egoism and "moral immobility" (*nravstvennuiu nepodvizhnost'*).[33] By linking false art with alcohol and opium, Tolstoy identifies it not as a source of new, perverse feelings but merely as a way to conceal an already extant moral turpitude—an inattentiveness to the world and other people. Once more we fail to find an example of art's dangerous power to possess. Instead, Tolstoy again chooses to describe a failed infection—and again, his own.

Tolstoy devotes multiple pages to narrating his bewilderment at a performance of *Der Ring des Nibelungen*:

> [O]pening his mouth in a *strange* way, [the actor] sang something incomprehensible. The music of various instruments accompanied the *strange* sounds which he emitted. From the libretto one was able to gather that the actor

had to represent a powerful dwarf, who lived in the cave, and who was forging a sword for Siegfried, whom he had reared. One could tell he was a dwarf by the fact that the actor walked all the time bending the knees of his trico-covered legs. This dwarf, still opening his mouth in the same *strange* way, long continued to sing or shout. The music meanwhile runs over something *strange*, like beginnings which are not continued and do not get finished. (*WIA* 122; *PSS*, 30:133; my emphasis)

Tolstoy flaunts his incomprehension by repeating the word "strange" (*stranno*) four times in one short paragraph. He stresses the work required to puzzle out the happenings on stage. His unresponsiveness, Tolstoy suggests, is not extraordinary. Instead, he posits that Wagner's fans actually share his own aversion but cannot admit it. "Everyone knows the feeling of distrust and repulsion that is always evoked by an author's evident calculation," Tolstoy writes (*WIA*, 126; *PSS*, 30:136).[34] All viewers, he speculates, feel the same distrust and incomprehension that he feels in response to Wagner. But they suppress this response because they "considered it their duty" to delight in the performance (*WIA*, 126; *PSS*, 30:137). What troubles Tolstoy is not the power of Wagner's art but the dishonesty of his fellow spectators.

What Is Art? thus offers almost no examples of successful infection, and certainly none so vivid as the examples of failed infection. Consequently, scholarship on Tolstoy's aesthetics frequently looks to other works—for example, *War and Peace, Anna Karenina*, and especially *The Kreutzer Sonata* to which I turn in the following chapter—to explicate the danger Tolstoy perceives in art's capacity to infect us with perverse feelings.[35] In the treatise itself what Tolstoy returns to over and over again is aesthetic unresponsiveness, his own as well as that of his peers. Fair or not, Wagner's acclaim demonstrates for Tolstoy not the artist's power to sway his audience but the "extent [to which] people of our circle and time have lost the capacity to receive real art" (*WIA*, 118; *PSS*, 30:129). It also reveals their efforts to hide their aesthetic unresponsiveness. Critics are the first who "lack the capacity to be infected by art and [they] therefore always especially prize works like Wagner's opera where it is all an affair of the intellect" (*WIA*, 130; 1 *PSS*, 30:40). Ordinary spectators emulate the critics: "'Oh yes, certainly! What poetry! Marvelous! Especially the birds!' 'Yes, yes! I am quite vanquished!'" (*WIA*, 130; *PSS*, 30:140). Most of his peers "will pass real works of art by, not only without attention, but even with contempt," because "the receptive feeling for art of these people is atrophied," Tolstoy laments (*WIA*, 133–34; *PSS*, 30:143–44). He indicts himself along with his peers: "I belong to the class of people whose taste has, by false training, been perverted. And therefore my old, inured habits may cause me to err" (*WIA*, 155; *PSS*, 30:163). Šilbajoris points out that "while maintaining the appearance of a reasoned argument,"

99

Chapter Three

What Is Art? really "communicates on the level of personal confession."[36] And what Tolstoy confesses, it seems, is his own struggle to become absorbed in the art of others. Tolstoy is troubled less by possession than by his failure to be possessed.

THE RESISTANT READER

Recognizing the way Tolstoy's concern about aesthetic unresponsiveness shaped *What Is Art?* changes how we understand his theory of infection. More than anything, it now looks like the expression of aesthetic fantasy. Emerson has suggested that because Tolstoy's "life and works were indeed one huge accumulating avalanche of self-expression," he longed for respite from the pressures of his own creative drive.[37] He "craved nothing more than those moments when he was infected himself . . . Tolstoy thrilled to the possibility that he could stand aside and be caught up."[38] The Platonic picture of aesthetic experience validates Tolstoy's dream of an artwork that could reliably sweep away its readers, and him first of all. Yet Tolstoy was too keen an observer of psychology and too honest a thinker not to articulate faithfully his own reactions to various artworks—his failures to be possessed. In his thinking and writing about art, Tolstoy recognizes his resistance to infection, and in doing so he participates in a strain of aesthetic thought that descends not from Plato but from Hume.

In his essay "Of the Standard of Taste," David Hume identifies an aspect of the phenomenology of reading that has received relatively little attention in aesthetic philosophy.[39] Hume observes that there are instances when readers refuse to engage with an author's fictions—namely, when they are asked to imagine a moral order vastly different from their own. Much of the time we have no trouble responding to art that depict worlds unlike the one we know, Hume writes:

> Whatever speculative errors may be found in the polite writings of any age or country, they detract but little from the value of those compositions. There needs but a certain turn of thought or imagination to make us enter into all the opinions, which then prevailed, and relish the sentiments or conclusions derived from them.[40]

We need not subscribe to the metaphysics of the ancient Greeks, for example, to sympathize with Odysseus's plight. It requires only a little effort to imagine what it might be like to believe in the Olympic pantheon or to value hospitality above other virtues, and thereby to engage with Homer's epic and delight in it. But it is another matter to delight in works that are averse to our moral sentiments:

But a very violent effort is requisite to change our judgment of manners, and excite sentiments of approbation or blame, love or hatred, different from those to which the mind from long custom has been familiarized. And where a man is confident of the rectitude of that moral standard, by which he judges, he is justly jealous of it, and will not pervert the sentiments of his heart for a moment, in complaisance to any writer whatsoever.[41]

For Hume, our sentiments—including our feelings of pleasure and displeasure—reveal our moral judgments. To take pleasure in an artwork that expresses something to which we are morally averse is, on this view, impossible: an artwork cannot please and displease me at once. We thus refuse to attend to such art.

The contemporary philosopher Tamar Gendler expands on this Humean insight. She asks why it is that we are capable of imagining all sorts of far-fetched scenarios and impossible worlds, yet we have trouble "imagining fictional worlds that we take to be morally deviant."[42] It is not that we *cannot* imagine such worlds, Gendler argues; we just refuse to do so. She proposes that moral truths are singular in that we expect them to hold for all possible worlds, so when a piece of fiction presents us with a deviant morality we require strong indications that we are not to "export" this morality into our own world. Otherwise, we will be "unwilling to follow the author's lead because in trying to make that world fictional, she is providing us with a way of looking at *this* world that we prefer not to embrace."[43] Put simply, we resist art that asks us to reject our moral commitments.

Tolstoy knew well Hume's writing, having read it in his youth and again in middle age, and he was likely familiar with the essay on taste: A heavily underlined copy of *Essays: Moral, Political, and Literary*, which includes this piece, sits in Tolstoy's library in Yasnaya Polyana.[44] Hume's omission from Tolstoy's catalogue of aesthetic theories in *What Is Art?* was likely due to his objection to taste as a governing concept in accounts of aesthetic enjoyment. Already in *Anna Karenina*, Tolstoy searches for a definition of aesthetic enjoyment irreducible to taste. By the time Tolstoy writes *What Is Art?* he is even more convinced that "all attempts to define what taste is must lead to nothing" (*WIA*, 44; *PSS*, 30:59). But while taste as a conceptual category holds no interest for Tolstoy, Hume's aesthetics is in other ways congenial to his own.

"Of the Standard of Taste" begins with the same paradox that troubled Tolstoy in *Anna Karenina* and again in *What Is Art?*: the paradox of aesthetic judgment that Kant formulated into the antinomy of taste. Our aesthetic preferences, like our gastronomic ones, seem to depend entirely on the idiosyncrasies of our senses. Some objects may please one person and displease another, and neither individual will be wrong in insisting on his own pleasure. And yet, as Hume notes, there is widespread agreement that John Mil-

Chapter Three

ton's talent, say, is greater than John Ogilby's. He therefore preserves the empirical possibility of universal agreement in our aesthetic judgments—a possibility Tolstoy also wished to defend (albeit on stronger grounds).[45]

Hume cannot deny, however, that disagreements do arise. He explains them by suggesting that our organs of aesthetic perception are very delicate and easily thrown off course. A spectator might be inattentive, he might not have experience making aesthetic judgments, or he might be consumed by prejudice that impedes his judgment. Hume suggests that aesthetic perceptions require a "perfect serenity of mind" and that achieving this serenity is, counterintuitively, an effortful process.[46] All aesthetic experiences require "impos[ing] a proper violence on [one's own] imagination."[47] What he means is that to be receptive to an artwork, the spectator must depart from his "natural position."[48] When confronted with works of the distant past or of another culture, the spectator "must place himself in the same situation as the [original] audience, in order to form a true judgment."[49] Hume proposes that this is not done "without some effort," since we are much more readily receptive to "pictures and characters, that resemble objects which are found in our own age or country."[50] But we find it harder still to forget the rivalries and affinities that distort our reception of the artworks of our own time: A proper judge of art "forgets his interest as a friend or enemy, as a rival or commentator."[51] If he cannot, then the "beauties and blemishes" of the work do not have "the same influence upon him, as if he had imposed a proper violence on his imagination, and had forgotten himself for a moment."[52] To properly experience an artwork, a critic must work to shed his prejudices and look past the contingencies of his own relation to the author.

The notion that aesthetic experience involves self-forgetting is not unique to Hume. Indeed, Hume's aesthetics shares this idea with Plato's otherwise quite dissimilar theory of art. What does stand out in Hume's essay is the notion that exemplary aesthetic experience—the kind of aesthetic experience that would then allow one to properly judge the work—*requires* self-forgetting and that achieving it is no easy feat. Most people are incapable of it: "A man of learning and reflection can make allowance for these peculiarities of manners; but a common audience can never divest themselves so far of their usual ideas and sentiments, as to relish pictures which no wise resemble them."[53] Far from being easy and automatic, the kind of "divestment" required by aesthetic receptivity is so difficult that it is beyond common audiences, Hume suggests; it is the special purview of critics. At the same time, Hume notes that an artwork can ask too much of its spectator, as when it compels him to sympathize with a moral perspective he finds abhorrent. Although Hume submits that aesthetic receptivity requires a certain spectatorial self-overcoming, he acknowledges that there must be some measure to the violence imposed on one's own imagination; it must be a *proper* violence.

102

Atrophied Aesthetic Sense

Tolstoy shares Hume's insight that divesting oneself of the contingencies of one's own "usual ideas and sentiments" is both difficult and essential to aesthetic experience. Indeed, it is in contemplation of this difficulty that Tolstoy begins to set down his thoughts on art. "We started to read Leskov's [*Zenon*] *the Goldsmith* in the presence of society ladies, [Ol'ga] Mamonova, [Aleksandra] Samarina," Tolstoy writes in his diary around the time he began to compose the cycle of essays that would culminate in *What Is Art?*[54] The society ladies, Tolstoy complains, were interested only in the aesthetic aspects of the work:

> I thought: All right, suppose all the power of fine art that I can imagine were summoned to express such a truth as obligates, such a truth as not only demands to be seen or listened to but that condemns one's old life and demands the new. Suppose there were such an artwork; it would not even stir the Mamonovas or Samarinas, and others like them.[55]

The unresponsiveness Tolstoy demonstrates over and over again in *What Is Art?* is diagnosed first in his own drawing room—in himself and in his guests. Tolstoy is struck by a thought that echoes Hume's observations: even the most brilliant artwork can fail to captivate its audience if it asks them to imagine a moral life radically different from their own.

Starting from this same insight, however, Tolstoy inverts Hume's hierarchy of readers and posits the need to impose a more radical violence on one's own imagination. Hume's cultured reader stands on high moral ground, and he is "just" in his unwillingness to "pervert the sentiments of his heart for a moment, in complaisance to any writer whatsoever."[56] Tolstoy would agree that a child or a peasant—those whom, following Rousseau, he believed to be innately morally righteous—should not trouble himself with art that asks him to imagine a moral universe different from his own. Such readers are infected by artworks immediately, without effort. But they are not the readers who ultimately interest Tolstoy; they are not whom he addresses in his writing on art. Tolstoy, like Hume, speaks to an elite, educated reader, and for him this reader is morally compromised. This reader belongs to a class of people whose wealth and privilege depend on the exploitation of the laboring masses. This reader is precisely the one who ought to alter the sentiments of his or her heart yet refuses to do so. The Mamonovas or Samarinas are blameworthy for their unwillingness to impose on their imagination the violence needed to radically change their (perverted) moral commitments. An upper-class reader, having lost his innate receptivity, must regain it through a radical, effortful self-forgetting—he must, Tolstoy suggests, impose an improper violence on his imagination.

Tolstoy's theory of art, as he articulates it in his treatise and the essays that precede it, stipulates that aesthetic response requires no interpretive

Chapter Three

labor and that interpretation is in fact a sign that something has gone wrong. This is surely one of the most suspect claims he makes in *What Is Art?*, and it has bewildered and irritated readers since the essay's publication. Emerson underscores the paradox of an author who was "profoundly committed to process in all areas of his moral philosophy and literary practice. But [who] in the realm of aesthetic theory . . . had no patience with forms of art that require for their appreciation prolonged or repeated exposure, arduous training, new languages, or complex techniques."[57] All this notwithstanding, it would be wrong to say that Tolstoy believed no labor was required in the task of aesthetic reception. Despite his ideal of instantaneous infection, Tolstoy suggests that a certain kind of labor *is* needed. What is needed is the willingness to radically reimagine one's own life. This task is no less arduous than learning a new language, and Tolstoy's appreciation of its difficulty is among the things that most appealed to Wittgenstein. Tolstoy and Wittgenstein, as R. W. Beardsmore observes, share the idea that what stands in the way of grasping great art is "not a matter of understanding, but of the will."[58] For Tolstoy, aesthetic unresponsiveness is one consequence of our refusal to reimagine our moral lives.

ART AS ANTIDOTE TO EGOISM

With its vivid depictions of violence, its lack of a straightforward moral lesson, and its elite rather than demotic register, Tolstoy's novella *Hadji Murat* appears to be the literary work most at odds with Tolstoy's discursive writing on art. Tolstoy composed it not long after he completed *What Is Art?* and the author himself sensed his failure to abide by his rules for art. "I kept wishing all this time to write something literary that would promote my own artistic demands, but couldn't do it," he wrote to Vladimir Chertkov.[59] For many scholars it is proof that Tolstoy the artist refutes Tolstoy the preacher, and F. I. Evnin speculates that writing *Hadji Murat* was a guilty pleasure for the author.[60] Others, however, contest this reading, suggesting that in many ways Tolstoy practices what he preaches. Susan Layton, for example, notices that in *Hadji Murat* Tolstoy privileges oral artworks—Dagestani songs and fables—over written ones, echoing his preference in *What Is Art?* for artworks that allow face-to-face communication between author and audience.[61] Edmund Heier notes that the novella answers Tolstoy's call in his treatise for art that inspires "indignation and horror at the violation of love."[62] As a literary work, of course, the novella does not straightforwardly endorse or deny Tolstoy's rules for art. And defending the supremacy of the artist or the preacher seems less compelling than investigating how in *Hadji Murat* Tolstoy uses literary means to plumb the same problem

104

Atrophied Aesthetic Sense

that concerns him in his philosophical treatise: the problem of aesthetic unresponsiveness.

Tolstoy's novella, completed in 1904 but published posthumously in 1912, explores the source and consequences of aesthetic unresponsiveness. It identifies an incapacity for aesthetic delight as an element of a broader imperviousness to others, the root of which Tolstoy locates in egoism. *Hadji Murat* complicates the apotheosis of the "inner voice" in Tolstoy's fiction. Tolstoy frequently lauded one's inner voice as the voice of conscience. By listening to one's inner voice, one casts off the falsifications of social life and approaches truth. *Hadji Murat*, however, inverts this scheme, so well established in both Tolstoy's fiction and discursive writing that critics rarely question it. Tolstoy's novella demonstrates that a corrupted inner voice might imperil us more than any influence from without. Instead of setting us on a righteous path, it allows us to persist in our immorality. Escape from this internal threat depends on our capacity to be attentive not to ourselves but to others. *Hadji Murat* posits that genuine aesthetic experiences can develop our capacity to be receptive to the external world and especially to other people.

The novella's first-person narrator walks home through a recently plowed field and notices a thistle plant the locals call "Tatar." The plant has been ploughed over but it nonetheless clings to life, reminding the narrator of a story he had "partly seen [himself], partly heard of from eye-witnesses, and in part imagined" (*HM*, 550; *PSS*, 35:6). He recalls the story of Hadji Murat, an Avarian military leader who, after decades of fighting the imperial Russian forces expanding into Dagestan and the Caucasus, surrenders to them. Betrayed by his onetime ally Imam Shamil, Hadji Murat turns to the Russians in hopes that they will help rescue his family, now imprisoned by Shamil. The Russians, uncertain of Hadji Murat's sincerity about fighting on their side, delay committing forces to assist him. They detain him and compel him to tell his life's story to the viceroy's aide-de-camp, Prince Loris-Melikov. In addition to encountering the military elite, largely indifferent to his plight, Hadji Murat also meets and befriends ordinary Russians—Butler, a young, idealistic officer; Marya Dmitrievna, the war-weary common-law wife of a major—who are, like he is, caught between two brutal forces, the Russian Empire and the Caucasian resistance under Shamil. When Hadji Murat hears of Shamil's threat to blind or kill his son, he is unable to wait any longer and escapes the Russian fort to attempt a rescue. The Russians pursue and finally kill him.

Tolstoy, as other readers have noted, relies heavily on parallelism in *Hadji Murat*, creating characters and scenes that rhyme with one another. This is most evident in the rhyming figures of Imam Shamil and Emperor Nicholas I, whom Tolstoy conceived of as "two poles of autocratic

Chapter Three

absolutism—Asian and European."[63] Throughout the novella Tolstoy distinguishes his hero, Hadji Murat, from the other two leaders in all the ways one might expect him to single out a praiseworthy military leader. Whereas the emperor and the imam are paranoid, impulsive, and brutal, Hadji Murat is brave, judicious, and kind to his men. But along with these expected traits, Tolstoy also underscores a trait that at first appears irrelevant to the description of a military commander. The emperor and the imam are both aesthetically unresponsive; Hadji Murat, in contrast, is moved by art. He takes great pleasure in his friend Khanefi's singing. Listening to the song with his eyes closed, he "always remarked in Russian—Good song! Wise song!" (*HM*, 641; *PSS*, 35:92). Evnin remarks that the Dagestani folklore that Tolstoy admired follows his hero like an aura throughout the novella.[64] Shklovsky likewise emphasizes this aesthetic dimension. He notes that when Tolstoy told the story of the historical Hadji Murat to his pupils at Yasnaya Polyana—years before writing the novella—he stressed that Hadji Murat died with a song on his lips.[65]

Through the characters of the emperor and the imam, Tolstoy offers us two portraits of unresponsive spectators. In my analysis of *Anna Karenina*, I showed that for Tolstoy (as for Kant) aesthetic response is characterized by the spectator's sense that his or her own interests and objectives are steered by the experience of admiring the artwork. We estimate the value of ordinary objects according to how well they address our demands. In contrast, the "beautiful" artwork in Kant and the genuine artwork in Tolstoy acquire what seems to be an unconditional value by making us feel that our obligation to admire them eclipses our own particular appetites and objectives. The appreciation of beauty, as philosopher Richard Moran explains it, involves the "recognition of a value to which my present interests and desires are themselves answerable or by which they are to be measured and hence a value that can create obligations (of attention, preservation, understanding, communicating, and so on)."[66] Instead of evaluating the artwork according to how well it meets my needs, I evaluate myself according to how well I meet my obligation to the artwork. The emperor and the imam in distinct ways avoid such experiences, which threaten to demote their own desires.

Emperor Nicholas seeks out only what Tolstoy considers false, or "ready-made," art. If a true artwork marginalizes the spectator's own demands, endowing him with a sense of obligation to admire the work, then a "ready-made" artwork inverts this effect. The false artwork is created according to an artist's calculations about what will please his audience. In *What Is Art?* Tolstoy calls such artworks "brain-spun" (*rassudochnye*), and he contrasts them with "sincere" (*iskrennie*) artworks (*WIA*, 72, 113; *PSS*, 30:85, 124). Sincerity, for Tolstoy, does not mean a lack of intention on the part of the artist. After all, Tolstoy defines art as a conscious activity in which the

106

Atrophied Aesthetic Sense

artist aims to infect others with his own feeling (*WIA*, 50; *PSS*, 30:64).[67] Sincerity means that the artist creates according to his own pattern of thought and does not simply echo that of his spectators. In genuine art, Tolstoy explains in his unpublished essay "About What Is Called Art" (1896), "there are always two people: one who produces the work of art, and one who receives it: the spectator, the listener."[68] In the ready-made artwork there is really only one person, the spectator. An artist who creates works based on deductions about his spectators' expectations and desires simply mirrors the spectators' accustomed ways of thinking.

With Emperor Nicholas, Tolstoy demonstrates that a preference for false art—what the author often referred to as "perverted taste" (*izvrashchennyi vkus*)—proceeds from aesthetic unresponsiveness. As in the case of Wagner, Tolstoy suggests that delight in false or brain-spun art is a disguise for aesthetic insensibility and a way of avoiding aesthetic experiences that might divert us from our own concerns. Nicholas is concerned most of all with gratifying his sensuous desires. Appetite shapes all his activity, including his encounters with art. Tolstoy draws attention to the emperor's protruding stomach and his fat cheeks with their "sausage-shaped" whiskers (*HM*, 615; *PSS*, 35:67). Even Nicholas's mental states are described in gastronomic terms: for example, his tryst with a young virgin at a ball leaves him with an "unpleasant after-taste" (*HM*, 616; *PSS*, 35:68). Tolstoy depicts the emperor's trip to the ballet as yet another instance of his search for sensuous gratification: "After dinner Nicholas drove to the ballet where hundreds of women marched round in tights and scanty clothing. One of them specially attracted him, and he had the German ballet-master sent for, thanked him and gave orders that a diamond ring should be presented to him" (*HM*, 624; *PSS*, 35:76).[69] The narration underscores the transactional nature of the performance. This is the ready-made artwork with which professional artists—the ballerinas and the ballet-master—seek to profit from meeting the spectator's expectations. The performance has the opposite effect of a genuine artwork, as Tolstoy conceived it. Masquerading as art, it never affords Nicholas the experience of aesthetic pleasure. Instead of marginalizing the emperor's established desires, it gratifies them. Instead of imparting to him new feelings, it mirrors his own mind.

Whereas Emperor Nicholas wards off experiences that decenter his desires by indulging in false art, Imam Shamil does so by abstaining from art altogether. Superficially, the emperor's sensuous indulgence seems counterposed to the imam's asceticism.[70] When Shamil returns to his seat of power in the village of Vedeno, he puts off satisfying his appetites for food, sleep, and sex to pray and attend to the affairs of government. Yet this asceticism does not present itself as something admirable. Indeed, Shamil's actions, no less than the emperor's, are guided by the desire for gratification and the

107

Chapter Three

wish to avoid anything that does not gratify him. While Nicholas is primarily concerned with his appetite for sex, Shamil is primarily concerned with his appetite for power. He abstains from sensuous indulgence to achieve a rational objective: to fortify his authority by displaying himself as a stern and pious leader. To create this impression of himself, he eschews art altogether. He does not ornament his dress or join his men in song to "produc[e] on the people just the impression and influence he desired and knew how to produce" (*HM*, 635; *PSS*, 35:86). Shamil's single-minded pursuit of power makes him unresponsive to the folklore that moves Hadji Murat. Both the emperor and the imam partake of the sort of aesthetic unresponsiveness that disturbs Tolstoy in *What Is Art?* But Shamil is perhaps still more blameworthy than the emperor, whose insensibility has been reinforced since childhood by false art. Shamil has every opportunity to attend to the traditional art of his people, yet he does not.

By depicting the emperor and the imam as unreceptive to art, Tolstoy points to the broader imperviousness of each to the world outside him, an imperviousness rooted in both cases in a relentless egoism. He contrasts this imperviousness with Hadji Murat's aesthetic receptivity and concomitant responsiveness to the demands made on him by his circumstances and by other people. The three leaders are juxtaposed in three scenes of deliberation. The emperor must decide the fate of a Polish student who in a fit of desperation attacked his professor. Shamil must decide whether to reconcile with Hadji Murat. And Hadji Murat must decide whether to attempt to rescue his family, though the attempt will almost certainly cost him his life. The three deliberating figures closely resemble one another: Nicholas thinks while "closing his eyes and bowing his head" (*HM*, 620; *PSS*, 35:72); Shamil, pondering, "closed his eyes and sat silent" (*HM*, 638; *PSS*, 35:89); and Hadji Murat "bowing his turbaned head remained silent a long time" before making a decision (*HM*, 651; *PSS*, 35:102). These three wordless deliberations support David Herman's claim that Tolstoy's text seeks foremost to depict silence. At the same time, it is significant that the silences of the three figures are distinct from one another, and not all silence is "pious," as Herman suggests.[71] The emperor and the imam may not speak out loud, but their inner voices never cease to chatter: they silence the outside world in order to hear the demands of their own egos. Hadji Murat, alternatively, silences his inner voice to attend to something other than himself. Whereas the emperor and the imam both reach their decisions quickly by listening to themselves, Hadji Murat thinks for a long time, and his deliberation is interrupted by moments of aesthetic delight at three artworks.

While deliberating, Emperor Nicholas hears an inner voice that, far from being the voice of conscience, articulates the best way to satisfy his lust for violence. The emperor needs only to "concentrate his attention for

Atrophied Aesthetic Sense

a few moments and the spirit moved him, and the best possible decision presented itself as though an inner voice had told him what to do" (*HM*, 621; *PSS*, 35:72). Without regard for the Polish student's suffering, Nicholas decides on a punishment that the narrator calls a "superfluous cruelty" (*HM*, 621; *PSS*, 35:72). He orders a gauntlet that is sure to kill the student, while at the same time boasting that, mercifully, he will uphold Russia's law against capital punishment by refraining from ordering an execution. "It pleased him to be ruthlessly cruel," the narrator explains, "and it also pleased him to think that we have abolished capital punishment in Russia" (*HM*, 621; *PSS*, 35:72). It is no spirit that moves Nicholas, but rather his wish to appease his racial hatred: "He had done much evil to the Poles . . . and hated them in proportion to the evil he had done them" (*HM*, 620; *PSS*, 35:72). The emperor uses the Polish student as a means for his own pleasure. In so doing, he exhibits a cruel egoism distinct from the naive egoism of Natasha Rostova in *War and Peace* or Dmitry Olenin in *The Cossacks* (1863). For these characters in Tolstoy's early works, self-love is an expression of natural vitality and a stage in the development of a love for others, as Donna Orwin has shown.[72] But Orwin argues that by the time Tolstoy writes *Hadji Murat* he has evolved on the question of self-love. He no longer considers it capable of "furnish[ing] a moral code to regulate behavior" and speculates that it "may even foster immorality."[73] In Nicholas, Tolstoy identifies an established and implacable egoism that makes it impossible to perceive anything outside one's own interests. It is the sort of egoism that inhibits a moral relation to other people.

Tolstoy attributes Nicholas's egoism to his separation from others. The narrator repeatedly underscores the monarch's isolation. The emperor moves among crowds of people, all the while speaking primarily to himself: "He began uttering aloud the first words that came into his head. 'Kopervine . . . Kovervine—' he repeated several times (it was the name of yesterday's girl). 'Horrid . . . horrid—' He did not think of what he was saying, but stifled his feelings by listening to the words" (*HM*, 617; *PSS*, 35:69). The emperor's connection with the world is further severed by the flattery of his subjects, the narrator explains: "Continual brazen flattery from everybody round him . . . had brought him to such a state that he no longer saw his own inconsistencies or measured his actions and words by reality, logic, or even simple common sense" (*HM*, 620; *PSS*, 35:71). Hardly anything that contradicts his own notions or demands reaches the emperor. And whenever the world does impinge on Nicholas, he, having grown used to this condition, tries to maintain his isolation both physically and psychologically: He retreats into his palace and he drowns out unpleasant thoughts with the sound of his own voice—"Kopervine . . . Kopervine." A thought about his brother's death visits Nicholas; to dispel the "feeling of sadness and vexation [that] came over him . . . he again began whispering the first words that came into

109

Chapter Three

his head" (*HM*, 618; *PSS*, 35:69). He moves in a vicious cycle where egoism leads to isolation and isolation reinforces egoism. Nicholas's predilection for ready-made art that appeases his desires is thus one instance of a more general condition: he is trapped in the echo chamber of his own mind.

One sees in Tolstoy's diaries and letters more and more frequent discussions of entrapment by egoism after the spiritual crisis he describes in his *Confession*. In one letter to Dmitry Litoshenko, Tolstoy describes walking out on a Sunday morning and seeing crowds of individuals—"janitors, policemen, cabbies"—wholly absorbed in their own work, executing their duties and discussing only their past and future work.[74] "It is so clear that all of them are absorbed in their affairs," Tolstoy observes, "They are soldered into one intricately twisted knot that not only is it impossible for them to change their lives, but they have no time, almost no opportunity, even to think about what a human life ought to be. For them to come to their senses, they need to break those bonds that pulled them into one knot. And the bonds are egoism, faith in egoism."[75] Their preoccupation with their own well-being robs them of the opportunity to contemplate what it means to be human, Tolstoy laments. This type of egoism is a form of bondage.

Tolstoy posits that such binding egoism—attributed to the emperor, people of his own class, and even the laboring people he observes on his Sunday outing—takes root in childhood. Children, especially of the upper classes, are inculcated with the imperative to pursue their own advantage; egoism becomes an intractable habit. "It is horrifying to see what rich people do to their children," Tolstoy notes in his diary.[76] "While the child is young, stupid, and passionate, they draw him into a life on the backs of other people, habituate him to this life."[77] Then, once the young person awakens to the fact that he exploits others to gratify himself, it is already too late for him to abandon the life he has gotten used to: "And now claw your way out as best you can: either become a martyr, rejecting everything you have gotten used to and cannot live without, or else remain a liar."[78] Though he condemns the upper-class way of life, Tolstoy expresses compassion for all those who have since childhood believed in the righteousness of pursuing their individual happiness. After a lifetime of setting one's own advantage above all else, how can the habits of egoism be overcome? Tolstoy hints that it cannot be accomplished on one's own. In the same diary entry, he speculates that transcending one's egoism requires the assistance of another, whether that other is a beloved person or God. Part of the tragedy of losing a loved one—"a child, a husband, a wife, a father, a mother"—is that an individual is "deprived of that which drew him out of himself, out of his egoism. Without [these loved ones] he is left in the most horrifying position a person can be in, if he is not a Christian—again, alone with himself."[79] Our love for other people draws us out of our state of confinement within ourselves. In the absence of such love, we, like Emperor Nicholas, hear only echoes of our own desires.

110

Atrophied Aesthetic Sense

Though egoism can be overcome with the help of another person, Tolstoy has greater confidence in conquering it through religious faith. People must replace their "faith in the pursuit of personal weal with faith in and service to God," he commands.[80] At the same time, as a keen critic of the church, he recognized that one might fool others and even oneself into believing that one serves God while in fact continuing to serve oneself. For Tolstoy, "efforts on one's own behalf, out of egoism, under the guise of efforts to serve God (most horrifying), society (less horrifying) and one's family (least horrifying)" are a "phariseeism, hypocrisy" that he considers to be what is "most horrible and harmful to humanity."[81] In other words, egoism masquerading as benevolence is even worse than the kind of brazen egoism displayed by the emperor in pursuit of his appetites. It is Shamil who exemplifies this most pernicious form of egoism.

Shamil's detachment from those around him resembles that of Emperor Nicholas: the imam is no less isolated in Vedeno than the emperor is in Saint Petersburg. When Shamil returns to his seat of power, he quickly rides past his people and retreats into the innermost courtyard of his house, in much the same way that Nicholas had retreated into his palace. And just as Nicholas keeps the world at bay by whispering to himself, Shamil seems to shut out the world by closing his eyes to it. Tolstoy repeatedly refers to "his small eyes always screwed up" (*soshchurennye*) (*HM*, 635; *PSS*, 35:86). Shamil, like Nicholas, retreats further into himself as he deliberates—in Shamil's case, over the fate of Hadji Murat's family. He gives his men the impression that he is communing with an otherworldly spirit: "he was listening to the voice of the Prophet, who spoke to him and told him what to do" (*HM*, 638; *PSS*, 35:89). But Shamil's decision after this silent rumination merely echoes what he had told himself previously: that reconciliation with Hadji Murat is impossible and that he should threaten violence against Hadji Murat's son to lure back the father and kill him. Shamil does not explain why he believes reconciliation is impossible, but the implication is that forgiving Hadji Murat's betrayal would threaten his own power. Shamil, like Nicholas, listens only to himself, to his inner voice. It is true that he does not make arbitrary decisions that suit his sensuous demands the way Nicholas does; his choices are more rational. But by listening to his inner voice, Shamil comes to a decision no less cruel than Nicholas's and perhaps more frightening, with its pretext of serving God rather than himself.

In his deliberations Hadji Murat hears no inner voice. Instead, as he contemplates his family's rescue, he attends to three artworks and is successfully infected by them. He first considers a Tavlinian fable about a falcon that returns home after living with humans who have dressed him in jesses with bells. The other mountain falcons, noticing the bells, peck the returning bird to death. "And they would peck me to death in the same way," Hadji Murat concludes, referring to Shamil's forces (*HM*, 652; *PSS*, 35:102). In the

111

Chapter Three

morning, after a night of contemplation, Hadji Murat encounters a second artwork: he hears his friend Khanefi's song about a dzhigit named Gamzad who, surrounded by Russian forces, fights to the death. Hadji Murat listens to Khanefi's song with such rapt attention that he neglects his prayer ritual—art breaks his habits—and in his distracted state spills the water for his ablutions. Khanefi's song reminds Hadji Murat of yet another artwork, a third: a song his mother, Patimat, once composed about her choice to bring violence on herself to save her son's life. Patimat's song displays her ethical and aesthetic capacities, which she bestows on her son.[82] With the example of his mother's sacrifice in view, Hadji Murat chooses to undertake a similar sacrifice for his son. The commander, famous for evading death, now decides on a rescue mission that will almost certainly result in his demise.

Scholars diverge in their assessments of Hadji Murat's success in transcending his egoism. Ani Kokobobo, reading Tolstoy's text in light of Sufism, suggests that "the life of violence seems to facilitate a journey of self-cleansing for Hadji Murat and a renunciation of the ego for the sake of something greater."[83] Orwin, on the contrary, argues that Tolstoy's hero ultimately "remains essentially self-absorbed."[84] To make her point, she adduces the violence Hadji Murat brings on innocent people by attempting to rescue his family. It seems that Tolstoy's hero can claim only partial success in transcending his egoism: to act out of love for one's family is still egoism, in Tolstoy's view, but it is surely a less virulent egoism than Shamil's and Nicholas's pursuits of personal satisfaction. But whether or not Hadji Murat falls short of the ideal of selflessness, it is significant that he attempts to "claw" his way out of egoism with the help of art. In diaries, letters, and other discursive writing, Tolstoy asserts that only a beloved other—and better yet, God—can draw us out of our abiding egoism. Here in his novella, however, he suggests that art, too, can help us escape our preoccupation with our own interests.

The significance of aesthetic receptivity as an antidote to egoism for Tolstoy helps explain one of the author's most puzzling (and troubling) directives to readers: to refrain, in encounters with art, from acting on one's own behalf. Tolstoy articulates this directive most explicitly in "About What Is Called Art":

> [The spectator] must not do anything himself. He only looks and listens and enjoys and plays. It is precisely the fact that the spectator does not exert himself, but rather allows the artist to possess him, that distinguishes artistic transmission from all other transmission.[85]

Art, as he explains, shares something with play. But where play allows us to exert our own powers—"flexibility, inventiveness, cleverness, and so on"—delight in art, Tolstoy insists, is "achieved passively through the reception of other people's feelings by infection."[86] Coming from an artist, the demand for a spectator to refrain from competing with the artwork with his own creative activity (including interpretive activity) seems self-serving, even tyrannical. Moreover, it is bewildering that someone ostensibly concerned with the danger posed by the charismatic artist would laud art that prevents the spectator from acting on his own behalf. But Tolstoy mischaracterized his own aesthetic apprehensions, and getting clear on what those were makes his rationale here much less dubious. The glorification of artistic possession makes sense only when we see that what he feared most, more than our vulnerability to others, was our propensity to remain consumed by our own pursuits.

Hadji Murat's aesthetic encounters allow him to experience a peculiar sort of idleness—an effortful restraint from action—that Tolstoy considered essential for breaking our habitual modes of thought. The emperor and the imam make their decisions quickly and act reflexively. Hadji Murat, with the help of three artworks, meditates all night long. He does what, for Tolstoy, few people are capable of doing: he does nothing.

The author who "more than anyone valued toil" would seem to be an unlikely advocate of idleness, observed Yuly Aikhenvald in his essay "In Praise of Idleness" (1922).[87] Many of Tolstoy's literary works are "as though sanctified with the breath of peasant labor at harvest."[88] Yet Aikhenvald suggests that the germ of his own essay, which had a considerable influence on Nabokov's aesthetics,[89] comes from Tolstoy. In making his case that idleness, not toil, is the state most befitting our nature, Aikhenvald invokes Tolstoy's essay "Not-Doing" ("Nedelanie," 1893). Tolstoy observes that "not doing"— arresting our ceaseless activity—is more difficult than the unthinking pursuit of our own affairs; and people persist in egoism and immorality not because they have no sense of right and wrong but because they cannot remain still long enough to reflect on their lives. In an echo of his letter to Litoshenko, Tolstoy asserts that ceaseless labor—"build[ing] railroads, factories . . . do[ing] missionary work in Japan or India . . . hold[ing] exams, writing scholarly essays, poems"—prevents people from "com[ing] to their senses and chang[ing] their understanding of life."[90] What is needed, according to him, is idleness.

He is not, as Aikhenvald notes, "preach[ing] laziness and indolence."[91] Tolstoy's idleness is not the bourgeois idleness he frequently disparaged. It is, rather, the hard-won idleness born of self-restraint. When we can compel ourselves to "stop doing," to "do nothing" we can "concentrate and think," Tolstoy argues, and decide to live less egoistically and more altruistically.[92] This is the form of idleness Aikhenvald, too, means to praise. Thomas Karshan, in his discussion of Aikhenvald's essay and its importance for Nabokov, emphasizes the ways in which the two of them broke with late nineteenth-century authors who "exalt work or satirise idleness."[93] Karshan, with good

Chapter Three

reason, counts Tolstoy foremost among these proponents of toil. Yet Aikhenvald, attuned to the complexity of Tolstoy's treatment of labor and idleness, sees not only differences but also key continuities between the great author's thought and his own.

Tolstoy, for Aikhenvald, "demands only that we finally look back at ourselves and ponder ourselves, instead of immersing ourselves head and shoulders in the fog (*durman*) of labor."[94] By employing the word "durman"—which Tolstoy used so frequently in connection with drugs, alcohol, sex, and false art—Aikhenvald stresses that the pursuit of our own affairs numbers among these other means to persist in our own insensibility. I share Jacob Emery's view that art and illness function analogously in Tolstoy's works: both dispel our *durman*. Both "make sensible in our bodies the knowledge that we must live better in a world where we are artificially separated from each other."[95] But unlike Emery, I attribute this analogy less to the social role played by art and illness than to the fact that each acts in a similar way on the individual. Illness gives us the chance to be idle. So does art. A receptive spectator partakes of the salutary state of not doing. Our attention is arrested; we are diverted from our habitual pursuits; we are given the opportunity to change our understanding of life. Aikhenvald serves as a mediating link between Tolstoy and Nabokov, who turn out to be closer than we might imagine in attributing a moral significance to idleness. Both believed that our capacity to divert our attention from ourselves at moments when our self-interest is most pressing—"to wonder at trifles" even in the face of "imminent peril," as Nabokov puts it[96]—is a moral virtue that can be inspired by aesthetic experience.

THE FEAT OF RECEPTIVITY

As *Hadji Murat* shows, Tolstoy valued art in part for its ability to induce in its spectators a state of reflective idleness. This explains why in his discursive writing Tolstoy—so often the champion of toil—lauds art that affords us a "rest from labor" (*otdykh ot truda*) an energetic cessation of activity.[97] This diversion from labor is essential, Tolstoy insists, not only for the upper classes—whose activity he often suspects to be senseless and unnecessary—but also for the laboring masses (*narod*). It is the latter who most urgently long for rest through art, Tolstoy explains, and he laments that upper-class artists fail to provide them with such rest.

But a defense of art on the grounds that it enables idleness poses a problem for Tolstoy, one that may have fueled his ambivalence to artmaking. The aesthetically receptive spectator is afforded the chance to escape his own notions and preoccupations. But what about the artist? It is undeniable

Atrophied Aesthetic Sense

that artmaking, at least in its early stages, involves receptivity: to one's surroundings and to one's own impressions. The process of crafting the artwork, however, seems to demand precisely the sort of labor Tolstoy disparages in "Not-Doing." It requires a keen attentiveness to the artwork at the cost of neglecting much of the rest of the world. It promotes the singular focus on one's own objectives that Tolstoy, perhaps too readily, equated with egoism. As long as he, Tolstoy, made art, he could not enter the state of receptivity that according to him is so important to enter. And if he cannot enter this state himself, how can he preach the virtue of it? The older Tolstoy likely registered this asymmetry between artist and spectator as a kind of hypocrisy, a hypocrisy that undermined the values he extoled. As he told Bernard Shaw, preaching fails when "preachers do not practice what they preach."[98]

Tolstoy's late works can be read as various attempts to confront the dilemma of the striving artist who exhorts others to stillness. He pursues three different strategies. One way to resolve his dilemma is to renounce artistic activity, as he comes close to doing in *What Is Art?* Another approach, which he takes in *Hadji Murat*, is to continue to "do"—to write the kind of literary work he had written throughout his life—in order to preach the virtues of "not doing." This strategy is problematic, of course, in that the content of *Hadji Murat* is at odds with the form: Tolstoy depicts the cessation of activity and concomitant receptivity within an exquisitely crafted text that manifests all the ambition and labor of artmaking. Neither strategy appears satisfactory. Tolstoy does not cease to write; on the heels of the publication of his aesthetic treatise, he composes *Hadji Murat*. At the same time, however, he chooses not to publish this novella. And while there were certainly more mundane reasons for this choice,[99] the contradiction between the novella's content and form perhaps contributed to Tolstoy's decision. Tolstoy finally hits upon a third approach in his sui generis literary endeavor, *The Circle of Reading* (1906; second edition 1910).[100] This text, a collection of the wise thoughts of others, promises to resolve the artist's dilemma not only in content but also in form. The very shape of the text offers Tolstoy the chance to exhibit the idleness and receptivity he commends.

The Circle of Reading—the project that occupied Tolstoy in the last years of his life—is an odd, hulking collection of texts and aphorisms on philosophical subjects like art, faith, and reason, drawn from the Bible, the Talmud, Buddha, Confucius, Plato, Blaise Pascal, Schopenhauer, John Ruskin, and many other sources, including Tolstoy's own essays and fiction. Its purpose is to serve as a calendar of daily wisdom. Each day offers between four and fifteen aphorisms, and the end of each week features a longer text, which is either a work of literature or philosophy. The book's publisher, Ivan Gorbunov-Posadov, who upon bringing out its second edition was prosecuted for publishing sayings that "galvanize the subversion of

Chapter Three

the established government and social orders in Russia," called *The Circle of Reading* Tolstoy's last great masterpiece.[101] As such, he declared, it "belongs not on the defendant's bench, but solely in the pantheon of the great works of world literature, most beneficial for all humanity."[102] The Symbolist writer Andrei Bely saw the book, in contrast, as evidence of Tolstoy's decline. Misled by a culture that devalued artistic means of expression, Tolstoy had renounced his art in favor of socioreligious writing; he silenced himself as an artist, Bely argues in his essay "Leo Tolstoy and Culture." Now, with *The Circle of Reading*, he had silenced himself as a prophet as well: "Tolstoy set out with the purpose that he, Leo Tolstoy, would give us his Tolstoyan word on life's truth. Then he began to cite the thought of other people, and Tolstoy the prophet dissolved in the end in these citations."[103] Gorbunov-Posadov's and Bely's divergent assessments of *The Circle of Reading* attest to the puzzling nature of this work, which, I will argue, is best understood as a formal solution to the artist's dilemma of receptivity. In "writing" *The Circle of Reading*, Tolstoy attempts to be at once the artist and the receptive reader.

Tolstoy's objective in composing *The Circle of Reading* evolved over the years that he spent contemplating, completing, and editing it. As he prepared the book's second edition, Tolstoy came to believe that *The Circle of Reading* expressed his own views so well that he recommended it to people who sought his opinion on this or that subject.[104] Then, in the last year of his life, he completed another compendium, *The Path of Life* (1910), which grew out of *The Circle of Reading* but departed from it in seeking to systematically present Tolstoy's own views on all aspects of life from God and faith to the government to the nature of science. Tolstoy undoubtedly ends up giving us his Tolstoyan truth and doing so in what Morson calls "absolute language": a language that appears to be impersonal, transhistorical, "limited neither by the contingencies of the moment nor by the anticipation of a response."[105] Morson shows how Tolstoy from his earliest writing made strategic use of such language, examples of which include proverbs, Biblical citations, and syllogisms. If one agrees with Morson that Tolstoy spent his life searching for a "speech center" unbounded by the historical, social, and individual circumstances of the speaker,[106] then Tolstoy's wisdom calendars are, in some sense, the culmination of this search. One might therefore echo Gorbunov-Posadov's assessment of them as Tolstoy's last great masterpiece.

At the same time, it is important to note that when Tolstoy first conceived *The Circle of Reading*, he set out with the explicit aim of *receiving* rather than issuing these timeless truths. He began to work on *The Circle of Reading* to satisfy his own desire to be a reader, to glean the wise thoughts of others on those subjects that were most important to him. The idea for a calendar of daily wisdom occurs to Tolstoy in 1884: "I need to compose for myself a Circle of Reading: Epictetus, Marcus Aurelius, Laozi, Buddha, Pas-

116

cal, the Gospels. And this will be useful for everyone."[107] Tolstoy recognizes how such a calendar would benefit him as a reader, though, as in his essays on art, he immediately generalizes from his own experiences, insisting that everyone else will be affected by it in the same way. "I know firsthand what power, tranquility, and happiness is bestowed on one by keeping company with such souls as Socrates, Epictetus, Arnold, Parker," Tolstoy writes to Chertkov.[108] Accounts of Tolstoy's work on *The Circle of Reading* all emphasize the evident pleasure the author took in the reading he did to complete the book. "How much happiness has there been for me in this work," Tolstoy tells his secretary Dushan Makovitsky. "How effortless this work, how much I have read!"[109] Makovitsky suggests that Tolstoy read approximately 150 books to compose and then revise his *Circle of Reading*.[110] Tolstoy delighted that this reading allowed him to "persist at such heights of thought."[111] Having completed the first edition of the book, he felt dejected to descend from these heights. "Recently, I felt how much I sank from that spiritual, moral height to which I was raised by having been in communication with those greatest, wisest people whom I read and whose thought I pondered for *The Circle of Reading*," Tolstoy confessed in his diary.[112] Perhaps unwilling to leave behind the peace and spiritual uplift afforded him by such reading, Tolstoy continued to search for texts to add to the calendar and produced another version of it in 1909, entitled *The New Circle of Reading, or For Every Day*. "He was not only the *Circle*'s author," Paperno remarks, "but also its dutiful reader, perusing it daily usually at bedtime."[113] And according to Nikolay Gusev, listening to Chertkov read from *The Circle of Reading* was the only thing that seemed to assuage Tolstoy's agitated delirium as he lay on his deathbed.[114]

Tolstoy was bewildered that many readers did not seem to share his elation at reading this book. "How can people live without *The Circle of Reading*?" he wondered aloud.[115] "I don't understand why people do not use *The Circle of Reading*," Tolstoy tells Gusev.[116] "What could be more precious than daily communication with the world's wisest people?"[117] Convinced of the benefits of the book Sofia Tolstoy called his "favorite child," Tolstoy frequently recommended *The Circle of Reading* to correspondents, sent gift copies to friends and acquaintances, and read it to his family circle and the peasant children at Yasnaya Polyana.[118] He was elated when he heard from his sister-in-law about a certain senator's wife who called *The Circle of Reading* her "second Gospel."[119] And he was exasperated by a review that claimed that this book was evidence of Tolstoy's "detachment from life, confinement within the self."[120] Detachment from life and confinement within the self were precisely what Tolstoy meant to transcend by reading the wise thought of other thinkers.

Despite his intention of giving voice to others, Tolstoy's book is hardly

Chapter Three

a monument to his own silence. That is especially clear when considering the trajectory of the work over time. *The Circle of Reading* is part of a series of books that Tolstoy composed with the aim of collecting wise thoughts. The first of these was the *Calendar of Proverbs for the Year 1887*, in which Tolstoy collected folk sayings. The calendar offers one proverb for each day of the year along with a short monthly text describing the peasants' duties for that month—for example, "Work in January," "Work in February," and so on. Here Tolstoy acts primarily as a chronicler and curator, though according to V. S. Mishin he did "enhance some well-known proverbs when these appeared weak to him."[121] We also hear Tolstoy's voice in the monthly readings, where, for example, he denounces the practice of peasant men going to work in the cities in wintertime because "they go to the cities not for extra earnings but for the temptations."[122] The next iteration of the calendar, and the immediate precursor to *The Circle of Reading*, is *The Thoughts of Wise People for Every Day* (1903). Here Tolstoy collects the wisdom not of peasants but of Epictetus, Marcus Aurelius, Buddha, Muhammad, and others. But alongside these citations, he also includes his own thoughts, marking them with an unassuming "L. T." With each month, the number of his personal contributions grows: none in January, two in February, three in March. Moreover, on certain days Tolstoy gives his own gloss on the aphorism of whomever he has quoted. With each version of the calendar, Tolstoy's own voice grows more prominent.

By the time of *The Circle of Reading*, Tolstoy's role has expanded well beyond curator and translator to that of commentator and coauthor. This calendar is no longer merely a collection of daily readings. Now each day of the year begins with a philosophical or moral quandary, often articulated by Tolstoy himself, which is then followed by aphorisms that reflect on the stated problem. Many aphorisms are still drawn from other sources, though often in Tolstoy's paraphrase (paraphrasings are signed "in accordance with so and so"—for example, *"po Kantu," "po Emersonu"*). But reflections from Tolstoy himself far outnumber those belonging to other thinkers, and on certain subjects, such as art, Tolstoy allots himself almost exclusive authorship. Each day concludes with a piece of practical advice, again authored by Tolstoy. In *For Every Day* (1909–10)—which Tolstoy composed after completing two editions of *The Circle of Reading*—and in *The Path of Life*, the last of the collections of wise thought, Tolstoy no longer feels the need even to affix his signature to his reflections. His voice permeates the texts; they are all his.

In prefaces to the two editions of *The Circle of Reading*, Tolstoy admits that he has reformulated many of the wise thoughts he included, so much so that readers might not find his citations in the original texts. Tolstoy explains that the discrepancies are due not only to the fact that he often read these texts in a language other than the original before translating them

118

Atrophied Aesthetic Sense

once more into Russian but also to his sense that many of the texts needed to be amended. When selecting passages from longer texts, "for the sake of clarity and wholeness," he would, where needed, "eliminate certain words and sentences," and sometimes not only substitute one set of words for another but actually express a thought in his own words.[123] In the preface to the first edition of *The Circle of Reading*, one senses Tolstoy's hesitation in making such emendations. He admits that some people will find his approach "criminal" and attempts to discredit this view as a misguided and "pernicious prejudice."[124] His purpose, he says, is to present the thought of the world's wisest people in its most potent form, even if that means making certain adjustments. The preface to the second edition is less apologetic: *"The goal of my book is not to offer literal translations of authors, but to make use of the great, fertile thought of different authors, to give readers daily access to a wide circle of reading that inspires the best thoughts and feelings."*[125] By partially erasing the origins of his citations, Tolstoy ostensibly wishes to present them as words belonging to everyone, as truths unbounded by context and so accessible and relevant to everyone. But as Morson points out, Tolstoy's "attempts to speak impersonally have become the mark of his personality."[126] In this light, Tolstoy's editorial gesture seems to do more than strip these citations of signs of their origins: it marks them with his own authorial signature. Far from dissolving into the words of others, Tolstoy comes to claim their words as his own.

The formal structure of *The Circle of Reading* registers Tolstoy's dueling impulses to listen and to speak. This clash is also subtly apparent in the content of his text. Given Tolstoy's careful attention to the shape of the book—"How important is the placement of each word, which word comes before and which after," he told Gusev—it is notable that the first day of his calendar is dedicated to questions of reading.[127] Tolstoy introduces the theme for January 1: "It is better to know a small amount of what is good and necessary than to know much of what is mediocre and unnecessary."[128] He then cites a passage from Ralph Waldo Emerson's published lecture "Books." "What great wealth there is in a small, select library," Tolstoy writes, slightly misquoting the original ("Consider what you have in the smallest chosen library"). He exalts the library still more than does Emerson. Tolstoy's passage continues more faithfully:

> A company of the wisest and wittiest men that could be picked out of all civil countries in a thousand years have set in best order the results of their learning and wisdom. The men themselves were hid and inaccessible, solitary, impatient of interruption, fenced by etiquette; but the thought which they did not uncover to their bosom friend is here written out in transparent words to us, the strangers of another age.[129]

Chapter Three

Emerson voices concerns that, as I argued earlier, also haunted Tolstoy: he observes that people remain obscure to one another for many reasons, from inclination to social constraint. We hide ourselves even from our closest friends. Reading, however, allows us to know another in a way that seems impossible in ordinarily life, Emerson suggests. Books, for Emerson, offer an extraordinary transparency, the same kind of transparency that Tolstoy longs for in his writing on art. (Nabokov, too, echoes this longing in envisioning a reader who shares the author's perspective completely.) Emerson goes on, "We owe to books those general benefits which come from high intellectual action."[130] Tolstoy gives this notion a Tolstoyan twist by misquoting it: "We owe to good books the most important spiritual accomplishments of our lives."[131] Tolstoy thereby attributes even greater significance to reading than the philosopher he cites. We make spiritual progress, he suggests, by attending to the wisdom of others—from peasant proverbs to Marcus Aurelius to Emerson himself.

But having begun his *Circle of Reading* with the notion that our spiritual achievements depend on our capacity to receive the words of others, Tolstoy immediately cast doubt on this idea. Three subsequent quotes—from John Locke, Seneca, and Henry David Thoreau—advise that one must read only great books, for much of what is written is trivial and unworthy of our attention. This is followed by a quotation from Schopenhauer warning against drowning out one's own voice with too much reading: "One ought to read only when the fount of one's own thought has run dry, which happens not infrequently even to the smartest person. But to scare off, for the sake of a book, one's own still unfortified thought is to commit a crime against the spirit."[132] Attending to other voices offers the opportunity for great spiritual feats, but it also poses the danger of stifling one's own thought. In private conversations, Tolstoy confidently settled this problem in favor of listening to oneself: "One needs to live according to one's own reason, conscience. Christ, Buddha must only lend assistance."[133] But both in his fiction, most notably *Hadji Murat*, and in *The Circle of Reading*, he demurs from such categorical resolutions. Instead, Tolstoy points up both the benefits and the dangers of quieting one's own voice, benefits and dangers that he navigates himself in composing his calendar of wisdom.

Tolstoy's most direct statement on the rewards of listening to others comes not in the form of a philosophical aphorism but in an afterword he appends to one of the weekly readings: Anton Chekhov's short story "The Darling" ("Dushechka," 1899). Many of the weekly readings—longer literary or philosophical texts—had to be translated, trimmed, or otherwise edited by Tolstoy to be included in his *Circle of Reading*. "The Darling" stands out in that it appears in the calendar almost unaltered. Yet it is perhaps the text most stamped with Tolstoy's own voice; it is the only weekly reading that

120

Atrophied Aesthetic Sense

is followed immediately by Tolstoy's interpretation of it. The "Afterword to 'The Darling'" (1908) is an apotheosis of the sort of receptivity Tolstoy attempted to practice but increasingly fell short of.

Chekhov's story begins with the heroine, Olenka, whom everyone calls Darling, listening to a desperate theater director, Kukin, monologue about his travails: the rain is keeping audiences away, the public is uneducated and does not understand his work, there is no money but the actors must be paid. Listening "silently and seriously," Olenka falls in love and adopts not only Kukin's cares but also the very language he uses to speak about them: "And whatever Kukin said about the theater and the actors, she repeated" (404, 405; *PSS*, 41:363, 365).[134] Kukin dies shortly thereafter, and Olenka soon finds herself listening to someone else, a lumber trader. After their first conversation, Olenka "heard his somber voice for the rest of the day" (406; *PSS*, 41:66). Olenka marries again, adopting her new husband's cares, his language, even the cadences of his speech: "she would always speak somberly and reasonably in imitation of her husband" (408; *PSS*, 41:368). Death strikes again, and Olenka again cannot live without sharing someone else's preoccupations, someone else's mind. A military veterinarian quartered at her home becomes her new lover, and she immerses herself in his world, concerning herself with the poor health of domesticated animals. Irritated, the veterinarian asks her to stop speaking with such enthusiasm about what is, after all, his specialty and not hers. Olenka is shaken: "But, Volodichka what am I to talk about?!" (409; *PSS*, 41:369). Life and language have meaning for Olenka only as long as there is another person whose words she can hear and share. When the veterinarian leaves town with his regiment, Olenka suffers:

> Now she was completely alone . . . But mainly, and this was worst of all, she no longer had any opinions. She saw objects around her and understood everything going on around her, but she could not form any opinion about anything, and she did not know what to talk about. And how awful it is not to have any opinions! You see a bottle standing there, for example, or it is raining, or a peasant is driving a cart, but what the purpose of a bottle is, or the rain or the peasant, what they all mean, you cannot say, and could not say even if you were paid a thousand rubles. (409–10; *PSS*, 41:369–70)

The stuff of the world is still there, but it loses all meaning without the opportunity to look upon the world together with someone else, to regard it in the same way as some other person. Chekhov depicts solitude in much the same way Tolstoy had in *Anna Karenina*. Without others, I can know what the world is but I cannot know what it means: Solitude is the absence of intersubjective agreement about the significance of the world. But Chekhov's

Chapter Three

heroine is spared the worst hazards of solitude; she does not experience the solipsistic self-absorption that comes to plague Tolstoy's Anna. Soon, Olenka's veterinarian returns to the village with his son, a student, and Olenka is brought back to life. She adopts the concerns of her new ward and experiences a joy beyond any she has known before.

As Makovitsky recalls, Tolstoy could not read "The Darling" without tears. While preparing the story for publication in *The Circle of Reading*, Tolstoy read it aloud, barely able to finish it as his "throat constricted from grief."[135] Having wiped his tears, Tolstoy then proceeded to read aloud his own afterword, which he also could not read without tears. What touched Tolstoy so deeply was Olenka's capacity to become completely absorbed in another's cares. In his afterword, Tolstoy suggests that Chekhov did not intend for his portrait of Olenka to be so sympathetic. He speculates that Chekhov had meant to portray her as an old-fashioned woman with little sense of self, thereby demonstrating "how a woman ought not to be."[136] But as a true poet, Chekhov was guided by his poetic sense, not his topical opinions. Instead of creating a figure of ridicule, he creates a "saintly, extraordinary soul of the Darling, with her ability to give her entire being to the one she loves."[137] Tolstoy compares Chekhov to Balaam, who meant to condemn the Israelites but blessed them instead: "[Chekhov] meant to knock down the Darling and trained on her the acute attention of a poet and elevated her instead."[138] Olenka's boundless receptivity does not make her pathetic in Tolstoy's view; it makes her "saintly."

Note the irony. Tolstoy praises Olenka—the consummate listener who adopts the language and cadences of others—in an afterword that speaks over and against another author. The very existence of this text, which claims the last word about Chekhov's story by suggesting that Chekhov says the opposite of what he means to say, attests to Tolstoy's incapacity for the receptivity he extols. This paradoxical predicament is not lost on Tolstoy—and as usual, he generalizes it. He submits that the transcendence of egoism and attentiveness to others that Olenka demonstrates is a special capability of women, not men. Modern women, Tolstoy laments, misguidedly believe that they need to aspire to do what men do and they forget that they are capable of things that men cannot do, such as "that highest, best, and most godlike endeavor—the endeavor of love, the endeavor of giving oneself completely to the one you love."[139] There is much to say about Tolstoy's essentializing views of women. But for my purposes, the salient point is that Tolstoy uses his gender to escape a contradiction, to escape, even, hypocrisy. He exalts a mode of being that he does not adopt himself. This is not to say that Tolstoy is insincere in his praise of Olenka or that he does not genuinely regret his own inability to do as she does. "Reading about women's vocation and what men cannot do (self-sacrifice) he nearly began to sob, and finished with tears," Makovitsky remembers.[140]

Atrophied Aesthetic Sense

Echoes of Tolstoy's own predicament—his difficulty in attending to voices other than his own—appear in another short story that he interpolates into his calendar: Guy de Maupassant's "Solitude" (1884). Tolstoy claimed that he had not encountered anywhere "a more heart-rending cry of despair of a lost person becoming conscious of his solitude" than in this Maupassant story.[141] The hero, an unnamed bachelor, asks the story's narrator to accompany him on a stroll on the Champs-Élysées and immediately proceeds to barrage the narrator with his thoughts, never stopping to let his companion respond. He tells his companion of his terror before the impossibility of knowing other people and making himself known to them: "what a terrible mystery—the unknown thought of another being . . . Always at the very bottom there remains the hidden corner of my 'I,' where no one can enter. No one has the power to open it, enter it, because no one resembles me, and no one ever understands anyone else."[142] We can never know how others experience the world. It therefore (this skeptic reflects) means something different to each of us. And no matter how much he tries to bare his soul, he remains alone:

> Knowing that I am condemned to terrible solitude, I look upon everything with indifference and do not give my opinion . . . Unable to share anything with people, I am indifferent to everything. My invisible thought remains unexplored.[143]

This cosmopolitan bachelor could not be more unlike Chekhov's provincial widow, yet their experiences of solitude have much in common. Left without a companion, Olenka sees the bottle, the rain, the peasant, but cannot say what any of it means. The bachelor, too, claims that in his solitude he only "looks at everything but does not give his opinion." Without the possibility of shared meaning, the characters feel that they can only observe the world; they cannot make sense of it. Olenka resists her solitude by listening, by sinking into the significations of others, and her receptivity, ultimately, is rewarded. Chekhov leaves her peaceful, happily listening to her ward muttering in his sleep. Tolstoy admires this receptivity and aspires to it with his *Circle of Reading*, but he continues, like Maupassant's gentleman, to loudly lament his own solitude with endless speech.

In his essays on art, in his fiction, and by his own example, Tolstoy demonstrates the difficulty of aesthetic receptivity. *What Is Art?* abounds with failures of infection. We are not truly possessed by the likes of Wagner, Tolstoy suggests, because the appeal of such "false" art lies precisely in the fact that it allows us to remain engrossed in ourselves. And true art fails to possess us because in our pervasive egoism we are loathe to attend to anything outside our own interests, least of all to art that asks us to imagine ways of life contrary to our own. In *Hadji Murat* Tolstoy shows us that our inca-

Chapter Three

pacity for aesthetic receptivity is indicative of a pernicious egoism. Art might lead us out of our habitual preoccupations with our own needs, but for it to do so we must retain or, more often, arduously regain our capacity to receive it by quieting the voice inside that in an unceasing monologue reiterates our own desires.

Hadji Murat and *The Circle of Reading* each in their own way exhort readers to practice the aesthetic receptivity Tolstoy fears might elude us and him. *Hadji Murat* does so in content only, leaving an incongruity between content and form.[144] The author models for us our predicament—our blinding egoism—and demonstrates how we might (at least partially) find our way out of it with the help of art.[145] Aesthetic experience, he suggests, can induce a productive idleness that enables us to look past our own needs. The hitch is that Tolstoy's novella imagines and prescribes to others a state of receptivity that the author himself, in laboring to write his novella, fails to enter. Tolstoy preaches idleness but continues to work, writing scholarly essays, philosophical tracts, and literary works. *The Circle of Reading*, more daringly, experiments with a literary form that would allow Tolstoy to practice what he preached. Yet even this formal solution is unstable, as we see in the book's content and especially in its evolving form. There is an ever-present temptation to speak out, to speak over—to move from quotation to paraphrase, from paraphrase to interpretation, and from interpretation back to the acts of creative expression he had hoped at the outset to subdue. Receptivity evidently cannot be attained once and for all; it requires daily practice.

The Platonic truism of art's dangerous power to possess is so pervasive in Western aesthetic thought that even Tolstoy repeats it, while keenly observing in his own work just how *hard* it is to become swept up by another's art. Our present reading debates, still in the grip of Plato's picture, ponder whether we ought to guard against aesthetic possession or allow ourselves its pleasures. But these pleasures are not always within our reach. Receptivity is not our natural state. It is a state we must work to enter and a state we must work to stay in. Even when he was failing at it, Tolstoy in his late writing shows us what that labor looks like.

Chapter Four

Suspicion on Trial

TO THE END of his life, Tolstoy was haunted by the idea that we might become imprisoned by our own minds; *The Circle of Reading* attests to that. Nabokov's concern about the blindness induced by our own obsessions manifests in the tragic solipsists and egomaniacs who populate his fiction early, middle, and late. Of course, these authors were not alone in recognizing that we are condemned to doubt the world beyond the self. The canon of modern literary doubters often centers on Samuel Beckett and Franz Kafka, but it includes many others. Tolstoy and Nabokov belong to this tradition, yet they depart from it as well. As Stanley Corngold observes, nothing could "quiet" Kafka's skepticism.[1] His fiction articulates that condition rather than attempting to quiet what could not be quieted. Tolstoy and Nabokov are not content to leave matters there. These authors are unique in recognizing as well as anyone the depth of the skeptical problem while still retaining hope that properly engineered fiction can assuage it.

Far from resigning themselves to skepticism, Tolstoy and Nabokov never stopped searching for a formal means of escaping it and helping their readers do the same. Three parables of suspicious reading—Tolstoy's *The Kreutzer Sonata* and Nabokov's unpublished dramatic monologue "Pozdnyshev's Address" and *Pale Fire*—illuminate their efforts to identify narrative strategies that would relieve their readers of doubt and inspire trust in the capacity of language to bridge the abyss between oneself and another— between author and reader. Both authors imagined that a certain kind of artwork, one in which the author and reader encounter each other in the right way, can offer the reader temporary relief from the burdens of doubt that cannot simply be willed away. Certainly the effect of this encounter depends on the reader. It would be naive to deny that the reader can read with varying degrees of attention, creativity, sympathy, and so on. But for Tolstoy and Nabokov, it would be just as naive to deny that the effect also depends on the text itself. From the author's perspective, the task is to construct such a text.

Tolstoy and Nabokov shared certain strategies for cultivating readerly receptivity and thereby dispelling skeptical doubt. In *The Kreutzer Sonata*

125

Chapter Four

and "Pozdnyshev's Address," Tolstoy and Nabokov, respectively, each set off what might be called controlled explosions of suspicion: they stimulate our suspicion to subsequently cast doubt on its virtues and point up the possibility of a more trusting attitude to the author's words. Ultimately, this approach does not entirely satisfy either author; each continues his search. Tolstoy abandons such narrative pyrotechnics in favor of writing tales so simple he hopes they cannot be mistrusted or misunderstood. For Nabokov, on the contrary, there is no hope of banishing such things. His *Pale Fire* amplifies narrative suspicion to demonstrate that the path to faith in our capacity to reveal ourselves to one another must lead *through* suspicion, not around it. For Nabokov, I argue, our impulse to suspect can be cultivated and deployed in ways that inspire belief, paradoxically, in the possibility of mutual recognition.

A SURFEIT OF SUSPICION

Tolstoy's *The Kreutzer Sonata* is told by an unnamed narrator traveling on a night train. The narrator listens to fellow passengers discuss modern-day relations between men and women. A quiet, solitary passenger grows excited by the conversation. He, Pozdnyshev, suddenly accuses the travelers of subtly referring to his own unhappy family life. When those unsettled by his accusation disperse, he offers to tell the narrator the story of how he killed his wife. Pozdnyshev recounts his sexual history, his cynical courtship of his wife, their unhappy marriage, and the arrival of a musician, Trukhachevsky, whom he suspects of having seduced her. Returning home one evening and finding her and the musician alone together, Pozdnyshev murders her. It is never confirmed that they were having an affair, but the court acquits Pozdnyshev nevertheless, justifying his actions as an attempt to defend his "outraged honor" (*KS*, 398; *PSS*, 27:49). Pozdnyshev explains the murder differently. He portrays himself as a victim of corrosive social forces, blaming his actions first on his vulnerability to the depraved customs of his social class— the gentlemanly habits of drinking alcohol and frequenting brothels—then on the inherent vileness of sexual love, and finally on the intoxicating effect of music. Pozdnyshev compares the impressions produced by music with those produced by hypnosis and argues that it was the terrible power of this art that seduced his wife and compelled him to kill her.

Tolstoy makes it hard for the reader to take Pozdnyshev's story of his own vulnerability at face value. Even if we share his suspicions of this or that social custom, we are also suspicious of Pozdnyshev himself. Why? First, because Tolstoy marks him as a paranoiac: Pozdnyshev believes people are speaking about him even though they are not, and he believes his wife has betrayed him even though the novella furnishes no proof of that. As Vladimir

126

Golstein observes, Tolstoy's decision to make his protagonist "vain, selfish, and self-righteous" primes us to reject Pozdnyshev's claims to be a "helpless passive entity."[2] Tolstoy, Golstein argues, "alerts us from the start that Pozdnyshev intends to turn his confession of murder into a narrative of justifications and evasions."[3] We have other grounds for suspicion. Pozdnyshev himself hints that his social explanations may obscure a more fundamental failing all his own: his unrelenting egoism, narcissism, and isolation—an isolation fueled, ironically, by his suspicion of the social world.

At several points in the story, Pozdnyshev reveals a connection between his egoism and his crime. He acknowledges that he felt his wife's body belonged to him "as if it were my own" (*KS*, 418; *PSS*, 27:68). And he admits that only after the murder does he recognize her humanity: "for the first time [I] saw a human being in her" (*KS*, 427; *PSS*, 27:77). These disclosures suggest that we ought (with Tolstoy's blessing) to read against the thrust of Pozdnyshev's social explanations for his crime, to see instead his self-absorption lurking behind what he has done. Tolstoy's friends, who responded to early versions of the story, understood Pozdnyshev in precisely this way: as an egoist rather than a mere victim of his circumstances.[4]

Pozdnyshev's brutality stems not from an excess but from a lack of vulnerability to the external world, an unresponsiveness to the people and things around him that is exacerbated by a distrust of them. He is not exactly a solipsist—he does not doubt the existence of other people—but he no longer believes that other people have thoughts and motives that differ from his. His wife's inner life is so hard to fathom that he can conceive of it only as a reflection of his own: "We were left confronting one another in our true relation: that is, as two egoists quite alien to each other who wished to get as much pleasure as possible each from the other" (*KS*, 380; *PSS*, 27:32). Pozdnyshev imputes to his wife his own egoistic and libidinous urges. This inability to imagine inner lives other than one's own is, for Tolstoy, tantamount to insanity. A formula appears in Tolstoy's diaries: "Madness is egoism, or conversely: egoism . . . is madness."[5]

And Tolstoy compels us to simulate this form of madness—Pozdnyshev's madness—in our own reading of and reasoning about the novella. As we read, we suspect both with and against Pozdnyshev, now adopting his perspective, now deconstructing his account. Tolstoy, as Morson has argued, is a master of "reader-implicating" fiction, and in *The Kreutzer Sonata* we are made to share Pozdnyshev's entrapment by adopting his suspicious hermeneutics.[6] In partaking of Pozdnyshev's predicament, having a taste of the madness it entails, we perceive a warning from the author: if you are not yet concerned about becoming trapped in your own mind, you ought to be. We recognize that Pozdnyshev's hermeneutic exertions lead only to further entrapment and isolation—he will, we intuit, continue to

Chapter Four

travel alone, buttonholing passengers whose own stories he admits he cannot absorb "because [he] continued to think about [his] own affairs"—and worry that such suspicious hermeneutics might do the same to us (*KS*, 417; *PSS*, 27:67).

The Kreutzer Sonata thus performs a kind of controlled explosion of readerly suspicion: instead of denying our deconstructive impulse, it recognizes it, sympathizes with it, and even encourages us to follow through on it, all within the safe confines of the story itself. Pozdnyshev, on the plane of the story, goes mad, but we, looking on with Tolstoy, learn our lesson.

~

In 1926, just four months after the publication of his debut novel, *Mary*, a young Nabokov had an occasion to retell Pozdnyshev's story. Nabokov's friends at the Berlin Journalists and Writers' Union invited him to play the role of Pozdnyshev at a literary event featuring a mock trial of Tolstoy's protagonist. Nabokov accepted the challenge and detailed his preparations for it in letters to his wife, Véra. First, he studied Tolstoy's novella: "I read 'The Kreutzer Sonata' today: a rather vulgar little pamphlet—although once it seemed very 'powerful' to me."[7] Then he composed his defendant's speech and rehearsed it with the other players: "I read my 'speech' at the committee meeting (praise and more praise . . . I am beginning to get sick of it: it even went as far as them saying I was 'subtler' than Tolstoy. Terrible nonsense, really)."[8] Finally, having performed his monologue, Nabokov, whose self-assurance antedated his masterworks, wrote to Véra that he had created a Pozdnyshev "completely different" from Tolstoy's original.[9]

Nabokov did indeed create a Pozdnyshev who departed from its model. He stripped the protagonist of his contempt for sexual love as well as his ambition to be an object lesson to his listeners. Whereas Tolstoy's Pozdnyshev presents himself as a warning against the general sins of sex and marriage, Nabokov's insists on the particularity of his marital strife: "I understand that it is not marriage itself that is sinful, but only my marriage that was sinful, because I sinned before love" ("A Monologue," 112; "Rech'," N38f).[10] In rewriting Pozdnyshev, Nabokov replaced the character's meditations on social ills with vivid recollections of the night he fell in love: "I recollect the smallest trifle of that outing, the color of the water, the reflection of the shrubs" ("A Monologue," 110; "Rech'," N38a). These precise, idiosyncratic memories reinforce the singularity of the character; it is hard to symbolize your entire social class when you are noticing the reflection of a particular shrub. Nabokov's Pozdnyshev declares: "I don't know anything. I only remember that I was too full of myself, too prejudiced against true passion, against true, transcendent love, to appreciate and let loose the new feeling I

128

felt that evening" ("A Monologue," 110; "Rech'," N38). True to his lifelong protest against moral generalization, Nabokov creates a Pozdnyshev who disavows any lessons to be learned from his life.

Nabokov's departures from Tolstoy attest to what the young author found most vulgar in the novella—namely, Pozdnyshev's absolutist condemnation of sexual love. But what Nabokov preserved is equally important. Nabokov retains Pozdnyshev's chief afflictions: his self-absorption and ensuing isolation. Like Tolstoy, Nabokov regards the character's blinding egoism as the root cause of his violence. Instead of doing away with Pozdnyshev's obsessive theorizing, Nabokov merely alters his theories and in fact inverts them. He presents Pozdnyshev's puritanical lessons as the source of his error, not as the result of his eventual revelation. In Tolstoy's version of their courtship, Pozdnyshev believes that he loves his wife when really he only lusts after her. The truth of their relationship is obscured by his belief that sexual desire and love can coexist. This false belief dooms his marriage. Nabokov's Pozdnyshev, in contrast, believes that he only lusts after his wife when really he loves her. The truth of their relationship is obscured by his belief that sexual desire and love cannot coexist. This false belief dooms his marriage. Nabokov's Pozdnyshev explains, "You see, in my blindness, I resolved that I needed only her body, and resolved that she knew this" ("A Monologue," 5–6; "Rech'," N38e). Nabokov inverts the content of Pozdnyshev's postmurder revelation. Love does not mask what is, in reality, lust; rather, that idea itself—the cynical idea that love is always, at bottom, lust—threatens to obscure love where it does exist.

A review of Nabokov's performance at the mock trial in the émigré newspaper *Rul'* declared that he had created an entirely new Pozdnyshev: "In [Nabokov's] inspired, creative rendering, Tolstoy's killer-philosophizer became a living, suffering individual who recognized his guilt before his murdered wife, before the possibility of real love that he had ruined."[11] The review responds to the greater self-awareness of Nabokov's Pozdnyshev, to his lyrical musings on the nature of love. It goes on to note that the changes Nabokov introduced posed some problems for the trial: "Such a departure from Tolstoy demanded that the trial's participants reckon with the existence of two Pozdnyshevs."[12] The mock trial was to end with a vote on the defendant's guilt, but Nabokov had altered Pozdnyshev so much that it now seemed there were two defendants. Which one was the audience to deliberate on? Were they judging Tolstoy's "killer-philosophizer" or Nabokov's "suffering individual"? Nabokov had created a subtler criminal who draws attention to his willingness to accept responsibility for the crime and thereby elicits the pity of his audience.

Yet the reviewer overestimated the extent to which Nabokov had altered the essence of Pozdnyshev's crime. Stripping Pozdnyshev of his stark

Chapter Four

ethical prescriptions, Nabokov makes him his own. But the monologue retains what is central to Pozdnyshev's tragedy and to Tolstoy's broad moral vision: the idea that brutality is born of unrelenting self-absorption fortified by distrust. And distrust not only of his wife and those near to him but also on a grand scale: Nabokov's Pozdnyshev, like Tolstoy's, once believed that women surreptitiously control the world. Both subscribed to this conspiracy "the same way some people believe the Freemasons govern the globe" and were inspired by it to judge women harshly, when in fact, as Nabokov's Pozdnyshev admits: "I did not know women at all, and I never gave a single thought to a woman's soul" ("A Monologue," 6; "Rech'," N38c). For all his Nabokovian alterations of Tolstoy's tale, Nabokov still depicts someone whose world is eclipsed by his own suspicious theories, his hyperactive ego, and the patterned chatter of his mind.

Indeed, it seems likely that Tolstoy's novella had once appeared powerful to Nabokov because, despite its moralizing, it portrayed precisely the kind of tragic monomania that concerned him, too, and that he would explore again and again in his fiction, most memorably in his Humbert Humbert. Nabokov's Pozdnyshev is an early prototype for this character, who, imprisoned by his own obsessions, attempts to escape by means of self-scrutiny but in doing so only entangles himself further. Nabokov's monologue, like Tolstoy's novella, argues that such hermeneutic exercises are futile. Neither author exonerates his Pozdnyshev, and neither liberates him. Tolstoy leaves him in the dark cell of his train compartment, immersed in his theories. Nabokov cheerfully reports to Véra that his own audience voted to convict him: "now I am already writing from jail."[13]

INFECTION AND AGITATION:
TOLSTOY'S IDEAL ARTWORK

The Kreutzer Sonata stimulates our suspicion with the aim to exhaust it and to underscore its pointlessness and perniciousness. The novella recommends trust to us by dramatizing the moral failures that result from its absence. The artwork offers a warning. But if suspicion is as engrained in us as these authors thought, then we need more than a warning to wean ourselves from it—and indeed Tolstoy believed that art could do more. Art that resists our attempts to assimilate it into our own thoughts and concerns can bring us into contact with the thoughts and concerns of another person, namely, the artist. With the musical piece that gives his story its name, Tolstoy models this effect of his ideal artwork.

Tolstoy never allows Pozdnyshev to escape his entrapment, but he does grant him one brief reprieve from it, during the performance by his wife

130

Suspicion on Trial

and Trukhachevsky of Beethoven's "Kreutzer" sonata. In this episode, which stands at the heart of his novella, Tolstoy suggests that a certain kind of aesthetic encounter is capable of liberating one from the strictures of one's own mind. As he listened to the sonata, Pozdnyshev recalls, he was moved to "forget myself, my real position" (*KS*, 410; *PSS*, 27:61). He explains that "music carries me immediately and directly into the mental condition in which the man was who composed it. My soul merges with his and together with him I pass from one condition into another" (*KS*, 411; *PSS*, 27:61). Pozdnyshev describes precisely the "infection with another's feeling" that Tolstoy considered "the very essence of art" and the grounds for its singular capacity to help us overcome our alienation from each other (*WIA*, 138; *PSS*, 30:147).

Aesthetic experiences connect characters throughout Tolstoy's fiction, but *The Kreutzer Sonata* illustrates the effect most vividly. In *What Is Art?* Tolstoy describes—hopefully, though not always convincingly—how art can dispel hostility and unite its appreciators: "Sometimes people who are together are, if not hostile to one another, at least estranged in mood and feeling, till perchance a story, a performance, a picture, or even a building, but most often of all music, unites them all as by an electric flash, and in place of their former isolation or even enmity they are all conscious of union and mutual love" (*WIA*, 150; *PSS*, 30:158). Through music, Pozdnyshev transcends his profound distrust and isolation, experiencing, if momentarily, a feeling of fellowship with others. He marvels at what is, for him, a novel experience: "What this new thing was that had been revealed to me I could not explain to myself, but the consciousness of this new condition was very joyous. All those same people, including my wife and him [Trukhachevsky], appeared in a new light" (*KS*, 412; *PSS*, 27:62). The new feeling Pozdnyshev describes is a more charitable relation to others. Where before Pozdnyshev had seen mere reflections of himself, shadows of his own desires, he now recognizes real human faces.

On the night of the performance Pozdnyshev revels in the feeling of fellowship, but on reflection he insists "it is a terrible thing, that sonata . . . in general music is a dreadful thing!" (*KS*, 410; *PSS*, 27:61). It is tempting to overlook the exalting effect of the sonata as it is played and to take Pozdnyshev's retrospective judgment at face value.[14] After all, in *What Is Art?* Tolstoy echoes Pozdnyshev's hysterical complaints against Beethoven's music. But one cannot simply read Tolstoy's later opinion of Beethoven into the story. For one thing, that opinion was complicated and inconsistent. Tolstoy denounced Beethoven's late period but praised the genius of his earlier works, possibly counting the middle-period "Kreutzer" sonata among these (*WIA*, 144; *PSS*, 30:134). An 1876 performance of the sonata partly inspired the novella, and Sofia Tolstoy attested to her husband's initial enthusiasm for the music: "Everyone was thrown into ecstasy, beginning with Lev Nikolaevich."[15]

Chapter Four

Moreover, according to her, a second performance, by their son Sergei, facilitated precisely the kind of familial closeness that Pozdnyshev experiences in the novella.[16] I mention these biographical facts not to confirm Tolstoy's approval of the sonata but only to challenge arguments that assume, on the basis of his late polemics, that Tolstoy simply endorsed Pozdnyshev's views.

A more compelling argument against the transformative power of the sonata rests on what seems like a fundamental tension in Tolstoy's aesthetics between his concept of amoral infectiousness and his notion that art promotes mutual love. Pickford identifies this tension and suggests that in *The Kreutzer Sonata* Tolstoy grapples with its ramifications. Implicit in Tolstoy's theory of infection, Pickford argues, is the Schopenhauerian idea that art, and especially music, "conveys affective contents . . . without the normatively structured motives that would be appropriate for them."[17] The spectator's feelings are excited but are not directed toward any particular object or activity. As a result, the spectator's agitation seems liable to be channeled in moral or immoral directions depending on the spectator's own disposition. Pickford concludes that Pozdnyshev is right to say the sonata had a "terrible" effect on him, not because it is itself immoral but because Pozdnyshev's evil disposition can only channel its excitement toward destructive ends.[18]

I agree with Pickford that the sonata excites Pozdnyshev's mental powers—he is keenly attentive to it—while arresting his activity. But I would not characterize this excitement as mere agitation. True, Pozdnyshev complains: "A dance is played, I dance and the music has achieved its object. Mass has been sung, I receive Communion, and that music too has reached a conclusion. Otherwise it is only agitating, and what ought to be done in that agitation is lacking" (*KS*, 411; *PSS*, 27:61). Yet moments later he admits that, far from simply irritating his senses, the sonata enables him to see the world anew. In one variant of the novella, Tolstoy is particularly explicit about the sonata's transformative effect. "That music drew me into some world in which jealousy no longer had place," Pozdnyshev says. "Jealousy and the feeling that evoked it seemed trifles not worth considering" (*KS*, 447; *PSS*, 27:333). Jealousy and what induces it—namely, sexual desire—are precisely what Tolstoy's protagonist comes to renounce after his wife's murder. Pozdnyshev claims that the first time he recognized his jealous torments as trifles was by his wife's deathbed: "And so insignificant did all that had offended me, all my jealousy, appear, and so important what I had done" (*KS*, 427; *PSS*, 27:77). In fact, this revelation is prefigured in Pozdnyshev's response to Beethoven's music. The sonata is not mere irritation—it is a glimpse of the moral transformation that Pozdnyshev would embrace too late.

On Pickford's reading, Pozdnyshev is driven to murder by his frustration that the "terrible" sonata—unlike a dance, unlike Mass—arrests his own action. This inhibition of one's own action, Pickford suggests, is part of the

132

danger of art that conveys affect without conveying any normative content. The sonata that inspired Pozdnyshev's frustration thus appears complicit in his sin. I propose, on the contrary, that the sonata only seems "terrible" to Pozdnyshev because it momentarily thwarts his egoistic pursuit of his own ends. It briefly arrests his activity—compels him to "do nothing"—and thereby enables Pozdnyshev to escape his accustomed, egocentric way of seeing the world. The fact that the sonata resists being easily absorbed into Pozdnyshev's thoughts and schemes makes it an exemplary artwork, and furnishes Pozdnyshev with a momentary reprieve from his mental torment. That it is only momentary—that he lapses back into torment and later commits murder—is evidence not of the sonata's complicity in his sin but of the limitations of the therapy it offers.

Consider the contrast between Beethoven's sonata and the inferior piece of music played just after it. His wife's performance pacifies his jealousy for a time; Pozdnyshev leaves on a business trip in high spirits. But after receiving a letter from her, he recalls the performance in a different light. He now remembers not the sonata but a different "impassioned little piece" by a composer whose name he cannot recall (KS, 414; PSS, 27:64). The fact that Pozdnyshev forgets the composer's name discredits the work. Throughout his fiction, Tolstoy assigns what he considers false or bad artworks to anonymous authors. And Pozdnyshev's murky recollection of the piece suggests that it did not elicit the keen attentiveness compelled by the sonata. Most important, this piece does not, as the sonata did, arrest Pozdnyshev's usual ruminations but rather gives them free rein. Pozdnyshev's suspicious imagination runs amok. Since Pozdnyshev sees habitually through the prism of sexual desire, he starts to decode the whole musical performance as evidence of an affair that had already taken place: "Was it not clear that everything had happened between them that evening?" (KS, 414; PSS, 27:64). Pozdnyshev begins to spin his own narrative of adultery and murder. An artwork that is not perceived as the expressive gesture of anyone in particular fails, Tolstoy suggests, to loosen the grip of our solipsism and may in fact tighten it.

I see the salutary (if short-lived) effect of the sonata as Tolstoy's way of partially resolving the aforementioned paradox of his aesthetics—the contradiction between his idea that art infects regardless of its moral content and his wish that art cultivate morality. It is true that the sonata itself does not directly convey moral content. All it seems to do is divert Pozdnyshev from his familiar obsessions and suspicions, from his usual frame of mind. For Tolstoy, though, that is not nothing. It is an effect few things are capable of achieving—not the game of backgammon Hume proposed as an antidote to solipsism and not an artwork that we experience as a purely passive object. What is needed is an artwork that resists us the way people resist us, that

133

Chapter Four

subjects us to its will no less than we subject it to ours, that expresses an outlook different from our own. The sonata confronts Pozdnyshev as something created by someone else for purposes other than his own and thus awakens him (as long as he hears it) to a reality not of his own making, inhabited by autonomous subjects who live alongside him in a shared world. For the first time, he sees them, in Kant's formulation, not as means but as ends in themselves. The sonata may be amoral in content, but the fact that Pozdnyshev "felt [it] as made by someone"—to borrow a phrase from Cavell—has for him a profound moral consequence.[19]

Pozdnyshev's own story has a similar effect on its captive and captivated audience, Tolstoy's frame narrator. Though he acquires from the murderer no moral knowledge and conspicuously refrains from affirming any of Pozdnyshev's ideas, the narrator at the end of Pozdnyshev's tale sees its teller's face clearly for the first time: "[he] smiled slightly, but so piteously that I felt ready to weep"—another recognition of another's subjectivity (*KS*, 428; *PSS*, 27:78). Echoing Kant, whose moral philosophy he admired, Tolstoy suggests that even art that does not impart moral content has a role to play in preparing us for moral action. Even if it has nothing to teach us, aesthetic experience can prime us for the ethical treatment of others merely by freeing us momentarily from our own thoughts and interests. Tolstoy's novella might be said to produce the moral effect it dramatizes by alerting us to our own suspicious impulse and compelling us, temporarily, to transcend it.

Tolstoy was ultimately unsatisfied with the moral capacity of art as he conceived it in the novella. Perhaps it seemed to him too weak and too fleeting. Emerson stresses that "once infected [Pozdnyshev] could not sustain that satisfaction."[20] His "ultimately corroded" reaction to Beethoven's music is evidence, she argues, of "the contradictory elements of [Tolstoy's] own infection theory."[21] Tolstoy fails to consider the way our involvement with an artwork might change over time; the artwork that initially had an exalting effect might, in time, distress or even derange us. Whether we agree with Emerson that the sonata's effect is eventually corroded or posit that its impression simply wanes and makes way for others—that is, the anonymous "impassioned little piece"—Pozdnyshev's fate makes one thing clear: even an exemplary aesthetic experience is not enough to teach people right from wrong or to save someone for long from his abiding egoism. It was perhaps a dissatisfaction with the limited power of aesthetic experience that moved Tolstoy to occasionally repeat the pronouncements of his protagonist and to disparage not only Beethoven's works but also his own. Later, in his essays on art, Tolstoy would argue that art should not only be aesthetically compelling (infectious) but also convey explicitly moral content.

The explanatory afterword Tolstoy appended to the novella has often been taken as an example of such straightforward moral instruction. Though he refers neither to his novella's plot nor to its protagonist, Tolstoy does seem

Suspicion on Trial

to echo in his own voice Pozdnyshev's praise of chastity. This has puzzled scholars. J. M. Coetzee wonders why "this incompetent diagnostician," a character we are compelled to disbelieve, "is given explicit support by Tolstoy as author in his 'Afterword.'"[22] In fact, though Tolstoy lauds chastity as a virtue, he does not endorse Pozdnyshev's morality here any more than he does in the story. The afterword is not as straightforward as it appears. Tolstoy writes, "Chastity is neither rule nor injunction, but an ideal."[23] The church gives us rules, Tolstoy says, but Christ gave us an unattainable moral example. By adhering to a set of precepts one might become self-satisfied, but in striving toward Christ's example one always possesses "an awareness of the degree of incongruousness one's behavior has in relation to ideal perfection." One is moved to "go beyond [oneself]."[24] Pozdnyshev follows the rule-based morality of the church, which in Tolstoy's view distorted Christ's teachings. Even in the afterword we are not meant to accept Pozdnyshev's precepts, which are at best a formalistic distortion of the ideal.

Tolstoy's afterword ends with the assertion that all rules of conduct recede in importance before the "renunciation of self and service for God and one's neighbor."[25] Above all, one must try to transcend oneself so as to be receptive to others. And that is just what Tolstoy's infectious artwork—even when he feared it could teach us, in its content, nothing at all—is designed to help us do.

PLEASURABLE TORMENTS, LOVINGLY PREPARED: NABOKOV'S VARIATION

Nabokov, no less than Tolstoy, feared that our skepticism and the generative activity of our own minds could impede our apprehension of the world. A character on his deathbed in *The Gift* suspects there is no afterlife: "There is nothing. It is as clear as the fact that it is raining."[26] Nabokov suggests the hubris of his doubt: "And meanwhile outside the spring sun was playing on the roof tiles, the sky was dreamy and cloudless, the tenant upstairs was watering the flowers on the edge of her balcony, and the water trickled down with a drumming sound."[27] Further on, the author offers an extended tutorial in good reading, which includes a warning against letting one's interpretive impulse run wild. The narrator recalls a piece of advice from his father, a famous naturalist:

> When closely—no matter how closely—observing events in nature we must, in the very process of observation, beware of letting our reason—that garrulous dragoman who always runs ahead—prompt us with explanations which then begin imperceptibly to influence the very course of observation and distort it: thus the shadow of the instrument falls upon the truth.[28]

135

Chapter Four

The careful observer must try to restrain the dragoman—reason, the professional interpreter—to keep from distorting the objects observed. The mind is an inveterate storyteller, weaving all sorts of plots and preventing us from seeing what is really there. By linking skepticism as well as our hypertrophied interpretive faculties with obfuscation, Nabokov echoes Tolstoy and anticipates contemporary critiques of suspicious reading.

But the younger author was more attuned than his predecessor to the pleasures of suspicion. Tolstoy saw our skeptical inclination primarily as a vice and a danger. In his discursive works—from *Confession* to *What Is Art?*—Tolstoy is tempted to declare that the struggle against his own skepticism has been won; his aesthetic treatise renounces his great works in favor of stories that exemplify the sort of unspoiled faith he attributed to Russian peasants. Lev Shestov noted bitterly that Tolstoy's denouncements in *What Is Art?* do little good for the peasants and are disastrous for everyone else—everyone who cannot discard their doubts as readily as Tolstoy claimed to have done. What such people need are artworks that commiserate with them by acknowledging their doubts: "They, of course, need this, and oh how they need it! But Count Tolstoy does not want it."[29] Shestov speculates that Tolstoy's late aesthetics were part of the author's effort to disguise from his followers the persistence of his own doubts, and, as I have shown, these doubts do persist in both the content and the form of his late works, including in *What Is Art?* Whether Tolstoy confronted skepticism head-on, as in *Anna Karenina*, or indirectly, as in his late works, skepticism for him was always a problem.

Nabokov, in contrast, recognized the suspicious disposition—which inspires us, among other things, to decode and decipher—not merely as an inescapable compulsion but also as something we might welcome for the pleasures it can provide. In *Speak, Memory* he elaborates on these pleasures in an extended comparison between the composition of a novel and that of a chess problem. "[A] great part of a problem's value," Nabokov explains "is due to the number of 'tries'—delusive opening moves, false scents, specious lines of play, astutely and lovingly prepared to lead the would-be solver astray."[30] In her critique of suspicion, Felski notes similar pleasures: "a sense of prowess in the exercise of ingenious interpretation, the striking elegance and economy of its explanatory schemes."[31] But in urging us to forego suspicion, she suggests that there are greater pleasures to be had from a trusting relation to the text. Nabokov rejects this dichotomy and insists that a good artwork offers both sorts of pleasures at once. A reader who tries to short-circuit the process of gradual unveiling and arrive at a chess problem's (or a novel's) "fairly simple, 'thetic' solution without having passed through the pleasurable torments" of false solutions, misses the point.[32] It is the "simple key move" discovered by the "roundabout route" prepared by the author that gives the reader the most "poignant artistic delight."[33]

136

Suspicion on Trial

Nabokov's Pozdnyshev performs for us an exercise in suspicious hermeneutics that far outstrips Tolstoy's. Tolstoy's Pozdnyshev had only one theory of his crime; Nabokov's has at least three. First, he offers the story of his crime as Tolstoy's character had told it: he suspects that the conventions of his class have led him astray. But hastily he turns his skeptical eye on himself, declaring, "I can't go on like this. I lied just now" ("A Monologue," 110; "Rech'," N38a). He then proceeds with a second account. Perhaps it was his false theories about women and sex that led him to stifle his affection for his wife, treat her roughly on their wedding night, and destroy their marriage. Nabokov's Pozdnyshev reverses himself twice more before resting his case. A third explanation suggests that the murder was not a failure to express his passion but that passion itself: "Maybe the murder that I committed was, in its way, the most natural act of my whole life—not only because bestial cruelty is natural, lawful everywhere in nature, but also because I for the first time gave full vent to my passion" ("A Monologue," 113–14; "Rech'," N38h). Once again he retracts his theory, calling this third account an "excuse" (*opravdanie*). Reversing himself a final time, he insists that the second explanation had to be the right one: he killed his wife by depriving her of affection and tenderness, "tenderness without which a woman cannot live" ("A Monologue," 114; "Rech'," N38g). But after so many reversals, so many rival explanations, we come to doubt all of them. We sense that there is no end to the revisions and reinterpretations, no ground beneath them.

In "Pozdnyshev's Address" Nabokov prefigures an essential thematic opposition that appears in much of his fiction: the tension between creative (including interpretive) virtuosity and the ethical treatment of others. Juxtaposing Nabokov's discursive remarks on art with his late novels, Richard Rorty argues that the author is at odds with himself. "Nabokov would desperately like artistic gifts to be sufficient for moral virtue," Rorty suggests; writers like George Orwell and Thomas Mann repel him because they deny this equation.[34] Yet Nabokov "knows that there is no connection between the contingent and selective curiosity of the autonomous artist and . . . the creation of a world in which tenderness and kindness are the human norm."[35] Nabokov's greatest contribution to "our knowledge of human possibilities," according to Rorty, is his "genius-monster[s]": characters who like Humbert and Kinbote are "both ecstatic and cruel, noticing and heartless, poets who are only selectively curious, obsessives who are as sensitive as they are callous. What [Nabokov] fears most is that one cannot have it both ways—that there is no synthesis of ecstasy and kindness."[36] Other scholars, too, have noted Nabokov's interest in the "heartless artist." Rampton sees it already in his early Russian fiction, and in particular in the 1932 novel *Kamera obskura* (later translated as *Laughter in the Dark*).[37] Julian Connolly similarly proposes that this novel "raises serious questions about the artist's relation-

Chapter Four

ship to the suffering of his fellow humans."[38] Toker identifies in Nabokov a lifelong "reservation about the Romantic quest for the infinite. This quest is beautiful and ennobling so long as it does not lead to the neglect of the finite."[39] Nabokov, as Rorty and others observe, was attuned to the ways our creative pursuits not only fail to save us from cruelty but might in fact reinforce cruelty by impeding our capacity to notice another person's pain.

Nabokov's Pozdnyshev can grasp his wife's suffering only when he ceases to relentlessly suspect and decipher—that is, to exhibit his peculiar form of creative activity. Toward the end of his monologue, Pozdnyshev is seized by the recollection of his wife's battered face:

> for the first time did I forget myself, my rights, my pride; for the first time I saw in her a human being . . . I understood all that I had done. I understood that it was I, I who had killed her—that it was because of me that she who had been living, moving, warm, now lay still, waxen, and cold, and that this could never, nowhere, by no means, be remedied. ("A Monologue," 113; "Rech'," N38f)

Significantly, these are the only sentences Nabokov quotes in toto from Tolstoy's story.[40] Their intertextuality endows these words with a stability denied to Pozdnyshev's shifting explanations, bolstering their claim to truth. By contrast with the unreliable accounts of the character, the words we recognize as those of the author (who else could have borrowed them from Tolstoy's text?) appear trustworthy. In the end, Nabokov, like Tolstoy, suggests that complex epistemological puzzles recede in importance before our ethical imperatives. He concludes the monologue with Pozdnyshev's entreaty of the audience: "Don't search for some especially profound reasons for my action" ("A Monologue," 113; "Rech'," N38g). Pozdnyshev declares: "It is simpler than all that. I killed a person" ("A Monologue," 114; "Rech'," N38h).

Here, as elsewhere in his works, Nabokov allots a modicum of self-awareness to his character but reserves the lion's share of it for the author and reader. Pozdnyshev can interpret his story and then interpret it again, but only from the higher perspective we share with the author can we glimpse the potentially endless vista of reinterpretations. The reader delights in Pozdnyshev's hermeneutic virtuosity but (ideally) comes to realize that this delight distracts us, and the narrator himself, from his ethical failures. Nabokov, as Naiman has observed, cultivates "hermeneutic anxieties" in his readers by confounding their capacity to determine whether they are reading well or overinterpreting.[41] I agree, but I make the further claim that Nabokov does this not only to prompt self-scrutiny but also to offer us a reprieve from it. The reader's suspicion of the fictive world is converted in the end into an appreciation of the artist's feat in evoking it. A "wise" reader, Nabokov suggests, pays attention not only to the conjured illusions but also, and most important, to the ingenuity of the artist in conjuring them: "watch[ing] the artist build his castle of cards and watch[ing] the castle of cards become a castle of beautiful steel and glass."[42] A trustful encounter between reader and author—each peering at rather than behind the other—is at the core of both aesthetic and moral experience in Nabokov, as it is in Tolstoy.

One could, of course, imagine self-interested reasons why these authors might have stressed the limitations of suspicious interpretation. After all, when we read suspiciously we deny the author's monopoly on meaning and claim it for ourselves. But, as I have argued, Tolstoy and Nabokov also had aesthetic and ethical motives for attempting to curtail our readerly freedom. Both worried that texts that offer free rein to our suspicious impulses and invite endless construals confine us to our established conceptual schemes, our intellectual habits. In the extreme case—Pozdnyshev's case—the mastery obtained over such passive texts verges, they feared, on solipsism. In creating works that seek to impose on us another's subjectivity, they hoped to free us from our own.

PALE FIRE: SUSPICION AS A PRECONDITION FOR ARTMAKING

As *The Circle of Reading* attests, Tolstoy wished to grant a reprieve from skepticism (and concomitantly from suspicion) not only to the reader but also to the artist. Nabokov had no such ambition. He rejected Tolstoy's striving for the absolute quiescence of skepticism. He deemed it not only impossible but indeed undesirable, since there are pleasures and possibilities associated with a skeptical disposition, particularly for the artist. Without denying the ways skepticism and suspicion might inhibit our receptivity to other people, Nabokov in his novel *Pale Fire* illuminates the positive potential of a skeptical temperament. Suspicion here is a double-edged sword. Nabokov does not contest that it can make one neglectful of other people. But he also suggests that it enables us to look past what appears at first glance to be an unbridgeable abyss between ourselves and others.

In "Pozdnyshev's Address" Nabokov largely echoes Tolstoy's strategy for circumscribing suspicion: like Tolstoy, he channels it toward the narrator and away from the author. He replicates this same strategy in many of his later texts, including major works like *Lolita*. There, too, hermeneutic exertions must in the end come to a halt before the fact of human suffering. In "Pozdnyshev's Address" and *Lolita*, as in *The Kreutzer Sonata*, readers are compelled to define themselves against the distrustful (and untrustworthy) narrator, whose suspicion fuels his egoism and paves the way for his moral

Chapter Four

failure. Not wishing to emulate the narrator's suspicion, readers adopt a more trusting stance toward the text and its author. In distrusting the narrator, readers partake of the pleasures of suspicious hermeneutics, yet in arriving at a rejection of suspicion they also enjoy what Wayne Booth called "the secret communion" of the author and reader "behind the speaker's back."[43] For a moment, they have faith that the text has allowed them to share another's perspective, namely, the author's. *Pale Fire* (1962), however, departs from this model; Nabokov does not lead his readers out of the labyrinth of suspicious interpretation. Instead, he troubles the very distinction between suspicion and faith.

Pale Fire, like Nabokov's earlier work *The Gift*, grapples with the limits of our access to other people, limits that are made particularly vivid by the experience of exile.[44] Although readers of *Pale Fire* have attended to the question of "what can be known by each mind, being only one mind," as Boyd puts it, scholarship tends to focus on the ways the text illuminates our finite knowledge of the cosmos rather than our no less finite understanding of other people.[45] And while most readings of the novel attend in some way to the linguistic skepticism inherent in its central conceit—a commentator radically misreads a poet's poem—few consider this skepticism within the novel's broader concern with the problem of other minds.[46] But doing so helps us recognize that the linguistic skepticism of Nabokov's mad commentator is unlike that which we find among poststructuralist and deconstructionist readers who would soon come by the multitudes. Rampton is not wrong to suggest that Nabokov anticipates Jacques Derrida.[47] But one should add that he also anticipates ways to counter Derridean skepticism. If deconstructionist readers like Paul de Man deploy "suspicious'" reading practices to stress the "duplicity, the confusion, the untruth"[48] in all language, then Nabokov's mad commentator deploys them precisely to avoid such conclusions. Only by reading suspiciously, this novel suggests, can we look beyond the myriad ways our communicative efforts fail us—the ways they fail to let us escape the confines of our own minds and share another's perspective. *Pale Fire* demonstrates that suspicion can paradoxically fuel the sort of idealism needed to persist in the creation and reception of art: it can help sustain one's faith in the power of art to convey a message from one person to another.

NEIGHBOR'S WINDOWS

Nabokov's two protagonists are neighbors in the Appalachian town of New Wye and colleagues at Wordsmith University. One, John Shade, is an American poet; the other, Charles Kinbote, is a European exile. The text of *Pale Fire* consists of two parts, each ostensibly authored by one of the two protagonists. The first part of the text is Shade's long poem, also titled "Pale Fire." Kinbote got ahold of the poem after the poet was killed by a bullet meant for someone else, and exploiting the distress of Shade's widow, received permission to publish a critical edition of it. The critical apparatus Kinbote produces—a foreword, commentary, and index—comprises the second part of the novel's text. Although Kinbote's voice guides us through the novel, we quickly learn that we cannot trust it. We see that in his commentary Kinbote seems to radically misinterpret Shade's work. On its face, the poem is Shade's artistic autobiography and an account of his daughter's suicide. Kinbote, however, sees in it allusions to his own tragic fate as the fugitive king of a distant northern land, Zembla. Shade's poem becomes an occasion for Kinbote to offer up, in the guise of criticism, his own fantastic tale. This tale may or may not be entirely fabricated. The narrator who calls himself Kinbote may be the Zemblan King Charles Xavier, but he is perhaps more likely to be a colleague of Shade's named Botkin, an obscure Russian émigré. The only thing certain is that Shade, born and bred in New Wye, is firmly rooted in this world, while Kinbote is a stranger to it.

Despite their biographical differences, Kinbote and Shade (and their texts) evince significant affinities. Indeed, these affinities are striking enough to have inspired a decades-long debate about the text's authorship, with commentators including Field, Boyd, Page Stegner, and D. Barton Johnson, suggesting a single author pens both the poem and the commentary, and disputing whether that author is Kinbote/Botkin or Shade, or (obliquely) Hazel Shade, as Boyd has proposed.[49] Other scholars, such as Ellen Pifer and Robert Alter, have alternatively refrained from contesting the novel's "basic fictional data."[50] Single-author readings are certainly made available by Nabokov's text, and they generate fascinating interpretations.[51] But my analysis follows Pifer's and Alter's in treating each protagonist as the author of one part of the whole text. Doing so illuminates the multiple facets of a skeptical disposition that Nabokov explores in his novel in part by evoking, as Pifer says, the "individual reality and unique differences" of these characters.[52]

Among other things, Kinbote and Shade share their concern with the limits that consciousness imposes on what we might know. Though this concern is ultimately more urgent for Kinbote, it is Shade who first introduces it in the text. His poem begins with the image of the mind straining to reach beyond itself:

> I was the shadow of the waxwing slain
> By the false azure in the windowpane;
> I was the smudge of ashen fluff–and I

141

Chapter Four

> Lived on, flew on, in the reflected sky.
> And from the inside, too, I'd duplicate
> Myself, my lamp, an apple on a plate:
> Uncurtaining the night, I'd let dark glass
> Hang all the furniture above the grass, (*PF*, 33)

For Shade, nightfall makes vivid the mind's enclosure within itself. The window is among the most symbolically rich images in *Pale Fire*, and it cannot be exhausted by a single interpretation. But one key function of the image, in Shade's poem and elsewhere, is to evoke the false promise of access to something outside the self. Shade looks out his window but sees first of all his own reflection. The elements of the outside world that do reach him mingle with this reflection; everything he perceives is stamped by his own image. In the guise of the waxwing, the poet imagines what it might be like to transcend the constraints of one's own consciousness. Yet despite this dream of escape, Shade does not seem oppressed by the mediation of the mind. There is little anguish in this reverie. Indeed, Shade delights in the way his consciousness transforms the stuff of the world.

The same epistemic limits plunge Kinbote into despair. Shade's poetic rendering of the confinement of consciousness is echoed in one of Kinbote's early notes. He, too, is most keenly aware of his psychic confinement at dusk. "The Goldsworth castle"—that is, the house Kinbote has rented for the year in New Wye from Judge Goldsworth—"became particularly solitary after that turning point at dusk which resembles so much the nightfall of the mind," Kinbote explains (*PF*, 96). He goes on to describe his terror as night descends:

> Stealthy rustles, the footsteps of yesteryear leaves, an idle breeze, a dog touring the garbage cans—everything sounded to me like a bloodthirsty prowler . . . I suppose it was then, on those dreadful nights, that I got used to consulting the windows of my neighbor's house in the hope for a gleam of comfort (see notes to lines 47–48). (*PF*, 96)

Confinement within the house becomes an objective correlative to Kinbote's sense of confinement within the self. Peering out of his own windows and into his neighbor's comforts him because it promises access to something outside himself—it lets him hope that he is not, after all, sealed off from others.

But windows betray the hope they inspire. They give Kinbote nothing more than "peeps and glimpses" (*PF*, 86). His peering is often obstructed in one of two ways, either by Sybil Shade or by the blooming garden between the two houses. Sybil, whom he repeatedly associates with domesticity—he

142

Suspicion on Trial

calls her a "domestic censor" (*PF*, 81) and a "domestic anti-Karlist" (*PF*, 74)—interferes by closing the shades. "Encroaching foliage" foils Kinbote still more often, "confus[ing] a green monocle with an opaque occludent, and the idea of protection with that of obstruction" (*PF*, 86). Kinbote boasts that by the time Shade begins his poem, Kinbote knows "exactly when and where to find the best points from which to follow the contours of [Shade's] inspiration" (*PF*, 88). And yet he admits that the summer vegetation "usually deprived [him] of a clear view of [Shade's] face; and perhaps nature arranged it that way so as to conceal from a possible predator the mysteries of generation" (*PF*, 89). It is fitting that Kinbote's fantasy of immediate access to the movement of another's mind is undermined by nature and by Sybil Shade as a symbol (to him) of ordinary life. Both remind Kinbote of the materiality of human being—of the physical bodies that confine us within ourselves and create an ineluctable distance between us.

One might object that it is not his metaphysical condition but rather his egoism that seals Kinbote within himself and disallows the possibility of intimacy with other people. But whether we believe Kinbote is sincerely interested in knowing another person or not, it is hard to deny that he longs for others to know *him*, and he therefore cannot help but shudder at the epistemic and metaphysical limits of human intimacy. Shade sympathizes with this fear. He imagines a soul's unrecognized despair among the possible horrors that can befall us in the afterlife:

> What if you are tossed
> Into a boundless void, your bearings lost,
> Your spirit stripped and utterly alone,
> Your task unfinished, your despair unknown. (*PF*, 53)

As Shade admits earlier in his poem, all our visions of the afterlife are hopelessly dependent on our experience of this life. It is in this life that one's despair may be unknown—that it might be fundamentally private and unshareable. Kinbote is certainly more aggressive in his desperate desire to reveal his despair. But the poet, too, tries to share with his neighbor his most intimate pain.

The neighbors take several evening strolls together and on these occasions each attempts to reveal himself to the other; an attempt that ultimately fails. Kinbote in a roundabout way—by recounting the history of Zembla and its revolution—tries to tell Shade of his loss: the loss of his homeland. At the same time, Shade in a similarly roundabout way tries to tell Kinbote of *his* profound loss: the loss of his daughter. Kinbote eventually learns (and explains to his readers) that what he initially took to be a pointless story about another neighbor's barn was actually Shade's way of speaking about

143

Chapter Four

his daughter. In a rare moment of pity for someone other than himself, Kinbote expresses regret that he "prevented [Shade] from getting to the point he was confusedly and self-consciously making . . . by filling in a welcome pause with an extraordinary episode from the history of [Zembla's] Onhava University" (*PF*, 187). Kinbote's commentary draws our attention to the fact that neither neighbor manages to communicate his pain to the other; neither manages to grasp the depth of the other's suffering. Kinbote goes on about Onhava University. Shade, though he means to be kind, fails to recognize the magnitude of Kinbote's loss when he dismisses the cataclysm that is Kinbote's exile as a "drab and unhappy past" (*PF*, 238).

In *The Gift* Nabokov gives us a protagonist in whom spiritual self-sufficiency and a skeptical disappointment with the limits of our intimacy exist in dialectical tension. In *Pale Fire* these strands of the dialectic come apart, with each protagonist embracing one side. Shade is no less aware of our ineluctable separateness from others than his commentator, but he is not oppressed by it. Why? Partly disposition, no doubt. But in part, perhaps, because his marriage has granted him an intimacy that approaches the boundary of what is possible in ordinary life. In the final canto of his poem Shade addresses Sybil:

> And all the time, and all the time, my love,
> You too are there, beneath the word, above
> The syllable, to underscore and stress
> The vital rhythm. One heard a woman's dress
> Rustle in days of yore. I've often caught
> The sound and sense of your approaching thought.
> And all in you is youth, and you make new,
> By quoting them, old things I made for you. (*PF*, 68)

The kind of understanding Fyodor longs for in *The Gift*, but does not receive from his mother, sister, or lover, is given to Shade by his wife. Indeed, Sybil combines elements of all those readers. She shares his childhood (having grown up in the same town), his sex life, and most importantly, his life's central tragedy. In Sybil, in the good fortune of finding his mate in his own little Appalachian town, Shade is afforded an experience of intimacy that nearly bridges that chasm between himself and another.

But if the Shades function as an expression of Nabokov's fantasy of perfect understanding, Kinbote serves to negate it, to reveal its illusions. The Shades' marital bliss finds its antithesis in Kinbote's estrangement from his (perhaps invented) wife Disa. This estrangement persists even in Kinbote's dreams: He turns to speak to her but she is gone and "the notes reaching him through a succession of hands said that she was not available; that she

144

Suspicion on Trial

was inaugurating a fire; that she had married an American businessman; that she had become a character in a novel; that she was dead" (*PF*, 211–12). Kinbote cannot imagine catching another person's approaching thought; instead he rehearses again and again the terrifying inaccessibility of the other. The Disa theme, as Michael Glynn observes, "speaks obliquely but eloquently of the pain of exile"—banishment from the "paradise" (Disa lives in the villa "Paradisa") of home.[53] Kinbote's exile appears to bring to the surface the metaphysical plight that Shade's rootedness obscures. His status as an émigré and a stranger—which of course he shares with his author—painfully illuminates his apartness from other people and conditions his reading of Shade's poem.

AWAKE ONE DAY UTTERLY UNABLE TO READ

Pale Fire, like *The Kreutzer Sonata*, centers on an experience of art, the artwork named in each title, each an artwork that compels its spectator to confront the limits of his own subjectivity. Shade's poem resists Kinbote in the same way that Beethoven's sonata resists Pozdnyshev; the poem and sonata both testify to one's coexistence with other people whose inner lives are like one's own in depth and complexity, but to which one has limited access. While for Pozdnyshev this experience is joyful, revelatory, for Kinbote it is shattering. This divergence in their responses stems from the divergence in their afflictions. Tolstoy gives us a protagonist whose egoism is so thoroughgoing that he fails even to recognize the subjectivity of others. Other people are merely the means to his own pleasures. His aesthetic encounter offers relief from this egoism by assuring him that he does not live among shadows of his own desires. Nabokov's protagonist never doubts that other people possess inner lives full of pleasures and pain inaccessible to him. His habit of peeping into Shade's windows attests to this conviction. But for him this knowledge is a source of suffering. Pozdnyshev does not need to access the inner lives of others—he only needs to know they exist. Kinbote, in contrast, cannot abide our mutual inaccessibility for it means that other people cannot know his pain. There is an undeniable egoism to Kinbote's wish for others to partake of his inner life, but this desire for intimacy also lends his character a pathos that Pozdnyshev lacks. And it complicates how we understand his inability to arrest his interpretive impulse.

For Kinbote, the encounter with Shade's poem reveals the abyss between oneself and another that he subsequently attempts to span by means of his hermeneutic exertions. Kinbote intimates his intention already in his foreword, suggesting that to appreciate Shade's poem one must look below the surface of his text. The final third of Shade's poem, he explains

Chapter Four

is extremely rough in appearance, teeming with devastating erasures and cataclysmic insertions, and does not follow the lines of the card as rigidly as the Fair Copy does. Actually, it turns out to be beautifully accurate when you once make the plunge and compel yourself to open your eyes in the limpid depths under its confused surface. It contains not one gappy line, not one doubtful reading. This fact would be sufficient to show that the imputations made (on July 24, 1959) in a newspaper interview with one of our professed Shadeans—who affirmed *without having seen the manuscript of the poem* that it "consists of disjointed drafts none of which yields a definite text"—is a malicious invention on the part of those who would wish not so much to deplore the state in which a great poet's work was interrupted by death as to asperse the competence, and perhaps honesty, of its present editor and commentator. (*PF*, 14)

Kinbote is ostensibly describing the discrepancy between the tangle of writing on the page and the poetic text that ultimately emerges. But he is also prefiguring the mode of reading he will undertake in his commentary. James Morrison proposes that what we take to be the "mistakes" of Nabokov's unreliable narrators—slips that clue readers in to their untrustworthiness—might in fact be "self-conscious strategies" deployed by them to tell their tales.[54] The charged language Kinbote uses to characterize Shade's draft—"devastating," "cataclysmic"—could be read as inadvertently exposing Kinbote's emotional disturbance and unreliability, which is further intimated by the divergence between him and his colleagues in their critical assessments of Shade's poem. At the same time, this "mistake" might not be a mistake at all, but Kinbote's way of revealing both his disappointment with Shade's poem and how he intends to overcome it. To see the text's wholeness rather than its gaps—to look past the devastating "erasure" of the Zembla theme—Kinbote will plunge below the text's "confused surface" and look upon its limpid depths. He will look beneath the poem's evident meaning for traces of his Zembla.

Readers of *Pale Fire* have long debated the motives that shape Kinbote's reading and his commentary. Pekka Tammi puts it simply: "Why would Kinbote as a narrator do all this?"[55] Insanity cannot be the answer, Tammi argues. It is "a bit facile to dismiss the narrative designs that [Kinbote] brings about as nothing but a madman's fancy."[56] Tammi observes that Shade tips us off that Kinbote's invention is not madness—"that is the wrong word," Shade says—but an artistic response to the pain of drab reality (*PF*, 238). But Kinbote offers us a still more substantial clue about the stakes of finding Zembla in Shade's poem, which are greater than Shade imagines. For Kinbote, finding Zembla means restoring his faith in the communicative promise of poetic language.

146

Suspicion on Trial

In the foreword, having subtly revealed his interpretive strategy, Kinbote, at the end of the next paragraph, sends his reader to "see [his] note to line 991" (*PF*, 15). This note is the only note that appears in Kinbote's foreword, and it is likewise marked by the fact that it is uninterrupted by directions to see other notes. Kinbote underscores its significance by refraining from his usual digressions and giving the reader a chance to read this particular note in full before going on to read the rest of the novel. The note refers to one of the last lines of Shade's poem: "Somewhere horseshoes are being tossed. Click, Clunk" (*PF*, 69). Kinbote comments:

> Neither Shade nor I had ever been able to ascertain whence precisely those ringing sounds came . . . but the tantalizing tingles and jingles contributed a pleasant melancholy note to the rest of Dulwich Hill's evening sonorities—children calling to each other, children being called home, and the ecstatic barking of the boxer dog whom most of the neighbors disliked (he overturned garbage cans) greeting his master home. (*PF*, 287)

First-time readers will not know what transpired between the evening described in the note and the moment Kinbote composes his commentary, but they might nevertheless be struck by Kinbote's serenity on this melodious evening. It stands in sharp contrast with the aggrieved, anxious narrator we meet in the foreword, who accuses his former university colleagues—"professed Shadeans"—of aspersions on his competence and honesty. Second-time readers will know that this moment of spiritual calm precedes Shade's death and Kinbote's reading of his poem. In this moment Kinbote experiences a spiritual tranquility that serves as a counterpoint to the despair he experienced on the night at the Goldsworth castle when he declared, "Solitude is the playfield of Satan" (*PF*, 95). On that night, oppressed by his isolation, Kinbote mistook the neighbor's dog for a "bloodthirsty prowler" (*PF*, 96). Now, the same hound's ecstasy at "greeting his master" intimates the presence of God.

Kinbote's spiritual height on this last evening with Shade is associated with both a faith in God and a faith in language. The sounds of indifferent nature during that lonely night at Goldsworth's—"Stealthy rustles, the footsteps of yesteryear leaves, an idle breeze . . . the sounds of new life in the trees cruelly mimicking the cracklings of old death in my brain" (*PF*, 96)—are replaced by human voices: "children calling to each other, children being called home." The image of children being summoned—especially in conjunction with the dog "greeting his master"—brings to mind a comprehending, benevolent Creator who will eventually summon his creations. But the children's calls to each other are no less important. They evoke the possibility of communion not only with God but also with other people. Kinbote's

Chapter Four

explicit exaltation of language further down in the note underscores the significance of this human community:

> We are absurdly accustomed to the miracle of a few written signs being able to contain immortal imagery, involutions of thought, new worlds with live people, speaking, weeping, laughing. We take it for granted so simply that in a sense, by the very act of brutish routine acceptance, we undo the work of the ages, the history of the gradual elaboration of poetical description and construction, from the treeman to Browning, from the caveman to Keats. What if we awake one day, all of us, and find ourselves utterly unable to read? I wish you to gasp not only at what you read but at the miracle of its being readable (so I used to tell my students) . . . [F]or a moment I found myself enriched with an indescribable amazement as if informed that fireflies were making decodable signals on behalf of stranded spirits, or that a bat was writing a legible tale of torture in the bruised and branded sky. (*PF*, 289)

Kinbote's ecstasy has to do with his belief in our capacity to speak to and to hear other people, to receive their communications, to follow their "involutions of thought." But even amid this exaltation there is a note of dread: "What if we awake one day, all of us, and find ourselves utterly unable to read?" Kinbote cannot wholly suppress his skeptical fear: What if we are wrong to believe we can express ourselves to one another?

Kinbote experiences precisely this dreadful awakening upon reading Shade's poem. We come to know Kinbote first as a commentator, but in the fabula of the novel his first actions are those of an artist: he has been telling Shade the fantastic story of Zembla's fugitive king—that is, himself. On this peaceful evening, Kinbote learns that the poet has completed his poem and takes this to mean that he, Kinbote, has successfully imparted his story to Shade—that he has successfully bridged the divide between self and other. The poem, in expressing (as Kinbote assumes it will) his own joys and sorrows, promises to both refute his skeptical doubt and affirm his skill as an artist. Kinbote's exaltation of the power of language in note 991 has as much to do with the celebration of his own achievement as Shade's. In the note that follows, Kinbote recalls the "agony" of seeing that "the complex contribution I had been pressing upon [Shade] with a hypnotist's patience and a lover's urge was simply not there" (*PF*, 296). The disappointment he experiences upon reading the poem is both metaphysical and artistic. Metaphysically, he again confronts the unbridgeable gap between one mind and another. Artistically, he confronts the failure of his own creative act. His signs have not been decoded. His exiled spirit has not made itself legible or found a home on the page.

The Kinbote we meet in the foreword has suffered a crisis of faith in his

148

art, and in the ability of his art to collapse the distance between himself and others. His response to this crisis is not, however, despair. In what Nabokov, following Shklovsky, might have called a "knight's move,"[57] an askew escape from the dialectic of faith and doubt, Kinbote turns his skeptical disposition against itself, deploying suspicious reading not as a means to reveal what is hidden but as a means to obscure what is obvious. Kinbote reads below the surface of Shade's poem—the surface that attests to his artistic failure and the distance between himself and the poet—to find evidence of his own genius, evidence of his and Shade's closeness: in short, evidence of Zembla. His suspicion promises paradoxically to affirm his faith in language and in his own capacity to wield it. Kinbote's dubious commentary, with its retelling of his Zemblan tale, is the testament to his revived artistic convictions. Having failed once before to tell his story, he now retells it with far greater artistry, weaving into it the text of Shade's poem and the story of Shade's death.

Kinbote's interpretive mode, as other readers have noted, appears congenial to Shade and Nabokov both. Alexandrov observes that "given the central importance [Shade] ascribes to patterning and coincidence in his life and art, it is certainly possible to infer that he may have recognized in Kinbote's seemingly fantastic story a corollary to his own."[58] Indeed, Nabokov's novel itself appears to authorize Kinbote's reading by offering parallels between poem and commentary that are invisible to Kinbote. For Alexandrov, these parallels serve as evidence of Nabokov's faith in a cosmic design beyond human comprehension. For Boyd, they complicate the ontology of *Pale Fire* and suggest that Hazel and John Shade author Kinbote's commentary from beyond the grave.[59] But putting metaphysics aside, one might simply say that by authorizing Kinbote's mode of reading, Shade and Nabokov partake of his mad faith in art.

THE PASSWORD IS HARMONY

Now we turn to the central irony of the novel. In his wish to affirm our capacity to commune with others, Kinbote ends up obscuring everyone but himself. It is hard not to recognize *Pale Fire* as a parody of academic editions, including perhaps Nabokov's own translation and commentary of *Eugene Onegin*. But Nabokov is not after laughs alone. *Pale Fire* illuminates the human pathos behind such endeavors. It recapitulates in fictional form the struggle manifested perhaps most vividly in Tolstoy's series of calendars of daily wisdom, and especially *The Circle of Reading*: the struggle between the desire to listen and the desire to speak. No reader could miss the fact that Kinbote eclipses Shade with his text; what is less immediately evident is that Kinbote begins from a sincere desire to hear the words of the poet. As

Chapter Four

with Tolstoy, though, this imperative to listen is imperiled and finally overwhelmed by the still stronger urge to speak. Kinbote's evolving relationship to Shade's poetry mimics Tolstoy's evolving relationship to the words of the wise men he admired. Both begin by translating, transcribing, and commenting, but end up reinterpreting, contesting, and replacing.

The emergence of Kinbote's voice and its gradual envelopment of Shade's is visible in the book's very form, the bracketing of the poem by Kinbote's reflections. But it is evident also in the content of Kinbote's notes, which show the steady amplification of Kinbote's desire to speak. As he tells us in the foreword, Kinbote had once attempted to translate Shade's poems. "My admiration for him was for me a sort of alpine cure," he explains (*PF*, 27). Expressing his wonder at what must be a "brain of a different brand than that of the synthetic jellies preserved in the skulls around him," Kinbote wishes to follow the course of Shade's thought:

> I am looking at him. I am witnessing a unique physiological phenomenon: John Shade perceiving and transforming the world, taking it in and taking it apart, re-combining its elements in the very process of storing them up so as to produce at some unspecified date an organic miracle, a fusion of image and music, a line of verse. And I experienced the same thrill as when in my early boyhood I once watched across the tea table in my uncle's castle a conjurer who had just given a fantastic performance and was now quietly consuming a vanilla ice . . . Shade's poem is, indeed, that sudden flourish of magic: my gray-haired friend, my beloved old conjurer, put a pack of index cards into his hat—and shook out a poem. (*PF*, 27–28)

The description of Kinbote's spectating echoes Nabokov's description of the exemplary spectator in his essay "Good Readers and Good Writers" (c. 1947/8). Conceiving of his relationship with Shade as an "alpine cure," Kinbote reprises Nabokov's use of mountain climbing as a metaphor for reading. "Up a trackless slope climbs the master artist," Nabokov writes in his essay, "and at the top, on a windy ridge, whom do you think he meets? The panting and happy reader."[60] And as in the essay, Kinbote compares the artist and the magician, and knows to attend not only to the conjuring trick but also to the conjurer who pulls it off. Kinbote's initial orientation toward the artwork and the artist is, by Nabokov's own lights, the proper one.

The progressive nature of Kinbote's ascendance as the major creative force in the book is crucial, of course, both to Nabokov's formal conceit and to Kinbote's own stratagem for retelling his Zemblan tale. At the same time, Nabokov's text suggests that Kinbote's propensity to speak over and against others is not entirely voluntary. It is a compulsion that he attempts to reign in but cannot. Kinbote offers us two interpolated conversations with Shade

Suspicion on Trial

that demonstrate this dynamic. The first exchange is preceded by Kinbote's apologies to his reader: "[Shade's] and my reader will, I trust, excuse me for breaking the orderly course of these comments and letting my illustrious friend speak for himself" (*PF*, 155). Kinbote endeavors to give Shade a voice by transcribing Shade's thoughts on literary reviews, Shakespeare, and teaching literature. Shade admits that he never responds to either praise or reproach in reviews: "I have never bothered to lean out of my window and empty my skoramis on some poor hack's pate" (*PF*, 155). He expresses his admiration for the Bard and explains his pedagogical method of "train[ing] the freshman to shiver, to get drunk on the poetry of *Hamlet* or *Lear*" (*PF*, 155). He speaks bitterly of bad readers, Freudians and Marxists first among them. As readers, we cannot know whether Kinbote has indeed faithfully transcribed an exchange with Shade or invented it in retrospect. What is clear, however, is that the voice that ostensibly belongs to Shade is distinct from Kinbote's own. It is not defensive or anxious, but rather calm and confident, more likely resembling the voice of Nabokov himself than his narrator. In other words, Kinbote *does* attempt to let Shade speak for himself, either by transcribing his words or by imagining what the poet would say on the subject of art. Real or invented, this episode attests to Kinbote's desire to inhabit a perspective other than his own.

The second conversation Kinbote includes in his commentary also demonstrates his wish to be attentive to Shade's thought. But the subtle difference in the way Kinbote presents this conversation in his text suggests a progressive failure to restrain his own voice. In the first conversation, Kinbote casts himself in the role of an unobtrusive interviewer who draws Shade out on various subjects:

> "When I hear a critic speaking of an author's sincerity I know that either the critic or the author is a fool." Kinbote: "But I am told this manner of thinking is taught in high school?" "That's where the broom should begin to sweep. A child should have thirty specialists to teach him thirty subjects, and not one harassed schoolmarm . . ." Kinbote: "Yes. I agree." (*PF*, 156)

Shade—echoing Nabokov's polemic with Tolstoy—disparages the exaltation of sincerity and simplicity, and Kinbote nods along in agreement. In the second conversation, the poet's voice is no less forceful or distinct. But Kinbote is no longer primarily a listener: he is an equal partner in the debate, as is evident from the formal dialogic form Kinbote gives his second conversation with the poet:

> SHADE: All the seven deadly sins are peccadilloes but without three of them, Pride, Lust and Sloth, poetry might never have been born.

151

Chapter Four

. . .

KINBOTE: Tut-tut. Do you also deny that there are sins?

SHADE: I can name only two: murder, and the deliberate infliction of pain.

KINBOTE: Then a man spending his life in absolute solitude could not be a sinner?

SHADE: He could torture animals. He could poison the springs on his island. He could denounce an innocent man in a posthumous manifesto.

KINBOTE: And so the password is—?

SHADE: Pity.

KINBOTE: But who instilled it in us, John? Who is the Judge of life, and the Designer of death? (*PF*, 224–25)

Kinbote here probes and contests Shade's convictions. He rejects Shade's agnosticism and makes a case for faith. He concludes the dialogue not with a statement from Shade but with his own argument for belief in God. Our narrator entertains Shade's perspective, but ultimately gives himself the final word.

Kinbote is not unaware of the cruelty of his self-absorption, the implacability of his desire to speak. His contrition about interrupting Shade's attempt to speak about Hazel with an episode from the history of Onhava University evinces his awareness that communicating his own inner life comes at the expense of being receptive to others. Writing his regretful note, Kinbote feels once again the urge to eclipse Shade and Hazel's story with his own: "That episode took place in the year of grace 1876" (*PF*, 187). This time he tries to restrain himself: "But to return to Hazel Shade" (*PF*, 187). He even attempts to make amends of sorts by including in his commentary the story of Hazel's trip to the haunted barn and her encounter with a spirit there. Kinbote transcribes Hazel's *Remarks*—notes from the visit, which include the spirit's encoded warning to her father about his impending death: "pada ata lane pad not ogo old wart alan ther tale feur far rant lant tal told" (*PF*, 188). Nabokov, according to Boyd, "noted privately" that this message warns Shade: "*Padre* should *not go* to the *lane* to be mistaken for *old Godswart* (worth) after finishing his *tale* (pale) *feur* (fire)."[61] Kinbote claims that he cannot make sense of the message, try as he might. Hazel's text thus resists Kinbote's dissection and recombination, and in this way her voice is granted a form of independence within the narrative. It cannot completely be assimilated into Kinbote's art, or, for that matter, into her father's.

It is possible that Kinbote has simply invented Hazel's *Remarks* along with the warning. (Of course, in a more global sense, this possibility haunts our attempts to say anything at all about the putative events of the novel.) This supposed transcription, after all, is immediately followed by an imaginative rendering of a third trip to the barn, a trip all three Shades make together, which Kinbote admits including for the sake of harmony. "There are always 'three nights' in fairy tales, and in this sad fairy tale there was a third one too," Kinbote says. "The minutes of that third session in the barn have not been preserved but I offer the reader the following scene which I feel cannot be too far removed from the truth" (*PF*, 190). But, just as in the case of his conversations with Shade, even if Kinbote invented Hazel's remarks and feigns ignorance of a message he himself devised, the inclusion of this text attests nevertheless to his desire to imagine himself into Hazel's inner life and differentiate her voice from his own. Hazel, as Michael Wood observes, "is Kinbote's rival in the poem, taking up what he thinks is his space."[62] This makes the presence of her *Remarks* in his own commentary all the more significant. Whether transcribed or invented, their inclusion suggests a capacity for empathy that is overlooked by readers like Rorty, who stress Kinbote's "remorseless pursuit" of the ecstasies of creative expression.[63] Kinbote may be incapable of seeing much beyond himself, but this incapability is tinged with regret.

Kinbote's awareness of the cruelty of his self-absorption and drive for self-expression is rendered vividly in his dreams of Disa. The queen he betrays with other lovers and eventually abandons becomes a repository for his exquisite guilt. In a note following shortly after the extended note on Hazel, Kinbote explains that though in waking life he was "casual and heartless," in his dreams of Disa he "made extraordinary amends" (*PF*, 209). Shade's "password"—his chief ethical principle—might be pity, but Kinbote's is harmony. "Harmony, indeed, was the reign's password," Kinbote tells us in an early note on the rule of Charles Xavier, the Zemblan king (*PF*, 75). Kinbote cannot be as receptive to others as he might wish—the pang of pity eludes him much of the time—but he can perhaps atone through the harmonies of his imagination.

Kinbote's desire to make amends through art complicates Rorty's opposition of Nabokov's "implausible moral philosophy" and his psychologically convincing literary fiction.[64] Nabokov's genius-monsters do not entirely refute the possibility of a "synthesis of ecstasy and kindness";[65] the fruits of creative ecstasy might, after all, offer some compensation for their initial inattentiveness to others. "It is one of the novel's central ironies," writes Dana Dragunoiu, "that Hazel gets a 'richly rhymed life'—replete with poltergeists and messages from the beyond—in a madman's commentary rather than in her father's poem."[66] Dragunoiu argues that for all his flaws "Kinbote's special brand of misreading is ultimately a gesture of courtesy and a declaration of love. His unreliable vision does what love is said to attain without effort and what courtesy attains with a great deal of it: namely, it makes the ugly beautiful."[67] Kinbote's intricate harmonies ennoble and immortalize Hazel's life in a way that Shade's pity cannot.

Chapter Four

It is hard to regret that Kinbote fails to quiet his own voice. Tolstoy, to our good fortune, failed there, too. Both Tolstoy and Nabokov recognize that creative work entails a certain sacrifice of one's own receptivity, but they diverge on the question of whether this sacrifice is worth making. In his lecture on Tolstoy's *The Death of Ivan Ilyich*, Nabokov acknowledges the struggle between "interest directed within oneself toward one's own inner life of vigorous thought and interest directed outward, toward the external world of people and tangible values."[68] But he objects to the way Tolstoy resolves this struggle by making inward-directed attention a sin; without this supposed sin, he thought, art would be impossible. Toker argues that Nabokov's literary works are "unified" by "the imperative need for reconciling human commitment with aesthetic or metaphysical pursuit."[69] The struggle between the urge to listen and the urge to speak is never resolved for him, but it becomes a source of creativity.

To the extent that Kinbote's suspicion enables him to sustain faith in his own art—faith that allows him to write down and present us with his marvelous "commentary"—one cannot condemn it either. It is illuminating to consider Nabokov's rendering of Kinbote alongside his earlier madmen Pozdnyshev and Humbert. *Pale Fire* and *Lolita* are, as Priscilla Meyer says, "explicitly paired works," but their similarities are meant "to emphasize the differences."[70] I have sought to draw out a key difference in the way Nabokov configures the relationships between reader, narrator-protagonist, and author. *Pale Fire* departs from the arrangement Nabokov established in "Pozdnyshev's Address" and used most potently in *Lolita*: an arrangement where the author and the reader stand in moral (and aesthetic) judgment of the narrator-protagonist. Here, the authoring consciousness of the novel appears to sanction Kinbote's faith in art and his means of sustaining it. We begin by suspecting Kinbote but end by suspecting with him.

Afterword

The Artful and the Artless

TOLSTOY, STRUGGLING WITH a new composition, explained that he could not proceed because he lacked "the energy of delusion necessary for all worldly work."[1] This evocative phrase—"the energy of delusion"—inspired the Formalist critics Boris Eikhenbaum and Viktor Shklovsky, who saw it as a key to understanding Tolstoy's creative drive. For Eikhenbaum the energy of delusion meant the author's sense of his world-historical purpose, for Shklovsky "a search for truth in the novel."[2] But Tolstoy's observation does not pertain to artmaking alone: he notes that *all* our endeavors require the energy of delusion.

That includes reading. Reading demands a faith in the communicative powers of language, in our ability to access another consciousness by way of the literary text. Not all readers are skeptics, so not all readers require such faith. But those who are, who do, cannot always summon that faith at will. Readers, too, can lack "the energy of delusion." For these readers, I have argued, Tolstoy and Nabokov sought to create artworks that might supply the delusion for them.

In their reckoning with skepticism, Tolstoy and Nabokov cover much of the same terrain. One might say they both tell the same story again and again: an introspective individual keenly attentive to his own impressions learns at last to recognize another's pain—or else, calamitously, fails to do so, and leaves that recognition to the reader. Yet in their mature works, this shared content takes radically different forms: Tolstoy's search for simplicity, Nabokov's flight into ever-ramifying complexity. Each not only picks his path but scorns the other one: narrative convolution appalls Tolstoy as much as simplicity does Nabokov. What are the implications of this divergence? How can such similar aims result in such diametrically opposed styles? In closing I want to consider two mature works of these two writers, apotheoses of their late styles, to suggest that the limitations of these contrasting strategies, each shrewdly perceived by the other, may indicate two basic boundaries beyond which pain cannot be communicated on paper.

In fall 1909, a year before his death, Tolstoy composed a series of very

155

Afterword

short tales, which Nabokov later dismissed as "simple tales for the people, for peasants, for school children."[3] One of them is called "Songs in the Village." It appears to be little more than a sketch of peasant life, drawn from Tolstoy's own impressions. The narrator (Tolstoy himself) relates a morning in Yasnaya Polyana on which he witnessed the peasants bidding farewell to young army recruits from their village. Throughout the narrative, Tolstoy attends mostly to sounds and sights, to the pleasures of the music and the beauty of the young villagers, whom he describes in some detail. Finally his gaze falls on a tall, spirited young man: " 'What a fine fellow,' I thought. 'This one will surely be assigned to some post in the guards.' "[4] Standing nearby is an old peasant whom Tolstoy does not at first recognize, Prokofii, a hard worker struck down time and again by various misfortunes. Tolstoy asks him who the young man is, but the peasant does not hear Tolstoy's question. When he repeats it, Prokofii mumbles something and turns away. Tolstoy persists:

> "I say: whose boy is that?"—I asked again and looked back at Prokofii.
> Prokofii's face crumpled, his cheeks quivered.
> "He's mine," he managed to say, and turning away from me and covering his face with his hand, he sobbed like a child.
> And only now, after these two words of Prokofii's, "he's mine," I felt not with reason alone but with my whole being the full horror of what was happening before me on that, for me, memorable, misty morning. All the disjointed, incomprehensible, strange things I saw—all suddenly took on for me a simple, clear, and horrible significance. I felt piercing shame at having looked upon this as an interesting spectacle. I stopped and, with the recognition of my dishonorable action, returned home.[5]

The story ends here, with Tolstoy's horror at his own voyeurism and complicity in a social order that steals children from their parents and sends them to war. The moral lesson is clear. But there is an aesthetic lesson here, too. Tolstoy suggests that the pain of a (possibly permanent) separation of parent and child is best communicated not with the many words Tolstoy has spent drawing this vivid scene, but by Prokofii's simple phrase: He's mine. "If you wish to say something," Tolstoy once wrote in his diary, "say it directly."[6]

Nabokov's short story "The Vane Sisters" (1958) is anything but simple. On "a compunctious Sunday after a week of blizzards," the narrator, a Frenchman and instructor of French literature, takes a stroll through the streets of his town (619).[7] He is particularly taken with the "brilliant icicles drip-dripping from the eaves of a frame house" (619). After some wandering, he observes that "the lean ghost, the elongated umbra cast by a parking

The Artful and the Artless

meter upon some damp snow, had a strange ruddy tinge" (620). It is then that he runs into his former acquaintance, D., and learns of the recent death of Cynthia Vane. Cynthia's younger sister, Sybil Vane, had been the narrator's student and had died by suicide after a failed love affair with D. Despite his mild fascination with Cynthia, the narrator recalls in a detached and mocking way their brief friendship after Sybil's death. He disdains Cynthia's vulgar friends and metaphysical notions, her theory that "her existence was influenced by all sorts of dead friends each of whom took turns in directing her fate" (624). Following his meeting with D., the narrator fears an encounter with Cynthia's ghost, which, as he notes by way of conclusion, fails to take place:

> I could isolate, consciously, little. Everything seemed blurred, yellow-clouded, yielding nothing tangible. Her inept acrostics, maudlin evasions, theopathies—every recollection formed ripples of mysterious meaning. Everything seemed yellowly blurred, illusive, lost. (631)

But these final lines of the story contain a hidden acrostic that indicates the narrator's mistake. Nabokov had to spell it out for *New Yorker* editor Katherine White, who (along with many others) missed it: "ICICLES BY CYNTHIA. METER FROM ME, SYBIL." In this hidden message, the Vane sisters claim credit for creating the lovely evening the narrator enjoyed the day before—the icicles, the ruddy parking meter. The narrator *had* encountered their ghosts after all. As Nabokov puts it, the sisters gave him "this gift of an iridescent day."[8] Nabokov was pained by White's rejection, but by no means did he deem the story a failure. On the contrary, he extoled its virtuosity: "My difficulty was to smuggle in the acrostic without the narrator's being aware that it was there, inspired to him by the phantoms," Nabokov explained. "Nothing of this kind has ever been attempted by any author."[9]

"Songs in the Village" demonstrates the culmination of Tolstoy's drive toward simplicity; "The Vane Sisters" marks the outer limit of Nabokov's narrative pyrotechnics. Yet the central drama of these radically dissimilar stories is one and the same. A keen-eyed spectator, capable of estranging habitual perceptions to see the world afresh, fails (at least at first) to grasp what is most important: another person's pain. Cynthia Vane rebukes Nabokov's narrator for this failure after he has artfully skewered her friends. One of these ridiculed friends had heroically rescued two people from drowning. Another friend, whom the narrator describes as the "the romping and screeching Joan Winter," has a child who is going blind (629). Each story ends with the recognition of pathos that had previously gone unnoticed. In Tolstoy, this recognition takes place within the narrative itself, and the nar-

157

Afterword

rator partakes in it. In Nabokov, it takes place only at the level of form, and only the (extremely adept or else tipped-off) reader partakes in it; the narrator persists in his blindness.

Why render this same predicament in such dissimilar ways—and why, moreover, condemn the other way of doing it? As this study has shown, Tolstoy first pursued other strategies for encouraging readerly receptivity, but in the end found artistic "simplicity" to be the best means of cultivating receptivity in the reader. A simple artwork—like Prokofii's simple phrase—is the way to draw readers out of themselves and alert them to the suffering of others. Tolstoy distrusted stylistic excess. "When people speak extravagantly, cleverly and floridly, they either wish to deceive you or to boast," he writes in *The Circle of Reading.* "One should not trust such people, should not imitate them. Good speeches are simple, understandable to all, and sensible."[10] For Tolstoy, rich prose and elaborate forms put the author's own virtuosity at the center of the work. The suffering that must be noticed and the reader who must notice it are always joined, in such works, by the author's ego, which distorts the process of recognition because it puts the reader on guard: he is being manipulated. In self-defense, the reader's gaze turns inward, toward his own agency or lack thereof, rather than outward, as the artist wants it to (or, at least, as Tolstoy wanted artists to want it to). To create an artwork capable of puncturing our self-absorption, Tolstoy thus strips away anything that might distract or divert us, anything that might earn our wariness or even our awe.

To Nabokov, nothing could be more suspicious than Tolstoy's putative simplicity. "Tolstoy's style is a marvelously complicated, ponderous instrument," he told his students at Cornell. In fact, "No major writer is simple. The *Saturday Evening Post* is simple. Journalese is simple. Upton Lewis is simple. Mom is simple. Digests are simple. Damnation is simple. But Tolstoys and Melvilles are not simple."[11] In a lecture at Stanford, Nabokov seems to go even further—to suggest that simplicity is always illusory and that the pursuit of it is bound to fail: "A writer knows that there are no objective words for describing an objective world. Neither of the two exist. You may reduce subject and style to their simplest combination and still not arrive at forming a standard sentence containing the truth and only the truth—that is, a truth that you cannot demolish or deepen."[12] What irks Nabokov is the pretense of a naive faith in the transparency of language, in the tidy alignment of word and world; and it irks him most of all in the case of Tolstoy, who recognized better than anyone the failures of our communicative gestures and made such failures central to his art. Tolstoy's insistence at the end of his life that the simplest syntax can convey our deepest verities therefore strikes Nabokov as a betrayal not only of Tolstoy's talent but also of the skeptical anxieties and insights the two authors shared. Tolstoy seems to be

The Artful and the Artless

shucking off the burden the two of them had borne together: no wonder Nabokov took Tolstoy's late simplicity, or feigned simplicity, so personally.

These two conjoint indictments—of egocentric artfulness on one side and affected artlessness on the other—point to the limitations of these two artistic strategies, which when taken to their extreme induce again the very distrust they are designed to dispel. In some ways the reception of Tolstoy's late work proves Nabokov's point and the reception of Nabokov's work proves Tolstoy's. If Tolstoy really wanted to bind his own virtuosity and banish his own ego, what do we make of readers like the Symbolist poet Alexander Blok who acclaimed his simple stories as "ingenious"?[13] If Nabokov's extravagance was really in the service of the sentiment he wished to convey, and not what Tolstoy might call boastfulness, what do we make of the proliferation of books and articles that attend less to the sentiment conveyed than to the wizardry of the author who conveyed it? Are these failures of reading or writing? Perhaps we have simply come up against the outer limit of a writer's ability to avoid a reader's suspicion, to anticipate it, to outwit it. These two authors set out to find some formal means of creating the sense that in reading we are accessing another mind. To create that sense, each had to subdue the reader's suspicion that they are being manipulated, which Nabokov did by absurdly heightening the degree of manipulation and subsuming it into the work, and Tolstoy did by trying to eliminate manipulation altogether. These techniques enjoyed striking success and have had a rich literary afterlife. But here, at their extremes, we see their limits. The skeptic who seeks perfect communion with another mind will always be disappointed; so, too, readers with novels.

~

Though he did not respond to Tolstoy's simple tales, Nabokov found in Tolstoy's great novels precisely the sense that he had encountered a consciousness other than his own. Nabokov celebrates this achievement in his 1928 poem "Tolstoy," written for the centenary celebration of Tolstoy's birth. Against the background of politicized efforts by Reds and Whites alike to monumentalize the author of the Russian national epic, the twenty-nine-year-old Nabokov evokes a human-sized Tolstoy, a Tolstoy whom, "with a feeling that he is our equal," we might address "by name and patronymic."[14] At first the poem's speaker laments that Tolstoy's life, unlike Pushkin's, has not turned into "legend." He blames "insidious technology"—the phonograph that "still preserves the cadence of his voice," the "archive of ancient films" in which Tolstoy appears "a nondescript old man of modest stature."[15] These things deprive the author's life of mystery and create only a false sense of closeness:

Afterword

> Yet there remains
> one thing we simply cannot reconstruct,
> no matter how we poke, armed with our notepads,
> just like reporters at a fire, around
> his soul.[16]

The deceptiveness of these documentary traces is then implicitly contrasted with the feeling of proximity generated by Tolstoy's own works:

> The people he created, thousands of them,
> transpire incredibly through our own life,
> lend color to the distance of recall—
> as though we actually lived beside them.[17]

Our sense of intimacy with Tolstoy's creatures extends to their creator himself. The poem concludes by underscoring the ultimate impenetrability of the great author, who, like Pushkin, took his secrets with him when he died. Yet it is joyful. Tolstoy's art has brought Nabokov as far as art can, to the brink of the knowledge he wants—knowledge of another's soul.

Notes

INTRODUCTION

1. "zarazhenie"; "[zritel'] sam ne delaet usiliia, a predostavliaet khudozhniku zavladet' soboi." Leo Tolstoy, "O tom, chto nazyvaiut iskusstvom" ["About What Is Called Art"], *PSS*, 30:252. When possible, I avoid gendered pronouns; otherwise, I default to whichever pronoun makes the most sense in context.

2. Vladimir Nabokov, "Good Readers and Good Writers," in *Lectures on Literature*, ed. Fredson Bowers (New York: Harcourt Brace Jovanovich, 1980), 3.

3. Leo Tolstoy, "Alyosha Gorshok," in *Tolstoy's Short Fiction*, ed. and trans. Michael R. Katz (New York: W. W. Norton, 2008), 284; Tolstoy, "Alyosha Gorshok," *PSS*, 36:58.

4. Nabokov, "The Death of Ivan Ilyich," in *Lectures on Russian Literature*, ed. Fredson Bowers (Orlando: Mariner Books, 2002), 238.

5. Mary McCarthy, "Bolt from the Blue: *Pale Fire* by Vladimir Nabokov," *New Republic*, June 4, 1962, https://newrepublic.com/article/63440/bolt-the-blue.

6. Nabokov, "Anna Karenina," *Lectures on Russian Literature*, 137.

7. "Dekart otvergaet vsyo sil'no, verno, i vnov' vozdvigaet proizvol'no, mechtatel'no. Spinoza delaet to zhe. Kant to zhe. Shopengauer to zhe." Tolstoy, *Dnevniki i zapisnye knizhki 1858–1880* [*Diaries and Notebooks 1858–1880*], *PSS*, 48:118.

8. Richard Popkin, "The High Road to Pyrrhonism," *American Philosophical Quarterly* 2, no. 1 (Jan. 1965): 18.

9. Popkin, "High Road to Pyrrhonism," 18.

10. Richard H. Popkin and Avrum Stroll, *Skeptical Philosophy for Everyone* (Princeton, NJ: Prometheus, 2001), 70.

11. René Descartes, *The Philosophical Writings of Descartes: Volume 2*, trans. John Cottingham, Robert Stoothoff, and Dugald Murdoch (Cambridge: Cambridge University Press, 1985), 275.

12. Arthur Schopenhauer, *The World as Will and Representation: In Two Volumes* (New York: Dover Publications, 1966), 1:104.

Notes to Pages 6–9

13. Schopenhauer, *World as Will*, 1:104.

14. Schopenhauer, *World as Will*, 1:104.

15. Ernst Michael Lange, "Wittgenstein on Solipsism," in *A Companion to Wittgenstein*, ed. Hans-Johann Glock and John Hyman (Chichester, England: Wiley-Blackwell, 2017): 165.

16. Ludwig Wittgenstein, *The Blue and Brown Books* (New York: Harper Torchbooks, 1965), 64.

17. Wittgenstein, "Notes for Lectures on 'Private Experience' and 'Sense Data,'" *Philosophical Review* 77, no. 3 (July 1968): 309.

18. Wittgenstein, *Blue and Brown Books*, 55.

19. Wittgenstein, *Blue and Brown Books*, 56.

20. Toril Moi invokes ordinary language philosophy, and Wittgenstein in particular, to dispel the idea that texts have a surface and a depth, which we might investigate through critique. This is a misleading picture of what we do as critics, she argues. We do not uncover anything but simply pay close attention to the features of a text and make sense of them in one way or another depending on what we find interesting, puzzling, and so on. Moi is certainly right that our picture of what a text *is* shapes how we relate to it. But she underestimates, I think, how hard it is for us to abandon these pictures. "Whether we write literary criticism to critique or to admire, to investigate or to explore, is up to us," Moi writes. This emphasis on choice does not acknowledge the difficulty of changing our notations. Moi, "'Nothing is Hidden': From Confusion to Clarity; or, Wittgenstein on Critique," in *Critique and Postcritique*, ed. Elizabeth S. Anker and Rita Felski (Durham, NC: Duke University Press, 2017), 47.

21. Wittgenstein, *Blue and Brown Books*, 57.

22. Wittgenstein, *Blue and Brown Books*, 57.

23. Wittgenstein, *Blue and Brown Books*, 57.

24. Wittgenstein, *Blue and Brown Books*, 57.

25. Stanley Cavell, *The Claim of Reason: Wittgenstein, Skepticism, Morality, and Tragedy* (Oxford: Oxford University Press, 1979), 45.

26. Cavell, *Claim of Reason*, 45.

27. Cavell, "Knowing and Acknowledging," in *Must We Mean What We Say?: A Book of Essays* (Cambridge: Cambridge University Press, 1976), 254.

28. Cavell, "Knowing and Acknowledging," 260.

29. Cavell, "Knowing and Acknowledging," 257.

30. Cavell, "Knowing and Acknowledging," 263.

31. Hannah Vandegrift Eldridge, *Lyric Orientations: Hölderlin, Rilke, and the Poetics of Community* (Ithaca, NY: Cornell University Press, 2016), 27.

32. Cavell, "Knowing and Acknowledging," 263.

33. Cavell, "Othello and the Stake of the Other," in *Disowning Knowledge: In Seven Plays of Shakespeare* (Cambridge: Cambridge University Press, 1987), 138.

Notes to Pages 9–13

34. Cavell, "Othello and the Stake of the Other," 138.

35. Cavell, "Othello and the Stake of the Other," 142. As Richard Eldridge and Bernard Rhie observe, for Cavell "skepticism is . . . an existential condition that is inevitably lived, whether destructively or productively." Cavell posits the possibility that through philosophical reflection we might inhabit this condition well. Eldridge and Rhie, *Stanley Cavell and Literary Studies: Consequences of Skepticism* (London: Bloomsbury Publishing, 2011), 1.

36. Nabokov, "Philistines and Philistinism," in *Lectures on Russian Literature*, 310.

37. Quoted in Viktor Shklovsky, "Art as Device," in *Theory of Prose*, trans. Benjamin Sher (Chicago: Dalkey Archive Press, 1991), 5; Tolstoy, *Dnevniki i zapisnye knizhki 1895–1899 [Diaries and Notebooks 1895–1899]*, *PSS*, 53:141–42.

38. Viktor Shklovsky, "Art as Device," 5; Viktor Shklovsky, "Iskusstvo, kak priem," in *O teorii prozy* (Moscow: Federatsiia, 1929), 13.

39. John E. Atwell, *Schopenhauer on the Character of the World: The Metaphysics of Will* (Berkeley: University of California Press, 1995), 96. Atwell quotes Schopenhauer, *World as Will and Representation*, 104.

40. In chapter 1 I discuss Tolstoy's paraphrase of Schopenhauer's reflections on theoretical egoism in *Anna Karenina*.

41. "(Kazalos' iasnee, kogda ia dumal.)" Tolstoy, *Dnevniki 1895–1899 [Diaries 1895–1899]*, *PSS*, 53:142.

42. Brian Boyd, *Vladimir Nabokov: The Russian Years* (Princeton, NJ: Princeton University Press, 1993), 262.

43. "Tret'ego dnia v noch' ia nocheval v Arzamase, i so mnoi bylo chto-to neobyknovennoe." Tolstoy to Sofia Tolstoy, September 4, 1869, *Pis'ma k S. A. Tolstoy 1862–1886 [Letters to S. A. Tolstoy, 1862–1886]*, *PSS*, 83:167.

44. "No vdrug na menia nashla toska, strakh, uzhas takie, kakikh ia nikogda ne ispytyval. Podrobnosti etogo chuvstva ia tebe rasskazhu vposledstvii; no podobnogo muchitel'nogo chuvstva ia nikogda ne ispytyval, i nikomu ne dai Bog ispytat'." Tolstoy to Sofia Tolstoy, September 4, 1869, *Pis'ma k S. A. Tolstoy*, *PSS*, 83:167.

45. Boris Eikhenbaum, "Commentary to 'Zapiski sumasshedshego,'" *PSS*, 26:853–54.

46. Aylmer Maud, "A Russian Philosopher," *Observer*, November 20, 1932, Proquest Historical Newspapers, 8.

47. Wittgenstein, "Notes for Lectures on 'Private Experience' and 'Sense Data,'" 309.

48. "Ia pokrichal, vsyo tikho. Nikto ne otkliknulsia." I altered the translation here to be more faithful to the original.

49. Henry Pickford, *Thinking with Tolstoy and Wittgenstein: Expression, Emotion, and Art* (Evanston, IL: Northwestern University Press, 2016), 36.

50. "[on] boialsia sumasshestviia, t. e. zhizni ne v obshchem vsem, a v svoem

163

Notes to Pages 13–17

osobennom mipe." Lev Shestov, "Otkroveniia smerti: Poslednie proizvedeniia L. N. Tolstogo" [*Revelations of Death: L. N. Tolstoy's Last Works*], *Sovremennye zapiski*, book 1(Paris, 1920), 84.

51. D. Barton Johnson, "'Terror': Pre-texts and Post-texts," in *A Small Alpine Form: Studies in Nabokov's Short Fiction*, ed. Charles Nicol and Gennady Barabtarlo (New York: Garland Publishing, 1993), 39–64.

52. Nabokov, "Terror," in *The Stories of Vladimir Nabokov* (New York: Vintage, 1996), 173–78; Nabokov, "Uzhas," in *Vladimir Nabokov: Sobranie sochinenii v chetyrekh tomakh* [*Collected Works in Four Volumes*] (Moscow: Pravda, 1990), 1:397–402.

53. Johnson, "Terror," 47, 48.

54. Explicit mention of Descartes appears only in Nabokov's English translation. In the Russian original Nabokov refers to the Cartesian method only obliquely: "ia iskal kakoi-nibud' tochki opory, iskhodnoi mysli, chtoby, nachav s nee, postroit' snova prostoi, estestvennyi, privychnyi mir, kotoryi my znaem."

55. "Zdes'—pouchitel'nost' i mudrost' rasskaza: besprichinnyi, misticheskii uzhas otstupaet pered prostym uzhasom chelovecheskogo goria, i ot strakha sobstvennoi smerti lechit smert' chuzhaia. V nashei strashnoi deistvitel'nosti misticheskii uzhas—kakaia-to roskosh'. I svoeobraznoi roskosh'iu takzhe iavliaetsia bezumie: ot nego ukhodish' kak v tesnyi egoizm, i ot drugikh, ot blizkikh, ot ostal'nogo mira zamykaet tebia sumasshestvie. V bezumie ne puskaiut real'naia beda i sostradanie. Bezumets povinen pered obshchestvennost'iu." Iulii Aikhenvald, "Literaturnyia zametki" ["Literary Notes"], *Rul'*, no. 1877, February 2, 1927, 2, https://dfg-viewer.de/show/?set%5Bmets%5D=https://content.staats bibliothek-berlin.de/zefys/SNP27230028-19270202-0-0-0-0.xml.

56. Shestov, "Otkroveniia smerti," 84.

57. Cavell, "The Avoidance of Love," in *Must We Mean What We Say?*, 267–353.

58. Paul Ricoeur, *Freud and Philosophy: An Essay on Interpretation*, trans. Denis Savage (New Haven, CT: Yale University Press, 1970).

59. Anker and Felski, *Critique and Postcritique*, 1.

60. Bruno Latour, "Why Has Critique Run Out of Steam? From Matters of Fact to Matters of Concern," *Critical Inquiry* 30, no. 2 (2004): 231.

61. Felski, *Limits of Critique* (Chicago: University of Chicago Press, 2015), 9.

62. Stephen Best and Sharon Marcus, "Surface Reading: An Introduction," *Representations* 108, no. 1 (2009): 9.

63. Ricoeur, *Freud and Philosophy*, 33.

64. See Plato, "Ion," in *The Dialogues of Plato: Ion, Hippias Minor, Laches, Protagoras*, trans. with commentary by R. E. Allen (New Haven, CT: Yale University Press, 1996), 9–22.

65. See, for example, Rita Felski's account of literary "enchantment" in *Uses of Literature* (Hoboken: John Wiley and Sons, 2008), 74. Felski suggests that proponents of critique exaggerate the danger of being swept up by our reading

Notes to Pages 18–20

and forget the pleasure of it—a pleasure that drew many of these same critics to literature in the first place. Amanda Anderson's nuanced treatment of "detachment" also proceeds from the presumption that detachment (as opposed to "partiality") must be cultivated. Anderson, *The Powers of Distance* (Princeton, NJ: Princeton University Press, 2001). Stephen Best and Sharon Marcus' rhetoric of "relinquishing," "embracing," and "deferring" to the text similarly associates critique with a willful resistance, and receptivity with yielding to our inclinations. Best and Marcus, "Surface Reading," 10.

66. Gabriel Josipovici, *On Trust: Art and the Temptations of Suspicion* (New Haven, CT: Yale University Press, 1999), 7.

67. Josipovici, *On Trust*, 21.

68. Josipovici, *On Trust*, 17.

69. Josipovici, *On Trust*, 17.

70. Eldridge and Rhie, *Stanley Cavell and Literary Studies*, 5.

71. Michael Fischer, *Stanley Cavell and Literary Skepticism* (Chicago: University of Chicago Press, 1989), 100.

72. Fischer, *Stanley Cavell and Literary Skepticism*, 101.

73. Michael Wood, *The Magician's Doubts* (Princeton, NJ: Princeton University Press, 1994), 19.

74. Roland Barthes, *The Pleasure of the Text*, trans. Richard Howard (New York: Macmillan, 1975), 27.

75. Anker and Felski, *Critique and Postcritique*, 9.

76. Felski, *Limits of Critique*, 36.

77. Felski, *Limits of Critique*, 42.

78. Zadie Smith, "Rereading Barthes and Nabokov," in *Changing My Mind: Occasional Essays* (New York: Penguin Books, 2010), 57.

79. Smith, "Rereading Barthes and Nabokov," 57.

80. Tyutchev's "Silentium!" (1830) famously declares, "A thought once uttered is untrue," and ironically commands the poet to silence. Tyutchev's meditation on the inadequacy of language to the task of poetic expression became, as Sofya Khagi observes, an "Ur-text" for Russian modernists. Khagi, *Silence and the Rest: Verbal Skepticism in Russian Poetry* (Evanston, IL: Northwestern University Press, 2013), 11. Though Tolstoy and Nabokov departed from Tyutchev in their skeptical outlooks, both authors greatly admired the poet. Nabokov alluded to "Silentium!" specifically in his own work. See Christine A. Rydel, "Nabokov and Tiutchev," in *Nabokov at Cornell*, ed. Gavriel Shapiro (Ithaca, NY: Cornell University Press, 2003); and Svetlana Pol'skaia, "Kommentarii k rasskazu V. Nabokova 'Oblako, ozero, bashnia,'" *Scando-Slavica* 39, no. 1 (1989): 111–23.

81. "Rabota mysli privodit k tshchete mysli. Vozvrashchat'sia k mysli ne nuzhno. Est' drugoe orudie—iskusstvo." Tolstoy, *Dnevniki 1858–1880*, PSS, 48:118.

82. "No chetvertaia stena neizvestnosti togo, chto delaetsia v dushakh drugikh liudei." Tolstoy, *Dnevniki [Diaries] 1895–1899*, PSS, 53:124.

165

Notes to Pages 20–25

83. "techenie i sut'." Nabokov, "Pamiati Iu. I. Aikhenval'da," *Rul'*, no. 2457, December 23, 1928, 4, http://zefys.staatsbibliothek-berlin.de/kalender/auswahl /date/1928-12-23/27230028. The above translation is mine. As I completed this manuscript, Brian Boyd and Anastasia Tolstoy published a translation of this essay in *Think, Write, Speak: Uncollected Essays, Reviews, Interviews, and Letters to the Editor*, ed. Brian Boyd and Anastasia Tolstoy (New York: Alfred A. Knopf, 2019), 82.

84. Tolstoy, *WIA*, 42; *PSS*, 30:60.

85. Nabokov, "A Commentary," in Alexander Pushkin, *Eugene Onegin: A Novel in Verse*, translated from the Russian with a commentary by Vladimir Nabokov, 4 vols. (New York: Bollinger Foundation, Random House Inc., 1964), 2:207.

86. Tolstoy, *WIA*, 152, 154; *PSS*, 30:149, 150.

87. Leona Toker, *Nabokov: The Mystery of Literary Structures* (Ithaca, NY: Cornell University Press, 1989), 3.

CHAPTER 1

1. Rancière makes a compelling case that the French Revolution ushered in a new aesthetic "regime" that no longer accepted a categorical distinction between the poetic and the prosaic. Of course, one might well see the erosion of this distinction as a more gradual process. Jacques Rancière, "Why Emma Bovary Had to Be Killed," *Critical Inquiry* 34, no. 2 (2008): 233–48.

2. "Odnim slovom, net, po-vidimomu, vozmozhnosti podvergat' somneniiu fakt, chto nashe esteticheskoe chuvstvo, podobno vsem drugim." Nikolay Chernyshevsky, *Esteticheskie otnosheniia iskusstva k deistvitel'nosti* [*Aesthetic Relations of Art to Reality*], in *Chernyshevskii N. G. Polnoe Sobranie sochinenii v 15 tomakh* [*Chernyshevsky N. G. Complete Collected Works in 15 volumes*] (Moscow: Goslitizdat, 1949), 2:37; 21.

3. "prekrasnoe to, v chem my vidim zhizn' tak, kak my ponimaem i zhelaem ee, kak ona raduet nas." Chernyshevsky, "*Esteticheskie otnosheniia*," 2:21.

4. "Estetika, ili nauka o prekrasnom, imeet razumnoe pravo sushchestvo vat' tol'ko v tom sluchae, esli prekrasnoe imeet kakoe-nibud' samostoiatel'noe znachenie, nezavisimoe ot beskonechnogo raznoobraziia lichnykh vkusov. Esli zhe prekrasno tol'ko to, chto nravitsia nam, i esli vsledstvie etogo vse raznoobrazneishie poniatiia o krasote okazyvaiutsia odinakovo zakonnymi, togda estetika rassypaetsia v prakh. U kazhdogo otdel'nogo cheloveka obrazuetsia svoia sobstvennaia estetika, i sledovatel'no, obshchaia estetika, privodiashchaia lichnye vkusy k obiazatel'nomu edinstvu, stanovitsia nevozmozhnoiu." Dmitry Pisarev, "Razrushenie estetiki" ["The Destruction of Aesthetics"], in *D. I. Pisarev Literaturnaia kritika v trekh tomakh* [*D. I. Pisarev Literary Criticism in Three Volumes*] (Leningrad: Khudozhestvennaia literatura, 1981), 2:329. Pisarev's italics.

166

Notes to Pages 25–29

5. "otpravit' ee tuda, kuda otpravleny alkhimiia i astrologiia." Pisarev, "Razrushenie estetiki," 328.

6. "V Pisareve khorosha smelost', s kotoroi govorit on." Nikolai Gusev, *Letopis' zhizni i tvorchestva L'va Nikolaevicha Tolstogo: 1891–1910* [*Chronicle of the Life and Works of Lev Nikolaevich Tolstoy: 1891–1910*] (Moscow: Gosudarstvennoe izdatel'stvo khudozhestvennoi literatury, 1960), 2:129.

7. Boris Sorokin, *Tolstoy in Prerevolutionary Russian Criticism* (Columbus: Ohio State University Press, 1979), 67.

8. Boris Eikhenbaum, *Tolstoi in the Sixties*, trans. D. White (Ann Arbor, MI: Ardis, 1982), 5.

9. See Donna Orwin's discussion of Tolstoy's friendship with Botkin. Orwin, *Tolstoy's Art and Thought, 1847–1880* (Princeton, NJ: Princeton University Press, 1993), 58–61.

10. "politicheskaia i, v osobennosti, izoblichitel'naia literatura." Tolstoy, "Rech' v obshchestve liubitelei rossiiskoi slovesnosti" ["Society of Lovers of the Russian Word"], *PSS*, 5:271–72.

11. "est' drugaia literatura, otrazhaiushchaia v sebe vechnye, obshchechelovecheskie interesy, samye dorogie, zadushevnye soznaniia naroda, literatura, dostupnaia cheloveku vsiakogo naroda i vsiakogo vremeni, i literatura, bez kotoroi ne razvivalsia ni odin narod, imeiushchii silu i sochnost'." Tolstoy, "Rech' v obshchestve liubitelei rossiiskoi slovesnosti," 5:271–72.

12. Eikhenbaum, *Tolstoi in the Sixties*, 7.

13. Sergei Taneev, *Dnevniki v 3 knigakh: 1894–1909* [*Diaries in Three Volumes: 1894–1909*] (Moscow: Muzyka, 1981), 1:109.

14. Ty prav. Odnim vozdushnym ochertan'em / Ia tak mila. / Ves' barkhat moi s ego zhivym migan'em— / Lish' dva kryla. / . . . / Vot-vot seichas, sverknuv, raskinu kryl'ia / I ulechu. Afanasii Fet, "Babochka" ["Butterfly"], in *Polnoe sobranie stikhotvorenii* [*Complete Collected Poems*] (Leningrad: Biblioteka Poeta osnovana M. Gor'kim, 1959), 303.

15. "vo vsyom predel, ego zhe ne preidyoshi. I predel etot ochevidnee vsego dlia menia v umstvennoi deiatel'nosti cheloveka." Tolstoy, *Dnevniki i zapisnye knizhki 1858–1880*, *PSS*, 48:118.

16. Tolstoy, *A Confession*, trans. Anthony Briggs (London: Hesperus Press, 2010), 47; *Ispoved'*, *PSS*, 23:33.

17. Tolstoy, *Confession*, 10; *PSS*, 23:7.

18. . "Odno iskusstvo ne znaet ni uslovii vremeni, ni prostranstva, ni dvizheniia." Tolstoy, *Dnevniki i zapisnye knizhk, 1858–1880*, *PSS*, 48:118.

19. "No 4-ia stena neizvestnosti togo, chto delaetsia v dushakh dr[ugikh] liudei, etu stenu my dolzhny vsemi silami razbivat'—stremit'sia k sliianiiu s dushami i drugikh liudei." Tolstoy, *Dnevniki i zapisnye knizhki 1895–1899* [*Diaries and Notebooks, 1895–1899*], *PSS*, 53:126.

20. Tolstoy, *WIA*, 149; *PSS*, 30:157.

Notes to Pages 29–38

21. Eduard Babaev, *"Anna Karenina" L. N. Tolstogo* (Moscow: Khudozhe-stvennaia literatura, 1978), 16.

22. Wittgenstein, "Notes for Lectures on 'Private Experience' and 'Sense Data,'" 309. Wittgenstein's italics.

23. Louis A. Sass, "'My So-Called Delusions': Solipsism, Madness, and the Schreber Case," *Journal of Phenomenological Psychology* 25, no. 1 (1994): 85.

24. Sass, "My So-Called Delusions," 85. Sass's italics.

25. Gary Saul Morson, *Anna Karenina in Our Time: Seeing More Wisely* (New Haven, CT: Yale University Press, 2007), 45.

26. Gustafson, *Leo Tolstoy: Resident and Stranger: A Study in Fiction and Theology* (Princeton, NJ: Princeton University Press, 1986), 437.

27. Babaev, *"Anna Karenina" L. N. Tolstogo*, 94.

28. "Kazhdomu kazalos', chto ta zhizn', kotoruiu on sam vedet, est' odna nastoiashchaia zhizn', a kotoruiu vedet priiatel'—est' tol'ko prizrak." I translate "prizrak" here as phantom, which is closer to the original than Pevear and Volo-khonsky's "illusion." Moreover, it underscores the connection to Schopenhauer. Schopenhauer observes that a "theoretical egoist [skeptic] regards and treats himself alone as a person, and all other persons as mere phantoms." Schopenhauer, *World as Will and Representation*, 104.

29. Amy Mandelker, *Framing Anna Karenina: Tolstoy, the Woman Question, and the Victorian Novel* (Columbus: Ohio State University Press, 1993), 113.

30. "Avtor obladal tem osobennym, nazyvaemym talantom, darom, kotoryi sostoit v sposobnosti usilennogo, napriazhennogo vnimaniia, smotria po vkusam avtora, napravliaemogo na tot ili drugoi predmet, vsledstvie kotorogo chelovek, odarennyi etoi sposobnost'iu, vidit v tekh predmetakh, na kotorye on napravli-aet svoe vnimanie, nechto novoe, takoe, chego ne vidiat drugie." Tolstoy, "Pre-dislovie k sochineniiam Gyui de Mopassana" ["Preface to the Works of Guy de Maupassant"], *PSS*, 30:4.

31. "talant uchit obladatelia ego, vedet ego vpered po puti nravstvennogo razvitiia . . . esli emu tol'ko budet dan khod." Tolstoy, "Predislovie k sochineniiam Gyui de Mopassana," *PSS*, 30:20.

32. Rimvydas Šilbajoris, *Tolstoy's Aesthetics and His Art* (Bloomington, IN: Slavica Publishers, 1991), 152.

33. "Nechto prezhde nevidimoe, neoshchushchaemoe, neponimaemoe liud'mi, dovedennoe do takoi stepeni iasnosti, chto ono stanovitsia dostupno im." Tolstoy, "O tom, chto est' i chto ne est' iskusstvo" ["About What Is and What Is Not Art"] (1889–90), *PSS*, 30: 220.

34. Morson, *Anna Karenina in Our Time,* 210.

35. Pickford, *Thinking with Tolstoy and Wittgenstein*, 49.

36. Pickford, *Thinking with Tolstoy and Wittgenstein*, 49.

37. "lechenie rabotoi." Tolstoy, *AK*, 257; *PSS*, 18:272.

Notes to Pages 38–41

38. "sovershenno novo i vazhno dlia vsekh liudei." Newness is the first of three key criteria for genuine art that Tolstoy enumerates in his essay "Ob iskusstve" (1889)—his earliest attempt to formally explicate his aesthetics. Tolstoy, "Ob iskusstve" ["About Art"], *PSS*, 30:213.

39. Tolstoy, *WIA*, 138; *PSS*, 30:147.

40. J. M. Bernstein, "Aesthetics, Modernism, Literature: Cavell's Transformations of Philosophy," in *Stanley Cavell*, ed. Richard Eldridge (Cambridge: Cambridge University Press, 2003), 111.

41. Bernstein, "Aesthetics, Modernism, Literature," 116.

42. Vladimir E. Alexandrov, *Limits to Interpretation: The Meanings of Anna Karenina* (Madison: University of Wisconsin Press, 2004), 87. Alexandrov's italics.

43. Cavell, "Music Discomposed," in *Must We Mean What We Say?* 188.

44. Tolstoy, "Ob iskusstve" ["About Art"], *PSS*, 30:213.

45. John Givens alternatively suggests that Anna is in fact moved by the expression of Christ's compassion—a compassion she desires from others. Givens, *The Image of Christ in Russian Literature: Dostoevsky, Tolstoy, Bulgakov, Pasternak* (DeKalb: Northern Illinois University Press, 2018), 99.

46. Laura Engelstein, *Slavophile Empire: Imperial Russia's Illiberal Path* (Ithaca, NY: Cornell University Press, 2011), 151–91.

47. Svetlana Evdokimova interprets this scene otherwise, suggesting that Tolstoy is on the side of the artist rather than the critic here. See Evdokimova, "The Drawing and the Grease Spot: Creativity and Interpretation in *Anna Karenina*," *Tolstoy Studies Journal* 8 (1995–96): 33–45. Contrary to this reading, I submit not only the textual analysis above but also Tolstoy's pronouncements on Nikolay Ge's painting of Christ. Golenishchev's remark echoes Tolstoy's own opinion that "Ge paints *beautifully* a painting of a worldly Christ. But this, of all things, cannot be the subject of a painting concerning any worldly events" (Ge pishet prekrasno kartinu grazhdanskogo Khrista. A eto odno, chto ne mozhet byt' siuzhetom kartiny iz vsekh grazhdanskikh sobytii). Tolstoy, diary entry dated March 13, 1870, *Dnevniki i zapisnye knizhki 1858–1880*, *PSS*, 48:118.

48. "nachinaiutsia raznye uklonchivye vosklitsaniia, v rode togo, chto 'ia nichego ne ponimaiu v zhivopisi!'"; "no vsegda poimut i otseniat zhiznennost' i talant, to est' imenno te kachestva, bez kotorykh khudozhestvennykh proizvedenii vovse ne sushchestvuet dlia publiki i k kotorym zritel' ostavat'sia ravnodushnym ne mozhet." Ivan Nikolaevich Kramskoi, "Ob Ivanove" [About Ivanov], in *Ivan Nikolaevich Kramskoi: Yego zhizn', perepiska i khudozhestvenno-kriticheskie stat'i 1837–1887* [*Ivan Nikolaevich Kramskoi: His Life, Correspondence and Critical Essays 1837–1887*] (Saint Petersburg: A. S. Suvorin, 1888), 650, https://elibrary.tambovlib.ru/?ebook=5661. See Engelstein's discussion of Kramskoy's assessment of Ivanov in Engelstein, *Slavophile Empire*, 168–71.

49. Jefferson J. A. Gatrall underscores the similarity between the fictional and nonfictional artists' biographies; for example, both live in poverty in Italy.

Notes to Pages 41–44

But Gatrall also suggests that it was perhaps Ivan Kramskoy himself who was "the most immediate model for the character Mikhailov," given Kramskoy's presence in Tolstoy's home and Tolstoy's active intellectual exchange with the artist in the years he worked on *Anna Karenina*. See Gatrall, "Tolstoy, Ge, Two Pilates: A Tale of the Interarts," in *From Realism to the Silver Age: New Studies in Russian Artistic Culture*, eds. Rosalind P. Blakesley and Margaret Samu (Ithaca, NY: Cornell University Press, an imprint of Northern Illinois University Press, 2014), 79–93.

50. "Dlia menia zhe [Kramskoi] interesen, kak chisteishii tip peterburgskogo noveishego napravleniia, kak ono moglo otrazit'sia na ochen' khoroshei i khudozhnicheskoi nature." Tolstoy to N. N. Strakhov, September 23–24, 1873, *Pis'ma 1873–1879 [Letters 1873–1879]*, *PSS*, 62:49.

51. "Merzkaia nasha pisatel'skaia dolzhnost'—razvrashchaiushchaia. U kazhdogo pisatelia est' svoia atmosfera khvalitelei, kotoruiu on ostorozhno nosit vokrug sebia i ne mozhet imet' poniatiia o svoem znachenii i o vremeni upadka." Tolstoy to N. N. Strakhov, November 17–18, 1876, *Pis'ma 1873–1879*, *PSS*, 62:295.

52. "Gorazdo luchshe ostanovit'sia na *Voine i mir*, chem pisat' *Chasy* ili t. p." Tolstoy to N. N. Strakhov, *Pis'ma 1873–1879*, *PSS*, 62:295.

53. Josipovici, *On Trust*, 22.

54. Josipovici, *On Trust*, 22.

55. I have altered the translation to be more faithful to the original and retain the stress on visual perception.

56. Gatrall, "Tolstoy, Ge, Two Pilates," 83.

57. Givens, *Image of Christ in Russian Literature*, 6.

58. Engelstein argues that Kramskoy attends to a similar self-reflexivity in Ivanov's *Christ*, treating it as an allegory for aesthetic (mis)apprehension. Engelstein, *Slavophile Empire*, 169.

59. In addition to the local ways that Tolstoy, as I suggest, undermines his characters' transcendent visions, Vladimir Alexandrov notes perhaps a more global undermining, that is, these visions are made suspect since they are presented in language, a medium whose fallibility Tolstoy underscores throughout the novel. Alexandrov, *Limits to Interpretation*, 111.

60. "V etu poezdku v pervyi raz ia pochuvstvoval, do kakoi stepeni ia srossia s toboi i s det'mi." Tolstoy to Sofia Tolstoy, September 4, 1869, *Pis'ma k S. A. Tolstoy 1862–1886*, *PSS*, 83:168.

61. "Ia mogu ostavat'sia odin v postoiannykh zaniatiiakh, kak ia byvaiu v Moskve, no kak teper' bez dela, ia reshitel'no chuvstvuiu, chto ne mogu byt' odin." Tolstoy to Sofia Tolstoy, *PSS*, 83:168.

62. Tolstoy, *Confession*, 13; *PSS*, 23:10.

63. Tolstoy, *Confession*, 56, 68; *PSS*, 23:40, 48.

64. Gustafson, *Resident and Stranger*, 434.

Notes to Pages 44–48

65. Irina Paperno, "*Who, What Am I?*": Tolstoy Struggles to Narrate the Self* (Ithaca, NY: Cornell University Press, 2014), 78.

66. Paperno, "*Who, What Am I?*" 47.

67. "Khudozhnik zvuka, linii, tsveta, slova, dazhe mysli v strashnom polozhenii, kogda ne verit v znachitel'nost' vyrazheniia svoei mysli . . . I [vera] byvaet i ne byvaet u menia. Otchego eto? Taina." Tolstoy, diary entry dated November 5, 1873, *Dnevniki i zapisnye knizhki 1858–1880, PSS*, 48:67.

68. "Sviaz' postroiki sdelana ne na fabule i ne na otnosheniiakh (znakomstve) lits, a na vnutrennei sviazi." Tolstoy to S. A. Rachinskii, January 27, 1878, *PSS*, 62:377.

69. Mandelker observes that Levin and Anna both "screw up" their eyes, but whereas Anna does it while "refusing to see," Levin does it to "see more clearly" (Mandelker, *Framing Anna Karenina*, 201). Morson suggests that Levin is determined to consider evidence that runs contrary to his own position, Anna, in contrast, is emblematic of society at large in "teach[ing] herself to exclude contrary evidence in order to assuage her guilt and allow herself to do what she wants" (Morson, *Anna Karenina in Our Time*, 171). Alexandrov notes that the recurrent "doubling" in Anna's eyes might be read as evidence that "Anna may not be 'seeing' her situation clearly" (Alexandrov, *Limits to Interpretation*, 199).

70. Thomas Seifrid, "Gazing on Life's Page: Perspectival Vision in Tolstoy," *PMLA* 113, no. 3 (1998): 436–48.

71. Justin Weir, *Leo Tolstoy and the Alibi of Narrative* (New Haven, CT: Yale University Press, 2011), 146.

72. As Tolstoy would have it, Elisabeth Stenbock-Fermor suggests, Anna's tragedy is one of a "woman's life in a large city" where "there was too much freedom from work and household worries (only one child)" and plenty of opportunity for sensuous indulgence. Stenbock-Fermor, *The Architecture of Anna Karenina: A History of Its Writing, Structure and Message* (Amsterdam and Philadelphia: John Benjamins), 91.

73. "Anna lishena etikh radostei zanimat'sia etoi zhenskoi storonoi zhizni, potomu chto ona odna, vse zhenshchiny ot nee otvernulis', i ei ne s kem pogovorit' obo vsem tom, chto sostavliaet obydennyi, chisto zhenskii krug zaniatii." Sofia A. Tolstaia, diary entry dated November 20, 1876, *Dnevniki. v dvukh tomakh* [*Diaries in Two Volumes*] (Moscow: Khudozhestvennaia literatura, 1978), 1:501.

74. See Morson's discussion of Dolly's visit to Anna in Morson, *Anna Karenina in Our Time*, 42–48.

75. Whereas I see Anna's artmaking as a primary motivation for her character, Weir and Mandelker regard it as compensatory for her social isolation and repression. Weir suggests that Anna's art is a mode of "symbolic" communication that substitutes for the failure of direct verbal communication (Weir, *Leo Tolstoy and the Alibi of Narrative*, 140). Mandelker sees her passionate adulterous affair—the grand narrative of Anna's life—as an attempt to reclaim a psychic

Notes to Pages 48–52

autonomy denied to her by a patriarchal society (Mandelker, *Framing Anna Ka-renin*, 159). Morson sees it still differently: Anna's aestheticization of her life reflects a belief that a true life is one lived with the dense plotting and emotional intensity of a romance novel. Morson, *Narrative and Freedom: The Shadows of Time* (New Haven, CT: Yale University Press, 1994), 72.

76. Buckler notes the multiple instances in which opera divas are invoked immediately before the narrative's attention turns to Anna, including, of course, the scandalous scene at the opera when the spectacle of Anna's disgrace rivals the star soprano Patti's performance. Buckler, *The Literary Lorgnette: Attending Opera in Imperial Russia* (Stanford, CA: Stanford University Press, 2000), 170.

77. Morson, *Narrative and Freedom*, 71–81.

78. Mandelker notes that "in addition to the three painted versions and the verbal portraits sketched by other characters, there are Anna's own ekphrastically presented self-portraits; that is, Tolstoy's framings of Anna's presentations of herself as an art object" (Mandelker, *Framing Anna Karenina*, 110).

79. "Esli u Anny byl talant, to eto byl talant aktrisy." Tolstoy, *Anna Karenina: Chernovye redaktsii i varianty* [*Anna Karenina: Draft Editions and Variants*], *PSS*, 20: 285.

80. Morson, *Narrative and Freedom*, 71.

81. Morson, *Narrative and Freedom*, 76.

82. "Odno mesto mozhet nravit'sia odnomu, drugoe—drugomu, i dazhe to, kotoroe nravitsia odnomu, ne nravitsia drugomu." Tolstoy, "K chitateliam" [To Readers]," *PSS*, 1:207.

83. Tolstoy, "Rech' v obshchestve liubitelei rossiiskoi slovesnosti," *PSS*, 5:271.

84. "Kogda vse sochinenie nravitsia odnomu cheloveku, to takoe sochine-niee, po moemu mneniiu, sovershenno v svoem rode." Tolstoy, "K chitateliam," *PSS*, 1:207.

85. "Chtoby dostignut' etogo sovershenstva, a vsiakii avtor nadeetsia na sovershenstvo, ia nakhozhu tol'ko odno sredstvo: sostavit' sebe iasnoe, oprede-lennoe poniatie o ume, kachestvakh i napravlenii predpolagaemogo chitatelia." Tolstoy, "K chitateliam," *PSS*, 1:207.

86. Weir, *Leo Tolstoy and the Alibi of Narrative*, 43.

87. Plato, "Symposium," in *A Plato Reader*, ed. Ronald Levinson (Boston: Houghton Mifflin, 1967), 143.

88. David Herman, "Allowable Passions in *Anna Karenina*," *Tolstoy Studies Journal* 8 (1995–96): 5.

89. Tolstaia, *Dnevniki* [*Diaries*], 1:502.

90. As Orwin has argued, the three main families in *War and Peace* offer us a hierarchy of virtues: the Kuragin siblings display a hypertrophied sensuality and little reason, the Bolkonskys (a slight improvement) are all reason and no feeling, and the Rostovs achieve a rather harmonious, though tenuous, balance of these qualities (Orwin, *Tolstoy's Art and Thought*, 124–29). Friedrich Schiller,

172

Notes to Pages 52–55

whose work Tolstoy knew and admired, defined our "aesthetic sense" precisely in terms of this balance of sensuousness and reason. Fittingly, the Rostovs are the most artistically gifted of the families in *War and Peace*.

91. Anna Berman, *Siblings in Tolstoy and Dostoevsky: The Path to Universal Brotherhood* (Evanston, IL: Northwestern University Press, 2015), 86.

92. "slaboi cherte kharaktera i liubov' ko vsemu Stepana Arkad'icha." Tolstoy, *Anna Karenina: Chernovye redaktsii i varianty*, PSS, 20:80, 55, 70.

93. Immanuel Kant, *Critique of Judgment*, trans. and ed. Werner S. Pluhar (Indianapolis: Hackett Publishing, 1987), §7, 55.

94. For an overview of Tolstoy's engagement with Schopenhauer's philosophy, see Sigrid McLaughlin, "Some Aspects of Tolstoy's Intellectual Development: Tolstoy and Schopenhauer," *California Slavic Studies* 5 (1970): 187–245. On Tolstoy's reading of Kant, see A. N. Kruglov, *Kant i Kantovskaia filosofiia v russkoi khudozhestvennoi literature* [*Kant and Kantian Philosophy in Russian Literature*] (Moscow: Kanon, 2012), 122–59.

95. Virtually all treatments of Tolstoy's aesthetics note Schopenhauer's influence. At the same time, it is important to remember that Tolstoy, as Eikhenbaum observed, made use of Schopenhauer but "broke" with him when the philosopher did not coincide with Tolstoy's own views. Boris Eikhenbaum, *Tolstoi in the Seventies*, trans. A. Kaspin (Ann Arbor, MI: Ardis, 1982), 100.

96. Schopenhauer, *World as Will and Representation*, 200.

97. Schopenhauer, *World as Will and Representation*, 196.

98. Schopenhauer, *World as Will and Representation*, 201.

99. Schopenhauer, *World as Will and Representation*, 199.

100. Schopenhauer, *World as Will and Representation*, 199.

101. Bart Vandenabeele, *The Sublime in Schopenhauer's Philosophy* (New York: Palgrave Macmillan, 2015), 43.

102. Schopenhauer, *World as Will and Representation*, 199.

103. Schopenhauer, *World as Will and Representation*, 199.

104. Vandenabeele suggests that sight for Schopenhauer "is the *aesthetic* organ par excellence, because it can be affected without this affection being experienced immediately as pleasant or unpleasant." He goes on to point out objections to such a claim. One might note "the common experience of the especially painful and unpleasant feeling caused by, for example driving out of a dark tunnel directly into blazing sunlight." Vandenabeele also observes that Schopenhauer, in later discussions of touch, contradicts the privileged position he ascribes to sight (Vandenabeele, *Sublime in Schopenhauer's Philosophy*, 42–43).

105. It is unclear how Schopenhauer's classification of hearing accords with his celebration of music, which he sets apart from all the other arts: "[M]usic is by no means like the other arts, namely a copy of the Ideas, but a *copy of the will itself*, the objectivity of which are the Ideas." Schopenhauer, *World as Will and Representation*, 257.

106. Moreover, Schopenhauer's ideas about sight were inspired in part by

Notes to Pages 55–57

Goethe's theory of color, which also interested Tolstoy. See Orwin's discussion in *Tolstoy's Art and Thought*, 130–32.

107. "neobyknovenno tonkoi taliei i shirokimi plechami." Tolstoy, *Anna Karenina: Chernovye redaktsii i varianty*, *PSS*, 20:146.

108. "Ona byla pokhozha na brata—to zhe krasivoe, svetloe i porodistoe litso i slozhenie, no sovershenno drugie glaza." Tolstoy, *Anna Karenina: Chernovye redaktsii i varianty*, *PSS*, 20:152.

109. Tolstoy, *Anna Karenina: Chernovye redaktsii i varianty*, *PSS*, 20:70.

110. "Iziashchnoi literature, polozhitel'no, net mesta teper' dlia publiki. No ne dumaite, chtoby eto meshalo mne liubit' ee teper' bol'she, chem kogda nibud'." Tolstoy to V. P. Botkin with fragment called "Son" [Dream], January 4, 1858, *PSS*, 60:247.

111. "Oni dvigali mnoiu, tak zhe kak i ia dvigal imi." Tolstoy to V. P. Botkin, *PSS*, 60:247.

112. "szadi sebia chto-to otdel'noe, neotviazno pritiagivaiushchee." Tolstoy to V. P. Botkin, *PSS*, 60:247.

113. "Vdrug ia pochuvstvoval szadi sebia chuzhoe schast'e i prinuzhden byl oglianut'sia." Tolstoy to V. P. Botkin, *PSS*, 60:247.

114. "i k nei sladko i bol'no tianula nepreodolimaia sila." Tolstoy to V. P. Botkin, *PSS*, 60:247.

115. "ona byla prelestna i schastliva. Ei nikogo ne nuzhno bylo, i ot etogo-to ia chuvstvoval, chto ne mogu zhit' bez nee." Tolstoy to V. P. Botkin, *PSS*, 60:248.

116. "bezzhalostnoe vospominanie." Tolstoy to V. P Botkin, *PSS*, 60:248. It should be noted that Tolstoy claims the fragment was inspired not by his own dream but by his brother's. Nevertheless, the context in which he narrates it suggests it to be an aesthetic fantasy he shares.

117. I disagree with Mandelker's interpretation of Vronsky's response to Anna as evidence that Tolstoy "rigorously rejects the Kantian notion of aesthetic disinterest" (Mandelker, *Framing Anna Karenina*, 79). Mandelker is certainly right to note that Vronsky's encounter with Anna is not free of desire, but she mischaracterizes the role of desire in Kantian aesthetics. Mandelker, I take it, uses Kant as shorthand for the aesthetic tradition as it was inflected by Schopenhauer. But unlike Schopenhauer, Kant does not banish desire from the aesthetic realm. In fact, the frustration of our desires is crucial to the psychological explanation Kant gives of our sense of obligation toward the beautiful object, the sense that we are *compelled* to admire it.

118. Richard Moran, "Kant, Proust, and the Appeal of Beauty," *Critical Inquiry* 38, no. 2 (Winter 2012): 308.

119. Moran, "Kant, Proust, and the Appeal of Beauty," 322. Moran explains that in the case of aesthetic pleasure we see a failure to recognize the value of a beautiful object not as a sign of deficiency in the object but as a failure of judg-

Notes to Pages 58–60

ment on our part. The beautiful is distinguished from the agreeable in that we consider such failure possible with regard to the former but not the latter.

120. Mandelker, *Framing Anna Karenina*, 110.

121. Kant, *Critique of Judgment*, §56, 211.

CHAPTER 2

1. "Khudozhnik oderzhim tvorchestvom. V etom—ego strast', ego (po vyrazheniiu Karoliny Pavlovoi) 'napast',' ego schast'e i gore, ego sviatoe urodstvo." Vladislav Khodasevich, "O Sirine," ["On Sirin"], in *Khodasevich V. F. Sobranie sochinenii v 4 tomakh* [*Khodasevich V. F. Collected Works in Four Volumes*] (Moscow: Soglasie, 1996), 2:390.

2. Nabokov, *Strong Opinions* (New York: Vintage Books, 1990), 183.

3. Nabokov, *Strong Opinions*, 114.

4. Nabokov, *Strong Opinions*, 18.

5. "Vnimanie Sirina ne stol'ko obrashcheno na okruzhaiushchii ego mir, skol'ko na sobstvennoe 'ia,' obrechennoe, v silu tvorcheskogo prizvaniia svoego, otrazhat' obrazy, videniia ili prizraki etogo mira." Vladimir Veidle, "Rets. *Otchaianie*" ["Review of *Despair*"], in *Klassik bez retushi: Literaturnyi mir o tvorchestve Vladimira Nabokova* [*Classic without Retouching. The Literary World about the Work of Vladimir Nabokov*], ed. N. G Mel'nikov and O. A Korostelev (Moscow: Novoe literaturnoe obozrenie, 2000), 127.

6. Al'fred Bem, "Pis'ma o literature: Chelovek i pisatel' (K stat'e Gaito Gazdanova 'O molodoi emigrantskoi literature')" ["Letters about Literature: The Person and the Writer (A Response to Gaito Gazdanov's 'About Young Émigré Literature')"], first published in *Mech.*, no. 18 (May 3, 1936), reprinted in Gaito Gazdanov, *Gaito Gazdanov: Sobranie sochinenii v piati tomakh* (Moscow: Ellis Lak, 2009), 5:304.

7. "On skoree bredit, chem dumaet, skoree vgliadyvaetsia v sozdannye im prizraki, chem v to, chto deistvitel'no ego okruzhaet." Georgii Adamovich, "Perechityvaia *Otchaianie*" ["Rereading *Despair*"], in Mel'nikov and Korostelev, *Klassik bez retushi*, 126.

8. "Emu kak budto ni do chego net dela. On sam sebia pitaet, sam k sebe obrashchen." Adamovich, "Perechityvaia *Otchaianie*," 126.

9. "[Nabokov] seems at times to have seen himself in a very special relation vis-à-vis readers: virtually no relation at all," Leland de la Durantaye has argued. "In artistic matters, their opinion is not of the slightest importance to him and their problems and pleasures do not seem to concern him." De la Durantaye proposes that Nabokov's reputation as a "cruel" artist was fueled in part by the fact that Nabokov showed "extraordinarily little concern for his readership." De la Durantaye, *Style Is Matter: The Moral Art of Vladimir Nabokov* (Ithaca, NY: Cornell University Press, 2007), 28, 30.

175

Notes to Pages 60–61

10. Nabokov, *The Gift* (New York: Vintage, 1991), 340; *Dar*, in *Vladimir Nabokov: Sobranie sochinenii v chetyrekh tomakh* [*Vladimir Nabokov: Collected Works in Four Volumes*] (Moscow: Pravda, 1990), 3:305.

11. In *Strong Opinions* Nabokov reiterated his purported aim to please himself alone by insisting that, as a fiction writer, he was indifferent to the opinions of critics: "the arrows of adverse criticism cannot scratch, let alone pierce, the shield of what disappointed archers call my 'self-assurance'" (146).

12. Vladimir Nabokov and Robert Robinson, "The Last Interview," in *Vladimir Nabokov: A Tribute* (New York: William Morrow, 1980), 122.

13. Nabokov, *Strong Opinions*, 241.

14. Nabokov, *Vladimir Nabokov: Selected Letters, 1940–1977*, ed. Dmitri Nabokov and Matthew J. Bruccoli (San Diego and New York: Harcourt Brace Jovanovich, 1989), 538.

15. Nabokov, *Strong Opinions*, 284, 290.

16. *Vladimir Nabokov: Selected Letters, 1940–1977*, 538.

17. *Vladimir Nabokov: Selected Letters, 1940–1977*, 393.

18. Nabokov writes to his wife, Véra: "[W]hat a pleasure it's been to read it to two people—to you and, the other day, to Mother. The third person who understood every comma and appreciated the trifles dear to me was my father." Vladimir Nabokov, *Letters to Véra*, eds. Ol'ga Voronina and Brian Boyd (London: Penguin Classics, 2014), 12; Vladimir Nabokov, *Pis'ma k Vere, Kommentarii Ol'gi Voroninoy i Braiana Boida* [*Letters to Vera, with commentary by Olga Voronina and Brian Boyd*] (Moscow: Azbuka-Attikus, KoLibri, 2017), 61.

19. Cited in Boyd, *Vladimir Nabokov: The Russian Years*, 419.

20. Eric Naiman, *Nabokov, Perversely* (Ithaca, NY: Cornell University Press), 2010.

21. Irina Paperno, "How Nabokov's *Gift* Is Made," *Stanford Slavic Studies* 4, no. 2 (1992): 313.

22. Brian Boyd regards Nabokov's relationship with his readers as a fundamentally generous one. Nabokov "writes with an acute awareness of the range and capacity of his readers," Boyd argues, and though Nabokov's formally difficult novels challenge the reader, he "spaces and grades his challenges, so that we can handle enough of them to continue at speed, so that we solve enough to want to look out for more" (12). Nabokov does not see the reader "as an antagonist whom he wants to outwit and convince of his own superiority" (8). Instead, he "lures" his readers to gradually discover the complexities of his novels, thereby training them to be more attentive to the complexities of the natural world. Boyd, *Nabokov's "Pale Fire": The Magic of Artistic Discovery* (Princeton, NJ: Princeton University Press, 1999). Blackwell likewise emphasizes the charity of Nabokov's tutelage. He proposes that in *The Gift* Nabokov models an ideal author-reader relationship, depicting an attentive reader who knows when to curb her imagination and thereby "lovingly and intimately activates the text."

176

Notes to Pages 61–68

Such a reader participates in an act of cocreation with the author; something we too could aspire to do, if we are similarly loving and attentive. Stephen H. Blackwell, *Zina's Paradox: The Figured Reader in Nabokov's "Gift"* (New York: Peter Lang International Academic Publishers, 2000), 140.

23. Naiman, *Nabokov, Perversely*, 1–14.

24. De la Durantaye, *Style Is Matter*, 42.

25. Saul Bellow, "On John Cheever," *New York Review of Books* 30, no. 2 (February 17, 1983): 38.

26. Four of the five chapters of *The Gift* appeared in serialized form in *Sovremennye zapiski* (1937–38). The émigré journal declined to publish chapter 4, which contains the fictionalized biography of Nikolay Chernyshevsky. In 1952 the New York–based Chekhov Press finally published the novel in its complete form. For a full discussion of the novel's composition and publication history, see Boyd, *Vladimir Nabokov: The Russian Years*, 391–446.

27. The formal structure of *The Gift* has been one of its most intensely debated aspects. Yuri Leving surveys the various ways critics have conceptualized the shape of *The Gift*, including as a fugue, a chess problem, a nesting doll, a Möbius strip, an infinity symbol, and an apple peel. See Leving, "Structure" in *Keys to "The Gift": A Guide to Vladimir Nabokov's Novel"* (Boston: Academic Studies Press, 2011), 205–13. For a more in-depth analysis of the novel's structure, see Sergey Davydov, *Teksty-Matreski Vladimira Nabokova* (Munich: Verlag Otto Sanger, 1982), 183–99; Irena Ronen and Omry Ronen, " 'Diabolically Evocative': An Inquiry into the Meaning of a Metaphor," *Slavica Hierosolymitana* 5–6 (1981): 371–86; and Toker, *Nabokov: The Mystery of Literary Structures*, 142–76.

28. Naiman, *Nabokov, Perversely*, 169.

29. Alexandrov (*Nabokov's Otherworld*, 115), Blackwell (*Zina's Paradox*, 123) and Alexander Dolinin (*"The Gift,"* in *The Garland Companion to Vladimir Nabokov*, ed. Vladimir E. Alexandrov [New York: Garland Publishing, 1995], 147.) read these scenes as evidence of Fyodor's empathetic self-transcendence. Dolinin, however, does describe Fyodor as "recreat[ing] and [appropriate[ing] the other as a potential fictional character." It is not entirely clear whether and how such an act squares with Fyodor's empathy toward others. Naiman presents an alternative perspective to these scholars.

30. Alexandrov, *Nabokov's Otherworld*, 113.

31. Vladimir Nabokov, *Speak, Memory: An Autobiography Revisited* (New York: Vintage, 1989), 218.

32. Nabokov, *Speak, Memory*, 218.

33. Alexandrov, *Nabokov's Otherworld*, 113.

34. Dolinin, *"The Gift,"* 153.

35. Cavell, "Knowing and Acknowledging," 242.

36. Cavell, "Knowing and Acknowledging," 261.

177

Notes to Pages 68–72

37. Cavell, "Knowing and Acknowledging," 263.

38. Nabokov, *Strong Opinions*, 10–11.

39. Sisson's discussion of cosmic synchronization broadens this concept beyond Nabokov's definition of it in *Speak, Memory*. Sisson suggests that such Nabokovian devices as the "catalogue of remote activity," the "juxtaposition of contrasting images," and the "fusion of the apparent contradictions of alternative realities," all allow the reader to simulate the experience of cosmic synchronization. Sisson, "Nabokov's Cosmic Synchronization and 'Something Else,'" *Nabokov Studies* 1 (1994): 158. Dana Dragunoiu also reminds us that Nabokov never let "his metaphysical yearnings congeal into dogma." He recognized the subjective nature of human thought and questioned even the fatidic patterns he claimed to recognize in his own life, worrying "that fate was a construct of the human mind." Dragunoiu, *Vladimir Nabokov and the Poetics of Liberalism* (Evanston, IL: Northwestern University Press, 2012), 71.

40. David Rampton recognizes in Fyodor's portrait of Chernyshevsky some of the same cruelty I see in his mind reading on the tram. Against commentators such as Andrew Field, who regard Fyodor's biography as ultimately humanizing Chernyshevsky, Rampton observes that "Chernyshevsky merits only a limited humanity from an art form which he was never willing to grant independent life." Rampton, *Vladimir Nabokov: A Critical Study of the Novels* (Cambridge: Cambridge University Press, 1984), 70.

41. Nabokov, "Pushkin, or the True and the Seemingly True," in Tolstoy and Boyd, *Think, Write, Speak*, 123. Originally published in French as "Pouchkine, ou le vrai et le vraisemblable," *Nouvelle revue française*, March 1937, 362–78.

42. Galya Diment, "Nabokov's Biographical Impulse: Art of Writing Lives," in *The Cambridge Companion to Nabokov*, ed. Julian W. Connolly (Cambridge: Cambridge University Press, 2005), 172.

43. Diment, "Nabokov's Biographical Impulse," 175.

44. Nabokov, "Pushkin, or the True and the Seemingly True," 124.

45. Dolinin, *"The Gift,"* 155.

46. Dolinin, *"The Gift,"* 155.

47. Monika Greenleaf has argued that, with regard to the father, Nabokov succeeds where Fyodor fails. In Konstantin Kirillovich, Greenleaf suggests, "the son rewrote a father uniquely tailored to himself, factually false but internally true to their shared nature." Creative reimagining may not allow Nabokov to divine the contents of his father's soul, but it does, as Greenleaf convincingly argues, allow for successful mourning. Greenleaf, "Fathers, Sons and Impostors: Pushkin's Trace in *The Gift*," *Slavic Review* 53, no. 1 (1994): 150.

48. "Uznavat' cheloveka znachit sozdavat' cheloveka." Nabokov, "Pamiati Iu. I. Aikhenval'da."

49. "O da, est' zemnaia vozmozhnost' bessmertiia." Nabokov, "Pamiati Iu. I. Aikhenval'da."

178

Notes to Pages 72–74

50. "Umershii prodolzhaet podrobno i raznoobrazno zhit' v dushakh vsekh liudei, znavshikh ego." Nabokov, "Pamiati Iu. I. Aikhenval'da."

51. "Kak ni filosofstvui, kak ni uteshai sebia vospriimchivost'iu piati svoikh chuvstv,—vse ravno, vse ravno podlinnogo cheloveka, togo edinstvennogo obraztsa, uzhe seichas net. On ushel k sebe domoi pozdno noch'iu, shel zaniatyi svoimi mysliami, techenie i sut' kotorykh nikto, nikto ne mozhet uznat'." Nabokov, "Pamiati Iu. I. Aikhenval'da."

52. The sweeping social reforms of the mid-nineteenth century initiated the growth of the reading public in Russia, and by the end of the century, "the mass reading public burst suddenly on the writer's world . . . as a phenomenon without precedent in cultural Russian history," according to Jeffrey Brooks. Although even in 1897 only 21 percent of the population claimed they could read, this figure marks a significant increase from previous decades. Many new readers were reading Tolstoy. As evident from both library records and publishing print runs, Tolstoy was tremendously popular with this new reading public. Brooks, "Readers and Reading at the End of the Tsarist Era," in *Literature and Society in Imperial Russia 1800–1914*, ed. William Mills Todd (Stanford, CA: Stanford University Press, 1978), 119.

53. Marc Raeff, *Russia Abroad: A Cultural History of the Russian Emigration: 1919–1939* (Oxford: Oxford University Press, 1990), 24.

54. Raeff, *Russia Abroad*, 77.

55. "propushchennaia, kak skvoz' miasorubku, skvoz' obshchii russkii krakh—i stavshaia davno besformennoi massoi. Eta chitatel'skaia massa okrashena v odin tsvet—bezrazlichnoi ustalosti." Georgii Ivanov, "Bez chitatelia" ["Without a Reader"], *Chisla* no. 5 (1931): 148.

56. "'russkii intelligent' . . . byl samym chuvstvitel'nym, vospriimchivym, blagodarnym chitatelem na svete"; "on krepko spit." Ivanov, "Bez chitatelia," 149.

57. Ivanov, "Bez chitatelia," 149.

58. Gaito Gazdanov, "O molodoi emigrantskoi literature" ["About Young Émigré Literature"], *Sovremennye zapiski*, book 60 (1936): 404–7, reprinted in *Gaito Gazdanov: Sobranie sochinenii v piati tomakh*, 1:747–866.

59. Vladislav Khodasevich, "O kinematografe" ["About Cinema"], *Poslednie Novosti* (October 28, 1926), reprinted in Khodasevich, *Sobranie sochinenii* 2:135–39.

60. Mark Aldanov, "O polozhenii emigrantskoi literatury" ["About the Situation of Émigré Literature"], *Sovremennye zapiski*, book 61 (1936): 400–408, reprinted in *Gaito Gazdanov: Sobranie sochinenii v piati tomakh*, 5:305–17.

61. Zinaida Gippius (Anton Krainii), "Polozhenie literaturnoi kritiki" ["The Situation of Literary Criticism"] *Vozrozhdenie* no. 10641 (May 1, 1928), 2, in *Gippius Z. N. Sobranie sochinenii* [*Z. N. Gippius Collected Works*] (Moscow: Dmitriy Sechin, 2012), 13:656.

62. Al'fred Bem, "V zashchitu chitatelia" ["In Defense of the Reader"], *Rul'*,

Notes to Pages 74–82

no. 3232, July 16, 1931, reprinted in *Gaito Gazdanov: Sobranie sochinenii v piati tomakh*, 5:300–304.

63. Dolinin, *"The Gift,"* 148.

64. Cavell, *Claim of Reason*, 442.

65. Cavell, *Claim of Reason*, 442.

66. Cavell, "Knowing and Acknowledging," 247.

67. Nabokov, "Good Readers and Good Writers," in *Lectures on Literature*, 1.

68. Vladimir Nabokov, *Nikolai Gogol* (New York: New Directions, [1959] 1961), 149.

69. Nabokov, *Nikolai Gogol*, 70.

70. Nabokov, *Strong Opinions*, 14.

71. Blackwell, *Zina's Paradox*, 100.

72. One finds a more acute version of Fyodor's distress at his best readers' misunderstanding in Nabokov's portrait of Gogol. Here, too, the ostensible danger posed by "bad" readers who merely seek information or entertainment turns out to be insignificant compared to the skeptical fear of being always and everywhere misinterpreted. Nabokov claims that "what seems to have tormented [Gogol] above all was the knowledge of being talked about by thousands of people and not being able to hear, let alone control, the talk" (Nabokov, *Gogol*, 58). In Gogol's case, apprehension about being misunderstood by all readers becomes pathological. An even more extreme manifestation of this pathology appears in the short story "Signs and Symbols" (1948), which was inspired by Nabokov's work on Gogol; see Boyd, *Vladimir Nabokov: The American Years* (Princeton, NJ: Princeton University Press, 1993), 117. A solipsistic young man imagines that "everything happening around him is a veiled reference to his personality and existence," and believes that he is profoundly misunderstood not only by people but by the world itself. All the objects that surround him "have a distorted opinion of him, and grotesquely misinterpret his actions" (Nabokov, "Signs and Symbols," in *Stories of Vladimir Nabokov*, 599–600). The young man shares the plight of the skeptic, who in longing for an impossible communion with the universe, fails to recognize our ordinary ways of knowing each other and responding to each other's pain. His mania, as Leona Toker points out, blinds him to his parents' love. Toker, "'Signs and Symbols' in and out of Contexts," 177.

73. Cavell, *Claim of Reason*, 440.

74. Cavell, *Knowing and Acknowledging*, 253.

75. Nabokov, *Strong Opinions*, 142.

76. Thomas Seifrid, "Nabokov's Poetics of Vision or What *Anna Karenina* Is Doing in *Kamera obskura*," *Nabokov Studies* 3 (1996): 9.

77. Seifrid, "Nabokov's Poetics of Vision," 9.

78. Blackwell, *Zina's Paradox*, 73–75.

79. The complex narrative structures of *The Gift* and the novel's shifts in perspective have fueled scholarly debate about the identity of *The Gift*'s author-narrator. Some commentators posit that Fyodor is its author. Others argue that

Notes to Pages 82–85

if the author-narrator is Fyodor, he must be an older Fyodor whose knowledge of the world he describes is greater than the character's. Still others propose that the author-narrator is someone else—an "invisible observer," in the words of Véra Nabokov—who nonetheless shares a certain style of thought with the protagonist (Leving, *Keys to "The Gift,"* 269). See Leving for an overview of the debate in his "Points of View," in *Keys to "The Gift,"* 265–70. More recently, Blackwell has argued that "the novel's implicit structuring persona is a *multistable* narrator." Blackwell, "Nabokov's *The Gift*, Dostoevsky, and the Tradition of Narratorial Ambiguity," *Slavic Review* 76, no.1 (2017): 148.

80. Blackwell, *Zina's Paradox*, 154.

81. Anna Brodsky, "Homosexuality in Nabokov's *Dar*," *Nabokov Studies* 4 (1997): 105.

82. Vladimir Nabokov, *The Annotated Lolita* ed. Alfred Appel (New York: Vintage Books, 1991), 60. See discussions of Humbert's "safe solipsizing" in de la Durantaye, *Style Is* Matter, 70–71; and Alexandrov, *Nabokov's Otherworld*, 168.

83. Nabokov, *Lolita*, 129.

84. Vladimir Nabokov, foreword to *Despair* (New York: Vintage International, 1965), xiii.

85. Alexandrov, *Nabokov's Otherworld*, 168. Comparing Fyodor and *Despair's* Hermann, Boyd argues: "For Nabokov the criminal ignores what the true artist knows, the gap between human desire and the frustrating world of fact. The performance and perfection of a work of art offer our only legitimate, albeit limited, escape from our life imprisonment within an evanescent and imperfect world. But art can function like that only if the artist has a firm grasp on the distinction between art and life." Boyd, *Vladimir Nabokov: The Russian Years*, 389.

86. Nabokov, *Strong Opinions*, 32.

87. Toker observes that with another of Humbert's famous exclamation "Reader, *Bruder!*" Nabokov forces us to confront in ourselves "a germ of the same tendency that reduces people to 'solipsized' objects in the novel's world." Toker, *Nabokov: Mystery of Literary Structures*, 207.

88. Cavell, "Othello and the Stake of the Other," *Disowning Knowledge*, 138.

89. Simon Karlinsky, "Vladimir Nabokov's Novel *Dar* as a Work of Literary Criticism: A Structural Analysis," *Slavic and East European Journal* 7, no. 3 (1963): 287.

90. Dolinin, *"The Gift,"* 152. Boyd notes that while Fyodor's factual biography differs from Nabokov's, the author nonetheless "passes on to his character all his essential passions—for his homeland, his family, his home, his language, his literature, his lepidoptera, his chess, his loves—and even surrounds him with the same accidentals, his émigré existence, his language teaching, his distaste for Berlin, his sunbathing in the Grunewald." Boyd, *Vladimir Nabokov: The Russian Years*, 463.

91. Paperno, "How Nabokov's *Gift* Is Made," 296.

181

Notes to Pages 85–88

92. Nabokov, *Nikolai Gogol*, 13.

93. Nabokov, *Strong Opinions*, 90, 156.

94. Nabokov, *Strong Opinions*, 104.

95. Nabokov, "*Anna Karenina*," in *Lectures on Russian Literature*, 231.

96. Nabokov, *Strong Opinions*, 55.

97. Nabokov, "A Commentary," in *Eugene Onegin: A Novel in Verse*, 207.

98. Nabokov, *Lectures on Literature*, 1.

99. Alexander Dolinin, "*Eugene Onegin*," in Alexandrov, *Garland Companion to Vladimir Nabokov*, 125.

100. Nabokov, "Style," in *Think, Write, Speak*, 189.

101. Nabokov, *Strong Opinions*, 63.

102. "dukhovnaia dvoitsa." Iulii Aikhenvald, "Pisatel' i chitatel'" ["The Writer and the Reader"], in *Pokhvala Prazdnosti: Sbornik statei* [*In Praise of Idleness: Collected Essays*] (Moscow: Kostry, 1922), 89.

103. "v svoikh stikhotvoreniiakh rasskazal Pushkin svoiu biografiiu tak, chto ona sdelalas' biografiei obshchechelovecheskoi. Peremenite imena, otdel'nye podrobnosti i fakty, i eto budete vy." Iulii Aikhenvald, "Pushkin," in *Siluety Russkikh Pisatelei* [*Silhouettes of Russian Writers*] (Moscow: Respublika, 1998), 1:73.

104. "Nado prosto ego chitat'"; "v samom techenii, v zvuchashchei radosti ego stikhov." Aikhenvald, "Pushkin," 1:71–72.

105. Michael Glynn, *Vladimir Nabokov: Bergsonian and Russian Formalist Influences in His Novels* (London: Palgrave Macmillan, 2007), 47.

106. Nabokov, *Lectures on Literature*, 2.

107. "Slovo zybko, slovo tumanno, i my, chitateli, ponimaem ego ne sovsem tak kak ono proizneseno avtorom." Aikhenvald, "Pisatel' i chitatel'," 88.

108. "Tol'ko net v etom nikakoi bedy, potomu chto dopolniat' pisatelia chitatelem neobkhodimo inache ne budet literatury." Aikhenvald, "Pisatel' i chitatel'," 88.

109. "Kazhdyi imeet pravo na samogo sebia." Aikhenvald, "Vstuplenie" ["Introduction"], in *Siluety Russkikh Pisatelei*, 24.

110. Nabokov, *Lectures on Literature*, 4.

111. Nabokov, *Nikolai Gogol*, 140.

112. Nabokov, *Nikolai Gogol*, 144.

113. Nabokov, *Nikolai Gogol*, 144.

114. Nabokov, "Pushkin, or the True and the Seemingly True," 125.

115. Nabokov, "Classroom Teaching Material, Creative Writing Course," box 10, reel 8, Vladimir Vladimirovich Nabokov Papers, Manuscript Division, Library of Congress, Washington, DC.

116. "ne usumnivshis' v sebe." Osip Mandel'stam, "O sobesednike" [About the Interlocutor] (1913), in *O. E. Mandel'shtam: Sobranie sochinenii v 4 tomakh* [O. E. Mandel'shtam: Collected Works in Four Volumes] (Saint Petersburg: Art-Biznes-Tsentr, 1993–97), 1:188.

182

Notes to Pages 88–91

117. Nabokov, *Strong Opinions*, 37.
118. Nabokov, *Vladimir Nabokov: Selected Letters, 1940–1977*, 391.
119. Nabokov, *Vladimir Nabokov: Selected Letters, 1940–1977*, 391.

CHAPTER 3

1. V. S. Mishin dates Tolstoy's initial efforts to articulate his theory of art to his conversations with the visual artist Vasiliy Petrov. Tolstoy first attempted to compose an essay on art in 1882. Mishin, "Istoriia pisaniia i pechataniia statei ob iskusstve i traktata *Chto takoe iskusstvo.*" [History of the Writing and Publication of (Tolstoy's) Essays on Art and the Treatise *What Is Art.*], *PSS*, 30:509.

2. Tolstoy, *WIA*, 155; *PSS*, 30:163.

3. Paul Guyer, *A History of Modern Aesthetics* (Cambridge: Cambridge University Press, 2014), 2:290.

4. Caryl Emerson, "Tolstoy's Aesthetics," in *The Cambridge Companion to Tolstoy*, ed. Donna Tussing Orwin (Cambridge: Cambridge University Press, 2002), 243.

5. Vladimir Nabokov, "Tolstoy: Miscellaneous Lecture Notes," holograph, unsigned and undated, album 14 (196–97), Vladimir Nabokov Papers 1918–87, Henry W. and Albert A. Berg Collection of English and American Literature, New York Public Library.

6. Nabokov, "Tolstoy: Miscellaneous Lecture Notes," album 14 (196–97).

7. Nabokov, "Tolstoy: Miscellaneous Lecture Notes," album 14 (196–97).

8. Nabokov, "Tolstoy: Miscellaneous Lecture Notes, album 14 (196–97).

9. Much of the previous scholarship on Tolstoy's aesthetic theory has taken one of these two paths. As Rimvydas Šilbajoris demonstrates, many of Tolstoy's contemporaries, both at home and abroad, rejected Tolstoy's association of aesthetic experience with ordinary emotions and were at pains to point out the flaws in his arguments (Šilbajoris, *Tolstoy's Aesthetics and His Art*, 180). More recently, scholars have attempted to highlight the coherence of some, if not all, of Tolstoy's aesthetic arguments. Gary Jahn shows that Tolstoy's aesthetic premises, when separated from his socioreligious ones, are not as "unreasonably narrow, exclusive, and arbitrary" as Tolstoy's detractors would have us believe. Jahn, "The Aesthetic Theory of Leo Tolstoy's *What Is Art.*" *Journal of Aesthetics and Art Criticism* 34, no. 1 (1975): 60. Henry Pickford, more ambitiously, undertakes a "reconstruction of Tolstoy's theory sufficient to constitute a viable alternative to 'interpretist' accounts of aesthetic understanding that derive from Derridean principles." Pickford, *Thinking with Tolstoy and Wittgenstein*, 6.

10. Tolstoy, "O Shekspire i o drame" ["On Shakespeare and On Drama"], *PSS*, 35:216. In her classic study of Tolstoy's aesthetics, Elena Kupreianova defends *What Is Art.* on the grounds that it expresses in theoretical terms the same "high civil consciousness" (vysokaia grazhdanstvennost') that she sees not

Notes to Pages 91–95

only in Tolstoy's art but also in Russian realism in general. Kupreianova, *Estetika L. N. Tolstogo* [*L. N. Tolstoy's Aesthetics*] (Moscow: Nauka, 1966), 323. Thomas Barran similarly reads *What Is Art?* as an expression of Tolstoy's sociopolitical views. Barran, "Rousseau's Political Vision and Tolstoy's *What Is Art?*," *Tolstoy Studies Journal* 5 (1992): 1–12. Richard Gustafson and Douglas Robinson, alternatively, see Tolstoy's aesthetics as a manifestation of certain personal, psychological traits. Gustafson, *Resident and Stranger*; and Douglas Robinson, "Tolstoy's Infection Theory and the Aesthetics of De- and Repersonalization," *Tolstoy Studies Journal* 19 (2007): 33–53.

11. "problema chitatel'skogo vospriiatiia okazyvalas' sviazannoi s ego fundamental'nymi filosofsko-esteticheskimi poiskami i postroeniiami." G. N. Ishchuk, *Problema chitatelia v tvorcheskom soznanii L. N. Tolstogo. Stat'i* [*The Problem of the Reader in L. N. Tolstoy's Literary Works: Essays*] (Tver': Tver. gos. universitet, 2004), 40–41.

12. "Dusha poddaetsia vliianiiu drugoi dushi. I chelovek vpolne svoboden, tol'ko kogda odin." Tolstoy, *Krug chteniia* [*The Circle of Reading*], *PSS*, 41:551.

13. Gustafson, *Resident and Stranger*, 19.

14. Shklovsky, "Iskusstvo, kak priem," 14.

15. Plato, "Ion," in *Ion, Hippias Minor, Laches, Protagoras*, 9–22.

16. Max Horkheimer and Theodor W. Adorno, *Dialectic of Enlightenment. Cultural Memory in the Present*, ed. Gunzelin Schmid Noerr, trans. Edmund Jephcott (Stanford, CA: Stanford University Press, 2002), 70, 64.

17. Bruce Robbins, "Not So Well Attached," *PMLA* 132, no. 2 (March 2017): 372.

18. Felski, *Uses of Literature*, 54.

19. Felski, *Uses of Literature*, 74.

20. Ludwig Wittgenstein, *Culture and Value*, ed. G. H. von Wright in collaboration with Heikki Nyman, trans. Peter Winch (Chicago: University of Chicago Press, 1980), 58.

21. "izvestnoe opredelenie iskusstva." Tolstoy to N. N. Strakhov, January 25, 1891, *Pis'ma 1890–1891* [*Letters 1890–1891*], *PSS*, 65:229.

22. "V tselom zhe poniatiem 'religioznogo soznaniia' okhvatyvaetsia u Tolstogo vsia sovokupnost' progressivnykh, s ego tochki zreniia, obshchestvennykh, nravstvennykh, sobstvenno religioznykh idei, sostavliaiushchaia dukhovnyi nerv postupatel'nogo razvitiia dannogo vremeni." Kupreianova, *Estetika*, 311.

23. Plato, "Ion," 15.

24. Plato, "Ion," 15.

25. Gustafson, *Resident and Stranger*, 370.

26. Gustafson, *Resident and Stranger*, 371.

27. Gustafson, *Resident and Stranger*, 339.

28. Gustafson, *Resident and Stranger*, 349.

29. Gustafson, *Resident and Stranger*, 369.

Notes to Pages 95–102

30. Gustafson, *Resident and Stranger*, 371.

31. Gustafson, *Resident and Stranger*, 339. Henry Pickford takes up the same thread in Tolstoy's aesthetics, arguing that Tolstoy's demand for art to express a moral message is motivated by his worry about art's essential amorality. Pickford traces the notion of art's amorality to Tolstoy's reading of Schopenhauer's theory of music, which, we might add, inherits in turn Plato's picture of art as a powerful vehicle for all sorts of feelings. Pickford, *Thinking with Tolstoy and Wittgenstein*, 91.

32. Stephen Halliwell, "Tolstoy, Opera, and the Problem of Aesthetic Seduction," in *Tolstoy and His Problems*, ed. Inessa Medzhibovskaya (Evanston, IL: Northwestern University Press, 2019), 174.

33. Tolstoy, "Dlia chego liudi odurmanivaiutsia?" ["Why Do People Stupify Themselves"], *PSS*, 27: 283.

34. "Vsiakii znaet to chuvstvo nedoveriia i otpora, kotorye vyzyvaiutsia vidimoi prednamerennost'iu avtora." Translation slightly altered to better reflect the original. Instead of "resistance" I have "repulsion" and instead of "predetermination" I have "calculation."

35. The need to supplement Tolstoy's arguments in his treatise with examples from his literary works is evident both in monograph-length treatments such as Pickford, *Thinking with Tolstoy and Wittgenstein*, and in article-length accounts such as David Herman, "Stricken by Infection: Art and Adultery in *Anna Karenina* and *Kreutzer Sonata*," *Slavic Review* 56, no.1 (Spring 1997): 15–36.

36. Šilbajoris, *Tolstoy's Aesthetics*, 129.

37. Caryl Emerson, "What Is Infection and What Is Expression in *What Is Art?*" in *Lev Tolstoy and the Concept of Brotherhood*, ed. Andrew Donskov and John Woodsworth (Ottawa: Legas, 1996), 114.

38. Emerson, "What Is Infection," 115.

39. See Tamar Gendler, *Intuition, Imagination, and Philosophical Methodology* (Oxford: Oxford University Press, 2010), 180.

40. David Hume, "Of the Standard of Taste," in *Essays: Moral, Political, and Literary*, ed. Eugene F. Miller (Indianapolis: Liberty Classics, 1985), 246–47.

41. Hume, "Of the Standard of Taste," 247.

42. Gendler, *Intuition*, 179.

43. Gendler, *Intuition*, 201.

44. Tolstoy relates reading Hume in diary entries from the spring of 1852. Tolstoy, *Dnevnik 1847–1854* [*Diaries 1847–1854*], *PSS*, 46:107, 113, 122, 126. In 1876 he requests and receives from Nikolay Strakhov French translations of Hume's philosophical writing. Letters from January 2 and February 15, 1876, *Pis'ma 1873–1879*, *PSS*, 62:237, 241. N. V. Kotrelev, *Biblioteka L'va Nikolaevicha Tolstogo v Iasnoi Poliane* [*Library of Lev Nikolaevich Tolstoy in Iasnaia Poliana*] (Tula: Dom Iasnaia Poliana, 1999), 3:526.

45. Hume, "Of the Standard of Taste," 230.

185

Notes to Pages 102–106

46. Hume, "Of the Standard of Taste," 232.

47. Hume, "Of the Standard of Taste," 239–40.

48. Hume, "Of the Standard of Taste," 239.

49. Hume, "Of the Standard of Taste," 239.

50. Hume, "Of the Standard of Taste," 245.

51. Hume, "Of the Standard of Taste," 239.

52. Hume, "Of the Standard of Taste," 239–40.

53. Hume, "Of the Standard of Taste," 245.

54. "Nachali chitat' Leskovsk[ogo] Zlatokuznetsa pri svetsk[ikh] baryshni-akh: Mamonova, Samarina." Tolstoy, *Dnevniki i zapisnye knizhki 1888–1889* [*Diaries and Notebooks 1888–1889*], *PSS*, 50:19.

55. "Tol'ko estetich[eskie] suzhdeniia, tol'ko etu storonu schitaiut vazhnoi. Podumal: nu pust' soberetsia vsia sila iziashchnykh iskusstv, kakuiu tol'ko ia mogu voobrazit', i vyrazit zhiznennuiu nravstvennuiu istinu takuiu, k[otoraia] obiazyvaet, ne takuiu, na k[otoruiu] mozhno tol'ko smotret' ili slushat', a takuiu, k[otoraia] osuzhdaet zhizn' prezhniuiu i trebuet novogo. Pust' budet takoe proizvedenie, ono ne shevel'net dazhe Mamon[ovykh], Samar[inykh] i im podobn[ykh]." Tolstoy, *Dnevniki i zapisnye knizhki 1888–1889*, *PSS*, 50:19.

56. Hume, "Of the Standard of Taste," 247.

57. Emerson, "What Is Infection," 107.

58. R. W. Beardsmore, "Wittgenstein on Tolstoi's *What is Art?*" *Philosophical Investigations* 14, no. 3 (July 1991): 201.

59. "Khotel ia vsyo eto vremia napisat' khudozhestvennoe, chto-nibud' takoe, chto sodeistvovalo by mnoiu zhe postavlennym trebovaniiam. No nichego ne mog." Tolstoy to Vladimir Chertkov, January 9, 1898, *Pis'ma k V. G. Chertkovu 1897–1910* [*Letters to V. G. Chertkov, 1897–1910*], *PSS*, 88:72.

60. F. I. Evnin, "Poslednii shedevr Tolstogo" ["Tolstoy's Last Masterpiece"], in *Tolstoi-khudozhnik: sbornik statei* [*Tolstoy-Artist: Collected Essays*], ed. D. D. Blagoi et al. (Moscow: Izd-vo Akademii nauk SSSR, 1961), 344.

61. Susan Layton, *Russian Literature and Empire: Conquest of the Caucasus from Pushkin to Tolstoy* (Cambridge: Cambridge University Press, 1995), 264.

62. Edmund Heier, "*Hadji Murat* in the Light of Tolstoy's Moral and Aesthetic Theories," *Canadian Slavonic Papers* 21, no. 3 (1979): 335.

63. Sergeenko, "Kommentarii *Hadji Murat*," 622. "dva poliusa vlastnogo absoliutizma—aziatskogo i evropeiskogo." Donald Fanger points out that, in addition to the similarities between the two rulers, "the Russian soldiers and officers and civilians have their functional and temperamental counterparts among the Chechens." Fanger, "Nazarov's Mother: Notes Towards an Interpretation of *Hadji Murat*," in *Mnemozina*, ed. Joachim T. Baer, Norman W. Ingham, and Stanley J. Rabinowitz (Munich: Fink, 1974), 97.

64. Evnin, "Poslednii shedevr," 383.

Notes to Pages 106–110

65. Viktor Shklovsky, *Lev Tolstoi: Zhizn' znamenitykh lyudei* [*Lev Tolstoy: Life of Renowned People*] (Moscow: TsK VLKTsM Molodaia Gvardiia, 1963), 743.

66. Moran, "Kant, Proust, and the Appeal of Beauty," 321.

67. Michael Denner identifies sincerity as the key characteristic that marks true art for Tolstoy, observing that it is the one characteristic that persists through all of Tolstoy's draft essays on art; Denner, "Accidental Art: Tolstoy's Poetics of Unintentionality," *Philosophy and Literature* 27, no. 2 (2003): 284–303. I agree with Denner about the significance of "sincerity" for Tolstoy, though I object to equating sincerity with the absence of intention. All art is intentional, and Tolstoy recognizes this in his definition of art: "Art begins when one person, with the object of joining another or others to himself in one and the same feeling, expresses that feeling by certain external indications" (*WIA*, 50; *PSS*, 30: 64).

68. "V iskusstve vsegda est' dva litsa: odin tot, kto proizvodit khudozhestvennoe proizvedenie, i tot, kto vosprinimaet: zritel', slushatel'." Tolstoy, "O tom, chto nazyvaiut iskusstvom" ["About What Is Called Art"], *PSS*, 30:251.

69. "Posle obeda Nikolai ezdil v balet, gde v triko marshirovali sotni obnazhennykh zhenshchin. Odna osobenno priglianulas' emu, i, pozvav baletmeistera, Nikolai blagodaril ego i velel podarit' emu persten' s bril'iantami." Translation slightly altered to better reflect the original.

70. The novella's orientalist tropes are not the focus of my analysis, but it is nonetheless worth noting that Tolstoy's engagement with them is far from simple. Susan Layton offers a useful discussion of the ways *Hadji Murat* both rehearses and undermines a Eurocentric perspective. Layton, *Russian Literature and Empire*, 269.

71. David Herman, "Khadzhi-Murat's Silence," *Slavic Review* 64, no. 1 (Spring 2005): 2.

72. In a discussion of *The Cossacks* and *War and Peace*, Orwin contends that, for the young Tolstoy, "If this desire for self-sacrifice does exist, it comes from within the same individual who loves himself." Orwin, *Tolstoy's Art and Thought*, 91.

73. Donna T. Orwin, "Nature and the Narrator in *Chadzi-Murat*," *Russian Literature* 28 (1990): 132.

74. "dvorniki, gorodovye, izvoshchiki." Tolstoy to Dmitry Litoshenko, February 7, 1889, *Pis'ma 1899–1900* [*Letters, 1899–1900*], *PSS*, 72:57.

75. "Tak iasno, chto vse oni pogloshcheny svoimi delami, tak vse skipeli v odin slozhno perepletennyi uzel, chto ne tol'ko izmenit' im svoiu zhizn', no podumat' o tom, chem dolzhna byt' zhizn' chelovecheskaia, im nekogda, pochti nevozmozhno. Dlia togo, chtoby im odumat'sia, nuzhno razorvat' im te stsepleniia, kotorye ikh stianuli v odin uzel. A stseplenie eto—egoizm, vera v egoizm." Tolstoy to Dmitry Litoshenko, February 7, 1889, *Pis'ma 1899–1900*, *PSS*, 72:57.

76. "Uzhasno smotret' na to, chto bogatye liudi delaiut s svoimi det'mi."

Tolstoy, *Dnevniki i zapisnye knizhki 1891–1894* [*Diaries and Notebooks, 1891–1894*], *PSS*, 52:115.

77. "Kogda on molod i glup i strasten, ego vtianut v zhizn', kotoraia vedetsia na shee drugikh liudei, priuchat k etoi zhizni." Tolstoy, *Dnevniki i zapisnye knizhki 1891–1894*, *PSS*, 52:115.

78. "I vybiraisia, kak znaesh': ili stan' muchenikom, otkazavshis' ot togo, k chemu privyk i bez chego ne mozhesh' zhit', ili bud' lgunom." Tolstoy, *Dnevniki i zapisnye knizhki 1891–1894*, *PSS*, 52:115.

79. "Tiazhest' poteri liubimykh liudei: rebenka, muzha, zheny, ottsa, materi, zakliuchaetsia, glavnoe, v tom, chto, lishaias' ikh, chelovek lishaetsia togo, chto vyvodilo ego iz sebia, iz svoego egoizma, i bez nikh on ostaetsia v samom uzhasnom dlia cheloveka polozhenii, esli on ne khristianin, opiat' odin s samim soboiu." Tolstoy, *Dnevniki i zapisnye knizhki 1891–1894*, *PSS*, 52:115.

80. "Tak chto nuzhno odno glavnoe—zamenit' etu veru v lichnoe blago veroi v sluzhenie Bogu." Tolstoy, letter dated February 7, 1889, *Pis'ma 1899–1900*, *PSS*, 72:57.

81. "Samoe uzhasno[e], vrednoe chelovechestvu eto fariseistvo, litsemerie: deiatel'nost' dlia sebia iz egoizma pod vidom deiatel'no[sti]—samoe uzhasn[oe]—dlia Boga, mene[e] uzhasnoe—dlia liudei, dlia obshchestva, i eshche menee durno[e]—dlia sem'i." Tolstoy, *Dnevniki, zapisnye knizhki i otdel'nye zapiski 1907–1908* [*Diaries, Notebooks and Miscellaneous Notes 1907–1908*], *PSS*, 56:236.

82. Shklovsky, the reader perhaps most attuned to the importance of art in the novella, stresses that Tolstoy had actually composed the text of Patimat's song, though he ultimately chose not to include it in the final version of the novella. Shklovsky, *Lev Tolstoi*, 747.

83. Ani Kokobobo, "Tolstoy's Enigmatic Final Hero: Holy War, Sufism, and the Spiritual Path in *Hadji Murat*," *Russian Review* 76 (January 2017): 46.

84. Orwin, "Nature and the Narrator in *Chadzi-Murat*," 136.

85. "[tot, kto vosprinimaet] ne dolzhen nichego sam delat', on tol'ko smotrit i slushaet i poluchaet udovol'stvie, zabavliaetsia. Imenno tem, chto on sam ne delaet usiliia, a predostavliaet khudozhniku zavladet' soboi, i otlichaetsia khudozhestvennaia peredacha ot vsiakoi drugoi." Tolstoy, "O tom, chto nazyvaiut iskusstvom" ["About What is Called Art"], *PSS*, 30:252.

86. "lovkosti, izobretatel'nosti, khitrosti i t. p."; "Iskusstvo—eto drugogo roda otdykh ot truda, dostigaemyi passivnym vosprinimaniem cherez zarazhenie chuvstv drugikh liudei." Tolstoy, "O tom, chto nazyvaiut iskusstvom," *PSS*, 30:252.

87. "Tolstoi bol'she, chem kto-libo, tsenil trud." Iulii Aikhenvald, "Pokhvala prazdnosti" [In Praise of Idleness] in *Pokhvala prazdnosti: Sbornik statei* [In Praise of Idleness: Collected Essays] (Moscow: Kostry, 1922), 6, https://babel.hathitrust.org/cgi/pt?id=ucl.$b150956&view=1up&seq=7.

Notes to Pages 113–116

88. "kak by osviashcheny dykhaniem krest'ianskoi strady." Aikhenvald, "Pokhvala prazdnosti," 6.

89. For discussions of Aikhenvald's influence on Nabokov, see Blackwell, *Zina's Paradox*, 25–36; Dana Dragunoiu, *Vladimir Nabokov and the Poetics of Liberalism*, 144–46; and Thomas Karshan, *Vladimir Nabokov and the Art of Play* (Oxford: Oxford University Press, 2011), 115–20.

90. "[chelovek] stroit zheleznuiu dorogu, fabriku, zaniat missionerstvom v Indii ili Iaponii . . . derzhit ekzamen, pishet uchenoe sochinenie, poemu, roman"; "odumaites', izmenite svoe ponimanie zhizni." Tolstoy, "Nedelanie," *PSS*, 29:199, 196.

91. "On etim ne propovedoval leni i prazdnosti." Aikhenvald, "Pokhvala prazdnosti," 15.

92. "ostanovit'sia, perestat' delat'"; "sosredotochit'sia i podumat'"; "liudi vmesto egoizma predalis' [by] al'truizmu." Tolstoy, "Nedelanie," *PSS*, 29:198, 195.

93. Karshan, *Vladimir Nabokov*, 115.

94. "on treboval tol'ko, chtoby my nakonets oglianulis' na sebia i o sebe podumali, a ne ukhodili s golovoiu v durman dela." Aikhenvald, "Pokhvala prazdnosti," 15.

95. Jacob Emery, "Art Is Inoculation: The Infectious Imagination of Leo Tolstoy," *Russian Review* 70 (October 2011): 642.

96. Nabokov, "The Art of Literature and Common Sense," *Lectures on Literature*, 374.

97. Tolstoy, "O tom, chto nazyvaiut iskusstvom," *PSS*, 30:252.

98. "propoveduiushchie ne ispolniaiut togo, chto propoveduiut." Tolstoy to Bernard Shaw, April 15–26, 1910, *Pis'ma 1910 [Letters 1910]*, *PSS*, 81:254.

99. Shklovsky speculates that Tolstoy wished to avoid disputes with his wife about copyright and proceeds from the publication. Shklovsky, *Lev Tolstoi*, 752.

100. Scholars have debated the generic classification of Tolstoy's *The Circle of Reading*. A. V. Golubkov suggests that *The Circle of Reading* resembles the encyclopedias of early modern Europe, before the transformation brought about by Diderot's *Encyclopédie*; Golubkov, "Entsiklopediia vs Kompendium: Lev Tolstoi i Zapadnaia Traditsiia" ["Encyclopedia vs. Compendium: Leo Tolstoy and the Western Tradition"], *Iasnopolianskii Sbornik* (2014): 304–24. S. Iu. Nikolaeva situates Tolstoy's calendar of wisdom within a religious rather than a secular tradition, comparing *The Circle of Reading* to liturgical texts; Nikolaeva, "Zhanrovoe Svoeobrazie Knigi L. N. Tolstogo *Krug chteniia*" ["The Generic Distinctiveness of Leo Tolstoy's Book *The Circle of Reading*], *Iasnopolianskii Sbornik* (2010):128–52.

101. "vozbuzhdaiushchie k nisproverzheniiu sushchestvuiushchego v Rossii gosudarstvennogo i obshchestvennogo stroia." N. N. Gusev, "*Krug chteniia* Istoriia pisaniia i pichataniia" ["History of the Writing and Publication of *The Circle of Reading*"], *PSS*, 42:579.

Notes to Pages 116–117

102. "Po moemu glubochaishemu ubezhdeniiu, mesto *Kruga chteniia*, etoi poslednei iz velichaishikh rabot L'va Tolstogo, ne na skam'e podsudimykh, a edinstvenno v Panteone velikikh, blagotvorneishikh dlia vsego chelovechestva proizvedenii mirovoi literatury." Gusev, "*Krug chteniia* Istoriia pisaniia i pichataniia," *PSS*, 42:580.

103. "Nachal Tolstoi s togo, chto on, Lev Tolstoi, skazhet nam svoe, tolstovskoe slovo o pravde zhizni; posle zhe on stal ssylat'sia na drugikh: v etikh ssylkakh v kontse kontsov rastvorilsia Tolstoi-propovednik." Andrei Bely, "Lev Tolstoi i kul'tura" ["Leo Tolstoy and Culture"], *O religii L'va Tolstogo* [*About Leo Tolstoy's Religion*], 152, https://www.prlib.ru/item/353778.

104. For example, Tolstoy advises a student who asks him what is meant by the word "God" to consult *The Circle of Reading*: "V otvet na pervyi vash vopros o tom, kak poniat' slovo 'bog,' posylaiu vam knizhechku, sostavlennuiu iz izdannogo mnoiu *Kruga Chteniia*, v kotoroi soedineny mysli o boge, s kotorymi ia soglasen." Tolstoy to Fridun Khan Badalbekov, December 28, 1908, *Pis'ma 1908* [*Letters, 1908*], *PSS*, 78:306.

105. Gary Saul Morson, *Hidden in Plain View: Narrative and Creative Potentials in "War and Peace"* (Stanford: Stanford University Press, 1987), 23.

106. Morson, *Hidden in Plain View*, 27

107. "nado sebe sostavit' Krug chteniia: Epiktet, Mark Avrelii, Laotsy, Budda, Paskal', Evangelie.—Eto i dlia vsekh by nuzhno." Tolstoy, *Dnevniki i zapisnye knizhki 1881–1887* [Diaries and Notebooks, 1881–1887], *PSS*, 49:68.

108. "Ia po sebe znaiu, kakuiu eto pridaet silu, spokoistvie i schast'e— vkhodit' v obshchenie s takimi dushami kak Sokrat, Epiktet, Arnold, Parker." Tolstoy to Chertkov, June 4–5, 1885, *Pis'ma k V. G. Chertkovu 1883–1886* [*Letters to V. G. Chertkov, 1883–1886*], *PSS*, 85:218.

109. "L. N: Skol'ko radosti dostavila mne eta rabota (*Krug chteniia*), kakaia ona byla legkaia, skol'ko ia nachitalsia!" D. P. Makovitskii, *U Tolstogo.* "*Iasnopolianskie zapiski*" *D. P. Makovitskogo* [*At Tolstoy's: D. P. Makovitskii's Notes from Iasnaia Poliana*], 1904–5 (Moscow: Izdatel'stvo Nauka, 1979), 1:126.

110. Makovitskii, *U Tolstogo*, 1:220.

111. "ia byl na takoi vysote mysli." Makovitskii, *U Tolstogo*, 1:154.

112. "V poslednee vremia ia pochuvstvoval, kak ia dukhovno spustilsia posle toi dukhovnoi, nravstvennoi vysoty, na kotoruiu menia podnialo moe prebyvanie v obshchenii s temi luchshimi, mudreishimi liud'mi, kotorykh ia chital i v mysli kotorykh vdumyvalsia dlia svoego Kruga Chteniia." Tolstoy, *Dnevniki i zapisnye knizhki 1904–1906* [*Diaries and Notebooks 1904–1906*], *PSS*, 55:120.

113. Paperno, *Who, What Am I?*, 154.

114. N. N. Gusev, *Zhizn' i uchenie L'va Tolstogo* [*The Life and Teaching of Lev Tolstoy*] (Moscow: Izdanie Obshchestva Istinnoi Svobody v pamyat' L. N. Tolstogo i Edineniia, 1920), 151.

115. "—Kak eto mogut liudi zhit' bez *Kruga chteniia!*" N. N. Gusev, *Dva goda*

190

Notes to Pages 117–119

s L. N. Tolstym: Zapiski byvshego sekretaria L. N. Tolstogo N. N. Guseva [Two Years with L. N. Tolstoy: Notes of L. N. Tolstoy's former secretary N. N. Gusev] (Moscow: Izdatel'stvo Posrednik, 1912), 284.

116. "Ia ne ponimaiu, kak eto liudi ne pol'zuiutsia *Krugom chteniia*?" Gusev, *Dva goda s L. N. Tolstym*, 145.

117. "Chto mozhet byt' dragotsennee, kak ezhednevno vkhodit' v obshchenie s mudreishimi liud'mi mira?" Gusev, *Dva goda s L. N. Tolstym*, 145.

118. "Izliublennoe detishche." Tolstaia, *Dnevniki*, 2:289.

119. "Eto moe vtoroe Evangelie." Gusev, *Dva goda s L. N. Tolstym*, 104.

120. "Chuvstvuetsia otorvannost' ot zhizni, zamknutost' v sebe." Gusev, *Dva goda s L. N. Tolstym*, 109.

121. "Tolstoi v nekotorykh sluchaiakh dopolnial izvestnye poslovitsy, kogda oni kazalis' emu slabymi." V. S. Mishin, *"Kalendar' s poslovitsami na 1887 god*: Istoriia pisaniia i pechataniia" [*Calendar of Proverbs for the Year 1887*: History of Writing and Publication"], *PSS*, 40:472.

122. "Ne za podatiami v gorod khodiat, a za soblaznami." Tolstoy, *Kalendar' s poslovitsami na 1887 god* [*Calendar of Proverbs for the Year 1887*], *PSS*, 40:13.

123. "perevodia nekotorye mesta, ia ne vsegda strogo derzhalsia originala, a inogda sokrashchal ego, vypuskaia nekotorye slova i predlozheniia . . . kogda schital zamenu etu neobkhodimoiu dlia iasnosti ponimaniia." Tolstoy, *"Krug chteniia*, predislovie" [*"The Circle of Reading*: Foreword"], *PSS*, 42:470.

124. "schitaetsia prestupnym"; "vrednyi predrassudok." Tolstoy, *"Krug chteniia*, predislovie,"*PSS*, 42:470.

125. "*tsel' moei knigi sostoit* ne v tom, chtoby dat' tochnye slovesnye perevody pisatelei, *a v tom, chtoby, vospol'zovavshis' velikimi, plodotvornymi mysliami raznykh pisatelei, dat' bol'shomu chislu chitatelei dostupnyi im ezhednevnyi krug chteniia, vozbuzhdaiushchego luchshie mysli i chuvstva.*" Tolstoy, *"Krug chteniia*, predislovie," *PSS*, 41:9. Tolstoy's italics.

126. Morson, *Hidden in Plain View*, 26.

127. "kak vazhno kazhdoe slovo kuda postavit', kakoe slovo ran'she, kakoe posle." Gusev, *Dva goda s L. N. Tolstym*, 87.

128. "1-e ianvaria: Luchshe znat' nemnogo istinno khoroshego i nuzhnogo, chem ochen' mnogo posredstvennogo i nenuzhnogo." Tolstoy, *Krug chteniia*, *PSS*, 41:11.

129. "Kakoe ogromnoe bogatstvo mozhet byt' v malen'koi izbrannoi biblioteke. Obshchestvo mudreishikh i dostoineishikh liudei, izbrannoe iz vsekh tsivilizovannykh stran mira na protiazhenii tysiach let, predostavilo nam zdes' v luchshem poriadke rezul'taty svoego izucheniia i svoei mudrosti. Sami liudi skryty i nedostupny, oni, mozhet byt', byli by neterpelivy, esli by my narushili ikh uedinenie i prervali ikh zaniatiia, mozhet byt', obshchestvennye usloviia sdelali by nevozmozhnym obshchenie s nimi, no mysl', kotoruiu oni ne otkryvali dazhe luchshim svoim druz'iam, napisana zdes' iasnymi slovami dlia nas, posto-

Notes to Pages 120–123

ronnikh liudei inogo veka." Tolstoy, *Krug chteniia*, *PSS*, 41:11. English text in Ralph Waldo Emerson, *Society and Solitude: Twelve Chapters* (Boston: Houghton, Mifflin, 1912), 190.

130. Emerson, *Society and Solitude*, 190.

131. "Da, my obiazany khoroshim knigam samymi glavnymi dukhovnymi blagodeianiiami v nashei zhizni.—Emerson." Tolstoy, *Krug chteniia*, *PSS*, 41:11.

132. "Chitat' sleduet tol'ko togda, kogda issiak istochnik sobstvennykh myslei, chto neredko sluchaetsia i s samym umnym chelovekom. No spugnut', radi knigi, sobstvennuiu neokrepshuiu mysl'—eto znachit sovershit' prestuplenie protiv dukha.—*Shopengauer*." Tolstoy, *Krug chteniia*, *PSS*, 41:12. Tolstoy likely draws from Schopenhauer's "On Reading and Books."

133. "[L. N.]—Zhit' nado svoim razumom, sovest'iu. Khristos, Budda dolzhny tol'ko pomogat'." Makovitskii, *U Tolstogo*, 126.

134. Anton Chekhov, "The Darling," in *Anton Chekhov's Selected Stories*, ed. Cathy Popkin (New York: W. W. Norton, 2014); "*Dushechka*," in Tolstoy, *Krug chteniia*, *PSS*. Page citations to "The Darling" are in text, followed by the Russian source *PSS*.

135. "szhimalo emu gorlo ot grusti." Makovitskii, *U Tolstogo*, 165.

136. "kakoiu ne dolzhna byt' zhenshchina." Tolstoy, "Posleslovie k rasskazu Chekhova 'Dushechka'" ["Afterword to Chekhov's story 'The Darling'"], *PSS*, 41:375.

137. "sviata, udivitel'na dusha 'Dushechki' s svoei sposobnost'iu otdavat'sia vsem sushchestvom svoim tomu, kogo ona liubit." Tolstoy, "Posleslovie," *PSS*, 41:375.

138. "on khotel svalit' Dushechku i obratil na nee usilennoe vnimanie poeta i voznes ee." Tolstoy, "Posleslovie," *PSS*, 41:377.

139. "muzhchiny ne mogut delat' togo vysshego, luchshego i naibolee priblizhaiushchego cheloveka k bogu dela,—dela liubvi, dela polnogo otdaniia sebia tomu, kogo liubish.'" Tolstoy, "Posleslovie," *PSS*, 41:376.

140. "Chitaia, v chem prizvanie zhenshchin, chego muzhchiny ne mogut (samopozhertvovanie), chut' ne zarydal i konchil so slezami." Makovitskii, *U Tolstogo*, 165.

141. "Ia ne znaiu bolee khvataiushchego za serdtse krika otchaianiia, soznaiushchego svoe odinochestvo, zabludivshegosia cheloveka, kak vyrazhenie etoi mysli v prelestneishem rasskaze 'Solitude.'" Tolstoy, "Predislovie k sochineniiam Gyui de Mopassana," *PSS*, 30:21.

142. "Kakaia strashnaia taina—neizvestnaia mysl' drugogo sushchestva . . . Vsegda na dne, na samom dne ostaetsia tainyi ugolok moego 'ia', kuda nikto ne pronikaet. Nikto ne v silakh otkryt' ego, voiti tuda, potomu chto nikto ne pokhozh na menia, i nikto nikogo ne ponimaet." I quote and translate from the Russian text published in *Krug chteniia*. Gi de Mopassan, "Odinochestvo" ["Solitude"], *PSS*, 41:565.

192

Notes to Pages 123–128

143. "Znaia, chto ia osuzhden na uzhasnoe odinochestvo, ia ravnodushno gliazhu na vsyo i ne vyskazyvaius' . . . Ne buduchi v sostoianii delit'sia nichem s liud'mi, ia bezuchasten ko vsemu. Moia nevidimaia mysl' ostaetsia neizvedan- noi." Mopassan, "Odinochestvo" ["Solitude"], *PSS*, 41:566.

144. David Herman makes an intriguing and persuasive argument that Tol- stoy "inscribes" silence into the structure of *Hadji Murat*. But, of course, there is no getting around the fact that the story must be told and so the author must speak; Herman admits that the strategy he describes is "difficult or even self- contradictory from a writer's standpoint." Herman, "Khadzhi-Murat's Silence," 2.

145. I read Tolstoy's hero as our model in *Hadji Murat*, though it is also pos- sible to regard the story's narrator as our best model, as Orwin has suggested ("Nature and the Narrator in *Chadzi-Murat*," 139). In either case, what is salient is that Tolstoy makes his point at the level of content.

CHAPTER 4

1. Stanley Corngold, *Lambent Traces: Franz Kafka* (Princeton, NJ: Princeton University Press, 2009), 135.

2. Vladimir Golstein, "Narrating the Murder: The Rhetoric of Evasion in *The Kreutzer Sonata*," *Russian Literature* 40, no. 4 (1996): 453, 454.

3. Golstein, "Narrating the Murder," 454.

4. See, for example, Vladimir Chertkov's and Nikolay Strakhov's responses in N. K. Gudziy, "Kommentarii: *Kreitserova sonata*" ["Commentary: *Kreutzer Sonata*"], *PSS*, 27: 584.

5. "Sumasshestvie eto egoizm, ili naoborot: egoizm . . . est' sumasshestvie." Tolstoy, diary entry dated January 29, 1895, *Dnevniki 1895, 1896* [*Diaries for the Years 1895, 1896*], *PSS*, 53:4.

6. Gary Saul Morson, "The Reader as Voyeur: Tolstoi and the Poetics of Di- dactic Fiction," *Canadian-American Slavic Studies* 12, no. 4 (1978): 477.

7. Nabokov to Véra Nabokov, July 6, 1926, in *Letters to Véra*, 125; *Pis'ma k Vere*, 147.

8. Nabokov to Véra Nabokov, July 12, 1926, in *Letters to Véra*, 139; *Pis'ma k Vere*, 160.

9. Nabokov to Véra Nabokov, July 13, 1926, in *Letters to Véra*, 142; *Pis'ma k Vere*, 163.

10. Vladimir Nabokov, "Rech' Pozdnysheva" ["Pozdnyshev's Address"] (1926), N38–N38j, Vladimir Nabokov Papers 1918–87, Albert A. Berg Collec- tion of English and American Literature, New York Public Library. The full text of Nabokov's work has appeared in the *Paris Review* under the title "A Mono- logue." I will cite this translation in what follows, but I will refer to the text more specifically as "Pozdnyshev's Address," which is the title Nabokov gave the

193

Notes to Pages 129–135

piece. Vladimir Nabokov, "A Monologue," introduction and translation by Tatyana Gershkovich, *Paris Review* 237 (Summer 2021): 106–14.

11. "V ego tvorcheskoi vdokhnovennoi peredache tolstovskii ubiitsa-rezoner stal zhivym stradaiushchim chelovekom, soznavshim svoiu vinu pered ubitoi zhenoi, pered pogublennoi im vozmozhnost'iu nastoiashchei podlinnoi liubvi." Raisa Tatarinova, "Sud nad *Kreitserovoi sonatoi*" ["Trial of *The Kreutzer Sonata*"], *Rul'*, no. 1709, July 18, 1926, https://dfg-viewer.de/show/?set%5Bmets%5D=https://content.staatsbibliothek-berlin.de/zefys/SNP27230028-19260718-0-0-0-0.xml.

12. "Takoe otstuplenie ot Tolstogo postavilo vsekh uchastnikov suda v neobkhodimost' schitat'sia s sushchestvovaniem dvukh Pozdnyshevykh." Tatarinova, "Sud nad *Kreitserovoi sonatoi*."

13. Nabokov to Véra Nabokov, July 13, 1926, *Letters to Véra*, 142; *Pis'ma k Vere*, 163.

14. Even critics who dismiss much of Pozdnyshev's monologue as madness tend to trust him on the sonata and dispute its salutary effect. (e.g., Gustafson and Herman). But I agree with Caryl Emerson that notwithstanding Tolstoy's late aesthetics, we should "remember that during the actual performance of the sonata in the Pozdnyshevs' drawing room, the outraged husband is moved, satisfied, ennobled." See Gustafson, *Resident and Stranger*, 369; David Herman, "Stricken by Infection"; and Caryl Emerson, "*What Is Art?* and the Anxiety of Music," *Russian Literature* 40, no. 4 (1996): 442.

15. S. A. Tolstaya, *My Life: Sofia Andreevna Tolstaya*, trans. John Woodsworth and Akradi Klioutchanski, ed. Andrew Donskov (University of Ottawa Press, 2010), 224; "vse prikhodili v vostorg, nachinaia s L'va Nikolaevicha," S. A. Tolstaia, *Moia zhizn' (v dvukh tomakh)* [*My Life: In Two Volumes*], ed. V. B. Remizov (Moscow: Kuchkovo pole, 2011), 1:253.

16. Tolstaya, *My Life*, 522; *Moia zhizn'*, 2:37.

17. Pickford, *Thinking with Tolstoy and Wittgenstein*, 90.

18. Pickford, *Thinking with Tolstoy and Wittgenstein*, 97.

19. Cavell, "Music Discomposed," in *Must We Mean What We Say?*, 198.

20. Emerson, "*What Is Art?* and The Anxiety of Music," 442.

21. Emerson, "*What Is Art?* and The Anxiety of Music," 442.

22. J. M. Coetzee, "Confession and Double Thoughts: Tolstoy, Rousseau, Dostoevsky," *Comparative Literature* 37, no. 3 (1985): 199.

23. Tolstoy, "Afterword to *Kreutzer Sonata*" (1890), in *"The Kreutzer Sonata" and Other Stories*, trans. by Louise Maude et al. (Oxford: Oxford University Press, 1999), 168; "Posleslovie k Kreitserovoi sonate," *PSS*, 27:78–92, 84.

24. Tolstoy, "Afterword to *Kreutzer Sonata*," 169–70; *PSS*, 27:85.

25. Tolstoy, "Afterword to *Kreutzer Sonata*," 172; *PSS*, 27:87.

26. Nabokov, *The Gift*, 312; *Dar*, *SS*, 3:279.

27. Nabokov, *The Gift*, 312; *Dar*, *SS*, 3:279.

28. Nabokov, *The Gift*, 330; *Dar*, *SS*, 3:296–97.

Notes to Pages 136–140

29. "Im, konechno, eto nuzhno—i kak eshche nuzhno! No gr. Tolstoi etogo ne zhelaet." Lev Shestov, *Dobro v uchenii gr. Tolstogo i F. Nittsshe: Filosofiia i propoved'* [*The Good in the Teaching of Count Tolstoy and F. Nietzsche: Philosophy and Prophecy*] (Berlin: Skify 1923), 63.

30. Nabokov, *Speak, Memory*, 290.

31. Felski, *Limits of Critique*, 110.

32. Nabokov, *Speak, Memory*, 291.

33. Nabokov, *Speak, Memory*, 291–92.

34. Richard Rorty, "The Barber of Kasbeam: Nabokov on Cruelty," in *Contingency, Irony, and Solidarity* (Cambridge: Cambridge University Press, 1989), 160.

35. Rorty, "Barber of Kasbeam," 160.

36. Rorty, "Barber of Kasbeam," 161.

37. David Rampton, *Vladimir Nabokov: A Literary Life* (London: Palgrave Macmillan, 2012), 54.

38. Julian W. Connolly, *Nabokov's Early Fiction: Patterns of Self and Other* (Cambridge: Cambridge University Press, 1992), 125.

39. Toker, *Nabokov: The Mystery of Literary Structures*, 11.

40. "[Ia] zabyl sebia, svoi prava, svoiu gordost', v pervyi raz uvidal v nei cheloveka . . . ia ponial vsyo, chto ia sdelal. Ia ponial, chto ia, ia ubil ee, chto ot menia sdelalos' to, chto ona byla zhivaia, dvizhushchaiasia, teplaia, a teper' lezhit nepodvizhnaia, voskovaia, kholodnaia i chto popravit' etogo nikogda, nigde, nichem, nel'zia." Nabokov is quoting verbatim from Tolstoy's text. The translation here is from Tolstoy, *KS*, 427–28.

41. Naiman, *Nabokov, Perversely*, 117.

42. Nabokov, "Good Readers and Good Writers," *Lectures on Literature*, 6.

43. Wayne C. Booth, *The Rhetoric of Fiction* (Chicago: University of Chicago Press, 1983), 304.

44. As Brian Boyd tells us, Nabokov corrected the English translation of *The Gift* while at work on *Pale Fire*. Boyd, *Vladimir Nabokov: The American Years*, 419.

45. Boyd, *Vladimir Nabokov: The American Years*, 446. Nabokov's interest in a "cosmic design" is at the center of Brian Boyd's important study of *Pale Fire*. Boyd notes the diversity of the novel's themes, which include "our human need for others." Ultimately, his reading foregrounds Nabokov's metaphysical concerns—his preoccupation with "the enigma of our origins and ends." Boyd, *Nabokov's "Pale Fire,"* 247, 249. Vladimir Alexandrov's seminal study *Nabokov's Otherworld* is still more overtly concerned with Nabokov's metaphysics and the unknowable "otherworld" that lies beyond this one. Alexandrov, *Nabokov's Otherworld* (Princeton, NJ: Princeton University Press, 1991). Many other excellent treatments of *Pale Fire* have debated whether the novel exhibits faith in a divine order. John Lyons, for example, sees in Nabokov's work an argument for

195

Notes to Pages 140–149

a "divine organizing principle." Lyons, "*Pale Fire* and the Fine Art of Annotation," *Wisconsin Studies in Contemporary Literature* 8, no. 2 (1967): 242. Robert Merrill alternatively considers *Pale Fire* to be "profoundly skeptical about such claims to cosmic faith." Merrill, "Nabokov and Fictional Artifice," *Modern Fiction Studies* 25, no. 3 (1979): 456.

46. Emma Lieber's treatment of the novel is a notable exception. "Nabokov," she argues, "ultimately leaves us all as solipsists and misreaders, and that it is precisely in this, oddly enough, that the depths of feeling and thought reside." I agree with Lieber that *Pale Fire* derives much of its emotional force from its reckoning with the incommunicability of individual experience, though I diverge from her sense of the novel as modeling a "graceful accommodation of otherness." Lieber, "Having Faith in Nabokov's *Pale Fire*,'" *Nabokov Studies* 11 (2007): 4, 7.

47. David Rampton, *Vladimir Nabokov* (London: Macmillan International Higher Education, 1993), 105.

48. Paul de Man, "Criticism and Crisis," in *Blindness and Insight: Essays in the Rhetoric of Contemporary Criticism* 2d ed. (Minneapolis: University of Minnesota Press, 1983), 9.

49. For a concise overview of the debate, see Pekka Tammi, "*Pale Fire*," in Alexandrov, *Garland Companion to Vladimir Nabokov*, 571–84. For a fascinating discussion of the historical Vasily Botkin as a link between Tolstoy and Nabokov, see Dana Dragunoiu, *Vladimir Nabokov and the Art of Moral Acts* (Evanston, IL: Northwestern University Press, 2021), 122–55.

50. Robert Alter, *Partial Magic: The Novel as Self-Conscious Genre* (Berkeley: University of California Press, 1975), 186; Ellen Pifer, *Nabokov and the Novel* (Cambridge: Harvard University Press, 1980).

51. Boyd, through an intricate and convincing deciphering of Nabokov's text, proposes that Hazel Shade "has herself 'begot' much of Kinbote's Zembla and, in a way quite unimagined by Kinbote, has shaped it so as to prompt her father to commit to verse the story of his lifelong quest for some escape from the limits of mortality. After death, Shade in turn begets Kinbote's Gradus fantasy and has it impart a shapeliness and suspense to the Commentary, even as he also fashions it into a meditation on the creative power unleashed by what seems the blind force of irresistibly advancing death." Boyd, *Nabokov's "Pale Fire,"* 248.

52. Ellen Pifer, *Nabokov and the Novel*, 111.

53. Glynn, *Vladimir Nabokov*, 88.

54. James Morrison, "Nabokov's Third-Person Selves," *Philological Quarterly* 71, no. 4 (Fall 1992): 499.

55. Tammi, "*Pale Fire*," 583.

56. Tammi, "*Pale Fire*," 583.

57. Nabokov, *The Gift*, 239; *SS*, 3:215.

58. Alexandrov, *Nabokov's Otherworld*, 203.

Notes to Pages 149–156

59. Boyd, *"Pale Fire,"* 248.

60. Nabokov, "Good Readers and Good Writers," *Lectures on Literature*, 2.

61. Boyd, *Vladimir Nabokov: The American Years*, 454.

62. Wood, *The Magician's Doubts*, 197.

63. Rorty, "Barber of Kasbeam," 164.

64. Rorty, "Barber of Kasbeam," 158.

65. Rorty, "Barber of Kasbeam," 160.

66. Draguniou, *Vladimir Nabokov and the Art of Moral Acts*, 145.

67. Draguniou, *Vladimir Nabokov and the Art of Moral Acts*, 155.

68. Nabokov, "The Death of Ivan Ilyich," *Lectures on Russian Literature*, 236.

69. Toker, *Nabokov: The Mystery of Literary Structures*, 15.

70. The parallels Priscilla Meyer identifies between the two novels range from crucial thematic concerns, including "the development of literature from its earliest oral stages through migration and metamorphosis," to plot devices, such as the violent confrontations between doppelgängers, to the "rosy stones" that adorn the lost paradise of each novel's protagonist. Meyer, *Find What the Sailor Has Hidden: Vladimir Nabokov's "Pale Fire"* (Middletown, CT: Wesleyan University Press, 1988), 215.

AFTERWORD

1. "Mne nedostaet toi energii zabluzhdeniia, kotoraia nuzhna dlia vsiakogo zemnogo dela." Tolstoy to A. A. Tolstaia, April 6, 1878, in *Pis'ma 1873–1879*, *PSS*, 62:408–9.

2. "Energiia zabluzhdeniia—eto poisk istiny v romane." Viktor Shklovsky, *Energiia zabluzhdeniia: Kniga o siuzhete* [*Energy of Delusion: A Book On Plot*] (Moscow: Sovetskii pisatel', 1981), 36; Boris Eikhenbaum, "Tvorcheskie stimuly L. Tolstogo" (1935) ["Creative Impulses of L. Tolstoy"], in *Raboty o L've Tolstom* [*Works on Lev Tolstoy*] (Saint Petersburg: Fakul'tet filologii i iskusstva SPbGU, 2009), 697.

3. Nabokov, "The Death of Ivan Ilyich," *Lectures on Russian Literature*, 238.

4. "Kakoi molodchina,—podumal ia.—Etogo uzhe verno zachisliat kuda-nibud' v gvardiiu." Tolstoy, "Pesni na derevne" ["Songs in the Village"], *PSS*, 37:18.

5. "—Ia govoriu: chei malyi?—peresprosil ia i oglianulsia na Prokofiia. "Litso Prokofiia smorshchilos', skuly zadrozhali. "—Moi eto,—progovoril on i, otvernu-vshis' ot menia i zakryvaia litso rukoiu, zakhliupal, kak rebenok. "I tol'ko teper', posle etikh dvukh slov Prokofiia: 'moi eto,' ia ne odnim rassudkom, no vsem sushchestvom svoim pochuvstvoval ves' uzhas togo, chto proiskhodilo peredo mnoiu v eto pamiatnoe mne tumannoe utro. Vsyo to razroznennoe, neponiatnoe,

Notes to Pages 156–160

strannoe, chto ia videl,—vse vdrug poluchilo dlia menia prostoe, iasnoe i uzhasnoe znachenie. Mne stalo muchitel'no stydno za to, chto ia smotrel na eto, kak na interesnoe zrelishche. Ia ostanovilsia i s soznaniem sovershennogo durnogo postupka vernulsia domoi." Tolstoy, "Pesni na derevne," 18.

6. "Esli khochesh' chto skazat', skazhi priamo." Tolstoy, diary entry dated July 18, 1893, *Dnevniki i zapisnye knizhki 1891–1894, PSS*, 52:93.

7. Nabokov, "The Vane Sisters," in *Stories of Vladimir Nabokov*, 619–31. Page numbers cited in text.

8. Nabokov to Katherine A. White, March 17, 1951, in *Vladimir Nabokov: Selected Letters*, 116.

9. Nabokov, printed letter, in *Encounter, Vladimir Nabokov: Selected Letters*, 286.

10. "Kogda liudi govoriat mudreno, khitro i krasno, to oni libo khotiat obmanut', libo khotiat velichat'sia. Takim liudiam ne nado verit', ne nado podrazhat' im. Khoroshie rechi prosty, poniatny vsem i razumny." Tolstoy, *Krug chteniia, PSS*, 41:106.

11. Nabokov, "The Death of Ivan Ilyich," *Lectures on Russian Literature*, 238.

12. Nabokov, "Style," in Boyd and Tolstoy, *Think, Write, Speak*, 187.

13. "Genial'neishee, chto chital,—Tolstoi—'Alesha-Gorshok.'"Alexander Blok, diary entry dated November 13, 1911, in *A. Blok. Sobranie sochinenii v vos'mi tomakh* [*A. Blok Collected Works in Eight Volumes*] (Moscow: Goslitizdat, 1963), 7:87.

14. Nabokov, "Tolstoy" (1928), trans. Dmitri Nabokov, *NOJ: Nabokov Online Journal* 3 (2009), http://www.nabokovonline.com/uploads/2/3/7/7/23779748/v3_11a_dmitri_nabokov_transl_tolstoy.pdf; http://nabokov-lit.ru/nabokov/stihi/368.htm (Russian text).

15. Nabokov, "Tolstoy."

16. Nabokov, "Tolstoy."

17. Nabokov, "Tolstoy."

Bibliography

Adamovich, Georgii. "Perechityvaia *Otchaianie*" ["Rereading *Despair*"]. In *Klassik bez retushi: Literaturnyi mir o tvorchestve Vladimira Nabokova* [*Classic without Retouching: The Literary World about the Work of Vladimir Nabokov*], edited by N. G Mel'nikov and O. A Korostelev, 123–26. Moscow: Novoe literaturnoe obozrenie, 2000.

Aikhenvald, Iulii. "Literaturnyia zametki" ["Literary Notes"]. *Rul'* no. 1877 (Berlin), February 2, 1927. https://dfg-viewer.de/show/?set%5Bmets%5D=https:// content.staatsbibliothek-berlin.de/zefys/SNP27230028-19270202-0-0-0-0 .xml.

——. "Pisatel' i chitatel'" ["The Writer and the Reader"]. In *Pokhvala prazdnosti: Sbornik statei* [*In Praise of Idleness: Collected Essays*], 84–94. Moscow: Kostry, 1922.

——. "Pokhvala prazdnosti" ["In Praise of Idleness"]. In *Pokhvala prazdnosti: Sbornik statei* [*In Praise of Idleness: Collected Essays*], 5–17. Moscow: Kostry, 1922.

——. "Pushkin." In *Siluety russkikh pisatelei* [*Silhouettes of Russian Writers*], 59–73. Moscow: Respublika, 1998.

——. "Vstuplenie" ["Introduction"]. In *Siluety russkikh pisatelei* [*Silhouettes of Russian Writers*], 14–40. Moscow: Respublika, 1998.

Aldanov, Mark. "O polozhenii emigrantskoi literatury" ["About the Situation of Émigré Literature"]. *Sovremennye zapiski* book 61 (1936): 400–408.

Alexandrov, Vladimir E, ed. *The Garland Companion to Vladimir Nabokov.* Garland Reference Library of the Humanities. New York: Garland Publishing, 1995.

——. *Limits to Interpretation: The Meanings of Anna Karenina.* Madison: University of Wisconsin Press, 2004.

——. *Nabokov's Otherworld.* Princeton, NJ: Princeton University Press, 1991.

Alter, Robert. *Partial Magic: The Novel as a Self-Conscious Genre.* Berkeley: University of California Press, 1975.

Anderson, Amanda. *The Powers of Distance.* Princeton, NJ: Princeton University Press, 2001.

Bibliography

Atwell, John E. *Schopenhauer on the Character of the World: The Metaphysics of Will.* Berkeley: University of California Press, 1995.

Babaev, Eduard. *"Anna Karenina" L. N. Tolstogo.* Moscow: Khudozhestvennaia literatura, 1978.

Barran, Thomas. "Rousseau's Political Vision and Tolstoy's *What Is Art?*" *Tolstoy Studies Journal* 5 (1992): 1–12.

Barthes, Roland. *The Pleasure of the Text.* Translated by Richard Howard. New York: Macmillan, 1975.

Beardsmore, R. W. "Wittgenstein on Tolstoi's *What Is Art?*" *Philosophical Investigations* 14, no. 3 (July 1991): 187–204.

Bellow, Saul. "On John Cheever." *New York Review of Books* 30, no. 2 (February 17, 1983): 30.

Belyi Andrei. "Lev Tolstoi i kul'tura" ["Leo Tolstoy and Culture"]. In *O religii L'va Tolstogo* [*About Leo Tolstoy's Religion*], 142–171. Moscow: Put' 1912. https://www.prlib.ru/item/353778.

Bem, Alfred. "Pis'ma o literature: Chelovek i pisatel (K stat'e Gaito Gazdanova 'O molodoi emigrantskoi literature')" ["Letters About Literature: The Person and the Writer (A Response to Gaito Gazdanov's 'About Young Émigré Literature')"]. In Gaito Gadanov, *Gaito Gazdanov: Sobranie sochinenii v piati tomakh* [*Gaito Gazdanov: Collected Works in Five Volumes*], 300–304. Moscow: Ellis Lak, 2009.

———. "V zashchitu chitatelia" ["In Defense of the Reader"]. *Rul'*, no. 3232 (Berlin), July 16, 1931. https://dfg-viewer.de/show/?set%5Bmets%5D=https://content.staatsbibliothek-berlin.de/zefys/SNP27230028-19310716-0-0-0-0.xml.

Berman, Anna A. *Siblings in Tolstoy and Dostoevsky: The Path to Universal Brotherhood.* Evanston, IL: Northwestern University Press, 2015.

Bernstein, J. M. "Aesthetics, Modernism, Literature: Cavell's Transformations of Philosophy." In *Stanley Cavell*, edited by Richard Eldridge, 107–42. Cambridge: Cambridge University Press, 2003.

Best, Stephen, and Sharon Marcus. "Surface Reading: An Introduction." *Representations* 108, no. 1 (2009): 1–21.

Blackwell, Stephen. "Nabokov's *The Gift*, Dostoevsky, and the Tradition of Narratorial Ambiguity." *Slavic Review* 76, no. 1 (2017): 147–68.

———. *Zina's Paradox: The Figured Reader in Nabokov's "Gift."* New York: Peter Lang International Academic Publishers, 2000.

Blok, Alexander. *A. Blok: Sobranie sochinenii v vos'mi tomakh* [*A. Blok: Collected Works in Eight Volumes*]. Vol. 7. Moscow: Goslitizdat, 1963.

Booth, Wayne C. *The Rhetoric of Fiction.* Chicago: University of Chicago Press, 1961.

Boyd, Brian. *Nabokov's "Pale Fire": The Magic of Artistic Discovery.* Princeton, NJ: Princeton University Press, 1999.

Bibliography

———. *Vladimir Nabokov: The American Years*. Princeton, NJ: Princeton University Press, 1991.

———. *Vladimir Nabokov: The Russian Years*. Princeton, NJ: Princeton University Press, 1990.

Brodsky, Anna. "Homosexuality in Nabokov's *Dar*." *Nabokov Studies*, no. 4 (1997): 95–115.

Brooks, Jeffrey. "Readers and Reading at the End of the Tsarist Era." In *Literature and Society in Imperial Russia 1800–1914*, edited by William Mills Todd, 97–150. Stanford, CA: Stanford University Press, 1978.

Buckler, Julie A. *The Literary Lorgnette: Attending Opera in Imperial Russia*. Stanford, CA: Stanford University Press, 2000.

Cavell, Stanley. "The Avoidance of Love." In *Must We Mean What We Say?: A Book of Essays*, 267–356. Cambridge: Cambridge University Press, 1976.

———. *The Claim of Reason: Wittgenstein, Skepticism, Morality, and Tragedy*. Oxford: Oxford University Press, 1979.

———. "Othello and the Stake of the Other." *Disowning Knowledge: In Seven Plays of Shakespeare*, 125–42. Cambridge: Cambridge University Press, 1987.

———. "Knowing and Acknowledging." In *Must We Mean What We Say?: A Book of Essays*, 238–66. Cambridge: Cambridge University Press, 1976.

———. "Music Discomposed." In *Must We Mean What We Say?: A Book of Essays*, 180–212. Cambridge: Cambridge University Press, 1976.

Chekhov, Anton. "The Darling." In *Anton Chekhov's Selected Stories: Texts of the Stories, Comparison of Translations, Life and Letters, Criticism*, edited by Cathy Popkin, 403–13. New York: W. W. Norton, 2014.

———. "Dushechka." In *Krug chteniia* [*The Circle of Reading*]. In *Lev Tolstoi: Polnoe sobranie sochinenii* [*Leo Tolstoy: Complete Collected Works*], 41:363–73. Moscow: Gosudarstvennoe izdatel'stvo Khudozhestvennaia literatura.

Chernyshevskii, Nikolai. *Esteticheskie otnosheniia iskusstva k deistvitel'nosti* [*Aesthetic Relations of Art to Reality*]. Vol. 2 of *Chernyshevskii N. G. Polnoe sobranie sochinenii v 15 tomakh* [*Chernyshevsky N. G. Complete Collected Works in 15 volumes*]. Moscow: Goslitizdat, 1949.

Coetzee, J. M. "Confession and Double Thoughts: Tolstoy, Rousseau, Dostoevsky." *Comparative Literature* 37, no. 3 (1985): 193–232.

Connolly, Julian W. *Nabokov's Early Fiction: Patterns of Self and Other*. Cambridge: Cambridge University Press, 1992.

Corngold, Stanley. *Lambent Traces: Franz Kafka*. Princeton, NJ; Princeton University Press, 2004.

Davydov, Sergey. *Teksty-Matreski Vladimira Nabokova*. Munich: Verlag Otto Sanger, 1982.

De la Durantaye, Leland. *Style Is Matter: The Moral Art of Vladimir Nabokov*. Ithaca, NY: Cornell University Press, 2007.

Bibliography

De Man, Paul. "Criticism and Crisis." In *Blindness and Insight: Essays in the Rhetoric of Contemporary Criticism*, 3–19. Minneapolis: University of Minnesota Press, 1983.

Denner, Michael. "Accidental Art: Tolstoy's Poetics of Unintentionality." *Philosophy and Literature* 27, no. 2 (2003): 284–303.

Descartes, René. *The Philosophical Writings of Descartes*. Translated by Robert Stoothoff, John Cottingham, and Dugald Murdoch. 3 vols. Cambridge: Cambridge University Press, 1985.

Diment, Galya. "Nabokov's Biographical Impulse: Art of Writing Lives." In *The Cambridge Companion to Nabokov*, edited by Julian W. Connolly, 170–84. Cambridge: Cambridge University Press, 2005.

Dolinin, Alexander. *"The Gift."* In *The Garland Companion to Vladimir Nabokov*, edited by Vladimir E. Alexandrov, 135–69. New York: Garland Publishing, 1995.

———. *"Eugene Onegin."* In *The Garland Companion to Vladimir Nabokov*, edited by Vladimir E. Alexandrov, 117–30. New York: Garland Publishing, 1995.

Dragunoiu, Dana. *Vladimir Nabokov and the Art of Moral Acts*. Evanston, IL: Northwestern University Press, 2021.

———. *Vladimir Nabokov and the Poetics of Liberalism*. Evanston, IL: Northwestern University Press, 2011.

Eikhenbaum, Boris. "Commentary to 'Zapiski sumasshedshego.'" In *Lev Tolstoi: Polnoe sobranie sochinenii* [*Leo Tolstoy: Complete Collected Works*], 26:853–54. Moscow: Gosudarstvennoe izdatel'stvo Khudozhestvennaia literatura, 1936.

———. Tolstoi in the Seventies. Translated by A. Kaspin. Ann Arbor, MI: Ardis, 1982.

———. Tolstoi in the Sixties. Translated by D. White. Ann Arbor, MI: Ardis, 1982.

———. "Tvorcheskie stimuly L. Tolstogo" (1935) ["Creative Impulses of L. Tolstoy"]. In *Raboty o L've Tolstom* [*Works on Lev Tolstoy*], 691–99. Saint Petersburg: Fakul'tet filologii i iskusstva SPbGU, 2009.

Eldridge, Hannah Vandegrift. *Lyric Orientations: Hölderlin, Rilke, and the Poetics of Community*. Ithaca, NY: Cornell University Press, 2016.

Eldridge, Richard Thomas, and Bernard Rhie. *Stanley Cavell and Literary Studies: Consequences of Skepticism*. London: Bloomsbury Publishing, 2011.

Emerson, Caryl. "Tolstoy's Aesthetics." In *The Cambridge Companion to Tolstoy*, edited by Donna Tussing Orwin, 237–51. Cambridge: Cambridge University Press, 2002.

———. *"What Is Art?* And the Anxiety of Music." *Russian Literature* 40, no. 4 (1996): 433–50.

———. "What Is Infection and What Is Expression in *What Is Art?*" In *Lev Tol-*

Bibliography

stoy and the Concept of Brotherhood, edited by Andrew Donskov and John Woodsworth, 102–15. Ottawa: Legas, 1996.

Emerson, Ralph Waldo. "Books." In Society and Solitude: Twelve Chapters, 187–221. Boston: Houghton, Mifflin, 1912.

Emery, Jacob. "Art Is Inoculation: The Infectious Imagination of Leo Tolstoy." Russian Review 70 (October 2011): 627–45.

Engelstein, Laura. Slavophile Empire: Imperial Russia's Illiberal Path. Ithaca, NY: Cornell University Press, 2009.

Evdokimova, Svetlana. "The Drawing and the Grease Spot: Creativity and Interpretation in Anna Karenina." Tolstoy Studies Journal 8 (1995–96): 33–45.

Evnin, F. I. "Poslednii shedevr Tolstogo" ["Tolstoy's Last Masterpiece"]. In Tolstoi-khudozhnik: sbornik statei [Tolstoy-Artist: Collected Essays], edited by D. D. Blagoi et al., 344–96. Moscow: Izd-vo Akademii nauk SSSR, 1961.

Fanger, Donald. "Nazarov's Mother: Notes Towards an Interpretation of Hadji Murat." In Mnemozina, edited by Norman W. Ingham Joachim T. Baer, and Stanley J. Rabinowitz, 95–104. Munich: Fink, 1974.

Felski, Rita. The Limits of Critique. Chicago: University of Chicago Press, 2015.

———. Uses of Literature. Hoboken, NJ: John Wiley and Sons, 2008.

Felski, Rita, and Elizabeth S. Anker. "Introduction." In Critique and Postcritique, edited by Elizabeth S. Anker and Rita Felski, 1–28. Durham, NC: Duke University Press, 2017.

Fet, Afanasii. "Babochka" ["Butterfly"]. In Polnoe sobranie stikhotvorenii [Complete Collected Poems]. Leningrad: Biblioteka Poeta osnovana M. Gor'kim, 1959.

Fischer, Michael. Stanley Cavell and Literary Skepticism. Chicago: University of Chicago Press, 1989.

Gatrall, Jefferson J. A. "Tolstoy, Ge, Two Pilates: A Tale of the Interarts." In From Realism to the Silver Age: New Studies in Russian Artistic Culture, edited by Margaret Samu and Rosalind P. Blakesley, 79–93. Ithaca, NY: Cornell University Press, an imprint of Northern Illinois University Press, 2014.

Gazdanov, Gaito. "O molodoi emigrantskoi literature" ["About Young Émigré Literature"]. Sovremennye zapiski book 60 (1936): 404–7.

———. Gaito Gazdanov: Sobranie sochinenii v piati tomakh [Gaito Gazdanov: Collected Works in Five Volumes]. Moscow: Ellis Lak, 2009.

Gendler, Tamar. Intuition, Imagination, and Philosophical Methodology. Oxford: Oxford University Press, 2010.

Gippius, Zinaida. "Polozhenie literaturnoi kritiki" ["The Situation of Literary Criticism]. In Gippius Z. N. Sobranie sochinenii [Z. N. Gippius Collected Works], 13: 44–9. Moscow: Dmitriy Sechin, 2012.

Givens, John. The Image of Christ in Russian Literature: Dostoevsky, Tolstoy, Bulgakov, Pasternak. DeKalb: Northern Illinois University Press, 2018.

Bibliography

Glynn, Michael. *Vladimir Nabokov: Bergsonian and Russian Formalist Influences in His Novels*. New York: Palgrave Macmillan, 2007.

Golstein, Vladimir. "Narrating the Murder: The Rhetoric of Evasion in *The Kreutzer Sonata*." *Russian Literature* 40, no. 4 (1996): 451–62.

Golubkov, A. V. "Entsiklopediia vs. kompendium: Lev Tolstoi i zapadnaia traditsiia" ["Encyclopedia vs. Compendium: Lev Tolstoy and the Western Tradition"]. *Iasnopolianskii sbornik* 27, no. 1 (2014): 304–24.

Greenleaf, Monika. "Fathers, Sons and Impostors: Pushkin's Trace in *The Gift*." *Slavic Review* 53, no. 1 (1994): 140–58.

Gudziy, N. K. "Kommentarii: *Kreitserova Sonata*" ["Commentary: *Kreutzer Sonata*"]. In *Lev Tolstoi: Polnoe sobranie sochinenii* [*Leo Tolstoy: Complete Collected Works*], 27:563–624. Moscow: Gosudarstvennoe izdatel'stvo Khudozhestvennaia literatura, 1936.

Gusev, N. N. *Letopis' zhizni i tvorchestva L'va Nikolaevicha Tolstogo: 1891–1910* [*Chronicle of the Life and Works of Lev Nikolaevich Tolstoy: 1891–1910*]. Vol. 2. Moscow: Gosudarstvennoe izdatel'stvo Khudozhestvennaia literatura, 1960.

———. *Dva goda s L. N. Tolstym: Zapiski byvshego sekretaria L. N. Tolstogo N. N. Guseva* [*Two Years with L. N. Tolstoy: Notes of L. N. Tolstoy's Former Secretary N. N. Gusev*]. Moscow: Posrednik, 1912. http://hdl.handle.net/2027/pst.000006398552.

———. "*Krug chteniia* istoriia pisaniia i pichataniia" ["History of the Writing and Publication of *The Circle of Reading*"]. In *Lev Tolstoi: Polnoe sobranie sochinenii* [*Leo Tolstoy: Complete Collected Works*], 42:557–83. Moscow: Gosudarstvennoe izdatel'stvo Khudozhestvennaia literatura, 1957.

———. *Zhizn' i uchenie L'va Tolstogo* [*The Life and Teaching of Lev Tolstoy*]. Moscow: Izdanie Obshchestva Istinnoi Svobody v pamyat' L. N. Tolstogo i Edineniia, 1920. http://hdl.handle.net/2027/umn.31951002298920j.

Gustafson, Richard F. *Leo Tolstoy, Resident and Stranger: A Study in Fiction and Theology*. Princeton, NJ: Princeton University Press, 1986.

Guyer, Paul. *A History of Modern Aesthetics*. New York: Cambridge University Press, 2014.

Halliwell, Stephen. "Tolstoy, Opera, and the Problem of Aesthetic Seduction." In *Tolstoy and His Problems: Views from the Twenty-First Century*, edited by Inessa Medzhibovskaya, 170–85. Evanston, IL: Northwestern University Press, 2019.

Heier, Edmund. "*Hadji Murat* in the Light of Tolstoy's Moral and Aesthetic Theories." *Canadian Slavonic Papers* 21, no. 3 (1979): 324–35.

Herman, David. "Allowable Passions in *Anna Karenina*." *Tolstoy Studies Journal* 8 (1995–96): 5–32.

———. "Khadzhi-Murat's Silence." *Slavic Review* 64, no. 1 (2005): 1–23.

———. "Stricken by Infection: Art and Adultery in *Anna Karenina* and *Kreutzer Sonata*." *Slavic Review* 56, no. 1 (Spring 1997): 15–36.

Bibliography

Horkheimer, Max, and Theodor W. Adorno. *Dialectic of Enlightenment: Philosophical Fragments*, edited by Schmid Noerr Gunzelin and translated by Edmund Jephcott. Stanford, CA: Stanford University Press, 2002.

Hume, David. "Of the Standard of Taste." In *Essays: Moral, Political, and Literary*, edited by Eugene F. Miller, 226–49. Indianapolis, IN: Liberty Classics, 1987.

Ishchuk, G. N. *Problema chitatelia v tvorcheskom soznanii L. N. Tolstogo. Stat'i* [*The Problem of the Reader in L. N. Tolstoy's Literary Works: Essays*]. Tver': Tver. gos. universitet, 2004.

Ivanov, Georgii. "Bez chitatelia" ["Without a Reader"]. *Chisla* 5 (1931): 148–52.

Jahn, Gary. "The Aesthetic Theory of Leo Tolstoy's *What Is Art?*" *Journal of Aesthetics and Art Criticism* 34, no. 1 (1975): 59–65.

Johnson, D. Barton. "'Terror': Pre-Texts and Post-Texts." In *A Small Alpine Form: Studies in Nabokov's Short Fiction*, edited by Charles Nicol and Gennady Barabtarlo, 39–64. New York: Garland Publishing, 1993.

Josipovici, Gabriel. *On Trust: Art and the Temptations of Suspicion.* New Haven, CT: Yale University Press, 1999.

Kant, Immanuel. *Critique of Judgment.* Translated and edited by Werner S. Pluhar. Indianapolis: Hackett Publishing, 1987.

Karlinsky, Simon. "Vladimir Nabokov's Novel *Dar* as a Work of Literary Criticism: A Structural Analysis." *Slavic and East European Journal* 7, no. 3 (1963): 284–96.

Karshan, Thomas. *Vladimir Nabokov and the Art of Play.* Oxford: Oxford University Press, 2011.

Khagi, Sofya. *Silence and the Rest: Verbal Skepticism in Russian Poetry.* Evanston, IL: Northwestern University Press, 2013.

Khodasevich, Vladislav. "O Kinematografe" ["About Cinema"]. In *Khodasevich V. F. Sobranie sochinenii v 4 tomakh* [*Khodasevich V. F. Collected Works in Four Volumes*], 2:135–39. Moscow: Soglasie, 1996. Original publication in *Poslednie novosti*, October 28, 1926.

———. "O Sirine," ["On Sirin"]. In *Khodasevich V. F. Sobranie sochinenii v 4 tomakh* [*Khodasevich V. F. Collected Works in Four Volumes*], 2: 388–95. Moscow: Soglasie, 1996. Original publication in *Vozrozhdenie*, February 13, 1937.

Kokobobo, Ani. "Tolstoy's Enigmatic Final Hero: Holy War, Sufism, and the Spiritual Path in *Hadji Murat.*" *Russian Review* 76 (January 2017): 38–52.

Kotrelev, N. V. *Biblioteka L'va Nikolaevicha Tolstogo v Iasnoi Poliane* [*Library of Lev Nikolaevich Tolstoy in Iasnaia Poliana*]. 3 vols. Tula: Dom Iasnaia Poliana, 1999.

Kramskoi, Ivan Nikolaevich. "Ob Ivanove" [About Ivanov]. In *Ivan Nikolaevich Kramskoi: Yego zhizn', perepiska i khudozhestvenno-kriticheskie stat'i 1837–1887* [*Ivan Nikolaevich Kramskoi: His Life, Correspondence and Critical Essays 1837–1887*]. Saint Petersburg: A. S. Suvorin, 1888, 647–62. https://elibrary.tambovlib.ru/?ebook=5661.

Bibliography

Kruglov, A. N. *Kant i kantovskaia filosofiia v Russkoi khudozhestvennoi litera-ture* [*Kant and Kantian Philosophy in Russian Literature*]. Moscow: Kanon, 2012.

Kupreianova, Elena. *Estetika L. N. Tolstogo* [*L. N. Tolstoy's Aesthetics*]. Moscow: Nauka, 1966.

Lange, Ernst Michael. "Wittgenstein on Solipsism." In *A Companion to Wittgenstein*, edited by Hans-Johann Glock and John Hyman, 159–74. Chichester, England: Wiley-Blackwell, 2017.

Latour, Bruno. "Why Has Critique Run out of Steam? From Matters of Fact to Matters of Concern." *Critical Inquiry* 30, no. 2 (2004): 225–48.

Layton, Susan. *Russian Literature and Empire: Conquest of the Caucasus from Pushkin to Tolstoy.* Cambridge: Cambridge University Press, 1994.

Leving, Yuri. *Keys to "The Gift": A Guide to Vladimir Nabokov's Novel.* Boston: Academic Studies Press, 2011.

Lieber, Emma. "Having Faith in Nabokov's *Pale Fire.*" *Nabokov Studies* 11 (2007): 1–9.

Lyons, John O. "*Pale Fire* and the Fine Art of Annotation." *Wisconsin Studies in Contemporary Literature* 8, no. 2 (1967): 242–49.

Makovitskii, D. P. *U Tolstogo. "Iasnopolianskie zapiski" D. P. Makovitskogo* [*At Tolstoy's: D. P. Makovitskii's Notes from Iasnaia Poliana*]. Vol. 1, 1904–5. Moscow: Nauka, 1979.

Mandel'stam, Osip. "O Sobesednike" ["About the Interlocutor"] (1913). In *O. E. Mandel'shtam: Sobranie sochinenii v 4 tomakh* [*O. E. Mandel'shtam: Collected Works in Four Volumes*]. Saint Petersburg: Art-Biznes-Tsentr, 1993–97.

Mandelker, Amy. *Framing Anna Karenina: Tolstoy, the Woman Question, and the Victorian Novel.* Columbus: Ohio State University Press, 1993.

Maud, Aylmer. "A Russian Philosopher." *Observer*, November 20, 1932, 8. Proquest Historical Newspapers.

Maupassant, Guy de. "Odinochestvo" ["Solitude"]. In *Krug chteniia* [*The Circle of Reading*]. In *Lev Tolstoi: Polnoe sobranie sochinenii* [*Leo Tolstoy: Complete Collected Works*], 41:562–67. Moscow: Gosudarstvennoe izdatel'stvo Khudozhestvennaia literatura, 1957.

McCarthy, Mary. "Bolt from the Blue: *Pale Fire* by Vladimir Nabokov." *New Republic*, June 4, 1962. https://newrepublic.com/article/63440/bolt-the-blue.

McLaughlin, Sigrid. "Some Aspects of Tolstoy's Intellectual Development: Tolstoy and Schopenhauer." *California Slavic Studies* 5 (1970): 187–245.

Merrill, Robert. "Nabokov and Fictional Artifice." *Modern Fiction Studies* 25, no. 3 (1979): 439–62.

Meyer, Priscilla. *Find What the Sailor Has Hidden: Vladimir Nabokov's "Pale Fire."* Middletown: Wesleyan University Press, 1988.

Mishin, V. S. "Istoriia pisaniia i pechataniia statei ob iskusstve i traktata *Chto takoe iskusstvo?*" [History of the Writing and Publication of (Tolstoy's) Essays

Bibliography

on Art and the Treatise *What Is Art?*]. In *Lev Tolstoi: Polnoe sobranie sochinenii* [*Leo Tolstoy: Complete Collected Works*], 30:509–16, Moscow: Gosudarstvennoe izdatel'stvo Khudozhestvennaia literatura, 1956.

———. *"Kalendar' s poslovitsami na 1887 god:* Istoriia pisaniia i pechataniia" [*"Calendar of Proverbs for the Year 1887*: History of Writing and Publication"]. In *Lev Tolstoi: Polnoe sobranie sochinenii* [*Leo Tolstoy: Complete Collected Works*], 40:471–74. Moscow: Gosudarstvennoe izdatel'stvo Khudozhestvennaia literatura, 1956.

Moi, Toril. "'Nothing Is Hidden': From Confusion to Clarity; or, Wittgenstein on Critique." In *Critique and Postcritique*, edited by Elizabeth S. Anker and Rita Felski, 31–49. Durham: Duke University Press, 2017.

Moran, Richard. "Kant, Proust, and the Appeal of Beauty." *Critical Inquiry* 38, no. 2 (Winter 2012): 298–329.

Morrison, James. "Nabokov's Third-Person Selves." *Philological Quarterly* 71, no. 4 (Fall 1992): 495–509.

Morson, Gary Saul. *Anna Karenina in Our Time: Seeing More Wisely.* New Haven, CT: Yale University Press, 2007.

———. "Anna's Omens." In *Narrative and Freedom: The Shadows of Time.* New Haven, CT: Yale University Press, 1994.

———. *Hidden in Plain View: Narrative and Creative Potentials in "War and Peace."* Stanford, CA: Stanford University Press, 1987.

———. "The Reader as Voyeur: Tolstoi and the Poetics of Didactic Fiction." *Canadian-American Slavic Studies* 12, no. 4 (1978): 465–80.

Nabokov, Vladimir. *The Annotated Lolita.* Edited by Alfred Appel. New York: Vintage Books, 1991.

———. "Classroom Teaching Material, Creative Writing Course." Vladimir Vladimirovich Nabokov Papers. Manuscript Division, Library of Congress, Washington, DC.

———. "A Commentary." In Alexander Pushkin, *Eugene Onegin: A Novel in Verse*, translated from the Russian with a commentary by Vladimir Nabokov in 4 vols. Vol. 2. New York: Bollinger Foundation, Random House, 1964.

———. *Dar.* In *Vladimir Nabokov: Sobranie sochinenii v chetyrekh tomakh* [*Vladimir Nabokov: Collected Works in Four Volumes.*], 3:5–330. Moscow: Pravda, 1990.

———. *Despair.* New York: Vintage International, 1965.

———. *The Gift.* New York: Vintage International, 1991.

———. *Lectures on Literature.* Edited by Fredson Bowers. New York: Harcourt Brace Jovanovich, 1980.

———. *Lectures on Russian Literature.* Edited by Fredson Bowers. New York: Harcourt Brace Jovanovich, 1981.

———. *Letters to Véra.* Edited by Ol'ga Voronina and Brian Boyd. New York: Alfred A. Knopf, 2015.

Bibliography

———. "A Monologue." Introduction and translation by Tatyana Gershkovich. *Paris Review* 237 (Summer 2021): 106–14.

———. *Nikolai Gogol.* New York: New Directions Books, 1961.

———. *Pale Fire: A Novel.* New York: Vintage International, 1989.

———. "Pamiati Iu. I. Aikhenval'da" ["In Memory of Iulii I. Aikhenval'd"]. *Rul'* no. 2457 (Berlin), December 23, 1928, 4. http://zefys.staatsbibliothek -berlin.de/kalender/auswahl/date/1928-12-23/27230028.

———. *Pis'ma k Vere, Kommentarii Ol'gi Voroninoy i Braiana Boida [Letters to Vera, with commentary by Olga Voronina and Brian Boyd].* Edited by Olga Voronina and Brian Boyd. Moscow: Azbuka-Attikus, KoLibri, 2017.

———. "Pushkin, or the True and the Seemingly True." In *Think, Write, Speak: Uncollected Essays, Reviews, Interviews, and Letters to the Editor*, edited and translated by Brian Boyd and Anastasia Tolstoy, 118–32. New York: Alfred A. Knopf, 2019.

———. "Rech' Pozdnysheva" ["Pozdnyshev's Address"] (1926). Vladimir Nabokov Papers 1918–87, Henry W. and Albert A. Berg Collection of English and American Literature, New York Public Library.

———. "Signs and Symbols." In *The Stories of Vladimir Nabokov*, 598–603. New York: Vintage International, 1996.

———. *Speak, Memory: An Autobiography Revisited.* New York: Vintage International, 1989.

———. *Strong Opinions.* New York: Vintage Books, 1990.

———. "Style." In *Think, Write, Speak: Uncollected Essays, Reviews, Interviews, and Letters to the Editor*, edited and translated by Brian Boyd and Anastasia Tolstoy, 187–90. New York: Alfred A. Knopf, 2019.

———. "Terror." In *The Stories of Vladimir Nabokov*, 173–78. New York: Vintage. International, 1996.

———. "Tolstoy: Miscellaneous Lecture Notes." Vladimir Nabokov Papers 1918–87, Henry W. and Albert A. Berg Collection of English and American Literature, New York Public Library.

———. "Tolstoy" (1928). Translated by Dmitri Nabokov. *NOJ: Nabokov Online Journal* 3 (2009). http://www.nabokovonline.com/uploads/2/3/7/7/23779748/ v3_11a_dmitri_nabokov_transl_tolstoy.pdf; http://nabokov-lit.ru/nabokov/ stihi/368.htm (Russian text).

———. "Uzhas." In *Vladimir Nabokov: Sobranie sochinenii v chetyrekh tomakh [Vladimir Nabokov: Collected Works in Four Volumes]*, 1: 397–402. Moscow: Pravda, 1990.

———. "The Vane Sisters." In *The Stories of Vladimir Nabokov*, 619–31. New York: Vintage International, 1996.

———. *Vladimir Nabokov: Selected Letters, 1940–1977.* Edited by Dmitri Nabokov and Matthew J. Bruccoli. San Diego and New York: Harcourt Brace Jovanovich, 1989.

Bibliography

Nabokov, Vladimir, and Robert Robinson. "The Last Interview." In *Vladimir Nabokov: A Tribute*, 119–25. New York: William Morrow, 1980.

Naiman, Eric. *Nabokov, Perversely*. Ithaca, NY: Cornell University Press, 2010.

Nikolaeva, S. Iu. "Zhanrovoe svoeobrazie knigi L. N. Tolstogo *Krug chteniia*" ["The Generic Distinctiveness of Leo Tolstoy's *The Circle of Reading*"]. *Iasnopolianskii sbornik* (2010): 128–52.

Orwin, Donna Tussing. *The Cambridge Companion to Tolstoy*. Cambridge: Cambridge University Press, 2002.

———. "Nature and the Narrator in *Chadzi-Murat*." *Russian Literature* 28 (1990): 125–44.

———. *Tolstoy's Art and Thought, 1847–1880*. Princeton, NJ: Princeton University Press, 1993.

Paperno, Irina. "How Nabokov's *Gift* Is Made." *Stanford Slavic Studies* 4, no. 2 (1992): 295–324.

———. *"Who, What Am I?": Tolstoy Struggles to Narrate the Self*. Ithaca, NY: Cornell University Press, 2014.

Pickford, Henry W. *Thinking with Tolstoy and Wittgenstein Expression, Emotion, and Art*. Evanston, IL: Northwestern University Press, 2015.

Pifer, Ellen. *Nabokov and the Novel*. Cambridge, MA: Harvard University Press, 1980.

Pisarev, Dmitrii. "Razrushenie estetiki" ["The Destruction of Aesthetics"]. In *D. I. Pisarev: literaturnaia Kritika v trekh tomakh* [*D. I. Pisarev: Literary Criticism in Three Volumes*]. Leningrad: Khudozhestvennaia literatura, 1981.

Plato. "Symposium." In *A Plato Reader: Readings from the Dialogues*, edited by Ronald Bartlett Levinson, 112–54. Boston: Houghton Mifflin, 1967.

———. "Ion." In *The Dialogues of Plato: Ion, Hippias Minor, Laches, Protagoras*, translated and commentary by R. E. Allen, 3: 9–22. New Haven, CT: Yale University Press, 1996.

Pol'skaia, Svetlana. "Kommentarii k rasskazu V. Nabokova 'Oblako, ozero, bashnia.'" ["Commentary to 'Cloud, Castle, Lake'"]. *Scando-Slavica* 39, no. 1 (1989): 111–23.

Popkin, Richard. "The High Road to Pyrrhonism." *American Philosophical Quarterly* 2, no. 1 (January 1965): 18–32.

Popkin, Richard, and Avrum Stroll. *Skeptical Philosophy for Everyone*. Princeton, NJ: Prometheus, 2001.

Raeff, Marc. *Russia Abroad: A Cultural History of the Russian Emigration: 1919–1939*. Oxford: Oxford University Press, 1990.

Rampton, David. *Vladimir Nabokov*. London: Macmillan International Higher Education, 1993.

———. *Vladimir Nabokov: A Critical Study of the Novels*. Cambridge: Cambridge University Press, 1984.

Bibliography

―――. *Vladimir Nabokov: A Literary Life*. New York: Palgrave Macmillan, 2012.

Rancière, Jacques. "Why Emma Bovary Had to Be Killed." *Critical Inquiry* 34, no. 2 (2008): 233–48.

Ricoeur, Paul. *Freud and Philosophy: An Essay on Interpretation*. Translated by Denis Savage. New Haven, CT: Yale University Press, 1970.

Robbins, Bruce. "Not So Well Attached." *PMLA* 132, no. 2 (2017): 371–76.

Robinson, Douglas. "Tolstoy's Infection Theory and the Aesthetics of De- and Repersonalization." *Tolstoy Studies Journal* 19 (2007): 33–53.

Ronen, Irena, and Omry Ronen. "'Diabolically Evocative': An Inquiry into the Meaning of a Metaphor." *Slavica Hierosolymitana* 5–6 (1981): 371–86.

Rorty, Richard. "The Barber of Kasbeam: Nabokov on Cruelty." In *Contingency, Irony, and Solidarity*, 141–68. Cambridge: Cambridge University Press, 1989.

Rydel, Christine A. "Nabokov and Tiutchev." In *Nabokov at Cornell*, edited by Gavriel Shapiro, 123–35. Ithaca, NY: Cornell University Press, 2003.

Sass, Louis A. "'My So-Called Delusions': Solipsism, Madness, and the Schreber Case." *Journal of Phenomenological Psychology* 25, no. 1 (1994): 70–103.

Schopenhauer, Arthur. *The World as Will and Representation*. 2 vols. New York: Dover Publications, 1966.

Seifrid, Thomas. "Nabokov's Poetics of Vision or What *Anna Karenina* Is Doing in *Kamera obskura*." *Nabokov Studies* 3 (1996): 1–12.

―――. "Gazing on Life's Page: Perspectival Vision in Tolstoy." *PMLA* 113, no. 3 (1998): 436–48.

Sergeenko, A. P. "Kommentarii *Hadji Murat*" ["Commentary to *Hadji Murat*"]. In *Lev Tolstoi: Polnoe sobranie sochinenii* [*Leo Tolstoy: Complete Collected Works*], 35:582–628. Moscow: Gosudarstvennoe izdatel'stvo Khudozhestvennaia literatura.

Shestov, Lev. "Otkroveniia smerti: Poslednie proizvedeniia L. N. Tolstogo" ["Revelations of Death: L. N. Tolstoy's Last Works"]. *Sovremennye zapiski*, book 1 (Paris, 1920): 81–106.

―――. *Dobro v uchenii gr. Tolstogo i F. Nittsshe: Filosofiia i propoved'* [*The Good in the Teaching of Count Tolstoy and F. Nietzsche: Philosophy and Prophecy*]. Berlin: Skify, 1923.

Shklovsky, Viktor. "Art as Device." In *Theory of Prose*, translated by Benjamin Sher, 1–14. Chicago: Dalkey Archive Press, 1991.

―――. *Energiia zabluzhdeniia: Kniga o siuzhete* [*Energy of Delusion: A Book on Plot*]. Moscow: Sovetskii pisatel', 1981.

―――. "Iskusstvo, kak priem" ["Art as Device"]. In *O teorii prozy*. Moscow: Federatsiia, 1929.

―――. *Lev Tolstoi: zhizn' znamenitykh lyudei*. [*Lev Tolstoy: Life of Renowned People*]. Moscow: TsK VLKTsM Molodaia Gvardiia, 1963.

Bibliography

Šilbajoris, Rimvydas. *Tolstoy's Aesthetics and His Art*. Bloomington, IN: Slavica Publishers, 1991.

Sisson, J. B. "Nabokov's Cosmic Synchronization and 'Something Else.'" *Nabokov Studies* 1 (1994): 155–77.

Smith, Zadie. "Rereading Barthes and Nabokov." In *Changing My Mind: Occasional Essays*, 42–57. New York: Penguin Books, 2010.

Sorokin, Boris. *Tolstoy in Prerevolutionary Russian Criticism*. Columbus: Ohio State University Press for Miami University, 1979.

Stenbock-Fermor, Elisabeth. *The Architecture of Anna Karenina: A History of Its Writing, Structure, and Message*. Philadelphia: John Benjamins, 1975.

Tammi, Pekka. "Pale Fire." In *The Garland Companion to Vladimir Nabokov*, edited by Vladimir E. Alexandrov, 571–86. New York: Garland Publishing, 1995.

Taneev, Sergei. *Dnevniki v 3 knigakh: 1894–1909* [*Diaries in Three Volumes: 1894–1909*]. Vol. 1. Moscow: Muzyka, 1981.

Tatarinova, Raisa. "Sud nad *Kreitserovoi sonatoi*" ["Trial of *The Kreutzer Sonata*"]. *Rul'*, no. 1709 (Berlin), July 18, 1926. https://dfg-viewer.de/show/?set%5Bmets%5D=https://content.staatsbibliothek-berlin.de/zefys/SNP27230028-19260718-0-0-0-0.xml.

Toker, Leona. *Nabokov: The Mystery of Literary Structures*. Ithaca, NY: Cornell University Press, 1989.

———. "'Signs and Symbols' in and out of Contexts." In *A Small Alpine Form: Studies in Nabokov's Short Fiction*, edited by Charles Nicol and Gennady Barabtarlo, 167–80. New York: Garland Publishing, 1993.

Tolstaia, S. A. [Sofia Andreevna]. *Dnevniki v dvukh tomakh* [*Diaries in Two Volumes*]. Moscow: Khudozhestvennaia literatura, 1978.

———. *Moia Zhizn' (v dvukh tomakh)* [*My Life: In Two Volumes*]. Edited by V. B. Remizov. 2 vols. Moscow: Kuchkovo pole, 2011.

Tolstaya, S. A. *My Life: Sofia Andreevna Tolstaya*. Edited by Andrew Donskov. Translated by John Woodsworth and Arkadi Klioutchanski. Ottawa: University of Ottawa Press, 2010.

Tolstoy, Leo. "Afterword to *The Kreutzer Sonata*." In *The Kreutzer Sonata and Other Stories*, 161–77. Oxford: Oxford University Press, 1997.

———. "Alyosha Gorshok." In *Tolstoy's Short Fiction: Revised Translations, Backgrounds and Sources, Criticism*, edited and translated by Michael R. Katz, 279–84. New York: Norton, 2008.

———. *Anna Karenina: A Novel in Eight Parts*. Translated by Larissa Volokhonsky and Richard Pevear. New York: Penguin Books, 2000.

———. *Anna Karenina*. Vols. 18–19 of *Lev Tolstoi: Polnoe sobranie sochinenii* [*Leo Tolstoy: Complete Collected Works*]. Moscow: Gosudarstvennoe izdatel'stvo Khudozhestvennaia literatura, 1934, 1935.

———. *Anna Karenina: Chernovye redaktsii i varianty* [*Anna Karenina: Draft*

Bibliography

Editions and Variants]. Vol. 20 of *Lev Tolstoi: Polnoe sobranie sochinenii* [*Leo Tolstoy: Complete Collected Works*]. Moscow: Gosudarstvennoe izdatel'stvo Khudozhestvennaia literatura, 1939.

————. *Chto takoe iskusstvo?* [*What Is Art?*]. Vol. 30:27–203. In *Lev Tolstoi: Polnoe sobranie sochinenii* [*Leo Tolstoy: Complete Collected Works*]. Moscow: Gosudarstvennoe izdatel'stvo Khudozhestvennaia literatura, 1951.

————. *A Confession*. Translated by Anthony Briggs. Hesperus Classics. London: Hesperus Press, 2010.

————. *Dnevnik 1847–1854* [*Diaries 1847–1854*]. Vol. 46 of *Lev Tolstoi: Polnoe sobranie sochinenii* [*Leo Tolstoy: Complete Collected Works*]. Moscow: Gosudarstvennoe izdatel'stvo Khudozhestvennaia literatura, 1937.

————. *Dnevniki i zapisnye knizhki 1858–1880* [*Diaries and Notebooks 1858–1880*]. Vol. 48 of *Lev Tolstoi: Polnoe sobranie sochinenii* [*Leo Tolstoy: Complete Collected Works*]. Moscow: Gosudarstvennoe izdatel'stvo Khudozhestvennaia literatura, 1952.

————. *Dnevniki i zapisnye knizhki 1895–1899* [*Diaries and Notebooks 1895–1899*]. Vol. 53 of *Lev Tolstoi: Polnoe sobranie sochinenii* [*Leo Tolstoy: Complete Collected Works*]. Moscow: Gosudarstvennoe izdatel'stvo Khudozhestvennaia literatura, 1953.

————. *Dnevniki 1895, 1896* [*Diaries for the Years 1895, 1896*]. Vol. 53 of *Lev Tolstoi: Polnoe sobranie sochinenii* [*Leo Tolstoy: Complete Collected Works*]. Moscow: Gosudarstvennoe izdatel'stvo Khudozhestvennaia literatura, 1953.

————. *Dnevniki i zapisnye knizhki 1881–1887* [*Diaries and Notebooks 1881–1887*]. Vol. 49 of *Lev Tolstoi: Polnoe sobranie sochinenii* [*Leo Tolstoy: Complete Collected Works*]. Moscow: Gosudarstvennoe izdatel'stvo Khudozhestvennaia literatura, 1952.

————. *Dnevniki i zapisnye knizhki 1888–1889* [*Diaries and Notebooks 1888–1889*]. Vol. 50 of *Lev Tolstoi: Polnoe sobranie sochinenii* [*Leo Tolstoy: Complete Collected Works*]. Moscow: Gosudarstvennoe izdatel'stvo Khudozhestvennaia literatura, 1952.

————. *Dnevniki i zapisnye knizhki 1891–1894* [*Diaries and Notebooks, 1891–1894*]. Vol. 52 of *Lev Tolstoi: Polnoe sobranie sochinenii* [*Lev Tolstoy: Complete Collected Works*]. Moscow: Gosudarstvennoe izdatel'stvo Khudozhestvennaia literatura, 1952.

————. *Dnevniki i zapisnye knizhki 1904–1906* [*Diaries and Notebooks 1904–1906*]. Vol. 55 of *Lev Tolstoi: Polnoe sobranie sochinenii* [*Leo Tolstoy: Complete Collected Works*]. Moscow: Gosudarstvennoe izdatel'stvo Khudozhestvennaia literatura, 1937.

————. *Dnevniki, zapisnye knizhki i otdel'nye zapiski 1907–1908* [*Diaries, Notebooks and Miscellaneous Notes 1907–1908*]. Vol. 56 of *Lev Tolstoi: Polnoe sobranie sochinenii* [*Leo Tolstoy: Complete Collected Works*]. Moscow: Gosudarstvennoe izdatel'stvo Khudozhestvennaia literatura, 1937.

Bibliography

———. *Hadji Murad.* In *Great Short Works of Leo Tolstoy*, translated by Louise Maude et al., 547–668. New York: Harper Perennial Modern Classics, 2004.

———. *Ispoved'* [*Confession*]. Vol. 23:515–36. In *Lev Tolstoi: Polnoe sobranie sochinenii* [*Leo Tolstoy: Complete Collected Works*]. Moscow: Gosudarstvennoe izdatel'stvo Khudozhestvennaia literatura, 1957.

———. "K chitateliam" ["To Readers"]. In *Lev Tolstoi: Polnoe sobranie sochinenii* [*Leo Tolstoy: Complete Collected Works*], 1:152–53. Moscow: Gosudarstvennoe izdatel'stvo Khudozhestvennaia literatura, 1935.

———. *Kalendar' s poslovitsami na 1887 god* [*Calendar of Proverbs for the Year 1887*]. Vol. 40:7–66. In *Lev Tolstoi: Polnoe sobranie sochinenii* [*Leo Tolstoy: Complete Collected Works*]. Moscow: Gosudarstvennoe izdatel'stvo Khudozhestvennaia literatura, 1956.

———. *Khadzhi-Murt* [Hadji Murat]. Vol. 35:5–118. In *Lev Tolstoi: Polnoe sobranie sochinenii* [*Leo Tolstoy: Complete Collected Works*]. Moscow: Gosudarstvennoe izdatel'stvo Khudozhestvennaia literatura, 1950.

———. *Kreitserova Sonata* [*The Kreutzer Sonata*]. Vol. 27:5–78. In *Lev Tolstoi: Polnoe sobranie sochinenii* [*Leo Tolstoy: Complete Collected Works*]. Moscow: Gosudarstvennoe izdatel'stvo Khudozhestvennaia literatura, 1936.

———. *The Kreutzer Sonata.* In *Great Short Works of Leo Tolstoy*, translated by Louise Maude et al., 353–449. New York: Harper Perennial Modern Classics, 2004.

———. *Krug chteniia* [*The Circle of Reading*]. Vols. 41–42. In *Lev Tolstoi: Polnoe sobranie sochinenii* [*Leo Tolstoy: Complete Collected Works*]. Moscow: Gosudarstvennoe izdatel'stvo Khudozhestvennaia literatura, 1957.

———. "*Krug chteniia*, predislovie" ["*The Circle of Reading*: Foreword"]. In *Lev Tolstoi: Polnoe sobranie sochinenii* [*Leo Tolstoy: Complete Collected Works*], 42:470–3. Moscow: Gosudarstvennoe izdatel'stvo Khudozhestvennaia literatura, 1957.

———. "Memoirs of a Madman." In *Tolstoy's Short Fiction*, translated by Louise and Aylmer Maude and edited by Michael R. Katz, 303–13. New York: W. W. Norton, 2008.

———. "Nedelanie" ["Not-Doing"]. In *Lev Tolstoi: Polnoe sobranie sochinenii* [*Leo Tolstoy: Complete Collected Works*], 29:173–201. Moscow: Gosudarstvennoe izdatel'stvo Khudozhestvennaia literatura, 1954.

———. "O Shekspire i o drame" ["On Shakespeare and on Drama"]. In *Lev Tolstoi: Polnoe sobranie sochinenii* [*Leo Tolstoy: Complete Collected Works*], 35:216–73. Moscow: Gosudarstvennoe izdatel'stvo Khudozhestvennaia literatura, 1950.

———. "O tom, chto est' i chto ne est' iskusstvo" ["About What Is and What Is Not Art"]. In *Lev Tolstoi: Polnoe sobranie sochinenii* [*Leo Tolstoy: Complete Collected Works*], 30:442–51. Moscow: Gosudarstvennoe izdatel'stvo Khudozhestvennaia literatura, 1951.

Bibliography

———. "O tom, chto nazyvaiut iskusstvom" ["About What Is Called Art"]. In *Lev Tolstoi: Polnoe sobranie sochinenii* [*Leo Tolstoy: Complete Collected Works*], 30:243–70. Moscow: Gosudarstvennoe izdatel'stvo Khudozhestvennaia literatura, 1951.

———. "Ob iskusstve" ["About Art"]. In *Lev Tolstoi: Polnoe sobranie sochinenii* [*Leo Tolstoy: Complete Collected Works*], 30:213–15. Moscow: Gosudarstvennoe izdatel'stvo Khudozhestvennaia literatura, 1951.

———. "Pesni na derevne" ["Songs in the Village"]. In *Lev Tolstoi: Polnoe sobranie sochinenii* [*Leo Tolstoy: Complete Collected Works*], 37:14–19. Moscow: Gosudarstvennoe izdatel'stvo Khudozhestvennaia literatura, 1956.

———. *Pis'ma 1873–1879* [*Letters 1873–1879*]. Vol. 62. In *Lev Tolstoi: Polnoe sobranie sochinenii* [*Leo Tolstoy: Complete Collected Works*]. Moscow: Gosudarstvennoe izdatel'stvo Khudozhestvennaia literatura, 1953.

———. *Pis'ma 1890–1891* [*Letters 1890–1891*]. Vol. 65. In *Lev Tolstoi: Polnoe sobranie sochinenii* [*Leo Tolstoy: Complete Collected Works*]. Moscow: Gosudarstvennoe izdatel'stvo Khudozhestvennaia literatura, 1953.

———. *Pis'ma 1899–1900* [*Letters 1899–1900*]. Vol. 72. In *Lev Tolstoi: Polnoe sobranie sochinenii* [*Complete Collected Works*]. Moscow: Gosudarstvennoe izdatel'stvo Khudozhestvennaia literatura, 1933.

———. *Pis'ma 1908* [*Letters 1908*]. Vol. 78. In *Lev Tolstoi: Polnoe sobranie sochinenii* [*Leo Tolstoy: Complete Collected Works*]. Moscow: Gosudarstvennoe izdatel'stvo Khudozhestvennaia literatura, 1956.

———. *Pis'ma 1910* [*Letters 1910*]. Vol. 81. In *Lev Tolstoi: Polnoe sobranie sochinenii* [*Leo Tolstoy: Complete Collected Works*]. Moscow: Gosudarstvennoe izdatel'stvo Khudozhestvennaia literatura, 1956.

———. *Pis'ma k S. A. Tolstoy 1862–1886* [*Letters to S. A. Tolstoy, 1862–1886*]. Vol. 83. In *Lev Tolstoi: Polnoe sobranie sochinenii* [*Leo Tolstoy: Complete Collected Works*]. Moscow: Gosudarstvennoe izdatel'stvo Khudozhestvennaia literatura, 1938.

———. *Pis'ma k V. G. Chertkovu 1883–1886* [*Letters to V. G. Chertkov, 1883–1886*]. Vol. 85. In *Lev Tolstoi: Polnoe sobranie sochinenii* [*Leo Tolstoy: Complete Collected Works*]. Moscow: Gosudarstvennoe izdatel'stvo Khudozhestvennaia literatura, 1935.

———. *Pis'ma k V. G. Chertkovu 1897–1910* [*Letters to V. G. Chertkov, 1897–1910*]. Vol. 88. In *Lev Tolstoi: Polnoe sobranie sochinenii* [*Leo Tolstoy: Complete Collected Works*]. Moscow: Gosudarstvennoe izdatel'stvo Khudozhestvennaia literatura, 1957.

———. *Lev Tolstoi: Polnoe sobranie sochinenii* [*Leo Tolstoy: Complete Collected Works*]. 90 Vols. Moscow: Gosudarstvennoe izdatel'stvo Khudozhestvennaia literatura, 1928–58.

———. "Posleslovie k *Kreitserovoi Sonate*" ["Afterword to *The Kreutzer Sonata*"]. In *Lev Tolstoi: Polnoe sobranie sochinenii* [*Leo Tolstoy: Complete*

Bibliography

Collected Works], 27:79–91. Moscow: Gosudarstvennoe izdatel'stvo Khudozhestvennaia literatura, 1936.

———. "Posleslovie k rasskazu chekhova 'Dushechka'" ["Afterword to Chekhov's Story 'The Darling'"]. In *Krug chteniia*. In *Lev Tolstoi: Polnoe sobranie sochinenii [Leo Tolstoy: Complete Collected Works*], 41:373–76. Moscow: Gosudarstvennoe izdatel'stvo Khudozhestvennaia literatura.

———. "Predislovie k sochineniiam Gyui de Mopassana" ["Preface to the Works of Guy de Maupassant"]. In *Lev Tolstoi: Polnoe sobranie sochinenii [Leo Tolstoy: Complete Collected Works*], 30:3–26. Moscow: Gosudarstvennoe izdatel'stvo Khudozhestvennaia literatura, 1951.

———. "Rech' v obshchestve liubitelei rossiiskoi slovesnosti" ["Society of Lovers of the Russian Word"]. In *Lev Tolstoi: Polnoe sobranie sochinenii [Leo Tolstoy: Complete Collected Works*], 5:271–72. Moscow: Gosudarstvennoe izdatel'stvo Khudozhestvennaia literatura, 1935.

———. "Son" ["Dream"]. In *Lev Tolstoi: Polnoe sobranie sochinenii [Leo Tolstoy: Complete Collected Works*], 60:246–52. Moscow: Gosudarstvennoe izdatel'stvo Khudozhestvennaia literatura, 1949.

———. *What Is Art?* New York: Bobbs-Merrill, 1960.

———. "Zapiski sumasshedshego" ["Memoirs of a Madman"]. In *Lev Tolstoi: Polnoe sobranie sochinenii [Leo Tolstoy: Complete Collected Works*], 26:466–74. Moscow: Gosudarstvennoe izdatel'stvo Khudozhestvennaia literatura, 1936.

Vandenabeele, Bart. *The Sublime in Schopenhauer's Philosophy*. New York: Palgrave Macmillan, 2015.

Veidle, Vladimir. "Rets. *Otchaianie*" ["Review of *Despair*"]. In *Klassik bez retushi: Literaturnyi mir o tvorchestve Vladimira Nabokova [Classic without Retouching: The Literary World about the Work of Vladimir Nabokov*], edited by N. G Mel'nikov and O. A Korostelev, 127. Moscow: Novoe literaturnoe obozrenie, 2000.

Weir, Justin. *Leo Tolstoy and the Alibi of Narrative*. New Haven, CT: Yale University Press, 2011.

Wittgenstein, Ludwig. *The Blue and Brown Books*. New York: Harper Torchbooks, 1965.

———. "Notes for Lectures on 'Private Experience' and 'Sense Data.'" *Philosophical Review* 77, no. 3 (July 1968): 275–320.

———. *Culture and Value*. Edited by G. H. von Wright, Heikki Nyman, and Peter Winch. Chicago: University of Chicago Press, 1980.

Wood, Michael. *The Magician's Doubts*. Princeton, NJ: Princeton University Press, 1994.

Index

"About What Is Called Art" (Tolstoy), 107, 112–13
"absolute language," 116, 119
Adamovich, Georgii, 60
aesthetic experience, 17–18, 50, 62, 92, 96, 102–3
aesthetic judgments, 21, 24–28, 40–41, 57, 101–2, 106, 154, 174n119
aesthetic objectivity, 26–29, 50–51, 53–54, 56, 58–59, 101–2, 106
aesthetic pleasure: and the agreeable, 53–55, 59; and desire, 56–58; and moral judgments, 100–101, 103
Aesthetic Relations of Art to Reality, The (Chernyshevsky), 24–25
aesthetics, defined, 25, 38, 93
aesthetic sense/cognition, 24–25, 42, 122, 172n90
aesthetic skepticism, 25–28, 38, 42, 49–50, 58–59. *See also* skepticism
"Afterword to 'The Darling'" (Tolstoy), 121–22
Aikhenvald, Yuly, 15–16, 72, 86–88, 113–14
Aldanov, Mark, 73–74
Alexandrov, Vladimir, 23, 39, 66, 149, 170n59, 171n69, 177n29, 195n45
Alter, Robert, 141
"Alyosha Gorshok" (Tolstoy), 3
Anderson, Amanda, 164n65
Anker, Elizabeth, 17, 19
Anna Karenina (Tolstoy): artmaking in, 14, 20–22, 34–36, 39–43, 48–50, 58, 99, 106; beauty and desire in, 48–49, 51–59; doubt in, 13, 29–31, 34, 43, 46–47, 49–50, 62, 75, 136; Nabokov on, 86; pleasure in, 36, 41, 43, 49, 52–55, 101; shared customs in, 33–34, 47–48, 50; solitude in,

30, 34–35, 45–47, 50, 122; staring/passive hyperconcentration in, 29–36, 38–39, 44–47; and transcendent vision, 39, 43, 49–50, 170n59; "uncertain artist" in, 20–21, 43–45, 50, 58–59, 66–67, 72, 91; "work cure" in, 37–38, 42, 44–45, 47–48; writing of, 41–42, 45, 52–55, 169n49
Appearance of Christ before the People, The (Ivanov), 40–41, 170n58
Appel, Alfred, 23, 61
Arnold, Matthew, 117
art: and acuity of vision, 35–36, 38–39, 54–55; and artistic imagination, 70–72; and artistic sincerity/simplicity, 106–7, 158–59; ascetic avoidance of, 107–8; on Biblical themes, 39–41, 43; as contrition, 152–54; and convention, 38–39, 41–42, 49; crisis of faith in, 148–49; defined, 24–28, 36, 38–39, 85–87, 90, 93–94, 106–7; as enchanting, 17, 58, 92–93; and energy of delusion, 155; and idleness, 112–15, 124, 133; as infection, 3, 22, 93–95, 97–100, 106–7, 112–13, 123, 131–32, 134–35; as intoxicating, 94–95, 98, 114, 126; as liberatory/transformative, 130–34; vs. life, 181n85; and moral judgments, 100–101, 103; and newness vs. significance, 38–40, 45; Platonic view of (as seductive), 17–18, 42–43, 56, 94–95, 97–98, 100, 102, 124; purpose of, 10, 20; "ready-made," 106–7, 110; and skeptical doubt, 28–29, 44–45; and solitude, 34–35; as subjective vs. objective, 21–22, 24–29, 50–51, 53–54, 56, 58–59, 101–2, 106; and Tolstoy's ideal artwork, 130–34; Tolstoy's muse of, 56–57; and transcendence, 29, 39, 43, 49–50, 181n85; true/genuine vs.

217

Index

art (*continued*)
    false, 94, 97–98, 106–8, 114, 122–23, 133; and uniting of souls, 29, 65, 69–70, 86–87, 131, 148–49, 159–60. *See also* author/artist; beautiful, the; creativity; receptivity; *What Is Art?* (Tolstoy)
"Art as Device" (Shklovsky), 10–11
Atwell, John, 10–11
author/artist: and genius/talent/virtuosity, 35–36, 42, 45, 55, 69–70, 88–89, 131, 138–39, 157–59; as heartless, 137–38; and ideal audience/reader, 79–83, 85, 87–89; and multilevel thinking/synchronization, 66–67, 69; and relationship with reader, 19–20, 62, 64, 72–74, 88–89, 125, 150; self-assurance/vanity of, 22, 41–43, 45, 49, 60–62, 66–67, 128, 148–49; solipsism of, 36, 60–62, 67, 69–70; "uncertain," 20–21, 43–45, 50, 58–59, 66–67, 72, 91. *See also* art

Babaev, Eduard, 33
Balaam, 122
Barran, Thomas, 183n10
Barthes, Roland, 18–20
Bateaux, Charles, 93
Baudelaire, Charles, 96
Baumgarten, Alexander Gottlieb, 93
beautiful, the: and desire, 55–59; as individual or shared, 24–27; Kantian view of, 52–54, 56–59; obligation to, 56–58, 106, 145; Platonic view of, 51–52; Schopenhauerian view of, 54; as source of frustration, 55–59; and subjective taste, 50–51, 53–54, 58–59, 93, 106; vs. the agreeable, 53–55, 59, 174n119. *See also Anna Karenina* (Tolstoy); art
Beckett, Samuel, 18–20, 125
Beethoven, Ludwig van, 42–43, 97, 131–34, 145
Bellow, Saul, 62
Bely, Andrei, 116
Bem, Alfred, 60, 74
Berlin Journalists and Writers' Union, 128
Berlioz, Hector, 97
Berman, Anna, 52
Bernstein, J. M., 38
Best, Stephen, 17, 164n65
Bible, 39–41, 43, 115–17
biography, 63–64, 67–72, 152–53

Blackwell, Stephen, 61, 78, 81–82, 177n29, 180n79
Blok, Alexander, 64, 84, 159
Bolshevik Revolution, 63, 73
"Books" (Emerson), 119–20
Booth, Wayne, 140
Botkin, Vasily, 26, 56, 196n49
Boyd, Brian, 11, 61, 140–41, 149, 152, 181n85, 181n90
Brodsky, Anna, 83
Brooks, Jeffrey, 179n52
Buckler, Julie, 48
Buddha, 115–18, 120
Bunin, Ivan, 73
Burke, Edmund, 93
"Butterfly" (Fet), 27

Calendar of Proverbs for the Year 1887 (Tolstoy), 118
Cavell, Stanley: and "acknowledgement," 8–9, 13, 68; and experience of art, 20, 39; and madman's guilt, 16; and other minds, 7, 62, 68, 72, 74, 79–81, 83, 134; and philosophical skepticism, 5–9, 74, 84; and poststructuralism, 18–19; and problem of pain, 7–8, 68, 74, 80–81
Chekhov, Anton, 64, 120–23
Chernyshevsky, Nikolay, 24–26, 63, 65, 70–71, 74, 76, 80, 177n26
Chertkov, Vladimir, 29, 104, 117, 193n4
Childhood (Tolstoy), 24, 26, 50–51
Christ, 40–41, 43, 120, 135, 169n47, 170n58
Circle of Reading, The (Tolstoy): "absolute language" of, 116, 119; aim and trajectory of, 22, 115–19, 124, 139, 150; and artist's dilemma of receptivity, 91, 115–16, 119, 121–25, 149–50; on the rewards of reading, 119–21; scholarly responses to, 189n100; on simplicity, 158
Coetzee, J. M., 135
communication/communion: and "absolute language," 116, 119; achieved through art, 29, 86–87, 94, 140, 146, 155, 158–60; vs. compulsion to speak, 150–52; vs. corporeality of the other, 83–84; with ideal/imagined reader, 79–83, 85, 87–89; impossibility of, 21, 32, 62, 76–79, 140, 159, 196n46; and misuse/inadequacy of lan-

218

Index

guage/linguistic skepticism, 6–10, 37–38, 68, 158, 165n80, 170n59, 171n75; reading as, 117, 119–20, 147–49; and shared customs, 33–34
Confession (Tolstoy), 29, 33, 43–45, 59, 110, 136
Confucius, 115
Connolly, Julian, 137–38
convention: artistic, 38–39, 41–42, 49; social, 45–47, 49–50
Corngold, Stanley, 125
Cossacks, The (Tolstoy), 109
creativity: and acuity of vision, 35–36, 38–39; and "imagined facts," 70–72, 152–53; vs. passivity, 112–15; readerly, 82, 87; and skepticism, 14–16, 28–29, 70, 148–49; and solitude, 34–35, 60–62; and suspicion, 140. *See also* art
critics, 61, 75–76, 89, 92, 99, 102, 157, 176n11

"Darling, The" (Chekhov), 120–23
Death of Ivan Ilyich, The (Tolstoy), 154
deconstructionism, 18–19, 140
Defense, The (Nabokov), 85
De la Durantaye, Leland, 23, 62 (qtd.), 175n9
De Man, Paul, 19, 140
Denner, Michael, 187n67
Derrida, Jacques, 140, 183n9
Der Ring des Nibelungen (Wagner), 98–99
Descartes, René, 5–6, 13, 15, 20, 31, 50
Despair (Nabokov), 181n85
"Destruction of Aesthetics, The" (Pisarev), 25–26
Devil, The (Tolstoy), 91
Diderot, Denis, 189n100
Diment, Galya, 70–71
disappointment: with limits of imagination, 70–72; reader's (with the text), 145–49; with "real" readers, 81–84; skeptical, 18–19, 43–44, 62, 68, 159
Dolinin, Alexander, 67, 71, 74, 85–86, 177n29
Dostoevsky, Fyodor, 80
doubt: and artistic expression, 28–29, 44–45; and author-reader encounter, 125; Descartes on, 5–6, 13; Levin's, 29–31, 34, 46; and modernists, 4; of own powers of observation, 65–67; and solitude, 30, 69–

70; vs. suspicion, 19. *See also* skepticism; suspicion
Dragunoiu, Dana, 23, 153, 178n39, 196n49
"Dream" (Tolstoy), 56–57
Druzhinin, Alexander, 26

egoism: of artist, 22, 41–43, 45, 158–59; and cruelty/brutality, 108–9, 126–29, 152–53; and estrangement, 10–11; as human condition, 95, 98, 123–24; vs. idleness, 112–15, 124, 133; and imperviousness to others, 105, 108–9; and isolation, 109–12, 143; and madness, 15–16, 126–30; and passion, 52; practical vs. theoretical, 10–11, 15, 33; of reader, 88, 158; and suspicion, 139–40; transcended, 110–12, 122, 133–35, 145
Eikhenbaum, Boris, 26, 155, 173n95
Eldridge, Hannah Vandegrift, 8
Eldridge, Richard, 18, 163n35
Emerson, Caryl, 90, 100, 104, 134, 194n14
Emerson, Ralph Waldo, 118–20
Emery, Jacob, 114
émigré community, 14–15, 60, 72–74, 129, 140, 144–45. *See also* Nabokov, Vladimir
empiricism, 21–22, 49–50, 85, 88
enchantment, 17, 58, 92–93
Engelstein, Laura, 170n58
Epictetus, 116–18
estrangement (*ostraneniia*): and perception, 9–16, 33, 39, 92, 156–58; vs. possession, 95–99. *See also* Shklovsky, Viktor
Eugene Onegin (Pushkin), 21, 86, 88, 149
Evdokimova, Svetlana, 169n47
Evnin, F. I., 104
Eye, The (Nabokov), 72

Fanger, Donald, 186n63
Felski, Rita, 17, 19, 92–93, 136, 16465
Fet, Afanasy, 27, 64
Field, Andrew, 23, 141, 178n40
Fischer, Michael, 18–19
Flaubert, Gustave, 80
For Every Day (Tolstoy), 118
Formalists, 85–87, 155
Foucault, Michel, 18
Frankfurt School, 92
French Decadents, 27
French Revolution, 166n1

Index

French Symbolism, 96–97
Freud, Sigmund, 17, 151

Gatrall, Jefferson J. A., 43, 169n49
Gazdanov, Gaito, 73
Ge, Nikolay, 169n47
Gendler, Tamar, 101
Gift, The (Nabokov): author-reader
relationship in, 62, 64, 72–74, 79–84,
176n22; Chernyshevsky biography in,
63, 65, 70–71, 74, 76, 80, 177n26; and
dangerous readers, 74–79, 135–36;
doubles in, 21, 62, 80, 84; failure of
communication in, 21–22, 65, 76–78,
83–84; and "imagined facts," 70–71;
imagined/ideal reader in, 79–85; and
impossibility of knowing or being known
by others, 64–70, 74–79, 83, 87, 140,
144; multilevel thinking in, 66–67, 69;
and other minds skepticism, 62, 67–70,
79–81; plot/structure of, 63–64, 180n79;
publication history of, 177n26; reading
of other people in, 64–67
Gippius, Zinaida, 73–74
Givens, John, 43, 169n45
Glynn, Michael, 87, 145
Goethe, Johann Wolfgang von, 173n106
Gogol, Nikolay, 21, 51, 76, 84–87, 180n72
Goldstein, Vladimir, 126–27
Golubkov, A. V., 189n100
"Good Readers and Good Writers"
(Nabokov), 150
Gorbunov-Posadov, Ivan, 115–16
Greenleaf, Monika, 178n47
Gusev, Nikolay, 117, 119
Gustafson, Richard, 33, 44, 91, 94–95,
183n10, 194n14
Guyer, Paul, 90

Hadji Murat (Tolstoy): and aesthetic
unresponsiveness, 22, 104–8, 110, 123–
24; and artist's dilemma of receptivity,
91, 115; and capacity to be moved by art,
106, 108, 111–14, 120, 124; egoism and
isolation in, 109–12; plot/structure of,
105–6, 193n144. *See also What Is Art?*
(Tolstoy)
Halliwell, Stephen, 98
Hegel, Georg Wilhelm Friedrich, 93

Heier, Edmund, 104
Herder, Johann Gottfried von, 93
Herman, David, 52, 108, 193n144, 194n14
Homer, 100
Hume, David, 22, 100–103, 133

idleness, 22, 112–15, 124, 133
infection of art: as amoral, 132–35; failed,
22, 93–95, 97–100, 123; and "feeling," 3,
106–7, 112–13, 131
"In Praise of Idleness" (Aikhenvald), 113–
14
Invitation to a Beheading (Nabokov), 61,
81, 85
"Ion" (Plato), 94
Ishuk, Gennadii, 91
isolation. *See* solitude
Ivanov, Alexander, 40–41, 170n58
Ivanov, Georgy, 73

Jahn, Gary, 183n9
Johnson, D. Barton, 13–14, 141
Josipovici, Gabriel, 18, 42–43
judgments: aesthetic, 21, 24–28, 57, 101–2,
106, 154, 174n119; moral, 100–101, 103,
154; of taste, 58–59, 106

Kafka, Franz, 18–20, 86, 125
Kamera obskura (Nabokov), 137–38
Kant, Immanuel: on beauty, 52–53, 58–
59, 106; and objectivity of aesthetics, 21,
53, 58, 101–2, 106; on pleasures, 53–54,
56–57; on taste, 58–59, 101, 106; Tolstoy
and, 5, 52–54, 56–58, 93, 118, 134
Karlinsky, Simon, 84–85
Karshan, Thomas, 113–14
Keats, John, 18
Khagi, Sofya, 165n80
Kharms, Daniil, 20
Khodasevich, Vladislav, 60, 73
Kierkegaard, Søren, 18–19
"Kindness to Authors" (Nabokov), 76
King Lear (Shakespeare), 9, 16
knowledge: of another, 72, 83, 88, 160; vs.
Cavell's "acknowledgement," 8–9, 13, 68;
and "epistemological ladder," 68–69; and
"imagined facts," 70–72, 152–53; and
"information," 85–88; lack of as creative
opportunity, 70–71; limitations of, 28–30,

220

Index

32, 43–44, 62, 160; and multilevel thinking, 66–67, 69; of self, 6, 52, 81; shared body of, 33. *See also* skepticism

Kokobobo, Ani, 112

Kramskoy, Ivan, 41, 169n49, 170n58

Kreutzer Sonata, The (Tolstoy): external forces in, 91; on force of art, 95, 99, 130–35, 145; vs. Nabokov's version, 14, 125–26, 128–30, 138; suspect narrator in, 22–23, 126–28, 130, 137, 139–40; as Tolstoy's ideal artwork, 130–32. *See also* "Pozdnyshev's Address" (Nabokov)

Kupreyanova, Elena, 94, 183n10

Lange, Ernst Michael, 6

Laozi, 116

Latour, Bruno, 17

Laughter in the Dark (Nabokov), 137–38

Layton, Susan, 104, 187n70

"Leo Tolstoy and Culture" (Bely), 116

Lermontov, Mikhail, 51

Leskov, Nikolay, 64, 103

Lessing, Gotthold Ephraim, 93

Leving, Yuri, 177n27

Lewis, Upton, 158

Lieber, Emma, 196n46

Liszt, Franz, 97

Litoshenko, Dmitry, 110, 113

Locke, John, 120

Lolita (Nabokov), 84, 89, 130, 137, 139, 154

loneliness. *See* solitude

Lyons, John, 195n45

madness: and egoism, 15–16, 126–30; and estrangement vs. perception, 11–16; and fear of being misunderstood, 180n72; of genius artist, 88–89; of moral isolation, 11–14, 46–47; of narrator/commentator, 140–41, 145–49; Tolstoy's Arzamas terror, 11–12, 43

Maeterlinck, Maurice, 96

Makovitsky, Dushan, 117, 122

Mallarmé, Stéphane, 96

Mamonova, Ol'ga, 103

Mandelker, Amy, 34, 48, 58, 171n69, 171n75, 174n117

Mandel'stam, Osip, 88

Mann, Thomas, 18, 137

Mansi (Vogul) people, 98

Marcus, Sharon, 17, 164n65

Marcus Aurelius, 116, 118

Marx, Karl, 17

Marxist critique, 76, 151

Mary (Nabokov), 84–85, 128

Maude, Aylmer, 12

Maupassant, Guy de, 35–36, 39, 41, 123

McCarthy, Mary, 3

Melville, Herman, 158

"Memoirs of a Madman" (Tolstoy), 11–15, 43

Merezhkovsky, Dmitry, 73

Merrill, Robert, 195n45

Metamorphosis, The (Kafka), 86

Meyer, Priscilla, 154

Milton, John, 101–2

Mishin, V. S., 118, 183n1

modernists, 4, 20, 85–87, 96–97, 125, 165n80

Moi, Toril, 7, 162n20

Moran, Richard, 57, 106

Morrison, James, 146

Morson, Gary Saul, 32–33, 37, 47–50, 116, 119, 127, 171n69, 171n75

Muhammad, 118

music, 54, 97–99, 126, 130–34, 147, 156

Nabokov, Véra, 61, 128, 130, 180n79

Nabokov, Vladimir: on artist as own audience, 60–62, 88–89; baroque style of, 3, 23, 136, 151, 155–59, 176n22; and Cavell, 68, 72–74, 80–81, 83–84; and cosmic synchronization, 69, 149, 195n45; and danger of own mind, 9–11, 125, 128–30; devices of, 178n39, 197n70; and doubles, 21, 62, 80, 84, 88–89, 120; empiricism of, 21–22, 85–88; and faith in capacity of art, 3, 23, 113–14, 125–26, 154; on Gogol, 21, 76, 85–87, 180n72; heroes and protagonists of, 84, 137–38, 146, 153–54; and his readers/critics, 60–62, 74–79, 85, 87–89, 138–40, 150–51, 157, 176n11; and idleness, 113–14; and "imagined facts," 70–72, 152–53; and labor of receptivity/creation, 16–20; lectures of, 76, 85, 90, 154, 158; and "moderate multiplication," 88–89; Platonism of, 62, 66; on Pushkin, 21–22, 86–88,

Index

Nabokov, Vladimir (*continued*)
149, 159; as reader, 85–88, 165n80; and
Schopenhauer, 6; and skeptical affliction,
3–5, 19–20, 155; supposed solipsism of,
60–62, 88–89; synesthesia of, 79, 82, 85;
on Tolstoy, 4, 90, 128, 154, 156, 158–60.
See also individual titles
Naiman, Eric, 61, 65, 138
*New Circle of Reading, or For Every Day,
The* (Tolstoy), 117
New Yorker, 157
Nietzsche, Friedrich, 17
Nikolaeva, S. Iu., 189n100
"Not-Doing" (Tolstoy), 113, 115

"Ob iskusstve" (Tolstoy), 169n38
Odysseus, 100
"Of the Standard of Taste" (Hume), 100–
103
Ogilby, John, 102
Orwell, George, 137
Orwin, Donna, 109, 112, 172n90, 193n145
Othello (Shakespeare), 9
Overcoat, The (Gogol), 86–87

pain: and attempt to share with others,
143–45, 155–58; as part of desire, 55–58;
problem of, 7–8, 68, 74, 80–81
Pale Fire (Nabokov): and conflicting desires
to speak/listen, 149–54; dual protagonists
of, 141–45; "genius-monster" in, 137;
and harmonies of the imagination, 152–
54; plot/structure of, 3, 23, 61, 140–41,
150; and suspicion vs. faith, 125–26, 139–
40, 146–49, 152, 154
Paperno, Irina, 44–45, 61, 85, 117
Parker, Theodore, 117
Pascal, Blaise, 115–17
Path of Life, The (Tolstoy), 116, 118
perception: of the artist, 34–36, 40–42, 54–
55, 66–70, 150; and associations/recollec-
tions, 79, 86; automized, 9–11; and desire, 55–58; estranged, 9–16, 33, 39, 92,
156–58; and madness, 11–16; and serenity of mind, 102; staring/passive hyperconcentration, 30–33, 35–36, 38–39, 45–
47; and superior vision of author/reader,
81, 87, 138–40, 149–50, 157–58
Perec, Georges, 18
Petrov, Vasiliy, 183n1

Pickford, Henry, 13, 29, 37, 132–33, 183n9,
185n31
Pifer, Ellen, 141
Pisarev, Dmitry, 25–26
Plato: and aesthetic experience, 17–18, 50,
62, 92, 97–98, 100, 102; and aesthetic
objectivity, 51–52, 56, 58; and artistic
perception, 42–43, 66–67; in *The Circle
of Reading*, 115; on power of art, 94,
124, 185n31
pleasure(s): vs. aesthetic delight, 28, 51;
authorial, 60–61, 88–89; "beautiful" vs.
"agreeable," 36, 53–55, 59; and gratification, 106–10; and moral judgments, 100–
101, 103; and poetic possession, 17–18,
95, 97–98, 112–13, 123–24; of reading,
17–20, 76, 117; sensuous, 24–28, 49,
53–55, 101, 107–8; as subjective, 93,
106; of suspicion, 136–40; from vanity,
41, 43, 49
Popkin, Richard, 5–6
possession, 17–18, 95, 97–98, 100, 112–13,
123–24
postmodernism, 71
poststructuralism, 17–18, 140
"Pozdnyshev's Address" (Nabokov): publication of, 193n10; suspect narrator in,
22–23, 137–40, 154; vs. Tolstoy's novella, 14, 125–26, 128–30, 138. *See also
Kreutzer Sonata, The* (Tolstoy)
"Preface to the Works of Guy de Maupassant" (Tolstoy), 35–36, 39, 41
problem of other minds: Cavell on, 7, 62,
68, 72, 74, 79–81, 83, 134; Nabokov and,
62, 67–70, 72, 74, 79–81, 140; Tolstoy
and, 28–29, 31, 34, 38, 40, 42, 72, 83,
134. *See also* skepticism
Proffer, Carl, 89
Pushkin, Alexander, 21–22, 70–71, 84, 86–
88, 149, 159–60
"Pushkin, or the True and the Seemingly
True" (Nabokov), 70–71, 88

radical critics (of 1860s), 24–26. *See also*
Chernyshevsky, Nikolay
Raeff, Marc, 73
Rampton, David, 23, 137, 140, 178n40
Rancière, Jacques, 166n1
readers: author's disappointment with,
81–84; and call for passivity/idleness,

112–14, 124, 133; as cocreators, 82, 87, 118–19; dangerous, 74–79, 135–36; and disappointment with text, 145–49; émigré, 72–74; as implicated in fiction, 127–28; as morally compromised, 99–100, 103–4; Nabokov and Tolstoy as, 85–88, 116–17; and Nabokov's taxonomy of good/bad/ideal, 3, 75–83, 85, 87–89, 151; nineteenth-century growth of, 179n52; and relationship with author, 60–62, 64, 72–79, 125, 138–39, 150, 176n22; resistant, 100–101

reading: "bad," 74–79; as communion, 117, 119–20, 147–49; defamiliarized, 61; and energy of delusion, 155; gendered understandings of, 19, 92, 122; and inhabiting author's consciousness, 86–87; of literary canon, 64, 84–86; of other people's minds, 64–68; pleasures of, 17–20, 76, 117; as process of revealing or obscuring, 77–78, 119–21, 149. *See also* suspicious reading/critique

receptivity: and amoral infectiousness vs. mutual love, 132–35; of artistic success or failure, 40–41, 51, 106; artist's dilemma of, 91, 115–16, 119, 121–24, 149–50, 154; and capacity to be moved by art, 106, 108, 111–12, 124; and conflicting desires to speak/listen, 149–54; and controlled suspicion, 125–26; and failure of responsiveness, 91, 95–96, 103–8; and feigned delight, 98–99; and idleness, 112–15, 124, 133; labor of, 16–18, 22, 91–93, 102–4, 124, 134–35; lack of, 76–77; liberatory/transformative power of, 130–34; and moral judgments, 100–103; and recognition of pathos, 155–58. *See also* suspicious reading/critique

Rhie, Bernard, 18, 163n35
Ricoeur, Paul, 16–17
Rimbaud, Arthur, 84–85
Robbins, Bruce, 92
Robinson, Douglas, 183n10
Romanticism, 18, 42, 138
Rorty, Richard, 23, 137–38, 153
Rousseau, Jean-Jacques, 44, 103
Rul', 15, 72
Ruskin, John, 115
Russian Civil War, 73

Samarina, Aleksandra, 103
Sass, Louis, 31, 33
Saturday Evening Post, 158
Schiller, Friedrich, 93, 172n90
schizophrenia, 31
Schopenhauer, Arthur: on artistic genius, 42; on dangers of reading, 120; on music, 54, 132, 185n31; on objectivity, 56, 58; on pleasure, 54–56; on radical doubt, 6–7, 15; on theoretical egoism, 10–11, 15–16, 33; and Tolstoy, 5–6, 10–11, 33, 54–56, 93, 115, 132; and transcendental essence of art, 50
Schumann, Robert, 97
seeing. *See* perception
Seifrid, Thomas, 46, 81
Seneca, 120
sensation: aesthetic, 24–28, 49–50; and the senses, 53–55, 101, 132, 147; and synesthesia, 79, 82, 85
Shakespeare, William, 9, 91, 151
Shaw, Bernard, 115
Shestov, Lev, 13–14, 16, 136
Shklovsky, Viktor, 9–11, 91–92, 149, 155, 188n82, 189n99
"Signs and Symbols" (Nabokov), 180n72
Šilbajoris, Rimvydas, 36, 99–100, 183n9
"Silentium!" (Tyutchev), 165n80
Sirin. *See* Nabokov, Vladimir
Sisson, J. B., 69
skepticism: active vs. passive, 74–75; aesthetic, 25–28, 38, 42, 49–50, 58–59; as affliction, 3–7, 9, 20, 155; cheerful, 70–72; and corporeality, 83–84, 143; and creativity/artistic creation, 14–16, 28–29, 38, 42–45, 70, 148–49; defined, 3–4, 19; and disappointment, 18–19, 43–44, 62, 68, 159; of external world, 7, 28, 31, 42; and fear of being misunderstood, 180n72, 196n46; and intense visual observation, 30–33; and limits of authorial strategies against, 155–59; linguistic, 140; loneliness of, 19–20, 123; and madness of moral isolation, 11–15, 46–47; and misuse/inadequacy of language, 6–10, 37–38, 68, 165n80, 170n59; of other minds, 7, 62, 68, 72, 74, 79–81, 83, 134; philosophical tradition of, 5–9, 16; and problem of pain, 7–8, 68, 74, 80–81; reprieve or release from, 15–16, 37–38,

Index

skepticism (*continued*)
138–39; succumbed to, 46–50, 75; and
"wall"/divide between people, 20, 28–
29, 71–72, 123, 125, 144, 148–49. *See
also* doubt; knowledge; problem of other
minds; solipsism; suspicion; suspicious
reading/critique
Smith, Zadie, 19–20
Society of Lovers of the Russian Word,
26, 51
Socrates, 51, 94, 117
solipsism: of artist, 36, 60–62, 67, 69–70;
and artistic creation, 14–15, 20–21; and
author-reader relationship, 79–81, 83,
88–89; defined, 6; and estranged perception, 11–14; and fear of being misunderstood, 180n72, 196n46; and longing for
double, 21, 62, 80, 84, 88–89, 120; mag-
nified by bad art, 133; and solipsizing
of the other, 83–84; and solitude, 122–
23; and staring/passive hyperconcentration, 30–33, 35–36, 38, 46–47. *See also*
skepticism
solitude: absence of intersubjective agreement as, 121–23; in *Anna Karenina*,
30, 34–35, 45–47, 50, 122; of artist,
60–62, 69–70; Barthesian, 19–20; and
confinement within the self, 142–43;
and egoism, 109–12, 143; of émigrés/
exiles, 73–74, 140, 144–45; as "force
for good," 91; and isolation of madness,
127, 129; Tolstoy's fear of, 28–29, 43–
44, 123
"Solitude" (Maupassant), 123
"Songs in the Village" (Tolstoy), 156–58
Sorokin, Boris, 25
Sovremennik, 26
Sovremennye zapiski, 14, 73, 177n26
Speak, Memory (Nabokov), 66, 72, 85, 136,
178n39
Spenser, Herbert, 93
Spinoza, Baruch, 5
Stegner, Page, 61, 141
Stenbock-Fermor, Elisabeth, 171n72
Stendhal, 18
Strakhov, Nikolay, 41–42, 93, 185n44,
193n4
Strong Opinions (Nabokov), 176n11
structuralism, 17

subjectivism, 21–22, 24–29, 50
suspicion: channeled toward narrator/
away from author, 22–23, 125–26, 139–
41; conceptualized, 4–5, 19; and faith
in power of art, 140, 146–49; hermeneutics of, 16–18, 23, 127–28, 137, 140;
and limits of authorial strategies against,
155–59; pleasures of, 135–36, 138–
40; stimulated in readers, 126–28, 130;
transcended, 130–34. *See also* doubt;
skepticism
suspicious reading/critique: Nabokov on,
125–26, 135–36, 139, 141, 149, 151–
52; scholars on, 4–5, 16–20, 124, 140,
162n20; Tolstoy on, 103–4, 125–26.
See also Kreutzer Sonata, The (Tolstoy);
Pale Fire (Nabokov); "Pozdnyshev's
Address" (Nabokov)
Symbolists, 96–97, 116, 159
Symposium (Plato), 51

Taine, Hippolyte, 93
Talmud, 115
Tammi, Pekka, 146
Taneev, Sergei, 26
taste, 58–59, 100–103, 106–7
"Terror" (Nabokov), 11, 13–16, 20
Thoreau, Henry David, 120
*Thoughts of Wise People for Every Day,
The* (Tolstoy), 118
Toker, Leona, 23, 138, 154, 180n72, 181n87
"Tolstoy" (Nabokov), 159–60
Tolstoy, Leo: on acuity of vision, 35–36,
38–39, 54–55; on aesthetics as objective/
universal, 21–22, 26–29, 50–51, 53–54,
58–59, 102, 106; on art as infection,
3, 22, 93–95, 97–100, 106–7, 112–13,
131–32, 134–35; on artistic convention, 38–39, 41–42; and artist's dilemma
of receptivity, 91, 115–16, 119, 121–24,
149–50, 154; ascetic style of, 3, 23, 151,
155–60; biography of, 11–12, 73, 131–
32; and Cavell, 6, 13; and Christology/
religion, 43–44, 94, 120, 135, 169n47,
190n104; and compendiums of others'
thoughts, 93, 115–20; and danger of
own mind, 9–11, 109–10, 125, 127–31;
on Descartes, 5, 20; and desire/call to
be possessed, 100, 112–13, 123–24; and

224

Index

dread of moral isolation, 11–15, 46–47; and *durman* (fog), 114; and energy of delusion, 155; and faith in capacity of art, 23, 44–45, 50, 111–14, 125–26; on habit/routine, 10–11, 43–44, 47–48, 50, 110, 113–14; and Hume, 100–103; and idleness, 22, 112–15, 124, 133; and inner voice, 105, 108–11, 120, 125, 133; and Kant, 5, 52–54, 56–58, 93, 118, 134; and labor of receptivity, 16–18, 91–93, 102, 104, 124; late aesthetics of, 90–91, 94–95, 104–5, 114–15, 126, 136; and limitations of human knowledge, 28–30, 43–44, 62; on Maupassant, 35–36, 39, 41; on moral capacity of art, 94, 130–35; on morality, 32–33, 35–36, 46–47, 109, 111–12; and muse of "pure art," 56–58; Nabokov on, 4, 64, 90, 128, 154, 156, 158–60; on newness and significance in art, 38, 45; as reader, 116–17, 165n80; and Schopenhauer, 5–6, 10–11, 33, 54–56, 132; and sincerity, 106–7; skeptical doubts of, 3–5, 20, 43–45, 136, 139, 155; and Wittgenstein, 6, 12, 93, 104; on women, 122, 130; and work/"toiling people," 44, 47–48, 113–14, 118. *See also individual titles*
Tolstoy, Sergei (Leo's son), 132
Tolstoy, Sofia, 43, 47–48, 117, 131, 189n99
transcendence: through art, 29, 39, 43, 49–50, 181n85; of constraints of consciousness, 142; of egoism, 110–12, 122, 133–35, 145; through reading, 117; self-consciousness and, 81; of suspicious impulse, 130–34
TriQuarterly, 61

Turgenev, Ivan, 26, 42, 64
Tyutchev, Fyodor, 20, 64, 165n80

Vandenabeele, Bart, 54
"Vane Sisters, The" (Nabokov), 156–58
Veidle, Vladimir, 60
Verlaine, Paul, 96
Vogul (Mansi) people, 98

Wagner, Richard, 97–99, 107, 123
War and Peace (Tolstoy), 42, 52, 54, 91, 99, 109
Watch, The (Turgenev), 42
Weir, Justin, 47, 171n75
What Is Art? (Tolstoy): and aesthetic unresponsiveness, 22, 99–100, 103–4, 108; "ecstasy" vs. "intoxication" in, 94–95, 98; on false art, 48, 94, 97–99, 106–8, 110, 123; on good vs. bad art, 94, 97–98; on incomprehension/failed receptivity, 91, 95–99, 123; "infection" in, 93–95, 97–100, 106–7, 123; moralizing of, 94, 96, 98–99, 103–4; on music, 97–99, 131; and rejection of subjectivism/taste, 26–29, 50, 101; responses to, 90–91, 94–95, 99–100; and Tolstoy's doubt, 99–100, 115, 123, 136; on true art, 94, 97–98, 106, 131. *See also Hadji Murat* (Tolstoy)
White, Katherine, 157
"Why Do People Stupefy Themselves?" (Tolstoy), 98
Wittgenstein, Ludwig, 5–9, 12, 20–21, 31, 33, 37, 93, 104
Wood, Michael, 19, 23, 153

Zenon the Goldsmith (Leskov), 103